Florida Thoroughbred

Needles, the first Florida thoroughbred to win the Kentucky Derby, May 3, 195
(by permission of Scott Dudley).

Florida Thoroughbred

Charlene R. Johnson

Foreword by John C. Weber

University Press of Florida
Gainesville Tallahassee Tampa Miami
Boca Raton Pensacola Orlando Jacksonville

Johnson, Charlene R.
Florida thoroughbred / Charlene R. Johnson.
p. cm.
Includes bibliographical references and index.
ISBN 0-8130-1198-1 (acid-free paper).
—ISBN 0-8130-1201-5 (pbk.: acid-free paper)
1. Thoroughbred horse—Florida—History. 2. Horse-racing-
-Florida—History. 3. Race horses—Florida—History. I. Title.
SF293.T5J62 1993 92-36966
CIP

The University Press of Florida is the scholarly publishing agency for the State University System of Florida, comprised of Florida A & M University, Florida Atlantic University, Florida International University, Florida State University, University of Central Florida, University of Florida, University of North Florida, University of South Florida, University of West Florida.

University Press of Florida
15 Northwest 15th Street
Gainesville, Florida 32611

Florida's climate is good for man and beast.

—Ben Jones, *veteran trainer*

Contents

Four Kingdom of the Sun

Five Appendixes

Illustrations

Color Illustrations

(following page 172)

Foreword

In 1991, Marion County commissioners approved a land-use plan that will be a method of mapping and controlling the growth of the county for many years to come. While it was a state-mandated assignment, the process in Marion County was unique in that it apart from the rest of Florida had a special industry to consider when planning county growth.

The impact of the thoroughbred industry on Marion County was clearly set forth throughout the planning process. While developers were not particularly pleased with the outcome, the fact is, the thoroughbred industry was recognized, paid homage, and preserved for the future in Marion County, therefore in Florida.

The fact that the thoroughbred industry is the third most important industry to Florida is undeniable. It is also fact that it has had a long, uphill struggle against some strong odds. In the early days, the thoroughbred industry came into existence only because of the perseverance of some dedicated believers. Their story is long overdue, and this book is vital so that we not forget who they were. Their faith and love of this beautiful sport is carried on today by more believers. In the past few years, still against many odds, the thoroughbred industry attained further legislative recognition with the passage of a Sunday racing bill, a family racing bill, and an intertrack wagering bill, all vital necessities for the health of the industry.

Today, Florida is the fourth largest state in the Union with the prediction that it will soon be the third largest. With the influx of so many potential racing fans, our industry should continue to grow in a positive way. Our progress today is closely charted by skilled turf writers and journalists who are familiar with the sport and the terminology. In the early years there weren't many turf writers in Florida; history has been hazy and in some cases incorrectly carried forward. As time passed it could have been lost. The research and interviews that Charlene Johnson did in ferreting out the early industry are invaluable for helping to clear up our past and put down on paper forever exactly how this important industry began in Florida. The history lover and the Florida lover will find much to enchant.

Florida Thoroughbred is long overdue. It should be an invaluable tool for all lovers of the sport of racing and the thoroughbred horse.

Today, the horses with sunshine in their veins stand proudly among the bluebloods of Kentucky and the best of Newmarket, England, and Chantilly, France. The Florida Thoroughbred Breeders' Association would like to recommend this book to every lover of horse and sunshine.

John C. Weber
President, Florida Thoroughbred Breeders' Association

Acknowledgements

Many, many people (and horses) have contributed to this book. It would be impossible to list all of those I spoke with and to whom I owe a great indebtedness, yet I would be terribly remiss if several were not mentioned, for without them the book could not have been written. Joseph O'Farrell's son Michael O'Farrell and Carl Rose's sons "Buddy" and "Happy" Rose provided extensive, invaluable scrapbooks kept by their fathers in the early years. Bonnie Heath, "Red" Vines, and several others also provided scrapbooks as well as personal reminiscences and photographs. The early South Florida material, which was virtually undocumented, was tremendously aided by the memories and actual footwork on the parts of Stefanie Zachar, daughter of Stefan Zachar, and Henry Taylor, whose father aided in the passage of parimutuel wagering. These people donated considerable "archive research" and documentation, which clarified numerous rumors and fallacies.

I must also thank the Florida Thoroughbred Breeders' Association and *The Florida Horse* for use of their libraries and photo files. Many of the pictures used in this book came from them.

Lastly, I thank the Chazal-Blair Insurance Agency and, more than anyone, Dick Chazal whose burning desire it was that this story be told. His faith and his support, financially and personally, are the real reasons this book exists today.

This book comes from the heart—not just mine, but the hearts of all those people I talked to who were so certain that good, competitive thoroughbreds could be raised in Florida. This book is for them and for their horses. In substance, it was written by them. Both people and horses truly have sunshine in their veins.

Charlene R. Johnson

Preface

Like an alligator, she rests in the water. Her head and shoulders nestle confidently in the protective curve of the mainland while her green and brown body curves languidly south, arcing away from the relentless, timeless pounding of the ocean surf on her eastern side and forming a protective curve for the gently lapping Gulf waters on the west. Her thick, wide shoulders hunch high, and a spiny backbone runs down the curve of her back, tapering to disappear in the bony knobs of a trailing tail that bobbles through the crystalline, lapping water.

She is richly green, lush with tropical growth and brilliant colors. She is the epitome of the dripping warmth of a romantic novel. She is home to an amazing and unique variety of land and marine life: the one-of-a-kind Everglades; the vanishing wetlands birds; the nearly extinct manatee, Florida panther, and Key deer.

The entire peninsula of Florida is made of an old coral reef, limestone. The limestone is the reason for this tale. It is Florida's wealth and her fragility. The human superstructure of living is devastating to the delicate, porous quality of the peninsula. Yet, the particularly high ridge of limestone deposits that form her backbone is the reason for the calcium richness of grass and water that make up Marion County in Central Florida. This ridge provides the essence of growing healthy bones and cartilage, which makes such areas so perfect for growing livestock.

From Tallahassee south through the center of the state runs the Ocala Ridge. Nearly 300 feet above sea level, it forms the "highlands" of the Sunshine State. Here thousands of springs have excellent runoff so there is no stagnant water, and the limestone base provides a foundation for the grass to hold moisture. Only in Kentucky, Ireland, and Florida do such widespread limestone areas exist. In these three areas is the highest concentration of thoroughbred breeding in the world.

Marion County and its county seat of Ocala is a country of rolling green hills and huge live oaks, miles of straight board fencing and manicured pastures and long, shady driveways. In the center of the paradoxical, flamboyant state of sunshine and humidity, hibiscus and cockroach, flamingo and alligator, exist horses: horses of every size, shape, color, and breed, but the thoroughbred predominates. Except for the dripping Spanish moss, it looks and feels like the bluegrass hills of Lexington, Kentucky, traditional breeding grounds of the blueblood thoroughbreds.

In the 1980s, Ocala became one of the fastest growing cities in the United States. Most of the attraction is because of the beauty of the land that supports and is maintained by the bustling thoroughbred industry, the third most important industry in the state after tourism and citrus. Here, among the undulating hills of Bahia and shaded by centuries-old oak trees, racehorses are born, raised, and trained to gallop on to national and worldwide acclaim. The Florida farmers have come a long way since the first scoffers told an early Florida breeder to stick to raising alligators and let Kentucky raise the nation's racehorses. Surely no horse could thrive in the heat and swampland of such a state. The horses themselves prove the critics wrong.

While Florida technically is well above the latitude designated "tropical," it nonetheless seems to defy global designations and is a "tropical-type" of environment. Early horses loved it. Florida is the richest source of prehistoric equine fossils found anywhere in the world.

In 1991, on a single horse farm north of Ocala, seven new species of horse were unearthed by University of Florida archaeologists who were called in when the proprietor turned up skulls while building a racetrack. Clearly, Florida was the site of successful horse breeding for millions of years. Following the mysterious disappearance of the horse from the entire North American continent, it was once again introduced to the continent through Florida by the Spanish conquistadors.

In 1494, Christopher Columbus brought twelve mares and two horses to the island of Haiti for the purpose of re-creating stock. Many of the later explorers would stop by the islands to pick up stock on their way to explore the main continent. It is probable that Juan Ponce de León brought horses with him when he landed on the shores of Florida in 1513 and named "La Florida" for the Easter season. It is unlikely that any survived. In 1527, Cabeza de Vaca brought forty-two horses to Florida as part of his entourage, but they, too, did not survive. On April 14, 1528, Panfilo de Narváez landed near present-day Charlotte Harbor with 600 men and 80 horses. His trip north was the first comprehensive exploration of Florida, a route that took him along the western shores north toward the Mississippi. These were the first white men to see the "Province of Ocali," or Ocale, a Timucuan Indian village. Men and horses sickened and died and were killed by Indians on this arduous journey. By the time they reached the Mississippi, only 247 men still lived. The remaining horses were sacrificed at this time so that the hair from their manes and tails could lash together makeshift boats; their hides were used to hold water.

In 1539, Hernando de Soto landed near Tampa Bay with citrus seed, 1,000 men, and 225 horses of royal blood. But he would sow more seed than just citrus. During his long and ruthless journey, de Soto reported the first horseraces and horse breeding overseen by humans on the continent. It is the escapees from this herd that started what would become wild horses spreading north and west through Mexico and into the American West, where they formed such an important part of American history.

In 1774, naturalist William Bartram described the area just north of Ocala as covered with "squadrons of beautiful, fleet Seminole horses on the great Alachua Savannah." But over a hundred years later, early Florida breeders would be scoffed at for their attempts to raise horses in Florida.

From 1923, when those who cared began to keep records, until 1970, only twelve farms were represented as the leading breeders of the year. All twelve of those farms were located in Kentucky. But in 1970, a non-Kentucky farm would finally break the stranglehold that state held over the most prestigious honor a breeder could earn. For two years in a row, Florida-based Harbor View Farm in Marion County would lead the nation's breeders in money won and races won.

Throughout the 1970s and into the 1980s, Florida breeders held an average of seven spots among the top twenty breeders every year, with Fred Hooper, Tartan Farms, Farnsworth Farms, Hobeau Farms, and Lasater Farm consistently among the leaders.

While Florida consistently produces approximately 9 percent of the national foal crop, Florida-breds equally consistently produce 15 percent of the stakes winners, indicating higher than average quality. In the late 1980s, Florida-breds took 26 percent of the stakes races worth $25,000 or more and 22 percent of the graded stakes races, which are the highest caliber of racing anywhere in the world. In 1990, state-breds won 394 stakes, averaging well over a stakes race a day, and earned nearly $125 million in purses in North America alone. Since 1955, when the Sunshine State earned its first national championship with Needles' two-year-old colt championship, to 1990, Florida has produced forty-five national championships, including four horses of the year, and seven international championships.

In 1990, there were nearly 600 thoroughbred farms in Florida, about 500 of them in Marion County, averaging 128 acres per farm. There are approximately 300,000 horses in Florida, while horsemen own over 1.6 million acres valued at close to $5 billion. Florida horse owners annually spend over $500 million on support services such as feed, veterinary fees, and supplies, not counting vehicles, land, and insurance. It is estimated that the thoroughbred industry makes up one-third of this economic impact. In Marion County alone, the thoroughbred industry is responsible for over 21,000 jobs and a payroll of almost $150 million. According to one report, thoroughbred horse farms, owners, and employees contribute more than $700 million annually to the local economy through employment, taxes, goods, and services.

The thrills provided by top caliber horses bred and raised in the southernmost state of the continental United States are many. Who will ever forget the duels between Harbor View's two-time horse of the year, Affirmed, and the Kentucky blue-blood Alydar? Or the hard-knocking, long-racing, three-time champion, Susan's Girl, much like her owner and breeder Fred Hooper? Or the poetry in motion of the incredibly long-striding Horse of the Year Conquistador Cielo? Or the blinding speed of Eillo, who won the first Breeders' Cup Sprint?

Long before the founding of Jamestown, Pedro Menéndez de Avilés founded the oldest settlement in the United States, St. Augustine, in 1565. The history of the sport of racing in Florida is as colorful and rich as the history of the state. While nations fought over whether the fragile, important finger into the sea was to be Spanish, English, French, or American property, the thoroughbred industry managed to get a strong foothold in Kentucky. Yet winter racing in Florida is older than the state. Since the beginning, Florida-breds have played a major role in the development of the thoroughbred in the United States. This, then, is not just the history of the Florida thoroughbred; it is the history of the thoroughbred in America, and it is the history of Florida.

Part One

Bright Sunshine

1 The Beginning

By the time that the United States finally acquired Florida in 1819, the huge territory had already been divided into two more manageable pieces by its earlier British owners and preserved by the Spanish during their second occupancy. East Florida was the Atlantic coastline, West Florida the Panhandle. The Americans liked the idea so well they went farther, and Middle Florida became the designation for the area from the Apalachicola to the Suwannee rivers, an area which, in the early 1800s, had a population of about 16,000.

In 1824, a capital was raised for Middle Florida on the high ground of an old Seminole village called Tallahassee. The capital was given the same name. By 1835, about 1,500 white people lived there, but the population was closer to 6,000 when the roving soldiers, the slaves who worked the cotton plantations, and resident mixed Indians (the mixes ranging from white-Indian and black-Indian to different Indian tribes) were counted. The faces were as colorful as the frontier life of the time. A railroad track had been laid to bring northerners, later to be called snowbirds, to the vast territory. But the rails were not strong enough to bear the weight of a steam locomotive, so mules pulled the train. And the people did come.

St. Augustine by this time was already recognized as a "health spa." Northerners with various maladies came to St. Augustine to cling to their fragile health in the healing sunshine. Other well-established towns at this time were Pensacola with its beautiful harbor where a naval station was built in 1830; Apalachicola; St. Joseph, nonexistent today, located near present-day Apalachicola; and Key West.

From the beginning, it appears to have been the attraction of the warmer weather that drew the thoroughbred industry south to Florida. Andrew Jackson, the father of Tennessee turf and influential in the development of the thoroughbred in America, became territorial governor in the 1820s and brought several good mares and a stallion from Tennessee, bred them, and raised foals behind the governor's mansion in Leon City, near Tallahassee. He also was the instigator of many race matches.

The first formal racing meets ever recorded in Florida were winter meets in the early 1800s. Until then, southern racing consisted of a meet at New Orleans, one in Tennessee, and one in Kentucky. From 1832 to 1848, there appear to have been three different racetracks in operation in Florida, sometimes with consecutive meets, sometimes just one of them running a meet a year. These were the Calhoun Course at St. Joseph, the Marianna Course about a mile north of Tallahassee (Marianna was an Indian trading center for early Florida), and the Franklin Track at Apalachicola.

In July 1832, the Tallahassee Jockey Club was formed and was duly listed in the August *American Turf Register and Sporting Magazine.* It conducted annual meets from 1832 to 1843 on the one-mile Marianna track.

The rules and orders of the Maryland Jockey Club, with slight alterations, served as guidelines. As listed in the September 1832 issue of the *American Turf Register and Sporting Magazine* (vol. 4, no. 1), the first officers elected were Major Romeo Lewis, president; Dr. Lewis Willis, vice president; Willis Alston, Esq., second vice president; Captain Thomas Brown, secretary and collector; Richard Hayward, Esq., treasurer. It was determined that "the first races will commence on the third Wednesday in December next and continue for four days. The track will be in fine order and will bear a comparison with the best courses in the Union. The purse will be good on each day. Thomas Brown, Sec'ry. Tallahassee, July 10, 1832." It was also moved in that first meeting that the Club subscribe to the *Turf Register.*

The March 1833 issue of the *American Turf Register and Sporting Magazine* (vol. 4, no. 7) reported the first official race meet in Florida history. The inaugural Tallahassee Jockey Club Races meet was indeed held Wednesday, December 19, 1832. The first recorded purse was $300 with an entrance fee of $20. The races were run in three-mile heats.

Crawford Sprowl's six-year-old bay horse, Platoff, by Kosciusko out of a dam by Hephestion, won both heats, the first in six minutes six seconds (written 6m.6s.) the second in 6m.12s. His only competitor was Willis Alston's chestnut five-year-old horse named

Mucklejohn, by Mucklejohn out of a dam by Potomac: "Mucklejohn bolted in the last quarter of the second heat making a spirited run at Platoff."

The second day the purses were $200 and run in two-mile heats. This time five horses competed, but Crawford Sprowl took this day as well with Gen. Andrew Jackson in four minutes three seconds carrying 118 pounds.

On the third day, Junius won the second of his one-mile heats by "nine inches" and the third heat by "six feet!" The fourth day, the finale, was listed as the Proprietor's Purse at $300 with an entrance fee of $10. The best in three of five one-mile heats would be the winner; entrance was free to all horses with an allowance of six pounds to the losing horses of the preceding day.

The meet in Tallahassee came to be considered one of the greatest meets in the country. For the week surrounding it, several thousand people were attracted to the small town for gala parties and elaborate affairs.

The Marianna Jockey Club conducted six annual meetings at the Apalachicola course between 1833 and 1839. On Wednesday, January 23, 1833, the Marianna Races commenced with many of the same horses competing and winning that had run at Tallahassee. On the fourth day of these races a colorful account in the May 1833 issue of the *American Turf Register and Sporting Magazine* read, "This was a beautiful contest between Mr. Malony's Weazel (the winner) and Mr. Sprowl's Bob Cotton. They were nearly equal. The weather was extremely fine and the turf in excellent order."

So the meets ran. Another six-day meet began Monday, December 15, 1834. On the nineteenth, the Jockey Club Purse of $500 attracted a field of two colts and one filly. The filly was J. J. Pittman's chestnut three-year-old, Mary Doubleday by John Henry out of a mare by Dundannon. She ran second in the first three-mile heat, third in the next. Her weight was listed in the April 1835 issue of the *American Turf Register and Sporting Magazine* (vol. 6, no. 8) as "Mary Doubleday, a feather, but her rider weighed 80 lbs.!"

The significant thing to note about Mary Doubleday, however, is found farther along in the race comments. "The filly is Floridian by birth and education, and ran under great disadvantage, the saddle having slipped on her shoulders in the first mile of the first heat, which prevented the rider from bracing her as he ought to have done." The first "Florida-bred" ever noted went on to win two of five races at the 1836 Tallahassee meet.

The first famous horse to come into the state for racing purposes was owned by General Thomas Brown, who later became the state's only Whig governor. According to the New Orleans *Daily Picayune,* Rienze (Autocrat–Fanny Kemble) won many races at the Calhoun Course in St. Joseph.

But early racing in Florida was doomed by government officials. By 1843, they deemed the sport a public nuisance and a hotbed of vice. After 1843, racing in Florida took a rest for about a half century.

Meanwhile, the rest of Florida was rapidly becoming civilized in the modern sense. The Timucua, Calusa, Apalachee, and other native Indians had long been cleared out, making way for the Seminoles—actually Creeks migrating away from encroaching white settlements in Georgia—to become the strongest tribe in Central Florida.

Already the United States had confronted the Seminoles in the First and Second Seminole Wars, the latter lasting from 1835 to 1841 and costing the U.S. government approximately $40 million. President Andrew Jackson was not fond of Indians and had encouraged Congress to pass the Removal Act in 1830, instructing all Indians to pack up and head west across the Mississippi. Despite their resistance, the last of the strong-willed Seminoles had either departed for Oklahoma and Arkansas reservations or had disappeared into the swampland, later to reappear as an important and colorful part of historical and contemporary Florida.

Though the Indian wars were declared over, the territory was far from stable. Following several years of debate, the Armed Occupation Act was passed in 1842 in order to get bodies into the wilderness to protect against further Indian encroachment. As long as a family abided by certain stipulations, it could obtain 160 acres of land free. This kind of generous inducement to settlers stimulated the first rush of immigrants to settle Central Florida.

Many of these settlers came from South Carolina, where their ancestors had settled in prerevolutionary days. The local hero in that area was General Francis Marion. On March 25, 1844, "Marion" was chosen as the name for the county, which in those days encompassed an area larger than the state of Rhode Island—far more than the 1,039,360 acres of today. Fort King, built on the site of present-day Ocala and one of several forts constructed in the territory by the Americans during the Second Seminole War, was the county seat.

Florida became a state in 1845, and at the first meeting of the assembly the name of Marion County was ratified. According to Eloise Robinson Ott and Louise Hickman Chazal, in their 1966 book, *Ocali Country*, the residential population of the county at that time included 947 whites, 523 slaves, and 5 free Negroes; taxes collected amounted to $669.84.

In 1846, plans for a new county seat to be named "Ocala" were begun and the original survey done. The area, chosen for its high ground and excellent water, was heavily agricultural from the start. Around 1849, choice land was selling for about forty-seven cents an acre. Some less desirable plots listed for as little as ten cents an acre. The trail leading into Marion County was widened so that wagon caravans carrying families could get through the wilderness more easily.

Between 1850 and 1860, planters moved into Marion County to grow sugarcane, tobacco, rice, and cotton. Fruit trees were grown for private use only. Fine cattle and horses were being raised at the same time.

By 1860, the value of Marion County's farms was second only to Leon County's, where Tallahassee is located. Marion County had the fifth largest population in the state. A plantation house, built during these times by Joseph Waldo from Edgefield, South Carolina, later was the last of the big plantations to be torn down—in this case to make room for Ocala Stud in the 1950s. In 1868, the city of Ocala was incorporated; the first official census in 1870 showed the county with a population of 10,804.

Between 1871 and 1875, serious citrus cultivation, which would later spread throughout the entire state, began in Marion County, largely due to the efforts of a Connecticut Yankee, Henry S. Sanford. Citrus groves rapidly began to replace the cotton and sugarcane fields, and today Florida accounts for about 70 percent of the nation's citrus acreage.

Meanwhile, in the rest of the country, horse racing was developing in its own American style. The first break with English ties came in the early 1800s when the British began their new style of "dash" racing. The Americans disdained it as a fad, so match racing and two- to three-mile heat racing continued until the Civil War.

In 1863, the formation of the Saratoga Association changed the concept of American racing. Up to this point, race meets were often held in fields or rough-cut tracks with few amenities attached to the event. Saratoga was already a health center and had several gaming opportunities available, as well as many luxurious accommodations. This New York spa and gambling resort was so popular that its progression to more formal racetracks was natural.

Leonard W. Jerome and his friend August Belmont proceeded to build Jerome Park on Long Island. A jockey club, formed to administer racing at Jerome Park, consisted of 1,300 of the nation's most socially, politically, and financially prominent people. August Belmont was its first president. In Kentucky, Colonel M. Lewis Clark organized the Louisville Jockey Club and conducted a race meet in 1875. One of the feature races of that year was a three-year-old event won by H. P. McGrath's Aristides. Thus began the Kentucky Derby, and there followed the construction of fancy race resorts around the country.

The first bookmaker to take bets on races opened for business in Philadelphia in 1866. Bookmakers were soon allowed on racetrack grounds everywhere.

In 1868, following twenty years of research, Colonel Sanford D. Bruce published the first volume of the *American Stud Book*. The book served the same purpose in the United States that the *General Stud Book* did in Great Britain—to record the lineage and race records of all thoroughbreds in the country.

Sometime between 1886 and 1888, a new ruling was adopted concerning the birthdate of thoroughbreds in North America. Until then the northern states used January 1 as their common date, while the southern states used May 1. The new ruling made January 1 the birthdate of all thoroughbreds in North America. This change made it easier to specify conditions for races restricted by the age of the competing horses. Such conditions were impossible without a standard date. For instance, the Kentucky Derby is for three-year-olds only. All horses born three years prior to the race are eligible, even if their calendar birthday happens to fall after the date of the race. They all become three-year-olds on January 1. In the 1980s, some 50,000 thoroughbreds were registered a year.

By 1894, 314 tracks were operating in the United States. There was little supervision or reciprocity among them. The disciplining of a trainer or jockey at one track was not necessarily honored anywhere else; a horse's performance might not be recognized from one track to another, and differing rulings simply confused the issues as well as allowed for dishonesty.

In 1890, Pierre Lorillard attempted to correct the problem of lack of uniform supervision with the formation of a seven-member

Board of Control. James R. Keene then expanded on the concept and in 1894 organized The Jockey Club in New York, patterned after the English Jockey Club. The Jockey Club became the racing authority, regulating and directing the whole of the turf sport. According to Tom Biracree and Wendy Insinger, in their 1982 *Complete Book of Thoroughbred Horse Racing,* today The Jockey Club is no longer judge and jury of racing because the states have taken over those roles. Instead, it is the keeper of the *Stud Book* and the official registry for the thoroughbred horse in the United States.

In 1880, the population of the new city of Ocala was listed at 803, all inhabitants residing around the central courthouse. By 1890, its population of 2,904 made it one of the largest towns in Florida, with a major commercial center and tourist resort.

In 1908, country racing was conducted in Florida when the first Marion County Fair opened with a racetrack as one of its attractions. One of the most successful fairs in Florida, it continued annually into the 1920s.

In 1909, a one-mile race course opened its inaugural meet at West Tampa, featuring the Thanksgiving Day Handicap. Jacksonville also opened racing that winter at Moncrief Park. Through 1911, Tampa, Jacksonville, and Pensacola were the major racing sites in Florida. By 1911, St. Augustine had become America's foremost winter resort. Many visitors would travel a few miles north to enjoy horse racing at Moncrief Park outside of Jacksonville. This track enjoyed immense popularity under the guidance of the flamboyant H. D. "Curly" Brown. Oral betting was in vogue then, and there were twenty-five to forty bookies at Jacksonville in contrast to three to five bookies handling the Tampa course.

Brown was practically a one-person official staff. Besides operating the track, he was racing secretary and starter. A souvenir program dated March 21, 1911, vividly describes Mr. Brown's idea of attracting the public to the races. The feature race was the Ladies' Day Handicap offering $600 to the winner. Five other races carried $400 awards. There were two cofeatures. One was a mule race at one mile for a $250 purse. The other was the Novelty Handicap race for winnings of $500. The competition in this race consisted of two thoroughbreds, two men, and two automobiles. Conditions stated that the two well-known runners, W. H. Williams and C. C. Dowlings, would race 525 yards. From a standing start, one automobile was to cover one mile and the other one and one-sixteenth miles. Unfortunately, what distance the thoroughbreds were to race was not listed, and as our source was a program announcement we do not know the winner.

By the turn of the century, a new wave of antigambling hysteria was sweeping the country. State after state banned bookmaking. By 1908, the number of racetracks in the United States had plummeted from 314 to 25. Even the glamorous Belmont was shut down during 1911 and 1912.

In 1911, the Florida legislature ruled that gambling was a nuisance and passed a law against betting (Bill #32 in the *Journal of the Senate*) by a vote of twenty-eight to zero. This prompted the Florida Live Stock Fair Association to disband racing for the following winter. Moncrief Park closed its gates, and there was no known racing in the state until 1916.

Nationwide, the closing of the tracks left Americans with many horses to sell, and they turned to England. In 1913, in an effort to prevent a flooding of the market, the English Jockey Club passed the Jersey Act, declaring that only horses traced in all their lines to animals previously registered in *The General Stud Book* would be accepted for future registration. Although all American thoroughbreds trace back in their tail-male lines (the subject's sire, his sire, and his sire, and so on) to the three English foundation sires—Eclipse, Herod, and Matchem—early American breeding necessarily included many half-bred mares. The offspring of these horses were allowed to race in England, but they could only be registered in the *Half-Bred Stud Book* and thus were denied any possibility for use as breeding stock.

While the Jersey Act was a crisis to American breeders at the time, in the end it resulted in today's superiority of American breeding. Once racing resumed, which it did after several years, Americans were still free to import good blooded stock, while the British had closed their doors on any fresh blood. The Jersey Act was finally repealed in 1949, when the British could no longer deny the obvious superiority of the American thoroughbred.

By 1925, Ocala, with a population of 6,500, was considered the most progressive section of Central Florida. It was the geographical center of the state, located on the Atlantic Coast Line and the Seaboard Air Line railroads as well as on the Dixie Highway. Most of the state's agricultural industry was in this area, making it a major source of corn, oats, cowpeas, peanuts, hay forage, citrus, and beans. Through Carl Rose, the highly important phosphate and limestone industries had been built up. Five mines produced

Carl Rose (left) with military friends at Rosemere Farm (by permission of W. Vines).

enough limerock to be used in 60 percent of all the road construction needs in the state. Tests on Ocala limerock run as high as 99.58 percent pure. Ocala–Marion County was about to undergo the second rush of population growth, this time the result of thoroughbreds rather than government incentive, and Carl Rose would once again play an important part.

There were now four major racetracks located in the state. One was at St. Johns (known as Keeney Park up to 1925, when its name was changed to St. Johns), another at Pompano, where tobacco tycoon R. J. Reynolds ran three meetings in 1924, 1925, and 1926.

(Another group would later open it in 1967 under the name Seminole Turf Club and conduct the first night racing in the state, but it would be short-lived). On the Gulf, there was a track called Tampa Downs (only one of the many names it would eventually carry), where in 1926 the first Florida Derby would run. The fourth track was Hialeah.

2

"Uncle Jimmy"

In 1907, James H. Bright moved to southern Florida, and the state would never be the same. He arrived with his brother Charles from St. Louis, Missouri, in search of broader horizons. In St. Louis, he and his family owned a successful business, the Imperial Laundry. Many early turf writers thought that Jimmy Bright was a retired muleskinner, basing that assumption on pictures of him with spotted mules. But he had only been the public relations man for his family's business. In that capacity, he found a pair of black and white spotted mules, hitched them to a wagon, set a Dalmatian dog on top, and the flamboyant composition became the Imperial Laundry's trademark—hence the mistaken impression that he had anything to do with mules. He did, however, have a passion for fast horses; whether thoroughbreds or standardbreds didn't matter. At one point, he owned the "champion runner" in the St. Louis area.

By the time he and Charles left St. Louis, they had narrowed their choice of horizons to Texas or Florida. On Jimmy's preference, they ended up in the Florida Everglades and bought vast quantities of land together. Jimmy eventually bought out Charles, who never did become accustomed to the strange environment of Florida. Jimmy's wife, Lulu, and his daughter Martha visited Florida only in the winter until 1919 when they moved to the state permanently.

A dapper gentleman, about five feet, seven inches tall and 130 pounds, "Uncle Jimmy," as everyone came to call him, was usually seen in a tidy blue suit with a little collar and a bow tie. His very presence spelled aristocrat. Among the many things he did to help the development of Florida was to introduce Brahma cattle to the state. Florida would become a worldwide leader in production of this hardy bovine, one of the few to thrive in the heat and humidity of South Florida.

Uncle Jimmy, ever ready to make a killing, immediately recognized the potential of land in South Florida which, except for the coastline, was virtually unpopulated. Throughout the history of the

James Bright, the man who started it all in South Florida. Photo by Leo Frutkoff (by permission of the FTBA).

Florida thoroughbred, real estate led the list of influential factors. Both in the South, with the establishment of racing, and later in the North, when breeding had a strong foothold, the businesses of real estate and horses have influenced one another and have grown together.

One of Bright's best friends was Glenn Hammond Curtiss (1878–1930), a world-renowned aviator of the day. According to Frank J. Cameron, in his 1964 book, *The Hungry Tiger*, it was Curtiss who in 1908 made the first public flight of one kilometer in his plane, the *June Bug*. He was the designer of the first successful amphibian planes, often called "flying boats" or "pontoon planes." His company, the Curtiss-Wright Company, expanded in 1917 and built planes for the United States, Great Britain, and Russia, including the famous "Jennies."

Curtiss and Bright became friends when Bright donated the use of his flat pastures west of Hialeah for Air Force pilots training during World War I. After the war, Curtiss and Bright formed a partnership named the Curtiss-Bright Company and bought up all the land around what is now Hialeah, Miami Springs, and Opa-Locka as well as a great deal of land around Lake Okeechobee, paying about $10 an acre for it. Theirs was the first big land speculation of any kind in South Florida.

They then met a young lawyer from Americus, Georgia, who had just been elected prosecuting attorney there. The lawyer was looking for a more imaginative position, so Bright and Curtiss invited him to come to South Florida and represent them as their attorney. Dan Chappell became the secretary of the Curtiss-Bright Company in the early 1920s, and they would all profit enormously from the venture.

Following this daring gamble, their problem became what to do with the land: how could they attract people to come and buy? Bright turned a portion of his land into successful dairy farming. On a much larger portion, he ran herds of beef cattle. He sold some to a dog track operation, which conducted afternoon racing and later introduced the first mechanical rabbit. Bright was entranced with the Everglades, which in those days were protected by a series of drainage canals. He was sure that this unusual and natural paradise should be an attraction if only he could figure out how to market it.

While living in St. Louis, Bright had been connected with various Missouri horse clubs. He had often engaged in racing and was an accomplished rider himself. The success of both the dog track, in which he had a hand, and a jai alai fronton he also helped start led him naturally to the concept of a horse track if one could be built in the marshy swampland.

Because he often rode his pony around the land, Bright was familiar with the quantities of marl in the neighborhood. If marl were just below the surface, a racetrack could indeed be constructed. When his friends heard the idea, they thought he had truly gone mad. Bright persevered in his search for the right person to carry out his dream. The search resulted in an offer from Joseph M. Smoot, a promoter from Buffalo, New York, who was also attracted to Florida by the real estate boom. A man of accomplished promotional talents, he was sure he could make a killing somehow in this fast-growing state. According to legend, Smoot hit town with an impressive wardrobe, a letter of introduction, and a gold-headed cane, which was to become his scepter when he later reigned over Hialeah. A gay, debonair attitude completed the picture.

After thoroughly checking Smoot's background, Bright turned over 160 acres of land to the city of Miami for the token price of

$10, requiring only that it be used for a racetrack. Smoot outlined a plan for organizing a jockey club and building a racetrack. Bright and Smoot gathered support from several leading Miamians, including Frank B. Shutts, a lawyer who once owned controlling interest in the *Miami Herald;* Ed Romfh of the First National Bank; and Luke Cassidy, Jack Cleary, John I. Day, Mars Cassidy, John B. Campbell, and William N. Urmey, all wealthy Miami businessmen. One man's dream of a racetrack in the wild, tropical Florida Everglades was about to become Hialeah. Building the track was no small project, however. Help came in the form of both advice and cash from many interested equestrians and investors. Eventually the basic facility, which would become one of the finest racing plants in the nation, was built.

The Miami Jockey Club opened its inaugural meet at Hialeah Race Track on January 15, 1925. In the November 24, 1963, issue of the *Miami News* ("The Story of Horse Racing in Florida"), one not-so-enthusiastic turf writer, Miller Davis, wrote in retrospect that Miami was still an "overgrown sandpit inhabited by real estate brokers and unemployed millionaires. . . . This was the heyday of the sailor straw hat for men and concave figures for women." The grandstand was one of the first built on a slant to the track in order to offer maximum visibility. But in 1925, it was merely concrete-and-steel functional, not at all glamorous. There was, in fact, very little glamor on opening day to even hint at what Hialeah would later become.

Trainer John Zoeller, who would manage John Hay Whitney's Greentree Stud Florida Annex in Ocala in the 1960s, was responsible for the first string of racehorses ever brought into Miami for racing. His recollections give a vivid account of what those first days were like. By the time he shipped his string from New York, they were dead tired. He knew they could not stay on the railroad car another day. But there was a problem getting to the track. There was no unloading platform in the tiny town of Hialeah, so the horses had to be unloaded in downtown Miami and walked the ten miles to the track. The grooms carried baseball bats for protection against the snakes. Although old Hialeah's backstretch could accommodate 1,000 horses, many stables were afraid to ship south to a meeting that might fold at any minute. John Zoeller did not brave the trip again until 1954. As Horace Wade wrote in the March 1954 issue of the *American Turf and Sport Digest* ("Tales of the Turf") at that time, Zoeller could not believe the changes that had taken place.

Hialeah Clubhouse during the opening meet in 1925 (by permission of *The Florida Horse*).

But in 1925 there was little to hint at the glamorous future. The dusty track was a peculiar greenish gold and mustard color, which did nothing to brighten the overall scene. A clear view of the backstretch clotheslines with their bedraggled rags flapping in the breeze was visible over an infield made less than festive with partially burned and charred weeds. The town of Hialeah itself did not enhance the prospect of a day of fun. Available entertainment included the afternoon dog races, jai alai, floating crap games, poker spas, bootleggers, and ladies of the night. Sometimes the boys about town played rough.

Yet on opening day, as if to prove Bright's predictions and fulfill his hopes, there was not an empty seat to be found. Fifteen thousand watched as Ivan Parke booted home the first winner ever at Hialeah—Braedalbane, who paid $9.20 to win. It was also Ivan Parke on Corinth, owned by Mose Goldblatt, who won the opening day feature, the Miami Handicap. The liquor, straight off the boat from Nassau, was supplied by Joe Smoot and flowed fast and free. The boxes were occupied by many of the famous of that day: John Philip Sousa, Gilda Grey, Joseph P. Kennedy, a disgruntled Al Jolson on his way back from Cuba (where he had temporarily lost his voice), Jimmy Walker (mayor of New York, who was made honorary president of the club for one day), Gloria Swanson in a blue foulard silk dress, Will Rogers, Bernard Gimbel, Albert Payson Terhune, and an unidentified Indian prince in a jeweled turban (who was the first to sign the guest book, albeit illegibly).

Luke Cassidy, the track's first general manager, decided that it was unladylike to bet and sent around an order that women would not be allowed to put their money down on their favorite horses. The women of the day had a different thought. Dressed in filmy georgette dresses belted low on the hip, with felt cloches pulled low over their eyebrows and amber beads swinging, they charged the windows in such numbers that they could not be halted. A sulking Luke Cassidy was forced to admit defeat.

Since pari-mutuel wagering was not legal in Florida, betting in those days was conducted in a number of surreptitious ways: by selling postcards depicting the horses in each race and cashing in the winning cards, by buying fake options on a horse with the track buying them back at prevailing odds if the horse won, and with "certificates" showing the amount deposited in a "purse" to which were added the wagers of all other persons backing that horse. The certificate also showed the horses' numbers and whether the "purchasers" expected them to win, place, or show. The money deposited into these purses was then distributed evenly among the "owners of the purse," with the track retaining about 5 percent. In this way, the tracks of the day attempted to get around the prohibition on gambling, which the courts had declared a "public nuisance." But providing a place to gamble was definitely illegal. According to the Florida Supreme Court's *Syllabus of the Court*, Pompano, a harness track north of Ft. Lauderdale, was taken to court on the charge at least once. Governor John Martin ignored the gambling problem as long as he could. But on March 9, 1927, the State Supreme Court upheld that gambling was illegal. The governor then was forced to close all the dog tracks, jai alai frontons and, after waiting just long enough for Hialeah to complete its season, the horse tracks. Hialeah did not open at all in 1928.

The Miami Jockey Club prospered through the 1926 and 1927 seasons, so much so that the surrounding dog tracks had to switch their racing times from afternoon to evening to avoid the competition. At that time, there were so many dog tracks in the area that it was referred to as "Dog Town." In 1931, Hialeah would purchase the closest dog track in order to expand its stable area and to bring in a railroad spur for the elite patrons of the horse track.

In 1929 the depression hit Florida in the same way it hit the rest of the nation. The land boom was over, and racetrack attendance plummeted. For a while it was feared the entire Miami Jockey Club operation would be abandoned. Late in 1929, Smoot sold out to J. H. Carstairs of Philadelphia. Carstairs, who apparently bought Hialeah only for an investment, quickly resold it in 1930, this time to a man who cared a great deal about what would happen to it, Joseph Early Widener.

Joseph E. Widener was the son of Peter Widener, and he inherited the Widener estate when his brother George died with the sinking of the *Titanic*. His passion for thoroughbreds started early in life despite his father's disapproval. He became vice-chairperson of The Jockey Club, a much more elitist organization in those days. This position was a small coup for a man who had spent his life trying to be a Philadelphia Main Line socialite. His significant impact upon the racing world is unquestioned. He refurbished Belmont Park and created in Hialeah what some would call the "Belmont of the South." An article in the *New York Times* read: "In 1931 and 1932 a great expansion of horse racing took place in various sections of the country all traceable to the pioneering efforts of Mr. Widener in Florida."

Many years later, Widener would be credited with instituting a mechanical pari-mutuel wagering system, first at Hialeah and later at Belmont. Although the system was about as personal as a robot, Widener argued that it was for the good of the public and that ridding the tracks of bookies provided a cleaner, more respectable atmosphere for the sport in general. His conviction paid off with higher than ever handles, purse distributions, and attendance following the installation of the new machines. Widener was a pioneer in attempting to ferret out drugged horses, "ringers" (one horse swapped for another), and other unsavory methods of attempted race fixing.

Widener was the master of Elmendorf Stud in the bluegrass heart of Kentucky. Here he stood such greats as Fair Play (sire of Man o' War) and raised the produce of August Belmont's bloodlines, since he had purchased a major portion of Belmont's racing stable. Widener was also well known for his world-renowned art collection, considered one of the greatest private collections in the world. It was donated to the National Gallery of Art in Washington, D.C., in 1940. This was the man who now claimed Hialeah.

With a group of associates that included Colonel Edward R. Bradley, Widener bought the Miami Jockey Club. Bright, who had been Hialeah's first president, remained on the board of directors until his death in 1959 and continued to be a stout booster of his dream track. Joseph Smoot went on to other projects, which will be discussed later in this book.

Widener changed the name of the track to Hialeah Park. The Miami Jockey Club became the Miami Racing Association, and it would henceforth operate under the same rules as those of the New York Jockey Club. He then installed Frank J. Bruen (1885–1939) as track manager. Bruen was the former vice-president and general manager of New York City's Madison Square Garden. Another major step had to be taken before Widener would put any new money into the track itself. The first $50,000 he spent went to Tallahassee, where he supported a move to get pari-mutuel wagering legally approved in Florida. This highly important step was made possible by the hard work and dedication of one man in particular: Dan Chappell, whose story follows in the next chapter.

3

"Mr. Racing"

Dan Chappell was born in Americus, Georgia. Shortly after finishing law school at Emory University in Atlanta and serving a term as prosecuting attorney in Americus, he was enticed to South Florida by his friends Jimmy Bright and Glenn Curtiss. After a brief time of commuting between Florida and Georgia, he moved south in 1925. The first mayor of the young town of Hialeah, Jack Grethen, appointed Chappell as Hialeah's first city attorney in the spring of 1925. Chappell drew up the charter for and presided over the meeting at which the town of Opa-Locka was incorporated on May 14, 1926.

About the same time, Dorothy Dekle, one of five beautiful sisters (several were beauty queens), moved to South Florida from Cornelia, Georgia, to be a school teacher. Chappell was immediately smitten. However, Dekle was also dating John Hay Whitney, commonly known as Jock Whitney. The son of Payne Whitney was of a class beyond the ken of most "commoners." Jock Whitney was heir to the largest private fortune in the United States at the time, was an outstanding Yale athlete, had an unmatched pedigree, and also owned some of the bluest-blooded horses in the world. He gave Dekle a Pierce-Arrow automobile, the latest fad of the day.

Dan Chappell was a big, outgoing man known for his light-colored suits and his Havana cigars. He usually wore a hat, which covered the expanding bald spot on his head. He was not a bit put off by the aristocratic Whitney. With the proceeds of his successful land deals burning a hole in his pocket, he did Whitney one better. He sent the lady an orangutan with a gold chain and a nameplate inscribed "Jock" around its neck. That terminated Dekle's romance with Jock Whitney, and she became Mrs. Dan Chappell. She and Dan had two daughters, Dorothy and Danna.

Late in the 1920s, the East Coast of Florida was suffering. The real estate boom, during which Chappell and Bright had made a fortune, was over, but the men were still left with a great deal of

Dan Chappell in 1925. Photo by Pictorial Press Photos (by permission of Dorothy Davis).

unsold land. The 1926 hurricane had destroyed much of the area. Cattle owners were blowing up dams that flooded their pastureland. Tourists were staying in the area only a day or two, then moving on to Cuba or New Orleans, where they could find racing and legal gambling. Something was needed to attract and keep the tourists.

Bright, Curtiss, and Chappell, laden with land they could not sell, decided to put Chappell into politics. He ran on an announced platform supporting pari-mutuel betting. Although the churches and newspapers opposed him, he managed to get elected to the Florida House of Representatives for Dade County. In 1929, Chappell's friend, Claude Pepper, was also a member of the Florida House. Since both men felt that legalized betting would attract business to the area, they began working on a bill to legalize pari-mutuel wagering. This was not the first year in which such an attempt had been made. In 1919, an attempt to nullify the antigambling bill that had been passed in 1911 had been unsuccessful.

Southern racing fans were up against more than just internal politicking for their gaming privileges. For many years, the Cuban lobby had been effective in eliminating Florida competition to its own racing industry. On May 31, 1925, the year Hialeah was born, the *Havana Telegram* published an article advocating no gambling in Florida. Many believed that lawyer James M. Carson, who sued and closed down the tracks in 1927 and 1928, was actually paid by Cuban interests.

In 1929, when Chappell, Pepper, and their associates began working to pass a bill legalizing pari-mutuel wagering, they were faced with Cuban lobbyists and Southern Baptists, both of whom were determined opponents. Money and religion held the line, and history repeated itself in 1929.

Although disappointed, Chappell was quick to realize that he had not prepared himself well enough or laid the groundwork adequately. More determined than ever, he did his homework before the next biennial legislative session. In 1931, with much more study and hard work under his belt, Chappell tried again. He had the full support now of J. E. Widener, who promised to turn Hialeah into a second Belmont Park if Chappell could get pari-mutuel wagering legalized.

Chappell first went to work on Governor Doyle S. Carlton, Sr. Florida was part of the strong Southern Baptist belt, and the governor was most definitely a Baptist. Somehow, Chappell managed to elicit a promise from Carlton that he would not veto the bill if indeed Chappell could get it adopted by the legislature. Chappell did not quit there, however. With fortunate foresight and as House majority leader, he made sure that several of the governor's own bills were held up until Chappell's gambling bill could get onto the floor. Chappell then found out that Carlton had given his promise to the preachers that he would veto the bill. At that point, Chappell told the governor that he could get a new floor leader; he and Carlton were through—and so was the governor's tax program. It

The ladies of Hialeah. Mrs. Dan Chappell is second from the left (by permission of Dorothy Davis).

would take three extra sessions to get Carlton's budget through the legislature.

S. P. Robineau and Walter Kehoe of Dade County were two legislators who supported Chappell's efforts. They introduced one of the gambling bills. On April 16, 1931, John W. Watson and A. M. Taylor introduced Bill 361, which consolidated House bills 190 (pari-mutuel wagering), 194 (creation of a racing commission), 195 (horse racing and dog racing regulations), and 514 (general regulation of pari-mutuel wagering). The revised bill focused attention on the state's percentage of the revenue, which would be aimed at education. The *Journal of the Senate* and the *Journal of the House of Representatives*, both for the twenty-third legislative session, contain information on these bills. All wagering bills were then referred to the Committee on Public Amusement.

John McDermott, in a June 13, 1976, *Miami Herald* article, "Horse Racing's Old Friend Recalls Big Economic Impact," reported that at the height of the battle in the Senate, a clergyman from Daytona Beach delivered a prayer: "'Taint right to taint education by using gambling money to educate our children." Senator Hayes Lewis of West Florida responded, "The only thing wrong with this gambling bill is that it 'taint enough." During this emotional battle, Chappell was personally threatened so many times that he sent his wife and two daughters back to Georgia to wait until the voting was over. The bill passed the Senate on May 14, 1931, by a vote of twenty to fifteen. It then passed the House as Senate Bill 361 on May 20.

On May 22, the *Miami News* predicted that Governor Carlton would allow the bill to become law without either approving or disapproving. The May 23 *Tallahassee Observer* reported that the governor was "maintaining a discreet silence." The attorney general and assistant attorney general of Kentucky sent an unsolicited message to Carlton: "Betting pari-mutuels on race tracks in Kentucky is demoralizing advocates of racing active in Kentucky politics. We urge you to veto the bill. Use our names if necessary." The *Miami News* reported that the Kentucky Court of Appeals had recently upheld the legality of the Kentucky pari-mutuel bill.

On May 29, the governor vetoed the bill. In his address to the Senate explaining his veto, he said: "It is unsound and unwise from an economic, political or moral standpoint to commit the State to a partnership in legalized gambling in any form. If we start with the pari-mutuel, where shall we stop?

"As a temporary expedient permitted by public officers in a spirit of liberality and under systems which some call legal and others a subterfuge, the racetrack has proven a doubtful if not dangerous experiment."

But Chappell was not through yet. He set out to get the veto overridden. Chappell had all but one of the required number of votes. Senator Arthur Gomez of Monroe County had agreed to vote in favor of the bill only if his vote was absolutely necessary. It was.

In the 1980s, Henry Taylor, Jr. was on the board of directors of Calder Race Track and was secretary and general counsel of Tropical Park, Inc. and of Calder Race Track, Inc. During the 1931 fight for the pari-mutuel bill, he was the eighteen-year-old son of the prominent Miami lawyer. He often chauffeured the representatives who were lobbying for support of their bill. Taylor remembers the episode well: "Senator Gomez was in Key West when it became necessary to override Governor Carlton's vote. I drove my father to lower Matecumbe where we met Senator Gomez. At that time the highway to Key West had not been completed. You would ride a ferry for awhile, drive for awhile, ride again. We picked up Senator Gomez, drove him to Miami and rode with him on the train from Miami to Jacksonville. Then we caught what was called a puddle-jumper, a one-car, diesel-powered arrangement, to Tallahassee. We stayed with him until the vote was taken, then took him back home."

It was a delightful coup. On June 4, just when the opposition was ready to celebrate victory, Senator Gomez was called upon to cast the deciding vote (twenty-six to twelve) in favor of legalizing pari-mutuel wagering in Florida. On June 6, the House followed suit with a fifty-five to twenty-six vote. Because of the veto, the dog track owners, whom the horse track owners had successfully shut out up to this time, rode in on a shirttail amendment.

One of the factors that helped in finally getting the bill accepted and the governor's veto overridden was the unique way Chappell appealed to the pocketbook of each county. He wrote into the bill that each of the sixty-seven counties would receive an equal portion of the state's share of taxable revenue from racing. The legislators could see the advantage of being able to finance their counties' governments, schools, and hospitals without having to tax local residents. To this day, that clause remains in effect. In the case of some of the poorer counties, pari-mutuel wagering has been the only source of educational support. The clause has also served as an example to other states requesting information in setting up similar programs. In the 1970s, another legislative act placed a cap of $446,500 on the amount received by each county, for a total of $29.5 million (FS 550.13). Once the public got used to having that income, it became very hard to give up the revenue, as Dan Chappell knew. Horse racing was in Florida to stay.

Immediately following passage of the new law, the legislature designated the land in the city of Hialeah upon which Hialeah Park stood to be the site of the first pari-mutuel gambling in Florida. Most of Dade County, where the Baptist faith was strong, still opposed gambling. The city council retaliated by adopting an ordinance prohibiting gambling in the city of Hialeah. Never one to be daunted, on June 16, 1931, Chappell and his friends introduced House Bill 102-X during a special session of the legislature. The bill abolished the charter of the city of Hialeah. They then enacted a revised charter for Hialeah with its own provisions for government, boundaries, and franchises.

Once again, Chappell and friends softened the blow with financial inducements. Their bill guaranteed that the City of Hialeah would receive a 10¢ head tax on every person who went to the racetrack to "relieve the people of Hialeah from the added burden by reason of the wear and tear on the city streets and added facilities necessary by reason of said racing activities." This bill was enacted into law as Section 10, Chapter 14832 of the Laws of Florida, Acts of 1931. Thus was the resistance of the Baptists overcome at Hialeah and in Florida. Although the religious influence would continue to be felt, the door was open at last.

Chappell was appointed city attorney of Hialeah to guarantee no further interference from the local people, who had been known to show up at city council meetings with shotguns and clubs. Most of the city commissioners fell under Chappell's persuasive influence, were charmed by gambling incentives, and came to appreciate a money-making operation. Within a few years, most would hold jobs at Hialeah Park as an additional source of personal income.

Senate Bill 361 stipulated a 3 percent takeout (money deducted from each mutuel pool for track revenue and taxes) for the state. It also provided for the formation of a state racing commission to govern all pari-mutuel activities. Carlton appointed, in his words, "men of the highest honor" to the commission: L. D. Reagin, representing the state at large; M. H. Mabry, representing the First Congressional District; R. L. Sweger, representing the Second Congressional District; M. R. Harrison, representing the Third Congressional District; and R. N. Dosh, representing the Fourth Congressional District.

Reagin, from Sarasota, was appointed chairperson of the first racing commission. He was a member of the Florida Railroad Commission and was the former editor and publisher of the *Sarasota Daily Times*, at one time the greatest revenue-producing weekly in the world, according to a June 29, 1931, *Sanford Herald* article. Mabry was in real estate and banking in Tampa. He was elected secretary of the commission. Sweger was editor of the *Gadsden County Times* in Quincy. Harrison was a Miami contractor with some background in building dog tracks. Dosh was the editor of the *Ocala Evening Star*, a newspaper that strongly opposed legalizing pari-mutuel wagering. By appointing Dosh to the racing commission, Governor Carlton hoped to quiet some of the outcry against the new bill. The "Governor's Baptist Racing Commission," as it was called by the press at the time, was considered to consist of men very similar to the governor. They would follow the letter of the law rather than its spirit. While much fun was poked at the men at first, their appointments did indeed calm the fears of most people, and a general feeling of acceptance finally prevailed. The first commissioners worked hard and conscientiously, with little guidance, at a job unfamiliar to them. The commission held its first meeting June 29, 1931. Harrison tendered his resignation immediately and was replaced by R.B. Burdine of Miami. Burdine was another highly respected businessperson who would be made the second chairperson of the commission early the following year due to questionable attitudes of Chairperson Reagin. Reagin began to enjoy his time spent at the tracks a little too much, and he was pressured by the other commissioners to resign the chair.

For the 1931 to 1932 racing season, twenty applications to hold meets were received from all over the state. After receiving a permit from the commission, each applicant then had to undergo a voting procedure by the general public in its respective county. By the winter racing season, only three permittees would actually conduct racing: the Miami Jockey Club (Hialeah Park), the Gables Racing Association (Tropical Park), and the Florida Jockey Club (St. Johns Park). In this first legal racing season, the Miami Jockey Club raced thirty-nine days, giving the state a total revenue of $258,772.23. Gables Racing Association raced thirty-four days and gave the state $127,537.86. The Florida Jockey Club, with only a ten-day meet, turned in $17,561.56. The revenue to the state from all pari-mutuel interests was $710,388.20, accordinging to the July 1932 Annual Report of the State Racing Commission.

The legalization of pari-mutuel wagering was the high point of Chappell's career, a coup which would earn him the honor of becoming the fourth person to be admitted to Florida's Racing Hall of Fame (instituted by and located at the Florida Thoroughbred Breeders' Association offices in Ocala, 1968) and the only living person to that date to be so honored. (By 1990, several more living honorees had been inducted.) December 26, 1981, fifty years after the first day of pari-mutuel racing, was declared Dan Chappell Day by the then metropolitan mayor of Dade County, Stephen Clark. Governor Bob Graham dedicated a marker at the site of old Tropical Park for the Historical Association of Southern Florida. The site is now a county park.

Chappell served for one more session of the state legislature in 1935. In 1936, at the urging of many supporters, he made a bid for

Dan Chappell in the 1950s (by permission of Dorothy Davis).

governor, running sixth in a field of fourteen candidates. Some felt that if a potential $200,000 supporter, Col. Henry M. Daugherty, had not died before getting the money to him, Chappell might have won. Chappell gave Claude Pepper so much time and support in his race for the U.S. Senate that he might have hurt his own race. Chappell also lost a congressional race in 1944 to an incumbent and lost a bid for the Dade County Commission in 1962. His political contributions to the state and to the thoroughbred industry have endured, however. In 1948, he was elected president of the Horsemen's Benevolent and Protective Association.

If Chappell's political career had peaked, his activities in the thoroughbred business were only beginning. His contributions to the industry would continue to be as dramatic when he later operated Sunshine Stud, north of Ocala. There he would stand an obscure son of Northern Dancer named Staff Writer, who became the sire of Timely Writer. Timely Writer went on to racing glory as a popular racehorse in 1982, but his timing was not as good as his name implied. The talent of the ill-fated colt was brought to a heart-wrenching end in front of millions, both at the track and on television, when he broke his leg during the Jockey Club Gold Cup and had to be put down.

Dan Chappell died just before the colt's glory, but his daughter, Dorothy "Dot" Davis, would live it for him. Staff Writer became another of Northern Dancer's unraced and previously unknown sons that made it to the big time. After years of heartbreak, Dan Chappell and his daughter had bred the big one.

4

The Friendly Track

Hialeah, which would later blossom into one of the most important tracks in the country, was not the first to open her gates following the legalization of pari-mutuel betting. Surprisingly, a new track beat Hialeah out of that history-making day, and in doing so, inaugurated a battle over dates that continues to plague Florida racing up to the present day.

Following the depression and the "public nuisance" ruling about gambling, many tracks closed down in 1927 and 1928. About the time racing was resumed at Hialeah in 1929, another track came into being halfway between St. Augustine and Jacksonville. Keeney Park was named after its owner, Frank Keeney, a Brooklyn theatrical man turned horseplayer. The track was operated by the Florida Jockey Club, and it featured not only racing with oral betting but also slot machines and a cabaret show at night. The reformers made the jumping joint even hotter, however, since it was difficult to conduct a meet against their opposition. Deciding the meet was not going well enough to fight for, Frank Keeney went out for a walk one day and never returned to racing. Keeney sold out to William Vincent "Big Bill" Dwyer and Bill Gallagher, who renamed the track St. Johns Park after the broad river that flowed nearby.

Big Bill was known as a big spender, as generous with strangers down on their luck as with his closest friends. He was a "soft touch," his money disappearing as quickly as he made it, which was very quickly. He had also been known as the "king of the rumrunners" back in New York during Prohibition. His luck and fortune ran hot and cold. At various times he was head of the famous Montalvo Stud, the New York American hockey team, and later the Brooklyn Dodgers team. He introduced professional ice hockey to New York. Dwyer also had a dark side: he faced death from an opposing rum-runner group, and he was in debt and in court many times. From July 1927 to August 1928, he served time in the Atlanta federal penitentiary for rum-running. This flamboyance often affected how he ran St. Johns Park, which he did until March 10, 1930.

It was in 1930 that Big Bill made his real impact on the Florida turf scene. It began when he threw an elaborate $50,000 party at the Biltmore Hotel in New York and invited every socialite in horse racing to attend. J. E. Widener, who dominated winter racing in Miami, was the guest of honor. Widener was seated at a huge horseshoe-shaped table. Curtains to one side opened, and there stood three of Widener's top thoroughbred racehorses in stalls. The horses were paraded along a special runway; the jockeys sported Widener's barber-pole white and red colors. Osmand, probably the best horse Widener ever owned, was one of the horses present. Widener was so moved that he wept and professed undying love for Dwyer.

That promise was to be short-lived. Almost immediately after the celebration, Dwyer abandoned St. Johns Park and purchased the deserted South Miami Kennel Club, a dog track near Coral Gables. Dwyer asked Widener to cooperate in running the two gambling interests together, under their combined management. Widener was incensed. Dwyer then announced his intention to turn his track into a thoroughbred track to run in opposition to Hialeah. He promptly named his new organization the Gables Racing Association. Hostile feelings between the two men were to smolder until their deaths.

Dwyer's first problem with the old dog track was that the grandstand faced west so that spectators were blinded by the setting sun during an afternoon program. Dwyer had the stand jacked up onto railcars, and mules turned it around to face the east. Seven weeks of reconstruction then followed, a task greatly assisted by the providential (and unusual) lack of rain. Dwyer further provoked Widener by stealing away Hialeah manager Frank J. Bruen to become manager of his new track. Bruen asked Widener if he could manage both tracks, but Widener would have none of it. Dwyer renamed his renovated racetrack Tropical Park.

Dwyer then applied for racing dates to begin on December 31, 1931, giving rise to the first conflict over racing dates in Florida. The newly formed Florida State Racing Commission had its unfamiliar work cut out for it. First, the commissioners had to determine exactly what their own authority was in establishing rules on racing dates. The only clear provision of the 1931 law was that the commissioners were allowed to allot only fifty days of racing to a single plant in any county. Could they then allow two tracks to run concurrently? Tropical Park and Hialeah were only about eighteen miles apart. The commissioners, with the help of the attorney general, determined that they did indeed have authority to permit concurrent operation of plants in a single county and to allot fewer than fifty days to a single plant. Then the commissioners had to consider how to allot the prime winter dates of January and February to the competing tracks. They finally ruled that Hialeah would get January 19 to March 11, while Tropical Park would get February 8 to March 31.

Neither track owner was happy. Each requested a hearing to present his arguments. The hearing was held on November 16, 1931. Even back then, the horsemen took sides. Dan Chappell represented Tropical Park at the hearings, while Desha Breckenridge, Fred Forsythe, and Colonel E. R. Bradley sent telegrams on behalf of Hialeah. The controversy was splashed across the sports pages of sizable newspapers all over the country.

Widener presented his case based on the past:

> Before any other track was a thought in Florida, a preamble was printed to give the people information as to what would be done this winter. It has attracted people from the largest stables, the kind of big turf people we need to make racing successful.
>
> Hialeah Park is to be run on a real sporting plan. The only other track so run is Arlington Park. Hialeah Park is to be modeled after the Arlington Park plan. The stockholders will never receive more than the legal return on their investment. All in excess is to go for charity. I, personally, have never taken a dollar from the sport but have given many to it. (Minutes, Meeting of the State Racing Commission, November 16, 1931)

Widener added that his track needed its requested dates (January 14 through March 5) in order to provide the quality of racing that people had come to expect from Hialeah. He stated that he did not mind if the Coral Gables association raced at the same time.

Dan Chappell stood up to represent the Coral Gables track. According to the November 16, 1931, minutes of the State Racing Commission, Chappell said:

> The racing law is now a state law. Every citizen and every county is interested. If Hialeah gets the dates they want, we'll go bankrupt. We have the friendliest feeling for the Hialeah track and hoped that the two tracks could work together harmoniously, but when they ask

> this Commission to award them all good dates and fix it so we could only lose money, it is unfair and we must protest.
>
> The Miami season, as is well known, reaches its height in February, and it would be unfair to give one track that month. We request fair consideration for our track.

After several hearings, the racing commission decided to cut Hialeah's meet back from forty-five to thirty-six days. Tropical would split its meeting, the first section running from December 26, 1931, to January 16, 1932. Hialeah would then run from January 14 through February 27, 1932, and Tropical would reopen from February 22 to March 19.

Again the Hialeah owners protested, insisting that they needed more days. Following the request for another hearing however, Commissioner M.H. Mabry wrote to Commissioner R.N. Dosh: "Changing these dates once was bad enough, but to change them again would, I feel, subject the commission to severe criticism." Mabry further suggested that with this year's warning, the following year would go much smoother. He felt sure the two tracks would iron out their own difficulties.

Little did he know how long the battle over dates would continue between the southern racetracks of Florida. The tracks have never been able to work out their difficulties about the prime dates. It would require rulings, hearings, fights, and lawsuits year after year in a battle that has done Florida racing little good. By the late 1980s, that very battle would spell the demise of Hialeah. The credibility of the Florida racing industry suffered among the horsemen who never knew where they would race, and who sometimes refused to chance the constant bickering. The battle over dates is a tradition as old as pari-mutuel wagering within the state. But back in 1931, it was a new and frustating dilemma for the racing commissioners, who were doing their best to be fair in their decisions. Just when they thought they had the problem taken care of, another track entered the picture.

The principals of St. Johns Park in St. Augustine were late in filing for their permit. However, after they were approved in their county, they insisted that the racing commission revise their dates allocation to give them some of the prime winter dates. On December 23, 1931, Resolution 811 came from the Mayor Commissioner T. Rogers Mickler, who represented St. Augustine in St. Johns County. The St. Johns principals requested eighteen days beginning on March 7, 1932, and asked the commission to close down racing in South Florida so that their track would have a fair

Tropical Park in 1948 (by permission of *The Florida Horse*).

chance. The principals insisted that they had worked as hard as anybody to get the pari-mutuel bill passed and deserved their time in the sun, too. They also insisted that racing was vital to the economy of St. Augustine.

The St. Johns principals were given ten days and did indeed compete with southern racing. However, they also suffered from lack of organization and business sense. Halfway through their ten-day meet, they asked to be allowed to close down, then changed their minds and decided to complete the meet. As far as can be determined from available records, that was the last time they held a meet.

So it happened that the first legal pari-mutuel horserace in Florida was run at 2:32 P.M. on Saturday, December 26, 1931, at Tropical Park. Because it ran the first "legal" meet, Tropical Park has often been called the oldest track in the state. Seven races were carded, each with a $1,000 purse. There were seventy-one entries for the day. Grandstand admission was $2.30 and clubhouse was $5.00. After weeks of dry weather, a heavy rain fell all morning of opening day. The skies cleared well enough by post time, however, leaving a fast strip and bringing out a crowd of about 5,000 undaunted fans.

The first race run under the new pari-mutuel law was a claiming event (a race in which other owners can purchase any of the horses entered for a specified price; this price, standard for all horses entered in the race, also determines the class of the race) for horses "of all ages." Fourteen horses were entered. The festive atmosphere of the day was enhanced by the many blue and yellow ribbons braided into the animals' manes and tails to commemorate Tropical Park's colors. The event was won by a two-year-old filly, Brown Supinet, owned and trained by M. J. Daly and ridden by Jimmy Stout (who later rode Johnstown to victory in the 1939 Kentucky Derby). The filly ran the six furlongs in 1:14 3/5, winning by half a length over a fast track. The three-year-old Leros, owned by James C. Ellis, president of the Dade Park track in Kentucky, won the featured Tropical Park Opening Handicap. Leros was trained by O. Johnson and ridden by Willie Carroll. Riders that day who later became famous included Jimmy Stout, Willie Carroll, Buddy Hanford, Herb Fisher, Georgie South, and Henry Mills. Four other riders later made their mark as trainers: Eddie DeCamillis, Otie Clelland, Joe Bollero, and Frank Catrone, who would win the Kentucky Derby in 1965 with Lucky Debonair. Because this was the first racing conducted under a racing commission, a state steward was in the stands: William Kennedy, appointed by Governor Carlton.

At first all did not run smoothly. Widener, furious at the turn of events after all his work and expense to get pari-mutuel wagering passed for his track, issued a statement that horses quartered at Hialeah would not be permitted to race at Tropical Park, and no owner or trainer who raced at Tropical Park would be permitted to race at Hialeah. Following strong suggestions on the part of the racing commissioners, Widener then held an interview with the *Miami News* stating that he had been misunderstood and requesting horsemen to help fill Tropical Park's race cards. The racing commission then ruled that any horses stabled at any track in Florida could not be ruled off any other track by mere virtue of their residency. Another racing commission ruling came about when Tropical Park's business dropped off during the end of its meet, when it ran a few dates concurrently with Hialeah. At Tropical Park's request to end the meet early, the commissioners once again had to decide if they could allow a track not to race its allotted days. They ruled that if dates were run in conflict with another track, a track could elect not to finish the meet. More importantly, however, they decided for the future that it would be best to avoid overlapping dates.

Overall, the meet was a popular and financial success. Tropical

Park became known as the "Friendly Track," a reputation it kept for fifty years, under five owners, nine general managers, and relocation to Calder Race Track in 1972. It was, in fact, the only Florida track to operate continuously for fifty years. Even Hialeah shut down for two seasons during World War II. For years, the opening of Tropical Park would signal the beginning of the thoroughbred season in Florida. It would not lose its significance until Calder entered the picture and changed the sport to a year-round proposition.

The stories about Tropical Park are colorful and worth telling. In one story, arriving fans saw orange-laden trees lining the clubhouse driveway every winter, no matter what the opening date. The oranges were tied to the trees by Tropical's superintendent, Henry Collins. Another story involved Lily B. Deming, one of the first women to get a trainer's license. She obtained her first license at Tropical Park in 1937. She won her first race there and later trained for Burt Bacharach.

Although Tropical Park appeared to be a success, the track did not necessarily help Dwyer, whose expensive tastes would still get him into trouble. Unable to live modestly, he continued to spend money on his Palm Beach home, threw outrageously elaborate parties (including one that cost him $154,000), and gambled whenever possible. In 1935, Dwyer nearly lost his whole track, as he had earlier lost a track near Cincinnati because of gambling losses. The nation's biggest bookmaker, Frank Erickson, loaned Dwyer $250,000 (including $57,000 to cover past-due pari-mutuel taxes) to keep the state from taking over the track. Erickson sent his own comptroller to keep an eye on the books. In 1938, Dwyer was sued by the federal government for $3,715,907 in unpaid taxes, interest, and penalties in Brooklyn. In 1941, the U.S. Marshal seized $200,000 worth of stock in the Gables Racing Association to satisfy a lien. Gradually, Dwyer's control of the track slipped away as others took over his stocks and his management. Dwyer was to die penniless but content. "I would not do a thing differently if I did it all over again," he stated, as reported by Horace Wade in *Turf and Sport Digest,* September, 1948.

In 1941, State Senator Ernest R. Graham (father of later governor Bob Graham) changed the course of Tropical Park's history by persuading Governor Spessard Holland to refuse the track a license until the track's ownership was changed. Columnists of the time had begun to write that a foul odor was tainting Florida racing. The

Chicago Guziks, Capones, Riccas, and Fishettis began to arrive, as did New York's emerging Mafia families, all of whom were taking syndicated control of some of the racing. In the summer of 1941, Graham charged in the state legislature that Tropical Park was controlled by gangsters and demanded an investigation of its officers. The Florida Racing Commission met to award dates to Hialeah but deferred action on Tropical Park. A new racing commission was appointed later in the year, and it joined Graham in the battle. It forced Frank Erickson, John Patton of "Chicagoland," and Owney Madden to sell their holdings in the track.

This was one of the boldest moves in racing history. If Tropical Park owners had fought back, the racing commission could have been in a very uncomfortable position. Considering the importance of the revenue racing brought Florida and the political implications involved, the commission's resolve to keep the track dark unless there was a change of ownership was nothing short of heroic. Following this brave move, 87 percent of the track was suddenly up for sale, and many potential buyers were interested. One group was headed by James Donn, who figures in Florida racing at a later date. But the commission approved the sale of the track to a group headed by three officials of the Automatic Totalisator, Ltd.: Harry Straus and Charlie and Gurnee Munn. Included in the group was an audacious journalist, Herbert Bayard Swope, who was made general manager.

In the fall of 1941, Walter Hall Donovan was recruited by the new owners of the track, and he managed it through the uncertain times of World War II. Donovan came to racing in 1933 when he was appointed secretary–member of the Florida State Racing Commission. He organized the National Association of State Racing Commissions (NASRC), the first nationwide racing organization, and served two terms as its president. He then became associate editor of *Turf and Sport Digest*. Donovan later resigned his post at Tropical Park when the president of Garden State Track, Eugene Mori, sought him out and offered him the position of managing director of that track while it was still being built. He went to work at Garden State Track in March 1943.

President Straus was killed in 1951 when his private plane crashed. Nat Herzfeld bought Tropical Park from the estate and imported Jerry Brady to run it. It was just before the 1953 to 1954 meet that Herzfeld received an offer he couldn't refuse. Herzfeld quickly turned a profit by selling the track to Saul Silberman and Ralph De Chiaro, who had successfully operated North Randall in Cleveland, and who were looking for a Florida track. Elmer Vickers, a former FBI agent in Miami, had been with Silberman in Cleveland and came down in 1954 as general manager.

Five foot, two inch tall Saul Silberman, sometimes called the "Little Napoleon of Horse Racing," was the second compulsive gambler to own Tropical Park. He was a would-be rabbi who couldn't stay away from the betting windows. So strong was his addiction that he had his own personal $50 daily double tote machine installed. He had to sign a waiver when it was installed relieving American Totalisator Company from liability if the machine malfunctioned. In spite of a quick temper that often kept Vickers busy soothing bruised feelings, Saul Silberman was the epitome of a host. Some of the stories about him include descriptions of how he used to strut about the grounds the day before Christmas handing out $20 bills. On other days, he offered surprise envelopes to random patrons who might find as much as $50 inside. He had Nathan's kosher hot dogs flown in from Coney Island for a post-race party every Saturday night of the meet.

It was also during Silberman's reign that a unique event in racing occurred. On December 30, 1959, the sixth race was declared official, but the decision was overturned one hour later. A photo finish between Deemster and Teacher had been decided by the placing judges in favor of Deemster. However, their decision was made from a wet print. One hour later when the print dried, it showed Deemster and Teacher reaching the wire in a dead heat. After considering his options, and with no legal necessity to do so, Silberman announced that a mistake had been made and winning tickets on Teacher would be honored ($5.30 to $2). In a rare attempt to be totally fair, Silberman even tried to honor those who insisted they had already thrown away their winning tickets by later announcing that claims could be filed for such winnings. As might be expected, the amount of the claims exceeded the money wagered on Teacher by about ten times.

Ten years later, another event unique to Florida occurred at Tropical. On January 8, 1969, an alligator decided to join in a race. To be precise, the animal was a South American caiman, similar to an alligator but having a longer snout. The caiman had been the pet of a backstretch employee who became disenchanted with it and

Saul Silberman was responsible for many colorful stories that came from Tropical Park in the 1950s. Photo by Leo Frutkoff (by permission of *The Florida Horse*).

turned it loose in the infield lake. During a one and one-eighth mile race, the Sunshine Endurance Handicap, the jockeys and their mounts rounded the clubhouse turn to find the caiman leisurely stretched across the track sunning itself. First and second place finishers, Swamp Rabbit and *Hans II were forced to leap the animal in their path and "ran their shoes off the rest of the race," according to their trainers. The caiman was removed from its adopted home later that day.

Business at Tropical Park was not without controversy under Sil-

*The asterisk is an old designation indicating the horse was imported from a foreign country.

berman's impetuous leadership. In 1957, the racing commission ordered him to dispose of his interest in the track because he was allowing bookmakers to make calls from his office. He fought the commission and won. Time and time again, Silberman bet himself and his track into trouble. He was bailed out by various people, including Vickers and W. L. McKnight, renowned leader of the Minnesota Mining and Manufacturing Corporation (3M). McKnight loaned Silberman so much money that eventually McKnight owned the track. Silberman had pledged 60 percent of his stock in the track to the Teamsters' Union. He pledged the remaining 40 percent to McKnight for his loans. When Silberman died suddenly, McKnight found himself about to be partners with the Teamsters' Union. He flew to Chicago, bought the pledge from the union, foreclosed that pledge on the 60 percent stock, and bought it at the foreclosure sale. Although Hialeah and Gulfstream (a new track, which will be discussed later in this book) principals attended the sale, they were afraid to bid without knowing the debts of Tropical Park.

In the mid-1960s, Stephen A. Calder, a real estate businessman, and Miami Beach architect Stefan Zachar had a vision of summertime racing in Florida, as strange a notion in concept as winter racing originally had been. In 1965, the state legislature had signed a bill authorizing summer racing. Although the three tracks in existence (Tropical, Hialeah, and Gulfstream) sponsored the bill, none of them applied for dates. However, Calder and Zachar did, first in 1965 and then again in 1966. If granted the dates, Calder explained, he would lease one of the existing tracks until his own track could be built. He was naturally reluctant to build until he knew he could get dates.

In their quest, Calder and Zachar solicited in their quest the help of McKnight, who had a personal goal as well. He had witnessed a multiple horse racing accident that influenced him to back the development of a better track surface. He agreed to help Calder if Calder would agree to experiment with a new synthetic surface designed by 3M. A test track was built in 1966 inside the main track at Tropical Park, and one race a day was run on it. Although three harness tracks had previously used the experimental surface, this was the first such track built for thoroughbreds. It was not popular with the horsemen, but McKnight insisted that it would work.

When Calder Race Course was built, therefore, it was a compromise. The main track was the synthetic surface with a covering of mixed sand and marl, the right mixture arrived at over a couple of

The groundbreaking of Calder Race Course in 1970 was also the beginning of summer racing in Florida. Left to right: Stephen Calder, William L. McKnight, Joe Benner (behind in hat), assistant to Calder; and Stefan Zachar. Photo by Leo Frutkoff (by permission of *The Florida Horse*).

years, and the grass track offered an alternative. The new facility was designed by Stefan Zachar, who incorporated years of his studies of the backside and track conditions into his designs. He had a dream of providing comfort for the patrons and the workers, not just for the elite. The plant was built north of the city with far better public access than the older Tropical Park track in the heart of

The paddock and saddling area at Calder Race Course in the early years. Photo by Leo Frutkoff (by permission of *The Florida Horse*).

rapidly developing Miami. Calder obtained his permit, then held the first Calder meet (the first summer thoroughbred racing meet in Florida) at Tropical Park, since his track was as yet unfinished in 1970. Calder Race Course finally opened its gates on May 6, 1971. At that point, since McKnight was involved with both tracks and since the accessibility of Tropical Park was becoming a major problem, Tropical Park held its last race day on January 15, 1972.

Calder's summer program was a success, raising the new track to one of the big three of southern Florida, holding two race meetings each year. It holds its own meet from May to November, emphasizing two-year-old and Florida-bred racing. The more prestigious and the richer of the two meets is the second and shorter one, called "Tropical-at-Calder," held from November to early January. It takes advantage of the first influx of winter tourists. So successful is this meet that in the late 1980s, it too began asking for winter dates, further adding to the competition in South Florida. James Binger, McKnight's son-in-law, was appointed by the McKnight estate to oversee the track upon McKnight's death. In 1979, Binger brought in Kenneth Noe to manage the track, and it continued to

Left to right: Dan Chappell, Jack Price of Carry Back fame, Everett Clay, publicity director for the FTBA and the tracks, and Senator Claude Pepper—at the dedication of a plaque at Tropical Park. The plaque was presented by the Historical Association of Southern Florida in commemoration of fifty years of racing. Photo by Turfotos (by permission of *The Florida Horse*).

increase in popularity and prestige. From 1980 to 1984, Calder Race Course invested $10.5 million in improvements. It has earned the respect of racing people and patrons everywhere.

In 1989, Tropical Park was a football–soccer field, an equestrian center, and a park for basketball, softball, and hiking. The grandstand still stands, a reminder of an exciting era of racing that smacked a little of the daring, the wild, and the never-to-be-forgotten.

5

The Queen of Bayou Racing

Although Hialeah would not, after all, be the first track to run legal racing dates, for many years it would be the most important. As soon as pari-mutuel wagering was approved, J. E. Widener proceeded to spend nearly $2 million remodeling Hialeah. Widener did not take this project lightly. First, he took his architect, Lester W. Giesler, on a grand tour of Europe from the classic turf courses of England to the casinos of the French Riviera. They also traveled to Belmont and Saratoga. From the impressions Giesler formed, he designed what became one of the most unique and beautiful racetrack facilities in America.

The drive through the main gate between perfectly matched royal palm trees is reminiscent of Saratoga's tree-lined walks. Both the spaciousness of Belmont and the elegance of English race courses can be detected in the large saddling stalls; and the open walking ring is similar to that of Longchamp outside Paris. The ugly clubhouse was transformed into a sweeping replica of a French château with wide verandas and balustraded terraces reminiscent of Monte Carlo. The new track was increased from one mile to nine furlongs (one furlong equals one-eighth of a mile) with a bougainvillea-rimmed turf course inside. The finishing touch was a lake in the infield boasting a tiny island in the shape of the State of Florida.

Widener's and Giesler's inspirations did not stop here. One dozen flamingos were imported from Cuba; peacocks arrived from India, pheasants came from Australia; parrots, toucans and a white jabiru stork were imported from Mexico; and crowned cranes were brought from Africa. So many and varied were the birds Widener imported that the infield was declared an Audubon wildlife sanctuary. Every bit as important as the adornments of the new Hialeah, however, were horses of the class owned by Widener, Colonel Edward R. (E. R.) Bradley, and their friends and associates. These fine horses would make Hialeah a winter racing mecca.

Hialeah became famous for the first captive breeding flock of flamingos. They are still the trademark for the track. Photo by Turfotos (by permission of *The Florida Horse*).

Today, with the advent of modern technology and advanced machinery, year-round racing is conducted all over America. But in the 1920s and 1930s, thoroughbred racing was considered a seasonal event, taking place from late spring through fall. Before Hialeah, the only winter racing took place in Cuba at Oriental Park. There, winter racing was a thriving business, powered by New York gambling interests and attended by East Coast people from the North who often wintered in Miami. The big horses and big gamblers were attracted by the $10,000 Cuban Grand National, which was the major race of the season. So jealous were the Cuban track owners of their exclusivity, that they actively funded the fight in the legislature, at the polls, and in the courts against the legalization of pari-mutuel wagering in Florida. The only other winter races were the $100,000 Handicap at Agua Caliente, across the border from California in Mexico, and several $10,000 features in New Orleans backed by Colonel Bradley.

The role that Colonel E. R. Bradley played deserves note here. Although he often stated that he was a gambler by profession,

Bradley was also a top-caliber horseman. His colonel's title was awarded by the State of Kentucky in recognition of his status as landowner and breeder of fine horses. Shortly after the turn of the century, Bradley turned the profits of several gambling ventures into a smart club in Palm Beach, Florida, the Beach Club, which quickly became the place to be if you were anybody. It was one of the first clubs to have a menu that did not list prices. Only nonresidents of Florida over twenty-four years of age were allowed to gamble at the Beach Club. Here cattle barons of the Southwest, big business tycoons from Chicago and Detroit, and railroad magnates from New York rubbed elbows.

In 1925, Bradley took over the somnolent Fair Grounds track in Louisiana and attempted to compete with the newly opened Hialeah Race Track. After an infusion of $1,250,000, the track still had failed to catch on, and Bradley disposed of it at a substantial loss. Apparently ready to join what he could not lick, he then became Hialeah's largest individual stockholder. During the blackness of the depression when no one, including other Hialeah investors, would help the suffering track, Colonel Bradley loaned $500,000 in cash to pull Hialeah through the rough times. According to Widener, Bradley never even asked for a written note on the loan.

Opening day, January 14, 1932, did not go totally according to plan. The flamingos flew away, never to be seen again. Widener did not hire enough ticket takers for the gates, and the long lines drew many complaints. Widener's overly strict attempts to keep his Turf Club exclusive resulted in its near desertion. Yet, Hialeah was a success. That first day, 8,128 people paid admission and wagered a total mutuel handle of $123,000. The Ziegfeld girls and the shimmy dancers were gone; in their place came Main Line Philadelphians, New York's 400, and many more socialites.

The new Australian Parimutuel Machine invented in the 1870s in France (*Paris-mutuel*) and further developed in Australia was installed by Automatic Totalisators, Ltd., and made its American debut on opening day at Hialeah. This machine mechanically recorded bets and kept up-to-the-minute odds. It was considered a financial success and went on to change the course of horserace wagering in the United States. Another precedent was set at Hialeah that year. After campaigning in Florida, William Woodward's Faireno went off to win the Belmont Stakes and be named best three-year-old of the year. Woodward was the first of a long string of owners who found the balmy air and warm sunshine of Florida far nicer than the icy North for winter training.

Financial distribution to each county from Hialeah as a result of the new racing law was just over $9,000. From the same meet, the state received $308,532. The estimated daily handle was $178,637. The 1932 to 1933 winter meet was as much a financial success as that of the previous winter. Each of the 67 Florida counties received checks for $10,641 from Florida State Comptroller J. M. Lee. Each check represented the county's share of the $700,900 revenue from the meet, which closed on April 1.

For this second meet, Widener imported more flamingos, clipped their wings, and fed them shrimp and dog biscuit. This diet agreed with them so well that they produced the first offspring ever hatched in captivity. Widener's vision of Hialeah as a "park" was one he fostered until the day he died. He insisted that Hialeah be considered a year-round park where racing happened to be conducted a few weeks in the winter. He continued to add plants and animals to his park until his death in 1939.

Hialeah became the scene of many more firsts in American racing. In 1933, Widener introduced turf racing (over a grass course) to the United States, something for which he had developed a fondness during his European travels. Six years later, on January 28, 1939, the first turf stakes race in America was the Miami Beach Handicap for $5,000-added. (A "stakes race" purse is made up of the entry fees paid by the horse owners; the track guarantees the "added" portion of the purse.) During the 1933 season, the saliva test (designed to discourage the drugging of horses) was first introduced at Hialeah by Dr. J. G. Catlett, veterinarian for the Florida State Racing Commission. Also in 1933, photo-finish cameras were used at Hialeah; they were destined to alter the course of American racing. In 1935, the Florida State Racing Commission revised the claiming rules in a manner that was adopted by the rest of the nation. Hialeah was the first track to use an electric timer, and it was the first race track in the United States to boast a beauty parlor.

Widener, as vice-chairperson of the board of directors of The Jockey Club, had prestige in social circles other than those of horsemen. He was therefore able to influence the upper echelon of East Coast society. He went to work on these people, and as a result, Hialeah quickly became the place to be in the winter. The fashionable set then began the trek from cool, elegant Saratoga in the summer to bright, fun-loving Hialeah in the winter. It was a time when one could enjoy a delightful lunch at the club and an afternoon of good racing with a few wagers won or lost. It was a time for camaraderie, dressing in one's summer finery (while snow storms swirled up north), and enjoying a colorful and fun-filled sport. The perfect complement to a day of racing was a visit to one of the many classy, popular nightclubs for an evening show.

Many of the regulars owned their own railroad cars. Dan Taylor, head of the railroad, designed a schedule to follow the day's races. The engine alone would leave Palm Beach in the morning and would be pulling ten to fifteen cars by the time it reached Hialeah, where it pulled up on the side track and parked. Connie Ring, who owned Three Rings Ranch; Mrs. Ted Sloane; and Joe Kennedy all had their own cars. The fun that went on in those cars was an important part of the day's entertainment. Equally important were the famous and infamous people one could be sure of seeing at Hialeah.

Widener and Bradley went even further to ensure the success of their newest project: they sent their own horses to winter in Florida. In 1935, Bradley sent his Black Helen to winter in Florida to prepare for the Kentucky Derby, and in 1936, Widener sent Brevity there for the same reason. The successes of those horses did much to advance the idea of winter racing.

Widener was also responsible for changing what was rapidly becoming an alarming custom of naming every three-year-old race a derby. Widener was afraid the word "derby" was losing its significance and announced that the Kentucky Derby was the only race worthy of that title. Widener then rechristened the Florida Derby, which had been run at Hialeah since 1929, the Flamingo Stakes.

In 1938, the famous trainer Ben Jones brought a brown colt named Lawrin to winter in Florida. This Woolford Farm-owned colt was the second to attempt and the first to win the Kentucky Derby after a winter campaign in Florida, which included a victory in the $25,000 Flamingo Stakes. Calumet Farm's Bull Lea was installed the favorite that year. But he was badly beaten back in the field when Lawrin sailed on to victory. The win was no fluke, for he went on to win nine races and total earnings of $126,275. Lawrin was the first of many horses to go on to win the Kentucky Derby after a winter of racing in the "Grapefruit State," the "Palm Tree State," and the "Gator State," as turf writers of the day referred to

Eugene Mori (right) and John Clark attending a horse sale in later years. Photo by Turfotos (by permission of *The Florida Horse*).

what would later become known as the Sunshine State. The high class of Florida racing was validated.

Following Widener's death in 1939, his son P. A. B. Widener II briefly held the reins of succession at Hialeah, then quickly handed John Clinton Clark the presidency in 1940. Clark had been an advertising executive in Binghamton, New York. Under his supervision, Hialeah continued as a winter racing mecca.

By 1942, the $50,000 Widener Cup was the richest and most important of the American (East Coast) winter races. In 1943, Joseph Kennedy bought Colonel E. R. Bradley's stock in Hialeah. Speculators believed that Kennedy bought the stock, not for himself, but for the young Alfred Vanderbilt, who was away at war. Since the stock did not amount to a controlling interest, the concern of the other stockholders soon abated.

Eugene Mori, a Binghamton, New York, sports enthusiast and advertising executive, had been a member of the board of directors since 1936. In 1954, when Clark announced his resignation, Mori and his associates purchased control of the track. Mori became

President Mori with Mrs. Lucille (Warren) Wright in front of the statue of Citation. Photo by Turfotos (by permission of *The Florida Horse*).

president in 1955. At the same time, he was president of Garden State Park in New Jersey and had interests in tracks in West Virginia and California. Mori, too, poured money into continuing the beautification of Hialeah. In 1957, after he enlarged and improved all of

Eugene Mori, Jr. followed in his father's footsteps as president of Hialeah (by permission of *The Florida Horse*).

the facilities, he commissioned a fountain by a local Italian sculptor, Thomas Famiglietti. The flamingo fountain featured side sprays and vertical jets shooting water twenty-four feet into the air. Later four bronze flamingos, sculpted by the same artist, were added, as were bronze plaques around the fountain to honor winners of the Flamingo Stakes. Mori also added an aquarium, a sidewalk cafe, and more floral gardens.

In 1962 his son, Eugene Mori, Jr., became president, while Gene Mori became chair of the board. "Junior" continued in the footsteps of his tasteful predecessors when he commissioned Famiglietti to sculpt a statue of Citation. The artist carefully studied the horse at Calumet and conferred often with Calumet trainer, Jimmy Jones, before the final bronze casting was done at the Bruno Bearzi Foundry in Florence. The statue of the 1947 and 1948 champion and Horse of the Year stands on a slab of green Carrara marble set in the center of a lily pond. It overlooks the clubhouse near the track where Citation scored some of his greatest victories in the Seminole, the Everglades and the Flamingo Stakes.

Eugene Mori with Diane Crump, the first woman licensed as a jockey. Photo by Turfotos (by permission of *The Florida Horse*).

By now Hialeah was indeed known as a park, an aviary, and a botanical garden. It was one of the finest tourist attractions southern Florida had to offer. On March 23, 1979, Hialeah Park was dedicated as a national historic site. In 1978, John Brunetti officially "bought" Hialeah after four years of negotiation. A thirty-year lease of the land upon which the track is located had to be negotiated with the City of Hialeah. To date, many people are confused about just who owns Hialeah.

Citation, Seabiscuit, Alsab, Whirlaway, Pensive, War Admiral, and Bull Lea were only a few of the great equine stars who helped make Hialeah the "queen" of southern racing. With Hialeah's longstanding success, a golden era for racing began in Florida. Attempts to emulate Hialeah were made, but no other southern track would ever match the reputation of the "queen" in her heyday.

6

The Track by the Sea

The indomitable Joseph Smoot, who first proved racetracks could survive in South Florida, went on from Hialeah to begin the building of Gulfstream Park and eventually Santa Anita in California. Before these successes, he perfected his skills with several failures. Smoot's first idea was to build a racetrack on an island in Biscayne Bay. He convinced Colonel Matt Winn, president of the American Turf Association, to join him as general manager of the proposed $2 million plant. The U.S. government refused to give him a permit to dredge an island, however.

In 1937, a new organization, the Hollywood Jockey Club, proposed a third track near Hallandale, Florida, in Broward County. Smoot, the force behind the project as usual, announced that he would capitalize the project for $1 million. The track would feature a $100,000 handicap, and he expected to share racing dates with Hialeah and Tropical Park. On August 3, Broward County voted 3,419 to 340 in favor of the new track. Smoot announced that construction would begin on August 15, with racing scheduled for January 20. The Florida State Racing Commission, however, refused the dates desired by the Hollywood Jockey Club, and the matter was taken to the State Supreme Court. The court ordered the commission to meet and grant the dates of February 3 through March 26 to the new track. President and promoter Smoot said he didn't think the track could be ready by February 3, but that a short meet would be held. However, on December 9, Smoot announced that the planned meet at the new track had been abandoned. Backers withdrew when it was obvious that construction was going nowhere. Smoot blamed the defalcation on the buffeting he felt he had been given by the racing commission on the matter of dates of operation.

When construction ceased and the assigned dates were apparently not going to be used, the racing commission revoked the track's permit. Through litigation, the permit was restored the following season. A twenty-eight-year-old contractor, John C. Horning, emerged as the chief stockholder by virtue of the amount of construction work he had already done for Smoot. Horning was from Pittsburgh and had been talked into being a partner with Smoot. But now Smoot dropped out of the picture. Horning planned to complete construction, open the track on January 11, and run it himself until March 4 ,1939. The track was located a little too far north of fashionable Miami Beach and West Miami to suit some critics. Others complained that it was in alligator swampland. But it had a magnificent view of the ocean, and Horning was sure it would attract patrons. He heavily invested his own money in it, and when that ran out, his mother, Mrs. Marie Horning, threw her savings in, too. By working day and night, workers and silent partners finished the stables and a 7,000-seat grandstand in time for the first race meeting of the Hollywood Jockey Club. John Letendre, who was in charge of the racing program, announced a minimum purse of $600. Optimism was high.

On February 1, 1939, with construction not quite complete, Gulfstream Park nonetheless opened, even though Hialeah Park was in full operation just an hour away. Because the new organization catered to horses of lesser rank, neither track experienced a shortage of horses. Would there be a shortage of patrons? On opening day, a crowd of 18,000 fans turned out and wagered $224,287. On the same day, Hialeah slumped from its usual $500,000 to $293,258. However, their curiosity satisfied, the patrons returned to business as usual at familiar Hialeah the following day. Gulfstream's mutuels on its second day of business totaled $69,424, and on its third day a paltry $65,928. When even on Saturday only $81,922 was shoved through the windows, the fledgling track was doomed.

The following Monday, manager John Letendre waited in vain for the person with the bankroll to show up with the cash to open the mutuel windows. Realizing that his backing had pulled out, Letendre recovered from shock long enough to announce over the loudspeaker system, "Gentlemen, I have bad news for you. The meeting is off." After thirty-two races and $23,300 awarded in purses, the new race meet was abandoned.

Why Gulfstream Park had such a poor beginning is a matter of speculation. From various magazine and newspaper articles of the time, we learn that Horning's financial backing was jerked out from under him, but not why. Some commentators felt that young

Horning knew nothing about racing, certainly not enough to run a track. Others blamed unidentified partners for encouraging Horning to pour his own money into the operation, promising their support later in the form of operating expenses, then backing out when the mutuel handle fell below $100,000. Perhaps these partners hoped Horning would go under so that they could buy him out for a pittance. The most popular explanation, however, was that competing with Hialeah was too much. In the words of a local writer, "The move appeared to lack wisdom." When Horning realized that he was through, he maintained his composure long enough to ensure that he was appointed receiver. The track became so tied up in legal knots and bankruptcy that it would be years before anything more could be done.

James Donn, son of a blacksmith, grew up in Scotland. Horses were a part of his life from the beginning, but flowers were his first love. In 1909, he set sail for America to find his fortune in a florist shop on Fifth Avenue. He quickly advanced to serving such clients as the Rockefellers, Goulds, Carnegies, and Twombleys. It was in New York that he also met and married Nellie Whitefield. In 1915, he was stricken with typhoid fever and advised by his physician to seek a warmer climate. He moved to Florida, a haven of tropical plants. When "Jimmy" first spotted the verdant flora of Florida, he knew he had found his home. He opened his first nursery on Fifteenth Avenue in Miami and named it Exotic Gardens. It was a shop that became internationally renowned.

Horse lovers were treated to his work when he was called in to beautify Tropical Park. He was responsible for turning that deserted track into a paradise by opening day. When the track operators at Tropical could not pay his bill, he instead accepted mortgage bonds that would mature in ten years. He quickly entered into management of the track, and because of his help, the track did not go under during hard times. Often he met the payroll out of his personal resources, paid off debtors, and ensured that the track kept running. When the bonds matured and new ownership took over, Donn was ready to try his hand at the business of horse racing again. Gulfstream naturally attracted his attention. Although Donn was a shrewd businessperson, he later recalled that the sad financial plight of Horning and his mother appealed to his sentimentality. He wanted to help the young man recoup some of his loss. Donn saw beyond the weeds, underbrush, and dust of the abandoned track and decided he liked the big steel and concrete

James Donn, the first president of Gulfstream Park. Photo by Turfotos (by permission of Gulfstream Park).

grandstand (which is still the only cantilevered racetrack grandstand in the United States), the track, and the infield lake. He set out to manage the track, not only to revive it, but also to get Horning's money back. It was not an easy task.

First, racing law had to be changed to permit three regular tracks. Bankruptcy court had to be dealt with, and politicians in Tallahassee had to be convinced that another forty days tacked on to the beginning of the racing season would be good for the state. Not until May 1944 would the bankruptcy referee finally award the sale of Gulfstream Park to the James A. Donn syndicate. Stefan Zachar, acting as silent partner, had by then purchased 90 percent of the outstanding claims at an average of 10¢ on the dollar.

Nineteen forty-three was a bad year for racing in Florida. Wartime gasoline rationing effectively ruined tourist travel to the tracks. Patriots of the time objected to the use of precious gasoline and rubber merely to attend horseraces. Neither Gulfstream nor Hialeah opened for the season. Tropical Park opened but closed five days early. At least 25 percent of the horses in Florida were shipped out to race elsewhere.

Donn spent the year preparing the facility and organizing his supporters, who included George W. Langford, a pioneer Miamian; Stefan H. Zachar, a Miami Beach architect and (as Charlie Gregg wrote in an August 1944 article for the *Miami Herald*) "Florida's largest breeder of thoroughbreds" at the time; James Mack, a well-known businessperson; William E. Leach, a breeder from Ocala; and Harold I. Clark, a hotel entrepreneur. To Donn fell the tasks of ironing out business and financial problems; to Clark, the restoring of the running strip and the attraction of thoroughbreds to the revitalized track; to Zachar, the refurbishing of the grandstand and club paddock; and to Leach, the supervision of the grounds.

In June 1944, Donn made Zachar vice-president and announced that the track would open in December. A fever of activity pervaded the stale, dusty plant, while critics and pessimists mocked that there was no way it could be ready in time. Construction work often continued after dark. Donn transplanted royal palms all around his track and planted petunias, hibiscus, geraniums, and orchid trees, which were soon to be famous. In a scant six months, the whole scene had changed from one of neglect to that of an attractive, modern track.

An article that appeared in *Tropic* on November 26, 1944, called it a "miracle" when the new Gulfstream meet, operating under the Gulfstream Park Racing Association, opened on December 1, 1944, sixteen days earlier than the usual start of the racing season. It was to be the longest racing season Florida had yet experienced. Many critics feared such a long season would ruin all three tracks and that the patrons would lose interest. The meet would not operate without its difficulties. Wartime restrictions left racing fans without adequate transportation. Although a new spur off the main railroad track existed for the unloading of horses shipped to the Hallandale track, there was no train service for the potential patrons.

Opening day at Gulfstream Park December 1, 1944. Mr. and Mrs. Stefan H. Zachar's Mucho Gusto heads the post parade (by permission of Stefanie Zachar).

Five hundred fifty stalls were prepared with a supportive number of races written, but only three hundred horses had arrived by opening day.

But Donn and associates held their meet. To those who participated, Donn showed his gratitude by announcing in an article written by Horace Wade in the *Turf and Sport Digest,* "Those horsemen who supported us can always return to Gulfstream Park, so long as I have a hand in the management." The curious and the well-wishers came. The mystery surrounding the history of the track, the knowledge of what magical beauty James Donn's landscaping could render, and of course the press (claiming that opening the track was an impossible task all along) assured that there would be a crowd. The split forty-day meet averaged $714,801 in daily wagering. It was deemed a success, and congratulations were due Donn, Zachar, Clark, and Leach. For twenty-nine years, Donn would manage the track by the sea and would eventually buy out his partners. In 1946, Gulfstream Park opened to an attendance of more than 20,000 fans and set an opening-day record for tracks in the State of Florida. It also reached a new high point for purse distribution. Hialeah, no longer the only game in town, now had a serious rival.

Inaugural Day lineup of Gulfstream Park players December 1, 1944. The four men standing in the center are (left to right) Stefan Zachar, James Donn, John Clark, and Mr. Shapiro, another principal. The rest are jockeys and employees assembled for the opening meet (by permission of Stefanie Zachar).

The next year, 1947, the "Hialeah Law" was passed as a direct result of competition over racing dates. This law divided the winter season into three forty-day winter meets and gave the lucrative "middle dates" to the best producer of revenue during the previous year. This practice naturally resulted in the same track getting the best dates each year because that was when tourist season was at its height. According to an article by Nancy Pyle, which appeared in a January 14, 1988, issue of the *Ocala Star Banner*, Gulfstream lost a Florida Supreme Court decision to overturn the law. The Hialeah Law remained in effect until 1971.

Dates continued to be a major issue for Florida horse racing. The matter was taken up in the state legislature during the late 1970s and 1980s. Finally in 1988, the legislature, despairing of the tracks ever agreeing, washed its hands of the affair and authorized deregulation. Now the tracks have to decide the issue of dates among themselves. Which track will hold meets at which times? Which tracks will compete side by side during the best dates? Bankruptcy seems inevitable for some track or tracks.

Gulfstream was also instrumental in initiating a thirty-minute delay of race result transmissions to hinder offtrack bookmaking. According to Nancy Pyle's January 14, 1988, *Ocala Star Banner* article, in 1950, Gulfstream and Tropical Park opposed what was

James Donn, Sr. and James Donn, Jr. in front of their racing plant. Photo by Turfotos (by permission of *The Florida Horse*).

James Donn, Jr. Photo by Jim Raftery (by permission of Gulfstream Park).

The paddock at Gulfstream Park in 1963. Beyond the enclosure is the Garden of Champions where the greatest horses to appear at Gulfstream are enshrined: among them Armed, Bold Ruler, Round Table, and Swaps. Photo by Turfotos (by permission of *The Florida Horse*).

The Florida Derby became a major prep race for the three-year-old classics. Besides the Florida Derby, Kentucky-bred Tim Tam went on to win the Kentucky Derby and the Belmont Stakes and be named champion three-year-old colt of 1958. Photo by Turfotos (by permission of Gulfstream Park).

In 1986 the new Gulfdome dining terrace was opened. The breezy minidomed dining terrace can accommodate 700 patrons in a delightful setting. Photo by Turfotos (by permission of Gulfstream Park).

Third in the family line of succession and president since 1989 of Gulfstream Park, Douglas Donn (by permission of Gulfstream Park).

called "Down Town Betting." The tracks' opposition forced Florida's attorney general to enforce the delay.

For several years, Donn admittedly had trouble lifting his track out of mediocrity. Most of the "big name" stables traditionally left town after Hialeah closed. But Donn worked hard, increased his purses, and introduced new stakes races. Equally instrumental to the success of Gulfstream Park was Horace Wade, who was made publicity director in 1944, the track's first year of operation. Later, Wade would also serve as racing secretary, director of racing, and race caller. He was also an eminent turf writer. Wade persuaded Donn to revive the Florida Derby in 1952. The Florida Derby, the first $100,000 stake ever offered in the nation, and the $50,000 Gulfstream Handicap were instant hits. The derby, along with Hialeah's Flamingo, quickly became one of the important winter prep races for the Triple Crown events (the Kentucky Derby, Preakness, and Belmont Stakes). Midway through the 1980s, the Florida Derby ranked among the nation's fifteen richest thoroughbred classics, with a guaranteed purse of $500,000 and live television coverage.

By 1954, only ten years after its reawakening, Gulfstream Park had become the elegant scene of the chic sport Donn had envisioned for so long and had worked so hard to develop. Gulfstream maintains that reputation to this day. Palms and orchids have been constantly added to upgrade and beautify the track. In 1959, a seven-furlong turf course was opened inside the main one-mile oval. That same year Joe Tannenbaum, recognized today as one of the world's foremost publicity directors, succeeded Wade. He was another well-known turf writer before he assumed his new position.

Gulfstream Park remains under the control of the Donn family. The late James Donn, Jr. succeeded his father as president in 1961. Douglas Donn, James Donn, Jr.'s son and the third generation of Donns at the track, took over in 1978. He had worked under his father in virtually every phase of track operation. Douglas Donn was dynamic and innovative. In 1988, he was one of the youngest presidents of a major thoroughbred plant. Through 1986, he guided Gulfstream to nine successive record seasons and directed a $10 million improvement program, which transformed the track into one of the world's showplaces of thoroughbred racing. Donn also instituted the Florida Derby Festival, an annual series of cultural,

The Florida Derby Ball is an annual black-tie event and the oldest ball associated with thoroughbred racing in Florida, dating back to 1954. For the ball, the Great Hall at Gulfstream is transformed into a sparkling vista of orchid, silver, and white decor with scores of ferns and flowers. Photo by Turfotos (by permission of Gulfstream Park).

An annual feature of Florida Derby Day special activities is the exotic animal race. In the past this has included llamas, Bengal tigers, Texas longhorns, Chinese zebus, aoudads, buffalo, elephants, and wooly alpacas. In 1986 it was ostriches. Photo by Turfotos (by permission of Gulfstream Park).

social, artistic, and athletic events to promote tourism and attract national attention to South Florida, particularly Broward County. The Florida Derby Festival is sponsored by the Order of the Orchid, a nonprofit organization for the promotion of tourism in Florida.

7

Sun Coast Racing

While both Hialeah and Gulfstream Park at some point laid claim to the Florida Derby, neither track was responsible for its conception or inauguration. This credit goes to an obscure, little track that was located not on the opulent eastern Gold Coast of Florida but on the Sun Coast overlooking the Gulf of Mexico.

In the late 1930s, promoters and investors were constantly attempting to compete with the lucrative racing in the southern tip of the state, mostly to no avail. The tourists simply loved South Florida. In 1937, Harry Kinsella filed an application with the State Racing Commission to operate a track in Volusia County near Daytona Beach; his request was denied. In August 1942, he tried again and was again denied. On December 11, 1939, actor George Jessel announced that a group he headed planned to operate a track in Hillsborough County; the first meeting was scheduled for December 1940. That, too, never came about.

But when Miami was nothing more than a fishing village, race meets were being held in Tampa and in nearby Ybor City, a bustling, unrestrained, cigar-making town. When bookmaking lost its glamor, racing ceased at the gulfside tracks around 1910. In 1926, under the guidance of Colonel Matt Winn (who seemed to have been determined to keep trying in the Sunshine State), a new track, appropriately named Tampa Downs, opened about fifteen miles north of the old track in Tampa. The choice of location, however, was not an easy one. The commercial town of Tampa, the conservative and retired persons' residential St. Petersburg, and the booming town of Clearwater were all about the same size. It was difficult to predict which would become the predominant city.

The site for a track was purposely chosen as a draw for all three cities. The track was located at a wide spot in the road, Oldsmar, named for and developed by the automobile magnate, R. E. Olds. Oldsmar was expected to grow into a bustling metropolis, which of course never happened. From the beginning, Tampa Downs was a pipe dream. So ambitious were Winn's early hopes that the Florida Derby was inaugurated when the track opened in 1926. Torcher won that first derby and collected his share of a $4,450 purse. This phenomenal amount of money would remain unmatched at the track for another twenty-two years. Not until 1948 would such a purse again be offered.

The first race meet could not finish before the plant closed down. The Florida Derby was transferred to Hialeah, and the original owners of the Oldsmar land took back their property. The Florida depression was continuing to take a terrible toll on land investors and businesses in the area. A second attempt to open the track was made in the early 1930s, before gambling was legal. Bettors made their wagers in one county and collected their winnings in another. On the back of each ticket, in very small print, was a proviso that if the purchasers were dissatisfied with their transactions after the race, they could redeem their tickets at slightly less than face value. Stoopers (people who pick up dropped and lost tickets) soon closed that meet. Joe Cattarinich, a French-Canadian who controlled a number of race tracks, also tried to reawaken the gulfside track and failed. In 1938, David Alexander of the *New York Morning Telegraph* reported that Lou Smith, manager of Rockingham Park in New Hampshire, planned to reopen the track at Tampa. Opening day was set for January 14, but this too never happened.

As the years passed, the stands and stables crumbled and were sold in pieces. Palmettos overtook the grounds. The track was used for dirt auto racing. During World War II, the army took over the remaining buildings and used the nearby forest for combat training.

In 1946, local attorneys C.C. "Milo" Vega and Frank Hobbs pushed through a referendum to legalize horse racing in Hillsborough County. Vega had at one time served as secretary to the Florida State Racing Commission. Vega and Hobbs were given dates to operate in 1947. With the help of Wilmington, Delaware, financiers John Kane and Harry Jacobs, the rush to transform the track was on. The army barracks at Oldsmar were being converted into stables when a hurricane struck. Most of the buildings were leveled. New construction began a mere two months before the scheduled opening. Governmental red tape required that new, nonessential construction be built only of old and used lumber with no more than six stalls per barn. This expensive construction was still going on when horses began to be shipped into these tiny barns

Sunshine Park in its heyday. The grandstand was designed by Matt Winn and is patterned after Churchill Downs (by permission of *The Florida Horse*).

dotting the backstretch. Luckily, the promoters found an abandoned county fair in New York, bought its barns, and shipped the lumber to Florida.

On opening day, January 23, 1947, the track looked like the real thing. About 400 thoroughbreds were on the grounds ready to run. The one-mile track with a chute for six-furlong dashes was in good shape. A modern totalisator, an odds board in the infield, and the new innovations from Hialeah—photo-finish cameras, urine and saliva tests—were all in place. The track was optimistically renamed Sunshine Park and became a favorite of Grantland "Granny" Rice, a famous turf writer of the day, for whom a stakes race would later be named. On opening day, however, the name of the new track proved to be an ironical joke. Day after day rain fell, dampening the track, bettor enthusiasm, and the mutuel handle. The investors lost about $25,000 a day.

There were many reasons for the poor beginnings of the Tampa track. Competition from well-established dog tracks in the area was keen. The West Coast tourist was more of a winter resident than were the flamboyant East Coast vacationers. These tourists knew less about the sport of racing than did the vacationers. But in 1947, the rain was probably the biggest factor in keeping attendance

The "roost" at Florida Downs in 1974 (by permission of *The Florida Horse*).

down. Despite that bad beginning, track officials felt optimistic about another season. Seven hundred horses showed up. But opening day was exceedingly glum when the handle barely broke $100,000. Drastic cuts in personnel, take, and worst of all, purses, were imposed in an effort to save the track. Purses reached an all-time low of $500.

But the promoters' prayers were answered. Just in time, the

weather turned balmy, greyhound owners had a falling-out with their track management, the dogs stopped running, and the Gasparilla Carnival (Florida's answer to the Mardi Gras) arrived, attracting half a million people. By the time the dog tracks ironed out their difficulties, the fickle fans had become accustomed to the sport of kings. The most valuable lesson learned during this meet was that a later scheduling of the races—to coincide with the Gasparilla Carnival and to assure better weather—would be advantageous. Vega, Kane, and Hobbs were assured a future in West Coast racing.

In February 1946, New Yorker M. Russell Dock and two associates purchased Sunshine Park. In 1953, Frank Hobbs became its president and general manager. While he was president (from 1953 to 1960), Dock and his associates built new barns and improved the three-story clubhouse. Hobbs is credited with raising the sport to a professional and successful level on Florida's West Coast. He was later joined by Fred Ballon and Dick West, who shared his enthusiasm for upgrading the facility and the sport.

In 1965, Chester H. Ferguson purchased a major interest in the track and the track assumed a new name, Florida Downs and Turf Club. Ferguson was the father of current owner Stella Ferguson Thayer. Ferguson renovated the track at a cost of $400,000. He used theme colors of maroon and gold and totally revitalized the clubhouse, dining rooms, grandstand, track, walking ring, saddling area, winners' circle, and pari-mutuel facilities. Ferguson added a new Visumatic timer, which assured accurate timing of races. Horace Wade continued to be the track manager. A new form of wagering, the "Florinella," was introduced at this first meet, held early in 1966. It was played on the last race of the day and was a combination of any two horses finishing first and second.

In 1973, Sam F. Davis bought the non-Ferguson interest in the track from the late William H. May. Davis became president and general manager and continued to be actively involved even after George Steinbrenner purchased Davis's share in 1980. Steinbrenner and Thayer gave the Gulfside track its current name, Tampa Bay Downs. When New York Yankees owner (and owner of a thoroughbred breeding farm, Kinsman Farm, in Ocala) George Steinbrenner bought 48 percent interest in the track in 1980, more improvements took place. Over $3.3 million were poured into the facilities, which are located on 508 acres, the largest tract of land for any racetrack in the United States. Stella Ferguson Thayer con-

Sam F. Davis entertains Leslie Combs, the master of Spendthrift Farms in Lexington, Kentucky, at Florida Downs. Photo by Bob Cicero (by permission of *The Florida Horse*).

A modern day facility, Tampa Bay Downs (by permission of *The Florida Horse*).

tinued to own 52 percent along with her brother, Howell (who was not an active partner), until 1986. But she and Steinbrenner had some differences of opinion, and she purchased the remaining 48 percent from Steinbrenner at a sheriff's auction.

Today Tampa Bay Downs (still called Florida Downs on some maps) is host to the Grade III Budweiser–Tampa Bay Derby. That race has attracted many top horses, which have gone on to do well in important races across the country and have thus enhanced the credibility of the Sun Coast track.

8

South Florida Breeding

Top-class racing was not the only contribution Uncle Jimmy Bright made to the young thoroughbred industry in Florida. From the start, he thought that Florida thoroughbred racing would receive a big boost if its more important patrons would also breed thoroughbreds within the state. He often remarked that any state that raised cow ponies with the durability and stamina of those being raised in Florida would have to raise good racehorses as well.

Bright's idea about raising thoroughbreds in Florida was mocked by out-of-state breeders, however, particularly by the bluegrass hardboots. During an elite party in Kentucky attended by many of the breeders of blue-blooded horses, Bright stood up and told all assembled that someday Florida would produce horses as good as those produced in Kentucky. The breeders retorted that he should stick to raising rattlesnakes and alligators; Kentucky would raise the nation's race horses. Bright also said, in an article by Everett Clay that appeared in the *Turf and Sport Digest* in August 1950, "It's my opinion that Florida is going to be one of the biggest horse-producing states in the Union. One reason is that Florida-breds have big, flat, strong bones. I've never seen a round-boned Florida-bred.

"We're getting better blood all the time. Another reason our horses can't miss being healthy is that they're out in the open all the time . . . from the day they're foaled. I only hope I stay around long enough to see a Florida-bred win the Flamingo." Bright lived to see Needles win both the Flamingo and the Kentucky Derby in 1956.

In the early 1930s, most of the land west of Miami on the edge of the Everglades was low, so Bright used land around Opa-Locka to begin raising thoroughbreds. In Hialeah, Bright's spread was named Bright's Ranch, and in Davie, he owned Martha Bright Farms (named after his daughter); the portion of that farm designated for the raising of thoroughbreds was called Martha Bright Ranch. Most chronicles indicate that this enterprise was started in the 1930s, but a metal survey marker still on the property was put down in 1920.

Mrs. John Cheatham, the former Martha Tinsley Bright, remembers that the first thoroughbreds were foaled in the 1920s, at the same time that Bright was fighting for a racetrack. The foals were by a stallion named Nor'easter (North Star III–*Bunchy, by Llangwm), which Bright acquired around 1926 from Mrs. John Hay Whitney. There was no attempt to register these foals, however. At some point, Bright also purchased land around Lake Okeechobee. Glenn Curtiss, over the objection of Bright, named an area there Brighton. In Brighton, some of Nor'easter's foals were raised to three-year-olds, then sold as polo ponies. Meanwhile, Bright was preparing his property back in Davie as his permanent breeding establishment. Once he moved to the Martha Bright acreage, he began breeding thoroughbreds; he wanted to race those he raised. Some of his acreage was planted in orange groves, and on some he grazed cattle and sheep.

In 1935, Bright planned to breed three thoroughbred mares: Rocky Day, Hillsaint, and Saxon Lady. Although at that time he appears to have owned a five-year-old stallion named Trimmer (Mad Hatter–Margin, by *All Gold), all of his first registered foals were by a stallion named Full Dress (Man o' War–Shady, by Broomstick). The mare Rocky Day (by Ormondale) bred to Full Dress resulted in the filly Martha's Queen. Martha's Queen was the first thoroughbred foaled in Florida (in 1936) to be registered with The Jockey Club. Hillsaint foaled a filly named Lady Florida, and Saxon Lady's filly was named Miami Maid. Both fillies were also sired by Full Dress; they were the second and third registered thoroughbreds born in the state.

In 1938 both Martha's Queen and Lady Florida hit the racetrack. Both failed to bring home any money. But in 1939, Martha's Queen became the first registered "Florida-foaled" winner when she won a race in Bel Air, Maryland. She earned $650 for the year, while a foal of 1937, Formal Dress, earned $25 that same year. Nineteen thirty-nine was the first year any Florida-foaled horses earned money at the track: a grand total of $675.

Bright was a charter member of the Florida Thoroughbred Breeders' Association and later was installed in its Hall of Fame. He lived into his nineties, remained clear-witted, and often traveled to Ocala for parties with other horsemen until his death on January 6, 1959. At the time of his death, Bright was still on the board of directors of Hialeah and president emeritus of the Florida Thoroughbred Breeders' Association. His wife, Mrs. Lulu Bright, remained interested in horses even after his death. She died on December 16, 1965, just hours before the seventh annual James Bright Memorial Handicap at Tropical Park.

Golden Shoe Farm, 105 acres located near Davie about thirty miles northwest of Miami, was owned by the young Miami Beach architect Stefan Zachar (already mentioned for his contributions at the racetracks) and his wife, Dorothy Elizabeth Lape "Billie". The property was actually a part of the original Martha Bright Farms. Under the Zachars, it became a model farm. Zachar came from Czechoslovakia in 1924 and settled in Miami in 1925. He had been a member of the Czechoslovakian boxing team, which competed in the 1924 Olympics in Paris. Before his architectural work became too pressing, he was the tennis champion of Miami Beach for several seasons. Zachar headed a large architectural enterprise and was widely known for his novel ideas. The U.S. Air Corps commissioned him to design air bases including Carlstrom Field, Arcadia Field, and Clewiston Field in Florida and others throughout this country and Brazil. Billie Zachar was born in Ohio and came from a long line of thoroughbred and standardbred owners. She herself rode and played polo. She met Stefan on the tennis court.

Jimmy Bright originally interested the Zachars in breeding thoroughbreds in 1940. They bred their mare, Cendrillon (Insco–Jacqueminot, by Pennant), to one of Bright's stallions, Stormscud (Hard Tack–Blustery, by *Sun Briar), in 1941, resulting in their first Florida foal, Smooth Gallop, born in 1942. As his interest in racing grew, Zachar began to study American racetracks and their shortcomings. He had very specific ideas on how to improve them to enhance the spectators' enjoyment of the sport as well as to provide clean, decent living quarters for stable help, in those days an uncommon consideration. Many of these ideas were incorporated in his later design for Calder Race Course.

Zachar was one of the founders of the Florida Thoroughbred Breeders' Association and was its first secretary. Mrs. Zachar was equally involved; she later held offices in the association and assisted her husband in his various track duties. Mrs. Zachar is believed to have been the first woman track announcer. In 1946, when there first were enough Florida-breds for restricted races (i.e., only Florida-breds could participate), the regular jockeys refused to

Mr. and Mrs. Stefan Zachar were very active in early racing and breeding in South Florida. Photo by Leo Frutkoff (by permission of *The Florida Horse*).

ride them and the track announcers refused to call the races. In those days, restricted races were very uncommon in any state; it is assumed that such races were considered lower-class. Mrs. Zachar therefore voluntarily called all the restricted races run at Hialeah because no one else would.

Although the Zachars are not well known today, they nonetheless deserve as much praise for their contributions to the breeding industry as to the racing industry. They were, after all, the second thoroughbred farm owners and breeders in South Florida, and the third in the state. Mrs. Zachar, whose daughter was born after a day at the races, had a passion for racing. She was still participating in the racing world up to her death in 1991. The Zachars were the first breeders to stand a major stakes winner, Mucho Gusto (Marvin May–Sweetheart Time, by Hanbridge), and the first to import a stallion from South America, *Hamilton II (=Lord Wembley–=Xirgu by =Movedizo) [equals sign indicates a horse in a country other than the U.S.].

Mucho Gusto at Golden Shoe Farm in 1944 (by permission of Stefanie Zachar).

The Zachars were friends of another ambitious breeder, Frederick C. Peters, who had a 4,500-acre farm in the Fort Lauderdale area. Peters had business interests all around the country and was one of the wealthiest men in America. He stood the famous Peace Chance (Chance Shot–Peace, by *Stefan the Great) on his Broward County farm. But after a son of that stallion, Four Freedoms (Peace Chance–*Nea Lap, by =Night Raid), won the 1944 Widener, Peters was persuaded to return the stallion to Kentucky. One of his foals, Uncle Edgar (Peace Chance–Beaming Gal, by Gallant Fox), was conceived in Kentucky but foaled in Florida. Uncle Edgar would be the closest claim to fame of any Peace Chance offspring with Florida connections.

Together, Peters and Zachar purchased the stallion Mucho Gusto, affectionately known by many racing fans across the United States as "Big Gus." Big Gus raced for nine years. He started 217 times and was in the money 129 times, with 61 wins and earnings of $101,880. He was a favorite with the crowd, even when he started his ten-year-old campaign with ankles the size of grapefruits.

Although Mucho Gusto was considered a hard-knocking horse (lots of starts, very little class), he had his moments of glory. As a four-year-old in 1936, he beat Seabiscuit at River Downs. As a six-year-old, he ran second to War Admiral in the Rhode Island Handicap. Mucho Gusto originally retired to Lexington in 1942, then was shipped to Florida the next year when Zachar and Peters purchased him to stand at Golden Shoe. Mucho Gusto went on to sire horses with his own durability. One son, Brezno (Mucho Gusto–Cendrillon, by Insco), foaled in 1946, raced for fourteen years, had 265 starts (including 33 wins), and was in the money 112 times. He earned a total of $54,508.

By 1944, the Zachars bought out Peters and owned the stallion themselves. With the stallion, seven mares, five weanlings, and a yearling, the Zachars were the largest thoroughbred breeders in the state until the mid-1940s. In 1945, Carl Rose wrote to Zachar, inviting him to move to Ocala and to bring Mucho Gusto with him so that there would be "at least two really well-bred stallions" there. Rose even offered to help Zachar buy land at $50 per acre. But the Zachars were well-established in Miami Beach, where Stefan was vice-president of Gulfstream Park and where both Stefan and Billie worked hard to get restricted races for Florida-breds. Their passion was for racing, and racing was in South Florida.

Mr. and Mrs. Tilyou Christopher (affectionately called "Mr. and Mrs. T") were also important early breeders in South Florida. Their blue and gold racing silks were well-known to turf followers from Florida to New England. Tilyou Christopher was the eleventh child of a family that had come to the United States from Italy before he was born. At the age of twenty, Christopher started an ice cream parlor in Lincoln, Maine. Lillian Grace Main, who was to become Chistopher's wife, was raised by her grandparents in Pennsylvania. She went to work for Christopher at his shop. The ice cream parlor business was not spirited enough for him, however. Christopher sold out to another brother and moved to Miami in the early 1920s; there he managed the used-car department of the Miami Willys Overland Company. In 1925, when there was a railroad embargo on shipping cars to Miami, he was in the right spot at the right time.

When the famous 1926 hurricane struck and destroyed the southern Florida economy, Christopher repossessed and resold many cars. He bought up cars from first the Franklin Car Company and then the Cord Car Company, when each went bankrupt.

Meanwhile, Lillian moved to Miami to be his secretary. Shortly thereafter, they were married. Business continued to grow as Christopher acquired a DeSoto agency, a Plymouth agency, and a Studebaker agency. In 1940, the DeSoto/Plymouth agency received an award from Chrysler; it had sold the most retail cars of any such agency in the United States.

In the early 1930s, Christopher began having mysterious fainting spells. His doctor advised him to find an outdoor hobby and take it a little easier at work. The Christophers took up riding at a local academy. When some distress sale property in the "boondocks" came up for sale, Christopher bought the land. Christopher Ranch was located three miles west of Miami's 36th Street Airport, later to be called International Airport. The area is now a large industrial complex. In the beginning, Christopher Ranch was used for weekend barbecues for the employees of Christopher Motors. But weekending at the farm was truly "roughing it," and soon only the owners were spending time there. Unfortunately, their saddle horses were costing money with no return. Harris Brown, who worked in Christopher's automobile agency, therefore advised Christopher to buy a few racehorses. Brown had been a trainer in Honduras. He had no intention of getting back into racing, but it was not long before he was indeed the Christophers' trainer.

The Christophers bred, imported, and raced many important horses extensively. One of their biggest contributions to the national industry (at a later date than we are presently discussing) was *Amerigo (=Nearco–=Sanlinea, by =Precipitation). Christopher imported the racing rogue from England, raced him in 1959 and 1960, then shipped him to Virginia to stand. *Amerigo had a very short career before his untimely death, but he had a profound influence on American bloodlines.

The first stallion the Christophers ever stood on their own farm was Sammie (Man o' War–*Thread, by =Gainesborough), who raced under the Christophers' colors. When he broke down, they retired him to their farm. The Christophers also bred both the first Florida-bred stakes winner, Donna's Ace (Sammie–Donna Leona, by Don Leon), and the first Florida-bred to win a major stakes race in North America, Liberty Rab. Liberty Rab's victory over the undefeated Battlefield in the Juvenile Stakes at Belmont Park in 1950 was a tremendous boost for Florida breeders.

Liberty Rab (Doublrab–Lady Liberty, by Liberty Limited) was sired by their prized stallion Doublrab (*Sherab–Double Shamrock,

Left to right: Mr. T. Christopher, Mrs. A. B. Christopher, Mrs. T. Christopher, and Judge Louis Bandel. Photo by Leo Frutkoff (by permission of *The Florida Horse*).

by *Double Entendre). This stallion was particularly appropriate for a fledgling breeding program. Outsiders mocked Doublrab because he came from very obscure breeding lines and raced for a long time, an apt description of many early Florida-breds. Doublrab was Illinois-bred. His sire, *Sherab (=Tetratema–Sherry, by =Maintenon), raced in England for the Aga Khan. When *Sherab had had one win in seventeen tries, he was sold for only $1,050 to the Chapell brothers of Rockford, Illinois. They raced him twenty-seven times in this country and were successful only once. Disgusted with their purchase, they sent *Sherab home to Illinois in disgrace to service an occasional lower-quality mare. Such a mare was Double Shamrock (*Double Entendre–Avisack II, by Leonardo II), and the offspring of that undistinguished mating was Doublrab.

An unverifiable but entertaining story is told about Doublrab. When he was a foal, Doublrab was sold to an iceman for $100 and was raised as a family pet in the back woodshed. The iceman and his family had faith in their horse, however, and decided to give the gray colt a chance on the track. Doublrab scored nine wins, seven seconds, and six thirds as a three-year-old and climbed steadily up the claiming ranks. (In claiming events, a horse's value is determined by the amount of money designated as the claiming price. Moving up the ranks therefore means entering increasingly higher priced races, referred to as a $5,000 claimer, a $10,000 claimer, etc. and the like).

The Christophers' acquisition of Doublrab is also the stuff of tall tales. Harris Brown liked the gray colt and wanted Christopher to buy him for $8,500. Brown finally convinced Christopher to swap a $3,500 claimer and pay $5,000 cash for the horse. The owner then raised his cash price to $5,500 and again Brown managed to persuade Christopher to go along. When Brown went to close the deal, however, the owner raised the cash price to $6,000 plus the claimer. Because the Christophers were at the theater, Brown went ahead and notarized the contract. Christopher blew up, and Brown offered to fund the $500 difference out of his own commissions when the horse won. Instead, Christopher found a buyer for the horse at a $500 profit. However, Brown sneaked the horse out of town and up to New York before the sale could be consummated. When the horse went on to set a track record in his first start under Brown, Christopher forgot his wrath.

Doublrab accumulated twenty-five wins, including many stakes races. He beat horses like Swing and Sway and Whirlaway. He equaled two track records and set a third at Aqueduct for six furlongs. He was voted the sprinter champion of 1942 by one voting poll. Mrs. Christopher, in whose name the colt raced, received many offers from Kentuckians to stand her gray champion. She turned the offers down and was the first breeder to keep in Florida a stallion coveted in Kentucky. Doublrab loved people and attention (or so some observers thought; others said that he was no fun to be around). In those days, stallions were kept in huge fields, not small paddocks. Whenever he saw people coming to visit, Doublrab would barrel toward them at full speed from wherever he was in the field. As Mr. T told a nervous visitor, Dorothy Chappell Davis, "Now just stand still, he won't hurt you." At the last possible second, Doublrab would skid to a stop and drop his head to be petted by the quaking visitors.

The Christophers began to summer in Saratoga. During that time, they bought good riding mares and thoroughbreds. These mares, when mated with Doublrab, consistently produced fast, well-mannered, gray horses that became fantastic lead ponies at the track. Trainers loved these ponies and created a demand for them. One year, James Donn sponsored a demonstration race at Gulfstream Park between the regular races featuring nothing but Doublrab lead ponies. The Christophers were also famous for raising their foals on goat's milk. In the early days, it was guessed that Florida grazing needed to be supplemented, but no one knew what to do. Many different supplements were tried. Despite the amusement engendered, the success of the Christopher "goat-foals" was hard to ignore.

When the industry moved to the Ocala area, the Christophers decided to get out of the breeding business. In 1955, they sold all their breeding stock to William Scottie McDade of Maryland. After Tilyou Christopher died in 1969, his wife carried on the racing end of the business as devotedly as before. After his death, she carried his picture everywhere. Mrs. T is remembered as a regal person, impeccably dressed and well-groomed. She had beautiful white hair and always wore a big diamond brooch, gloves, and hat whenever she stepped out of the house. In the early 1970s Mrs. Lillian T. Christopher became the first horsewoman in the state to be honored by any organization when she was named Florida's First Lady of the Thoroughbred Industry by the Farm Managers Club. Several years later, she was killed in a car accident.

Charles O'Neil, Jr., one of the largest liquor distributors on Florida's East Coast, was a longtime racing owner whose green and white silks were well-known in East Coast racing circles. In the earlier years, many of his horses and partnerships went with Carl Rose up to the Ocala area. O'Neil also had a beautiful 160-acre farm of his own, Pine Island Farm, in Broward County. By 1950, he stood three stallions there: leading sire Ariel Game (to be discussed later), Jakajones (Johnstown–Wound Up, by Stimulus) and Galedo (Gallahadion–Torpedo, by Man o' War). O'Neil's brother Roscoe was also involved in the industry.

A number of other persons became involved in the racing and breeding industry. B. L. Whitten was a famous Miami eye surgeon who campaigned a modest stable of race horses. He also had several mares on a Dade County farm. George E. Woollard was a Miami Beach doctor. He built a showplace farm in Broward County. J. H. Yarborough was a well-known veterinarian in the area. Hunter L. Lyon was equally well-known and had been long associated with both the racing and breeding industry. His first thoroughbred was foaled on his farm in 1944. Lyon brought Liberty Franc to stand in

1945. Dr. C. C. Collins and Dr. H. H. Humphries started C & H Farm in Duval County near Jacksonville. They acquired the stallion On Location (*Teddy–Cinema, by Sweep). Other people in the breeding business in South Florida at about this time included H. H. Horn, who had a farm in Dade County. He was the head of public works for the City of Miami Beach.

Since Dan Chappell associated with horse people and loved the track, it was only a matter of time before he was also in the breeding business. His interest was not immediate. Early on, Chappell decided that the cost of stallion fees was outrageous. When he calculated the cost of buying a yearling at a public auction, as opposed to trying to breed to the same sire and get that horse to the sale, he thought it was most sensible to buy. For many years, he simply purchased horses. He first owned horses in 1943, when the war brought about a racing moratorium in Florida. Panic set in among horse owners with hungry horses and no means of paying the bills. Suddenly, horses were cheap. Chappell bought Buzfuz (Zacaweista–Polyata, by Polydor), an unraced gelding, in the spring of 1945 for $2,000. The horse went on to become a stakes winner of $286,740, with thirty-five wins to his credit. Chappell was so pleased with his first purchase that he immediately bought another gelding: Lets Dance. The horse had a bad habit of striking his own elbows and therefore required special shoes and special care after every race. Lets Dance went on to reward his owner and trainer by becoming their second major stakes horse, eventually equaling a world record. Chappell's horses turned stakes winning into an art form. Buzfuz was the sprinter, and Lets Dance was the distance horse. Therefore, Buzfuz was often entered to act as the rabbit for his stablemate. Buzfuz learned his lesson so well that after killing off the opposition, he would then relax for a final spurt of his own at the end of the race. The two horses ran first and second more than once, including in the Seminole Handicap. Lets Dance went on to win the San Pasqual, defeating the famous Armed. He would retire with total earnings of $224,725 and like his stablemate, with thirty-five wins.

Naturally Chappell was by now hopelessly lost to the industry. It was only a matter of time before he started breeding as well as racing horses. He developed a small farm near Davie named Sunshine Stable. Later, he would move to the Ocala area. His Davie farm became Paul Mellon's Toujour L'Amour, but today it is a warehouse storage facility.

Chappell's daughter, Dorothy "Dot" Davis, remembers her early racing days in Miami as a young girl. "When one of our horses was running I would skip school to go watch," she recalled. "I'd go to the principal and tell him that my filly was running tomorrow and I wouldn't be in school the next day. He'd say, 'Well, you come to school until noon, then I'll go with you.' And he would. We'd go out, eat lunch and watch the horse race then come back to school! You couldn't do that today." She remembers that her father played similar games. He used to take the Catholic bishop to the track between services on Sunday. Dot took over her father's business after he died.

9

The Florida Thoroughbred Breeders' Association

On the evening of September 11, 1945, nine of the Florida breeders met in Hunter Lyon's office in the Security Building in Miami to form a breeders' organization. At this time, there were twenty-one breeding farms in the state, twenty-seven Florida-foaled yearlings, and thirteen horses that were two years old or older.

The nine members present chose eleven people—Jimmy Bright, Dan Chappell, Charlie O'Neil, Dr. C. C. Collins, Dr. B. L. Whitten, Dr. J. H. Yarborough, Tilyou Christopher, Dr. George Woollard, Hunter Lyon, Stefan Zachar, and Carl Rose—to be the first directors of the Florida Thoroughbred Association, as it was originally called. The first officers elected were James Bright (president), Carl Rose (vice president), Stefan Zachar (secretary), and Charles O'Neil (treasurer). The charter provided that anyone who owned thoroughbred mares or stallions and maintained them for breeding purposes could be a member of the nonprofit organization. Annual membership dues were set at $25 and initiation fees the same. The officers then voted to name the fledgling organization the Florida Thoroughbred Breeders' Association.

Dan Chappell was asked to prepare the charter and the constitution of the association. He would later be made president and remained in office until 1957 when he resigned, stating, "I have been president longer than I think any man should hold the job." Chappell also drew up the original contract for the Florida Breeders' Sales Association in 1957. When he died in 1981, he was the last surviving member of the eleven original board members.

Following the organizational meeting, the first formal meeting of the group was held at the Columbus Hotel in Miami on March 1, 1946. At the meeting, a committee was appointed to meet with

Organizational meeting of the Florida Thoroughbred Breeders' Association in September of 1945. Left to right, standing: Charles A. O'Neil, Dr. J. H. Yarborough, Dan Chappell, C. Burlinghame, Hunter Lyon, Stefan Zachar, and Dr. George E. Woollard. Left to right, sitting: Mr. and Mrs. David Nossek, Carl Rose, and C. C. Collins (by permission of Carl Rose, Jr.).

President Straus of the Gables Racing Association in order to discuss Florida-bred races. During this same meeting, several more members were added; Sam Murray, Fred W. Hooper, and two men whose first names were apparently unknown to secretary Zachar, namely Mr. Ferris and Mr. Lowery.

On June 3, back at the Security Building, the board of directors met in a special session to appoint a committee to represent the organization at the meeting of the Florida State Racing Commission in July. At this meeting, Hunter Lyon was chair of the board, Stefan Zachar was secretary, Charlie O'Neil, Jr., was treasurer, and Jimmy Bright was president. Appointed to the special committee were Carl Rose, Dan Chappell, and Hunter Lyon. During this meeting, it was also decided that the organization pay dues and join the National Association of Thoroughbred Breeders of America. Registration of Florida-bred foals was also established. It was decided that all foals born before 1946 could be registered without fee following proof of their Florida-bred status. The first registration certificate ever issued by the association was for Franc's Cracker (Liberty Franc–Justa

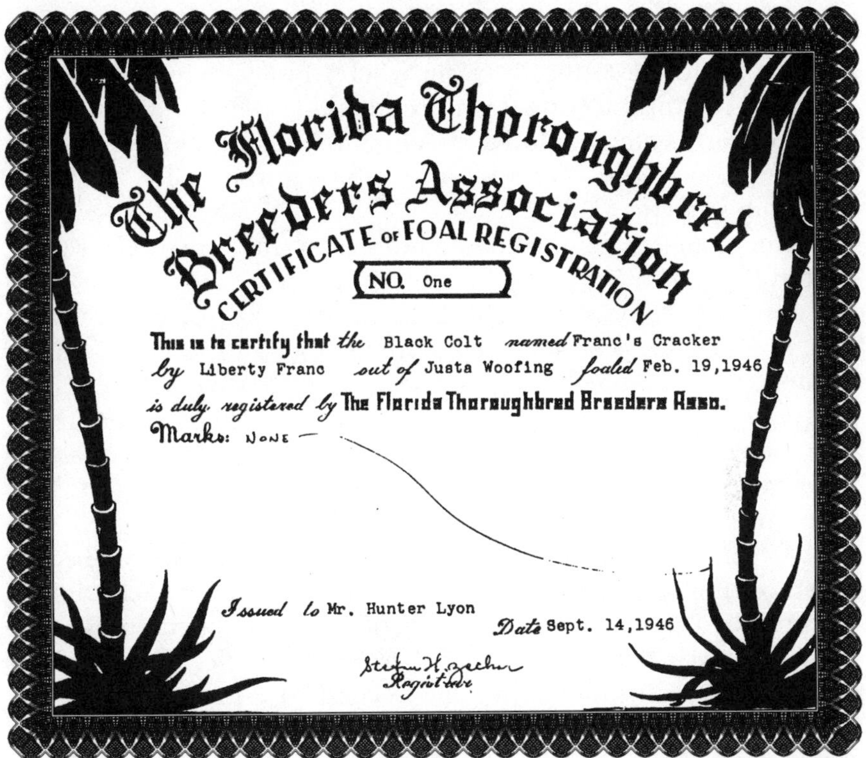
The Florida Thoroughbred Breeders Association
CERTIFICATE OF FOAL REGISTRATION
NO. One

This is to certify that *the* Black Colt *named* Franc's Cracker *by* Liberty Franc *out of* Justa Woofing *foaled* Feb. 19,1946 *is duly registered by* The Florida Thoroughbred Breeders Asso.

Marks: NONE

Issued to Mr. Hunter Lyon

Date Sept. 14,1946

Stefan H. Zachar
Registrar

Memorabilia—the first registration blanks used by the Florida Thoroughbred Breeders' Association. The certificate reproduced above was in 1946 the first issued by registrar Stefan H. Zachar (to Hunter Lyon, Sr. for his black colt Franc's Cracker). Franc's Cracker contested the first running of the Florida Breeders' Stakes at Hialeah in 1948 in his breeders' colors and was beaten a head by Mrs. T. Christopher's home-bred filly Rablim.

Woofing, by Good Goods), foaled February 19, 1946, and bred by Hunter Lyon. Fees from that point on would be $2.00 before a foal reached one year of age; $10.00 after the first year. Nonmembers would pay $10.00 for the first year; $50.00 thereafter. The directors also adopted a resolution to ask the Florida State Racing Commission at its next meeting to bar horses from Florida-bred races except those registered with the association. Thus began the first formal registry for Florida-breds.

Two rules passed by the racing commission gave encouragement to the Florida breeding program. One provided a five-pound allowance to Florida-breds in open competition within the state. The other rule provided that the three major tracks pay $250 to the breeder of any Florida-foaled horse each time that horse won a race at a recognized course within the state. On June 21, 1947, the board met at the Hotel Marion in Ocala where they were guests of Carl Rose. During this meeting it was decided that the Florida-bred registration certificate should be attached to The Jockey Club certificate and kept as one. They also raised the registration fee for members from $2.00 to $5.00.

The next meeting of the board of directors was held the following year at the Seven Seas Restaurant in Miami on November 10. The minutes note that Mrs. Stefan Zachar was the secretary. David Nossek was added to the list of board members, and a guest, Merrit Buxton, also attended. At this meeting, Dan Chappell read the charter and constitution he had prepared. It was moved that these documents be recorded in the circuit court. A motion to establish the next meeting, the purpose of which was to elect officers, was then carried. The meeting was set for January 16, 1949.

That meeting was held at the Flamingo Hotel in Miami Beach. The recording secretary, Jane Ackerman, presided while election of the president took place. Jimmy Bright was nominated and unanimously reelected to that position, Carl Rose was elected vice-president, Tilyou Christopher became second vice-president, Everett Clay was elected executive secretary, and Charles O'Neil was made treasurer. A copy of the proposed letterhead was approved, and the question of an official address for the association was raised. Ev Clay was then elected registrar. Hunter Lyon, Dan Chappell, Fred Hooper, Stefan Zachar, David Nossek, Dr. Woollard, Dr. J. H. Yarborough, and H. H. Horn were elected to the board of directors. Hunter Lyon was elected chairperson of the board. Pressing business included the motion to solicit Gulfstream's James Donn to sponsor a Florida–Cuban race similar to Tropical Park's sponsorship. (Tropical Park donated $5,000 and expenses). A membership committee was formed to pursue the idea.

In 1949, the association became affiliated with the National Association of Thoroughbred Clubs. Hunter Lyon and Dan Chappell were to represent Florida at the national association's quarterly meeting in Lexington, Kentucky, on July 23.

The meetings continued in South Florida at various locations. In 1950, the association had thirty-four members. Hialeah had contributed $2,500 to the association, while Gulfstream had pledged $1,000. A motion was carried requesting breeders to donate 10 percent of their breeders' awards to the association effective that year. Humphrey Finney, secretary of the Maryland Horse Breeders' Asso-

The FTBA struggled in the early days for recognition and support from the tracks as well as other areas. The Florida Breeders' Stakes race was the first restricted race just for Florida-breds. Here at a presentation in 1961 when Fair Gal, bred by Sunshine Stud, won are (left to right) L. Hebert, trainer; Dan Chappell, owner; Walter Donovan of Hialeah; William Hartack, jockey; and Abe Mersky, co-owner of Sunshine Stud. Photo by Leo Frutkoff (by permission of *The Florida Horse*).

ciation (and later involved with Fasig-Tipton, a sales company that operated in Florida), had loaned the association the film *The Maryland Horse,* which all enjoyed.

In 1951, several more names appeared on the roster of members from the Ocala area, including Elmer Heubeck and Mrs. William Leach. Also in 1951, a motion was passed allowing the association to preside over the awarding of the breeders' awards. The association would submit lists of the Florida-bred winners to the tracks. The earlier practice had required breeders to apply to the tracks themselves, because breeders' awards were made by each track. Motion was made to ask the tracks to reserve a certain number of stalls for Florida-bred horses. In addition, each track was asked to increase the number of Florida-bred races to one per condition book (the publication in which the track announces its races, with purses, eligibilities, and weight considerations; condition books are published every few of weeks, so there is usually more than one book per meet).

In 1952, a motion to ask the commissioner of agriculture for his support in getting the tracks to allot 5 percent of their stall space to Florida-breds was carried. In 1954, Elaine Roberts, wife of jockey Porter Roberts, became the first woman director of the Florida Thoroughbred Breeders' Association. In 1955, the minutes record that in 1954, there were 176 Florida-bred starters with 97 winners, 230 races won, and purses totaling $570,942. Marked Game was the leading Florida-bred to date. By then, the association had fifty-six members from seven counties in the state. (Today there are over fourteen hundred members, many of whom live out of state but leave their mares in Florida.)

At the July 10, 1955, meeting, there was much discussion about a magazine, *Florida Thoroughbred,* published by the Florida Bloodstock Agency. President Chappell appointed special committee members Carl Rose, Everett Clay, Bonnie Heath, Joseph O'Farrell, Tilyou Christopher, and himself to discuss the implications of this magazine. This special committee would meet on July 15 in Ocala. Most of the members were new breeders from the Ocala area. The Ocala meeting marked the first real indication of the future direction of the breeding industry in Florida. (The magazine proved to be short-lived, but it existed long enough to preempt the name. Hence, today's magazine is named *The Florida Horse.*) Also during the July 10, 1955, meeting, a motion was passed to request the racing commission to waive the five-pound allowance previously allowed for Florida-breds in stakes races. A motion to request all four tracks to present Florida-bred two-year-old races once a week was also passed.

At the January 13, 1957, annual meeting, discontent was expressed in a plea for more efficient operation of the association. Members were particularly concerned about Florida-bred races and the notification of members. A meeting was arranged on January 27 to discuss reorganization of the association, which was accomplished by the November 1957 meeting. A nominating committee and mail balloting for the election of officers was established, as were monthly meetings and, for the executive committee during racing season, weekly meetings.

Until 1958, most horses were not raced until late in the summer of their second year. With the advent of winter racing in Florida and since Florida weather permitted earlier training and condi-

In later years, the officers of the FTBA were mostly from Ocala. Several who played key roles are (left to right) Grant Dorland of Roseland Farm, Elmer Heubeck of Rosemere Farm, Bonnie Heath of Bonnie Heath Farm, and Pat Farrell, field secretary for the FTBA (by permission of the FTBA).

tioning, Florida began instituting earlier and earlier two-year-old races. At first these races were disliked; it was felt that the horses were simply too young. But in time, two-year-old races became an accepted part of the racing year. (There are still those who protest and refuse to race their youngsters that early, however.) In 1958, the same year the association voted to endorse early two-year-old racing, Carl Rose of Ocala was appointed president, and in 1959 he was voted chairperson of the board. In 1960, a motion was carried to request permission to use the Florida state flag on the Hialeah program next to Florida-bred entries. The Florida Thoroughbred Breeders' Association eventually persuaded the *Daily Racing Form* to start designating state-bred status. Also in 1960, Bonnie Heath was elected president.

In 1961, meetings began to be held consistently in Ocala. At first, the Florida Thoroughbred Breeders' Association conducted business out of an old tack room in the Needles Barn at Dickey Stables in Ocala. The organization then moved to a small stone building that had housed a beef barbecue. This structure boasted a big fireplace and jalousied windows, but it lacked indoor plumbing. In 1961, association members decided to meet three times a year

More active FTBA members included these three enjoying the sun at Hialeah: (left to right) George Cavanaugh of Pinecrest Farm; Douglas Stewart of Shady Lane Farm; and Everett Clay, who not only was publicist for Hialeah but was one of the first turf writers to regularly write about the fledgling industry in Florida. Photo by Leo Frutkoff (by permission of *The Florida Horse*).

The new FTBA building in Ocala. Photo by Art Kunkel (by permission of the FTBA).

instead of just once and also declared that board members would be elected for staggered terms. Hence, three board members were elected for one year, three for two years, and three for three years.

In 1962, the problem of the designation of Florida-breds was again discussed. Members suggested using the outline of the state of Florida with an "F" inside it. This symbol would be placed on programs next to the names of Florida-bred horses.

In October 1966, the association moved into its new building at the Golden Hills Country Club in Ocala. Offices of *The Florida Horse* and the Florida Breeders' Sales Company were also at Golden Hills. In 1987, the association again expanded its office space. This time, major construction to add several new offices and remodel the entire Golden Hills building took place. Only the breeders' association was housed in this building.

The breeders' association would be instrumental in most of the major legislation passed regarding the important racing and breeding industries. In 1949, the association first attempted to get legislation passed to allow tracks to be open on Sundays and holidays. Not until 1986 would the bill finally pass the legislature, making Florida the last state in the nation to get Sunday racing. In 1974, the breeders' association attempted to get the "Family Bill" (or "Minors Bill") passed. The bill would allow minors to attend races with their families. Time and again that bill, too, would be defeated. Finally in 1988, the Family Bill, which allows minors to attend the races with their parents, passed. In 1977, band-aid legislation provided tax relief and raised breeders' awards from 10 to 15 percent. Such problems as these and problems of the tracks (such as dates and regulation) continue to be concerns of the Florida Thoroughbred Breeders' Association.

By the early 1960s, the fledgling breeding industry had become well established in the midsection of the state. Ocala had already earned its reputation as a major breeding center. In 1968, the FTBA voted to open a Hall of Fame to honor its only Horse of the Year, four divisional champions, five dams of champions, two top-caliber racehorses, and its leading sire. The unveiling occurred on October 6, 1968, as part of Ocala Week. In future years, Ocala's place as a major breeding center would rank second in the world only to Lexington, Kentucky.

Part Two

Coming Up Roses

10

The Man Who Brought Kentucky to Florida

A letter to the editor written by S. L. "Sid" Kilgore of Lakeland appeared in the *Orlando Sentinel* on June, 3, 1957:

> There is a man among you who I feel has earned in the fullest possible way the gratitude of his neighbors and his city, his county, his state, for having done more for the whole people there than any single individual or group of individuals. . . .
>
> Carl Rose had the vision of Florida's wonderful road system years ago and saw in his mind's eye these roads built of lime rock and at a time when it took real courage and determination to go ahead with something new, he pioneered the use of lime rock for Florida roads and secured approval from the then infant State Road Dept., for the first lime rock road. Thus his vision was the beginning of the greatest industry in Marion County and one of the greatest in Florida. . . .
>
> Through his vision and faith and encouragement he has brought to the attention of the nation and of the whole sporting world the value of Marion County limestone land which has resulted, even now, in another great industry for his home county and city, in the form of horse breeding farms that in time will rival Kentucky. The surface has only been scratched in this great new undertaking and all of this is because of the foresight and hard work of this wonderful man.
>
> When the new courthouse is completed, I should like to see a great statue of Carl Rose cast in bronze standing alongside one of his thoroughbred horses, also life-size in bronze, and these mounted on a base of Ocala limerock concrete, placed on the grounds as an expression of the appreciation of the people of Marion County and the City of Ocala for his wonderful foresight and vision and unselfish contribution to the welfare of his neighbors and that his memory may not be lost to the future citizens of our state and ever remain an inspiration to others.

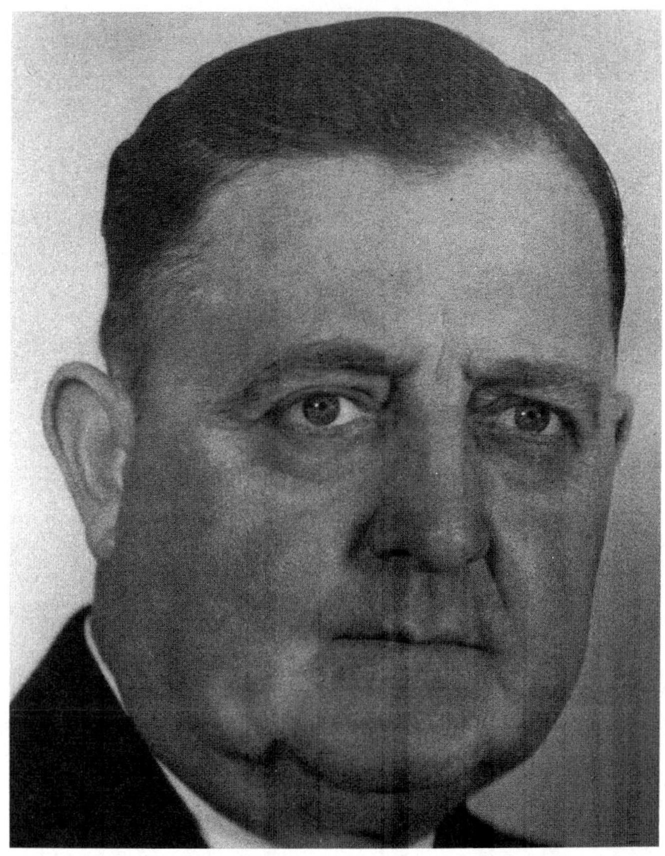

Carl G. Rose (by permission of the FTBA).

While the thoroughbred industry waxed and then began to wane in South Florida, a new breeding industry was just getting started in the north-central part of the state around Ocala and Marion County. Marion County and its neighboring counties are unique to Florida in the richness of their soil, which is indicated by huge live oaks (a particular type of oak tree that grows very slowly to massive heights and has an extensive yet somewhat shallow root system; it therefore cannot exist in sandy soils, as it would topple) growing in the midst of rolling, lush, green fields reminiscent of Kentucky. Unlike sandy South Florida with its barren pine runs and swampy Everglades, this country was green, comparatively cool, and inviting. The outcroppings of limestone were evidence of the solid base beneath the topsoil. It was the limestone that drew the first thoroughbred breeder to Ocala.

Carl Graham Rose has been given many titles in Florida history.

Mr. and Mrs. Carl Rose (by permission of W. Vines).

He is considered the father of the thoroughbred industry in the state and is also called the father of Florida's limerock industry. Highway 200, a major highway in Ocala, is named Carl G. Rose Highway in his honor. Carl Rose was born on June 6, 1892, on a farm in Bourbon, Indiana, where his father, Graham Rose, was active in the draft horse and mule business. Graham Rose was responsible for importing many fine horses to the United States from Germany, France, Belgium, and England for breeding purposes. Carl's education ended with high school. In a speech he gave on April 30, 1957, he told people that his college education consisted of "going through college one day when he was visiting the university in Gainesville." Yet he had drive, ambition, and a dogged determination. When his mind was made up, he could not be swayed.

In April 1916, Carl Rose came to Florida with his wife, Ann, and year-old son, Graham, by slow train through the bluegrass section of Kentucky. Rose later decided that the trip through Kentucky qualified him for appointment to the State Racing Commission, since no other member of the commission had ever been there. He came to Florida to be the superintendent of a construction company that had a contract to build the first asphalt road in the state. An oyster-shell base with very little durability had been used for road material up to this time.

As he worked with various road materials, Rose learned that a strip of limestone stretched from the Florida Panhandle through the north-central section of the state and down some of the West Coast, taking in most of Marion County. Rose had the material tested for purity at the Pittsburgh Testing Laboratory and sought approval for its use in road building from the newly formed State Road Department. The U.S. Bureau of Public Roads approved, and the department granted authorization. By the 1930s, eleven limestone mines were in operation in the state. Today, limestone is used in concrete, fertilizer, and building materials, and it is also a road substrate material.

Rose first went to Ocala in 1917 as one-third owner of a sand-dredging operation on Lake Weir. He did the work, and his partners furnished the capital. In 1918, he moved his residence to Ocala. Land was selling for $5 to $10 an acre, and Rose bought up thousands of acres of the virgin, green countryside. Although he bought and sold land continuously, he probably owned some 20,000 acres at different times. He ran cattle on much of his land and began selling property to anyone he could entice to the area; Rose charged up to $200 an acre.

Rose was earning a respectable reputation as a successful contractor, large landowner, and civic-minded leader. He was very active in the Chamber of Commerce. According to a July 19, 1988, article in the *Ocala Star Banner,* in the early 1930s, the chamber enacted work relief projects that resulted in the construction of a water softening plant, city auditorium, athletic field and grandstand, cold storage plant, slaughterhouse, tree-planting program, and beautification of approaches to the city. Rose was also active in the Harry Anna Crippled Children's Home of Umatilla.

While building forty-four miles of asphalt road in Volusia County (the longest such road in the state at that time), Rose developed a fast friendship with a young lawyer, Dave Sholtz. This relationship would figure strongly in Rose's future success, when Sholtz was elected governor in 1932. When Sholtz took office in January 1933, he replaced the old racing commission with his own supporters. He appointed B. F. Paty chairperson of the board and made Walter H. Donovan secretary. Upon Paty's resignation at the first commission meeting in Tallahassee, however, Sholtz asked Rose to fill the position. This appointment pleased Ocala residents. Rose served as chairperson of the commission from 1933 to 1936.

Rose had little experience to recommend him for the position (other than, of course, his train trip through Kentucky on his way to Florida). But the little knowledge he had gained from his father's involvement with horses was more than the other four members of the commission could claim. They, like most people in Florida north of Miami, had never been to a racetrack or a horse farm. The racing commission consisted of five members, one from each congressional district and one from the state at large. The commission was responsible for eight or nine dog racing plants as well.

While Rose was chairperson, the Don Meade case came to light. Meade was famous for race "etiquette" violations. In 1936 the Florida Racing Commission taped conversations Meade had with other jockeys that proved he was involved in race-fixing. Rose got much of the credit for clearing up the facts and meting out the punishment. According to the ruling at the time, E. R. Bradley's contract rider was cited for "unsatisfactory riding and violation of racing rules." Meade was suspended by the Hialeah stewards. His license was then revoked by the Florida Racing Commission; it was not reinstated until 1939. Rose was credited with cleaning up many of the unsavory aspects that had begun to taint South Florida racing.

But the most important result of Rose's service on the commission was that it piqued his interest in the thoroughbred industry. He became intrigued with raising thoroughbreds in the state. Jimmy Bright encouraged him to experiment. Dr. J. G. Catlett, the racing commission's veterinarian, and Rose often discussed how to produce horses in the limestone sections of Marion County. From his father's horse raising experience, Rose had learned that limestone land and water were excellent for growing healthy bone in young stock. He had already had success raising cattle on his limestone land. In Illinois, another thoroughbred entrepreneur, John Daniel Hertz (of Hertz Rent-a-Car), had grown weary of Kentuckians' boasts about their minerals and bluegrass. Hertz moved his nursery from Kentucky to Cary, Illinois, to prove that a good horse could be raised outside Kentucky. Carl Rose decided he could do the same thing in Florida that Hertz was doing at Leona Farm in Illinois.

When Rose completed his stint as racing commissioner, his interest in thoroughbreds was so great that he could not possibly stop there. Almost immediately, he acquired his first thoroughbred brood mare, Jacinth, from a disgusted Marshall Field (Chicago's leading department store magnate). The mare was passed on to Rose with Field's curt statement, "She can't be trained." Rose did not bother to refute Field's judgment. At the tender age of twenty-two months, Jacinth (*Jacopo–Calycanthus, by Brown Bud) became Rosemere Farm's foundation mare, eventually producing

Rosemere Farm in 1936 (by permission of W. Vines).

Carl Rose and a young Jacinth with one of her many foals (by permission of W. Vines).

Carl Rose holds Jacinth at age twenty-one in 1957 with her fourteenth foal, Thyminth (by permission of FTBA).

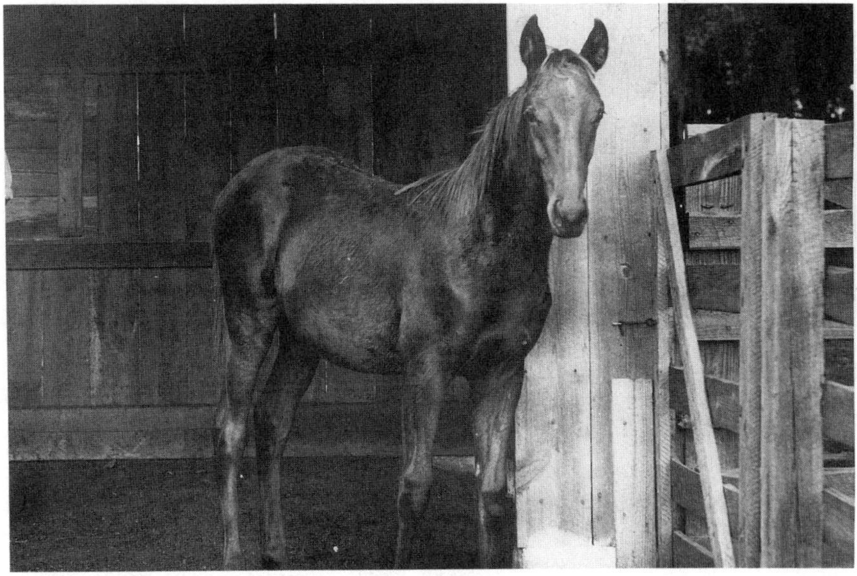

Rosemere Rose was Jacinth's first foal and the first thoroughbred foaled in Marion County. She was born in 1939. Photo by Gleason's (by permission of W. Vines).

fourteen foals, all of which were winners. (The last was Thyminth, foaled in 1957, who completed the record with a win on September 1, 1959. Incredibly enough, at the age of thirty-two, Jacinth had one more foal, but it died shortly after birth.) Rosemere Rose, Jacinth's first foal, by Full Dress, was the first registered thoroughbred foaled in Marion County. She was born in 1939 and became the first of Rose's horses to hit the racetrack. Rosemere Rose would not be his first winner, however.

Purchasing Jacinth was Carl Rose's first step toward developing and promoting Marion County as a prime area for raising thoroughbred racehorses. An activity that started out as a hobby would soon become his passion. Rose was the first to admit that one of the reasons the industry appealed to him was because he owned so much land in Marion County. He had purchased most of the land because of the limestone he knew was just below the tough Bahia grass. To market the property as prime horse farm land looked like excellent mathematics to him.

His horses grazed in belly deep grass near a segment of the Tampa-to-Jacksonville stagecoach trail. Several natural springs of clear, cold water had been the site of coach stops in years gone by. A huge, rambling plantation house still stood, a relic of Civil War days. In 1992, some of the land he owned is still horse farms (including Ocala Stud), but a larger portion is now the Central Florida Community College, the Industrial Center, and the Paddock Mall.

Rose and Charlie O'Neil owned a lot of the land together. The main portion of the early Rosemere Stock Farm was located on Highway 74, called Dunellon Road, southwest of Ocala. Originally, the farm was a little more than 3,000 acres. This vast piece of real estate was gradually whittled down as Rose encouraged more and more people to buy land and start horse farms. The last piece that he and O'Neil bought was turned into Rolling Acres, later to be the main thoroughbred section. Rose and O'Neil paid the exorbitant price of $20 an acre for 700 acres on what is now Highway 200 to Truxton P. Drake, a cattle and restaurant owner. Someone told O'Neil that it was too high a price; it should have been only $12 to $13. In the ensuing argument, Rose settled it with the flip of a coin, the loser to buy the property. Rose lost . . . and won. A popular turf writer in the 1930s and 40s, Jimmy Loftus of the *Ocala Star Banner* wrote in the *Turf and Sport Digest* of April 1940 that Rose was "one of the sport's strongest bulwarks in the flower state" and quoted Rose as saying, "Florida is known for its Hialeah Park and its Tropical

Park and its Widener Cup, but soon Florida will be known as a flourishing state for breeding horses."

On March 30, 1940, the first thoroughbred stallion to stand in Marion County arrived at Rosemere Farm. Major Frank L. Carr of the U.S. Army Remount in Lexington, Kentucky, had come to inspect the farm and to authorize the placing of a good remount stallion there. Because the army was winding down its cavalry division and no longer needed its horses, it used army stock to encourage the breeding of better horses all over the country. Carl Rose and Major Carr together chose a dark bay seven-year-old, Green Melon (Whichone–*Rambling II, by =Essexford). The stallion had been bred by Robert Sterling Clark and was a consistent winner at Hialeah. At this time, stock at Rosemere consisted of one stallion, two mares, two yearlings, and, according to the *Turf and Sport Digest,* January 1942, "three fine saddle mares with colts at their sides." Rose told a local newspaper, "This country has everything necessary to raise fine horses. Rich fertile soil, flowing spring water and groves of magnolias, walnuts, pines and live oaks to furnish shade." He added that the climate was virtually insect-free and averaged seventy-four degrees.

By 1943, about 325 of Rosemere's 3,100 acres were devoted to the equine operation; the rest of the land was turned over to polled Herefords and Tennessee walking horses. A half-mile track was constructed for $100, the cost of grading it out of the fine Ocala soil. Here the young horses received their early training and conditioning before being sent to Miami to race and to be sold.

In 1943, Green Melon was returned to the Remount, and a new stallion was purchased to replace him at Rosemere. Canadian-bred Suffern (Sweepster–Saffron, by Marathon) was a winner of fourteen races and $18,245. He stood his first season at Rosemere in 1944. In December 1943, Rosemere had its first winner at the track. It was also the county's first homebred to win a race. Gornil (Green Melon–Jacinth, by *Jacopo) won at Tropical Park. Her owner thus became the first Florida breeder to collect a breeders' award of $250 from the track.

By 1945, most of the twenty-one breeding farms in the state were in southern Florida, with a few located in Jacksonville and one in St. Augustine. But Rosemere Farm in Marion County had become the largest of all. Everett Clay, Hialeah's publicity director, wrote in the May *Florida Cattleman,* "One of these winters a Florida-bred race horse will come thundering down the stretch at Hialeah to win Florida's big horse race, the Widener. This isn't any wild

Carl Rose with the 1944 colt by Green Melon out of Wise Helen, Rosemere Count (by permission of H. C. Vines).

dream. The state has been steadily gaining ground. Admittedly it is still small change, but there's talk already of a race at one of south Florida's three tracks every season for Florida-breds." He added that five foals reportedly had been dropped that spring, and that perhaps a dozen were expected for the following spring.

In July 1945, a real coup for the fledgling breeding industry occurred when Carl Rose sold a Florida-bred yearling to Henry H. Knight's Almahurst Farm in Kentucky. The colt, Rosemere Count, was out of a Kentucky-bred mare, Wise Helen, who had been sold to Almahurst. Almahurst at the time stood three of the nation's top stallions, including the 1940 Kentucky Derby winner, Gallahadion. In stressing the significance of this sale, in July 1945, the *Ocala Star Banner* reported that this event was "equal to a universal demand by California for Florida citrus fruit." The recognition this sale attained for Rose was worth more than the check he put in his pocket.

By this time, Rosemere's Rolling Acres was becoming a local attraction. Nine horses were in training under O'Neil's trainer,

In 1943 races at Rosemere Farm attracted visitors from all over central Florida (by permission of W. Vines).

T.J. "Tom" Tault, whom O'Neil had shipped up from South Florida. O'Neil at this time was firmly behind the development of the industry in North Florida and was moving most of his operation to Ocala. The training track was the scene of much excitement most mornings. Town spectators and passing vacationers were always seen lined up along the rail to watch the morning workouts. The track was located on a main highway near the municipal airport, and many passers-by could not resist stopping to see what was going on. On Sunday afternoons, racing with some minor betting on the side was the weekend sport for much of the town. Those who were there in the late 1930s and early 1940s remember that the sheriff collected tickets at the door. By July 1945, Rolling Acres was the natural place for a local race meet sponsored by the Marion County Fair Association. About 2,000 spectators attended the race.

Rosemere Farm was gaining so much popularity throughout the nation that visitors were coming from far away to see the novel thoroughbred farm in Florida. The tradition of the "Rosy Order of the Gate Openers" was begun for the tourists who visited Rosemere. Visitors disembarked from the farm vehicles to open and close the numerous gates on the farm; there were about 1,000 gates, which kept the polled Herefords, Tennessee walking horses, quarter horses (owned by boarders), and thoroughbreds in their respective places. Visitors even received formal membership cards proving that they were esteemed members of the Rosy Order once they had been initiated. In June 1945, there were over 500 members. Visitors were always welcome. If Rose was not busy with his contracting company, auto agency, or other business ventures, he would conduct the tours himself.

In September 1945, Rosemere Farm-bred Rosemere Chief won the third race at Washington Park in Chicago, earning his breeder more honors. In December, Carl Rose discussed his ponies in the Sunday *Sentinel Star*: "Marion County's lime rock will grow stronger horses faster than any spot in Florida. When enough people discover this, that $25 and $30 an acre land will jump to $100 an acre!"

Rose made an announcement several weeks later, just before the end of the year, of his intention to begin raising horses on a major scale at Rolling Acres Farm. To help him accomplish his goal, he hired a new farm manager, Elmer Heubeck, Jr., a veteran of the racing industry from Reisterstown, Maryland. Hiring Heubeck was one of the best moves Rose had yet made, not only for his own personal growth as a thoroughbred breeder, but also for increasing the knowledge of horsemanship in Marion County.

11

The Horseman

Elmer Heubeck graduated from the University of Maryland in 1939 with a degree in animal husbandry. He had grown up in the horse country of Maryland and Virginia, where neat, picturesque farms on rolling, smoothly manicured hills came into being during the Civil War era. He married his college sweetheart, Harriet, in 1940. They immediately moved to Hialeah, where Heubeck trained and worked under major trainers such as Guy Bedwell.

After World War II broke out, the Heubecks returned to Maryland. There Heubeck worked first as farm manager for W. L. Brann at Glade Valley Farm and later for C. E. Tuttle. When Tuttle decided to move his operation to Oregon, Heubeck, who was then a new father, opted not to go. In 1945, Heubeck placed a work-wanted advertisement in a weekly magazine, the *Blood-Horse*, an ad that Carl Rose answered. In an interview with Rose, Heubeck was at first dubious about a thoroughbred career in Florida: "Like most people, all I'd seen of Florida besides the tracks, was riding up and down Highway U.S. 1 along the coast. It didn't look like horse country to me," Heubeck recalled.

Rose sent his good friend Joe Kelleher to interview Heubeck, but no one knows who asked more questions. In the end, both Joe Kelleher and the Heubecks decided to give Rosemere Farm a try. When they arrived at Rosemere, however, they very nearly turned back. Heubeck recalled: "All the fencing was barbed wire; the horses ran out with cattle on several thousand acres. Mr. Rose liked animals being around and with all of the pigs, sheep, chickens and hound dogs, it looked like Noah's Ark! And the sand, the palm trees, the weird bugs down here—it sure didn't look like horse country the way we knew it!" But the Heubecks also saw the potential of the rolling hills, the thick grass, and the limestone deposits. These deposits not only purified the water but also provided the sort of solid-soil foundation necessary to support the great live oaks, the best canopy available against the heat. The

Carl Rose holds Jacinth and Pekaki in 1946, both with foals by Suffern at their sides. Jacinth's would be named Ann Rose while Pekaki's would become Suffki (by permission of W. Vines).

Heubecks moved from Maryland with their son, Kerry, who was still a baby; Harriet's pet cocker spaniel; and two of Heubeck's own mares. Until their house was completed at Rosemere, they lived in Ocala.

Heubeck began working on the fencing soon after his arrival. He managed to convince Rose, who believed in the "natural" way of doing things, that barbed wire was not natural for a high-strung thoroughbred. Gradually, the offensive barbs receded to the section of farm that was used for cattle alone. Woven wire topped with a board took its place in the pastures, and board fencing dressed the barn area. New barns took the place of open sheds. While Heubeck recognized that in Florida the horses could indeed be left to "nature" a little more than they could in the frozen North, he interceded on their behalf more than Rose had.

When the Heubecks arrived at the farm, there were eight mares belonging to Rose and four more belonging to Rose's longtime friend and partner, Charlie O'Neil. Heubeck immediately began to train three yearlings: one by Suffern; one purchased by Rose at Pimlico; and a third owned by G. J. Egan of Clermont, a citrus grower and packer brought into the thoroughbred industry by Rose.

By the time Heubeck arrived at Rosemere Farm, a pattern for raising and racing the young stock had already been established. O'Neil customarily purchased the Rosemere two-year-olds to raise and race himself. He would pay for them out of their ensuing purses. With the arrival of Heubeck, winning races was an imme-

Elmer Heubeck leads his bevy of horses and riders around the Rosemere track. He is followed by George May and two other riders (by permission of W. Vines).

diate result. "Back then, Mr. Bright could promote Florida-bred races at Hialeah since he had donated the land for the track, but the races were pretty poor, they were easy to win, so we were successful right away," said Heubeck. With the advent of Heubeck and the successes at the track that followed, Rosemere began to produce more stock than O'Neil cared to buy, and Rose began to think his juveniles were worth more than O'Neil was willing to pay for them.

By 1949, several years after Heubeck's arrival, a new pattern developed. Training began every September 1. Every November 15, a vanload of yearling colts and fillies were shipped from Rosemere to Hialeah. By March 1, the end of the Hialeah season, most of those horses were sold, some through the claiming ranks but most outright. Heubeck stayed with them until the last one was sold before heading back to Rosemere. In an interview Heubeck remembered:

> Carl Rose was one of the few men who could get ten stalls at Hialeah during the season for his two-year-olds. That was something like the second coming of Christ, so we decided to take advantage of it to sell our horses.
>
> Once potential buyers saw our horses work a fast three furlongs or after they showed what they could do in a race, we didn't have any trouble at all selling them. Rose's whole idea right from the start was commercial. He never had a real racing stable; he bred to sell and we took the horses to the track to show and sell there.

Bringing the youngsters into the barn at Rosemere. Horse-safe fencing was at Heubeck's insistence (by permission of W. Vines).

From this practice, which was very unusual at a time when most breeders sought the prestige of racing the "big one" themselves, was later born the concept of the two-year-olds in training sale. Sometimes, Heubeck remembered, horses in training would be used by the cowhands as cow ponies when they were short of stock. Not only were they broken in by the end of such an experience, they were nimble and accustomed to a wide variety of surprises. Another important part of the training was unplanned: the proximity of the farm to the airport. This location turned out to be invaluable to horses that were going to be racing at Hialeah near Miami's by-now-huge international airport. Rose's young horses paid no attention to the sound of aircraft overhead.

The Rosemere-trained stock ran on to fame and fortune, proving that the limerock man had been correct. Again in an interview Heubeck recalled the South Florida–raised stock as being very small (doubtless due to the poorer quality of soil and water) and credited Rose with foresight in moving the breeding industry north to Marion County. "I don't think the breeding industry would have gotten off the ground if it hadn't moved north," he reflected.

From the beginning, the underdog breeders of Florida emphasized environment over pedigree. Rose was the first. The media often took potshots at Floridians' attempts to raise blue bloods among the palm trees and laughed at the pedigrees and the smallness of the animals in the early days. "Mr. Rose refused to spend money on horses," Heubeck admitted in an interview. "He used the remount stallions, and a few Kentucky breeders who got to know him when he was a racing commissioner would give him some of their culls. I think the most he ever paid for a horse was $200.

Ready for a day's work are several riders, including George May and Jerry Harrison. Photo by Floria State News Bureau (by permission of *The Florida Horse*).

When his horses started winning races, people just couldn't understand why. It blew them away!" Yancey Christmas, an old friend of Heubeck's in Maryland, decided it had to be something in the soil since the breeding was nonexistent "[Elmer Heubeck] certainly couldn't train a horse!" However, he also stated that "if Heubeck could train those Florida-breds, he could probably train a billy goat!"

Another method of acquiring stock for Rosemere was to wait for the end of the meet at "Shoeshine Park," as Sunshine Park used to be called by the locals. The trainers and owners who had not had a good meet and could not afford to pay their bills or ship their horses elsewhere would often sell their stock cheaply. Rose picked up several decent mares that way. At the end of each meet, he would have a vanload of horses hauled back to the farm, where he would resell any he did not want. One day, when he was unloading a van containing such a group, someone offered Heubeck about $2,000 for a gelding in the lot. Heubeck snatched it immediately, knowing it had to be the best profit he had ever made for his penny-wise boss. The good-looking gelding, as it turned out, belonged to someone else, and Rose had shipped it with his own stock as a favor.

Heubeck found out immediately that Rose was actively involved in running his farm. He rode the lead pony on the training track, walked hots at Hialeah (race horses just off the track after exercise or racing are called "hots," and the people who walk them to cool them off are called "hot-walkers"), and helped break the babies. "He could rattle off the pedigree, breeding history and personality of every horse on the farm," Heubeck remembered. One of Rose's unique theories concerned the feeding of his mares, which, like all Florida stock, were fed outside. He always liked to put one more tub of feed on the ground for his pasture mares than there were mares in the field. That way, he reasoned, whenever a fight ensued there was always another tub to move on to.

Rose took a personal interest in the people who worked for him, as well. Shortly after the Heubecks arrived in Florida, Harriet's beloved cocker spaniel was bitten by a rattlesnake and died. Harriet remembered that episode very well. "Mr. Rose was always very brusque, he didn't like to show emotion. He would come by every morning with the paper and toot his horn for me to come and get it and this one morning, here's this boxer puppy in the back seat of his car. 'I don't believe in buying the same breed back, but you need a puppy, so I bought you a puppy!' he said to me. I named him C.G., and he loved it! C.G. used to travel in his truck with him all over the farm."

His thoughtful habit of buying the morning paper for all his employees (there were four or five working for Rose when the Heubecks arrived) sometimes ended in comical results. One morning, as Rose came out of Reese's Snack Bar (now the California Federal Bank), where he purchased his papers, he was greeted by the chauffeur of an impressive-looking limousine parked at the curb. "Boy," the chauffeur addressed him, "my lady would like to purchase one of your papers." Rose agreeably gave him a paper, took the proffered nickel and went back in for another newspaper.

Rose was also known for his active involvement in the community. He was the president of the Marion Construction Company, the Ocala Limerock Corporation, the Marion Motor Company, and the Ocala Insurance Company. He continued to be very involved with the Crippled Children's Home. He always liked youngsters. Many young jockeys got their start at Rosemere Farm: Ocala-born Jimmy Duff went on to become a leading jockey nationally; Frank Hanes, who was born in Montgomery, Alabama, but raised in

Aerial view of Rosemere Farm (by permission of W. Vines).

Ocala, started in 1944 at Rosemere, then took a contract with O'Neil. Darl Norman from Chicago started at Rosemere, as well. Porter Roberts, who with his wife, Elaine, would later own Millwood Farm, exercised all the Rose horses on the farm. He also jockeyed many of them, as well as other early Florida-breds, to wins at the track. Don Roswell, Gene Martin, and Max Pryor all began at Rosemere. By 1948, Harry Trotsek of Miami Springs and Louisville was sending jockey trainees to Rosemere. He would hold the contract on their services, and the contract would be sold to owners when the boys reached seventeen. A few other jockeys who started at Rosemere went on to become trainers and owners in their own right later: George May, a trainer and owner with his wife, Ruth, of Mayfair Farm in Ocala; Pat Hunter, who would later manage Savin Farm; Donny Jordan, a Calder trainer; Sam Davis, Manny Tortora, and John Thornberry, all trainers today.

Rose was extremely influential in encouraging people to move into the area as landowners and as new horse breeders, whether they were already breeding elsewhere or had never raised a horse in their lives. "Mr. Rose was absolutely sold on this land. He bent over backward to help anyone who wanted to buy land and start a farm in the area," Heubeck recalled "He'd help them find the land—often it was his to sell—but it didn't have to be. He'd get in the well-drillers, builders, fencing, everything. Some people thought he was too much help."

The second annual race meet was held at Rose's Rolling Acres' half-mile track in 1946, which was Heubeck's first year there. This was one of the biggest events of the year for Ocala, attracting 3,500 people or more from as far away as Orlando, Tampa, and Jacksonville. The races included a match race between Ariel Game (Ariel–Play Dis, by Display), a colt owned by O'Neil, who had gotten the horse from a Canadian whiskey manufacturer, and the highly regarded quarter horse Alexander Border, owned by Otis Cowart. Ariel Game won by a nose. He would go on to have great influence on early Florida breeding. Other events included "slow" and "fast" cow pony races and a free-for-all for thoroughbred and quarter horse colts over fifteen months of age. These young animals were shooed riderless down a lane.

Nationally, 1946 was the year Florida-breds were beginning to be noticed outside of the state. At Monmouth Park, Rosemere Dee and Rosemere Sis won three races. Other Florida-breds who won at Monmouth and other Atlantic Coast tracks included animals bred by Mrs. Christopher, O'Neil, the Zachars, and D. R. Duxtad of Miami. Carl Rose was invited to Garden State, where manager Walter Donovan publicly recognized him for the success of his Rosemere-bred horses. Five scenes from the award-winning film *The Yearling* (starring Gregory Peck, Jane Wyman, and Claude Jarman, Jr.) were shot on the picturesque farm. Reporters were coming around the farm "in the boonies" regularly; the *Miami Herald* and newspapers from Lexington, Kentucky, were printing stories about Rosemere. In the *Thoroughbred Record* of March 1, 1946, Horace Wade wrote: "Nothing is too good for the Rose horses. . . . Carl Rose believes in giving his horses all of the fresh air and sunshine they can absorb. It is his contention that air and light are necessary ingredients for the well-being of any thoroughbred and he sees they get plenty of both. There is running water in every paddock; and no expense has been spared in giving the horses every equine luxury."

By mid-September 1946, Rose had sent a total of six Marion County-bred horses into competition, with total earnings of $32,775. With two years required to raise the first starters and two years during the war when racing was banned, this figure was the result of five years invested. All the winners were out of Jacinth, which prompted Rose to purchase three more *Jacopo mares. The earnings record for Marion County horses (which were still just Rosemere horses) was:

Rosemere Rose	$9,320
Lucy S.	$7,220
Rosemere Dee	$6,360
Rosemere Chief	$5,195
Gornil	$2,420
Rosemere Sis	$2,260

Only one horse sent to the track by Rose, Ramel, was as yet a non-winner; he would shortly become one.

It was this outstanding success that at last prompted Rose to turn the management of his limestone business over to his oldest son Graham so that he could run his farm full-time. Graham, a graduate of Oglethorpe University in Atlanta, was well versed in the road construction business. Rose's other children were Donald ("Buddy"), nineteen years old; Carl, Jr. ("Happy"), fifteen; and Lettie Ann, eight. All helped with the horses.

Rose had been successful in selling off chunks of his farm in 4,000- to 5,000-acre parcels at $200 an acre, a clear profit over his original $10 to $20 per acre investment. Gradually, the horses were being moved onto Rolling Acres, the northern section of the farm. At this point, Rosemere was still about 1,400 acres of lush, rolling Bahia grass. Suffern was standing for $100, and in November 1946, Ariel Game was retired to the farm after three years of racing and total earnings of $17,325. On November 24, 1946, Rose said in an interview with the local newspaper, the *Sentinel Star*, "We're waiting for the day when a Florida-bred and trained horse wins the Kentucky Derby or some other big stakes race. Then our new industry will be over the hump." Only two months later, Donna's Ace became the first Florida-bred to win a stakes race.

12

Hit the Dirt Running

From 1945 to 1948, Florida blossomed as a winter training ground, completely disproving previously held theories that racehorses should be given the winter off. In December 1944, Charles Gregg wrote an article, "In Support of Winter Racing," for the *Turf and Sport Digest:* "Figures show that horses trained in the warm tropical sunshine get the best share of turf events during the succeeding months of the year." Gregg used statistics from mid-April through June to prove the value of winter conditioning. During that interval, Florida-trained horses took the $10,000 Excelsior, the $25,000 Wood Memorial, and the $5,000 Experimental in New York. In Maryland, they took the $7,500 Rowe Memorial, the $5,000 Bowie Kindergarten Stakes, the $7,500 Southern Maryland Handicap, the $25,000 Chesapeake Stakes, and the $7,500 Gittings Handicap. Florida-trained horses performed equally well in the bluegrass and New England regions. During two weeks in April, they took fourteen major events.

By running against good competition in good races later in the year, juveniles that had wintered in Florida and raced earlier than those in other parts of the country were proving that they lost none of their effectiveness and were not ruined by early racing. Older horses that trained continuously in Florida instead of being given the winter off, as once was the case, were equally effective against their rested competition. As time went on, the trainers learned that their charges would benefit from a rest, but the timing of such a "vacation" would no longer be dependent on the weather or the season.

Many of the best stables were represented at the southern tracks. Calumet, the world's leading money-winning stable, wintered its entire string under the royal palms. Greentree Stable, Coldstream Stud, and Walter P. Chrysler were just a few of the many recognizable names. Ben Jones was a prime example. For a number of years, he had been bringing his yearlings and his older horses to train in

Florida. In 1944, within eight weeks after the season's closing at Hialeah, his horses Pensive, Twilight Tear, and Sun Again won the Kentucky Derby, the Preakness, the Dixie Handicap, the Pimlico Oaks, the Rowe Memorial, the Southern Maryland Handicap, the Acorn Stakes, the Coaching Club American Oaks, the Princess Doreen, and the Skokie handicaps and took second place in the Belmont and Suburban. Calumet Farm netted over $250,000 from these performances.

Florida had firmly established the tradition of year-round racing. The top stars of the sport now wintered in Florida or California. The Widener was *the* winter race, rivaled only by the Santa Anita Handicap. Both were ten years old in 1947.

Florida-based owners were doing as well as the winter residents with non-Florida-bred stock that they owned and trained in Florida. By the end of the 1946 to 1947 season, six of the sixteen stakes offered at the southern tracks were won by horses flying the colors of owners based in Florida. All told, Florida owners gathered in some $140,000 in purse money that season. Most successful were Mr. and Mrs. Edward Moore of Miami Beach. Their Circle M Farm's Cosmic Missile finished the 1947 season as one of the top earners in the nation. Fred Hooper's Education was the leading money-winning two-year-old of 1946; the Hoopers lived in Coral Gables. Dan Chappell's Buzfuz and Lets Dance and Jacob Sher's Frere Jacques, one of the nation's best turf horses, were other notables.

The "palm tree circuit" was no longer a laughing matter. The only thing left to prove was that horses born and raised in the state could do as well as those only trained and raced there. On Monday, January 21, 1946, the first race held exclusively for Florida-breds took place at Hialeah over the Nursery Course. This was a three-furlong chute that opened into the homestretch so that the youngsters would not have to negotiate a turn in their first starts. The race carried a purse of $2,500. It was the result of much hard work by Jimmy Bright, Dan Chappell, and Tilyou Christopher. The three men had urged John C. Clark, then president of Hialeah, to hold the race. According to the *Turf and Sport Digest*, August 1950, Clark was very gracious; he put his arm around Bright and said, "If you think we should run a race, Mr. Bright, we will." By making this race an annual event, the track recognized the efforts of the Florida breeders and the importance of their work in the racing industry, as well. Unfortunately, not all the tracks were equally supportive. Some considered the big stables that shipped horses in for the winter more important than the new breeders in their own state.

Entered in this inaugural race were three Florida-breds from Broward County, one from Dade County and one from Duval County. Also in that same issue of the *Turf and Sport Digest,* when jockey Andy LoTorco was boosted into the saddle of the favorite, a filly named Sweet Hash, he looked around and uttered what was to become a famous joke, "There ain't much to hang onto is there?" The filly, bred by Fred C. Peters in Broward County and owned by Paradise Farm, did her best to offset the joke by racing on to win by two lengths. In the winners' circle, where everyone milled about, grinned, and shook hands, Bright, never one to rest on his laurels, announced to Clark, "Pretty soon now we'll have enough horses for you to run a stakes." True to prediction, a stakes race for Florida-breds took place only two years later.

In the mid-1940s, the tourist season was bringing in more business than Miami had ever seen before. Hotels were jammed; they had no trouble demanding an outrageous $20 a night and more. Owners of private homes rented out every spare room they had. According to the *Blood Horse,* "We have never seen such a madhouse as Miami is. . . . Inflation rules everywhere . . . gambling seems to flourish . . . and one sees the license plates of every state in the Union and every Dominion province." Handles and attendance reached record highs.

Late in December 1946, Mrs. T. Christopher's Donna's Ace (Sammie–Donna Leona, by Don Leon) became the first Florida-bred to account for a stakes race when she sped to victory at Tropical Park in the $10,000-added Ponce de Leon Handicap. This test for juveniles was conducted over one and one-sixteenth miles in 1:45 1/5. Donna's Ace won by a length over what was considered to be a very competitive field. In 1947, Florida-breds won fifty races at recognized tracks across the United States. In June 1947, Charles Gregg of the *Turf and Sport Digest* wrote of the young breeding industry in the state: "No champion has as yet charged out of Florida into the glare of the national spotlight. . . . Of the thirty-six home-breds sent up to the racing wars thus far, 31 of them have triumphed in open competition. And that, viewed from any angle, is some sort of record."

At last the home tracks in Florida began taking note of these successes and offering support to the struggling Florida breeders. On February 6, 1948, Florida breeders got their first stakes race. The Florida Breeders' Stakes would be contested over Hialeah's three-furlong Nursery Course. In promotional interviews about the race, Carl Rose was heard to say, "I have great admiration for Kentucky and other states as breeding centers, but I believe that Florida has everything they have but snowdrifts." In October, twenty-four horses were nominated to the stakes race by twelve owners. By the day of the big race, there were seven starters: three from Broward County, three from Dade County, and one from Marion County. The Marion County horse was Charlie O'Neil's Suffazon, bred by Rose.

Sam McCormick, secretary-treasurer of Hialeah, another Kentuckian who helped turn Hialeah into an outstanding race course, said during a prerace interview, "I remember when a friend of mine was told he couldn't raise Irish potatoes in this section of Florida. Today he ships $2 million worth in a single year off his acreage. When I first arrived in Florida, I was told it was impossible to breed good horses here. This afternoon when an all Florida-bred field goes to the post in the Breeders' Stakes, it will prove the pessimists and cynics wrong." Hunter Lyon made the observation that this was the best crop of two-year-olds yet produced in the state. "Most of the youngsters are large and no excuses or apologies need be offered for them."

By special invitation a number of sportswriters were on hand for the event, along with 13,841 fans. Sires represented in this stakes were Doublrab, Mucho Gusto, Liberty Franc, and Suffern. Mrs. T. Christopher's Rablim (Doublrab–Over Limit, by Liberty Limited) won. He was Doublrab's first stakes winner. Runner-up was Hunter Lyon's Franc's Cracker. Doublrab was also the sire of fourth runner-up Bundlrab. Jimmy Bright presented the trophy. The race was followed by the annual breeders' dinner at the Columbus Hotel. The dinner was a little more jubilant this time than usual.

The Florida Breeders' Stakes was the first of what became a yearly event. In 1963, it was renamed the Carl Rose Stakes. The purse was increased to $10,000 in 1949 and to $15,000 in 1953. By 1958, the dates were moved back to the end of February and finally to March to allow the youngsters a little more growing time and racing experience. In the early years, Dade County breeders, particularly the Christopher Ranch, dominated the race. By the mid-fifties, however, the balance of power had swung to Marion County. Eight of the first twelve winners were foaled in Marion County: four from Rosemere, one from Dickey Stables, and later, three from Ocala Stud. Two winners of the stakes went on to national fame. King Hairan won eight other stakes in 1956; he was the first two-year-old since Man o' War to win nine stakes.

Carl and Ann Rose with Luther Evans, president of the Florida Turf Writers (by permission of W. Vines).

My Dear Girl, winner in 1959, went on to become juvenile filly champion.

Elmer Heubeck's mare, Leonardtown (Solace–Laurel, by Manager Waite), was a dominant factor in the stakes. She produced three winners: Werwolf in 1949, Wolf Gal in 1953, and Merriwolf in 1954. In November 1948, Heubeck shipped thirteen horses to Barn X at Hialeah to complete their training and to offer them for sale. When the 1949 meet opened, Rosemere had ten two-year-olds. By the end of the meet, every one was sold. Rose's breeding operation showed a profit for the first time. It was also the first time a Florida breeder ever sold out his entire crop of two-year-olds since the Florida Thoroughbred Breeders' Association had been formed. These sales demonstrated that there was national interest in Florida-breds, or at least Rosemere-breds. One horse sold to Pennsylvania owners; one to Clermont, Florida; one to Chicago; one to Miami; two to Massachusetts; and one to Venezuela.

The average price for this lot was $7,500. Werwolf, however, was sold for $12,500 and became the subject of national interest.

Heubeck's Werwolf was purchased by Mrs. J. G. Smyth of New York, along with a Rosemere-bred colt, Dalpark; the two horses were sold for $20,000. Werwolf had already won his first race with Porter Roberts in the saddle in the second fastest time of the meet: three furlongs in :33 3/5. Following that performance a prophetic line appeared in the February 13, 1949, *Miami Herald*: "Don't be surprised if Ocala becomes the Lexington of Florida."

This was the second year of the Breeders' Stakes race, and there was a vast improvement in the field. Two of the horses, including Werwolf, were already winners. In the first year, all had been maidens. Werwolf won, and Smyth prepared to ship her two new horses to her racing stable in California. The *Blood Horse* of February 28, 1949, noted this move: "She is certainly a brave woman. . . . If one of these (Werwolf or Dalpark) should win a stakes on the west coast, she'd need a body guard. Also I would be glad to contribute to one because I think the situation would be amusing!" Werwolf was the best Florida-bred to date, going on to capture the Florida-bred juvenile championship. (Florida championships had not yet become well-recorded, well-organized, annual events.) At this running of the stakes, several papers and turf magazines agreed with Hunter Lyon's observation that this year's crop was bigger and better looking than ever. "No excuses need be made for them; they would look good in open races," was one written comment.

In 1948, a series of races was set up for the best Florida-breds and Cuban-breds. The series was put together by the Florida Thoroughbred Breeders' Association and some of the larger breeders in Cuba. There were to be two races each spring, one for two-year-olds and one for older horses, pitting five of each country's or state's best horses against each other for fields of ten. The series would be run at Oriental Park in Cuba and at Tropical Park in alternate years. The first Florida-Cuba race was held on March 21, 1948, at Oriental Park. Donna's Ace ran second to Cuban-bred Mayito in the older horses' race. Many of the visiting Florida breeders were put up with great hospitality at the beautiful farms of the rival Cuban breeders.

The series continued for several years. Doug Donn requested that Gulfstream host the Florida segment in 1950. The inaugural Rivalry Purse, as the two-year-old segment at Gulfstream was called, was advertised as "representing the cream of Cuban and Floridian breeding farms." Liberty Rab and Mr. A. B., winner of the 1950 Breeders' Stakes, were early favorites. Liberty Rab won, Fair Game came in second, and Mr. A. B. was third. The day was a festive one, with Cubans providing the rumba band.

A series of races instituted by the FTBA was the Florida/Cuban series held at one of the Florida tracks and at the Cuban track Oriental Park shown here. Oriental Park was purchased by Dan Chappell and associates but it became a terrible loss when Castro forced Americans out of Cuba (by permission of *The Florida Horse*).

One result of this series was Dan Chappell's interest in the Oriental Park race course. The track was vacationland itself, with gambling of every sort provided right at the track. Sumptuous dining and dancing, slot machines, and lottery ticket sellers provided the atmosphere of an adult playground. Oriental Park had been in operation since January 14, 1915, and was known as "Millionaire's Paradise." It was the winter mecca for Americans before Hialeah became a success. Chappell and several friends thought that the track would make an excellent investment. Chappell checked with his political connections in Washington to determine the state of affairs between America and Cuba. He was assured that his money would be safe. Cuba would not be allowed to become a Communist state. Chappell and his friends purchased the track in the late fifties and spent several million dollars on its rehabilitation. To raise money for the project, Chappell sold several good mares, including the dams of later-produced O'Calaway and My Dear Girl.

Fidel Castro was delighted with the American investors. He

June 25, 1959. Dan Chappell disembarks in Havana (by permission of Dorothy Davis).

welcomed with open arms the signs that the United States would be on his side. On opening day, Castro was there to present a trophy for one of Chappell's own homebreds, Set n' Go. Thirty-four thousand people walked through the turnstiles, more people than Hialeah had ever seen on a single day. For twenty glorious days, Chappell and associates saw the fruits of their labors ripening. Then suddenly it was over. Castro was faced with a country full of hungry people. Dwight D. Eisenhower turned a deaf ear to his pleas. In desperation, Castro turned to Russia in 1960. Before the Americans were shipped out, they were forced to sign papers leaving Oriental Park in Castro's hands. The entire investment was lost, never to be retrieved. Today Oriental Park, which discontinued racing in 1963, is a storage lot for old but functioning automobiles and buses. Present-day Calder sponsors an annual Oriental Park Hall of Fame Day. This practice was initiated in 1979, in honor of some of the various Cubans who have had an influence on the American racing industry.

Another race was initiated by Gulfstream Park following the success of the Cuban series. This race was a four and one-half furlong allowance race for Florida-breds. President James Donn agreed to match dollar for dollar any share of the purse donated by the winning owners to the treasury of the Florida Thoroughbred Breeders' Association. Rosemere Cindy won the first year. Her owners donated half their winnings, while Elmer Heubeck donated half of his fourth-place money. Donn matched the total of $1,500, making the association's coffers $3,000 richer. In 1954, President Clark of Hialeah initiated another Florida-bred race, a three-furlong event for maiden two-year-olds.

In those early days, the tracks supported local breeders by agreeing to pay bonuses of $250 to winning owners of Florida-breds in open races. Hialeah, Gulfstream, and Tropical Park each paid a special sum to the winning trainer of Florida-breds, as well. In the 1951 to 1952 season, Hialeah paid out an astounding $2,500 to state breeders for ten wins in open races. Smaller Sunshine Park meanwhile paid the winning breeders $100.

It had become apparent that two-year-old racing was becoming a major commodity for the state. The breeders acknowledged that and began selectively breeding for that precocious early speed. Sunshine Park joined in the backing of two-year-old racing. W. Frank Hobbs became president and general manager of Sunshine Park in 1953; he was principally responsible for the rejuvenation of racing on the West Coast. In 1955, he was joined by a group that included Fred Ballon (chairperson of the board) and Dick West (vice-president).

Carl Rose, Joe O'Farrell, and Bonnie Heath went to Hobbs to request support for two-year-old racing. Hobbs arranged for more stables to house 100 yearlings; half were designated as Florida-breds. A special three-furlong chute, which his associates nicknamed "Hobbs's Course," was built for the short baby races. Hobbs held his first two-year-old races in mid-January 1957. By 1958, he had instituted the Florida Breeders' Futurity, a four and one-half furlong, $2,500-added, two-year-old stakes race. The first edition was run on March 15, 1958. A filly, Indian Maid, won that inaugural, then raced on to over $200,000 in earnings, thus assuring the success and credibility of that race. Hobbs continued writing the baby races into the condition books even when the handle for those races was only 80 percent of what the older horse races brought. He believed in the benefit of the two-year-old races to the industry. Saul Silberman, president of Tropical Park, scheduled the

Joe O'Farrell of Ocala Stud and Dan Chappell of Sunshine Stud were instrumental in getting the tracks to write Florida-bred restricted races. Photo by Leo Frutkoff (by permission of FTBA).

first running of the Florida Breeders' Championship (also known as the James H. Bright Memorial Stakes). The first running was to take place on December 30, 1959. This race was for Florida-bred two-year-olds and carried a $7,500-added purse. These early races were the forerunners of a series of races, the Florida Stallion Stakes series. These races were started in 1980 and proved to be the most popular and profitable state series ever devised.

By 1951, racing was considered one of the most important industries in the state. A June 24, 1951, article in the *Florida Times Union* mentioned the millions of racing dollars given to each county as well as the "countless sums spent by race-conscious tourists and those actively involved with the industry." Florida was the only state to aid education at its racetracks. As early as the 1950s, six special days were set aside at the three southern tracks. Every university in the state would receive one day's take; the privately funded University of Miami received three days' worth. The proceeds on these days amounted to $1 million. Despite the successes of horse racing and the income to the state that it produced, it would be 1961 before the first breeders' bill passed. That bill allowed for one Florida-bred preferred race per day. Further legisla-

The Florida Breeders' Futurity held at Sunshine Park beginning in 1958 was one of the supportive races the tracks offered the Florida breeders. In this running in 1961 First Banker owned by Sunshine Stable noses out Roy Howard's General Mark. The winner was timed in 1.00 2/5 and paid $15.70 to win. He earned $9,548.50 (by permission of *The Florida Horse*).

tion in 1961 provided for the Florida Thoroughbred Breeders' Association to take over the awarding of breeders' awards, which were set at 10 percent of the gross purse.

At this point, it is time to introduce a man who, if he was not yet an Ocala-based breeder, had almost as much influence on the progress of the Florida industry as did those breeders who lived in Ocala. He had a home in South Florida, but he kept his stock in Alabama. Because he began shipping his mares across state lines to drop their foals and claim Florida-bred status, the breeding rules were changed. Mares were required to be bred back to Florida stallions or proof of domicile within the state had to be provided. Something had to be done: this man was winning many of Florida's restricted purses.

13

My Way

Although Fred Hooper did not actually move to the Ocala area until the 1960s, his influence was strongly felt in both the racing and breeding industries almost from the beginning. Hooper's later influence on the Florida breeding industry is legendary. He has won more awards than any breeder nationwide. For years, he has been listed among the top breeders nationally and has earned the Eclipse award twice (this award is given to the nation's leading breeder). Hooper has won the Jockey Agents' Benevolent Association Man of the Year award and has earned the Florida Turf Writers' Horseman of the Year award, among others. He is the breeder of two champions as well as many other top class stakes horses. The two champions, Susan's Girl and Precisionist, are also millionaires. Until 1991, Precisionist was the leading money earner of all time for Florida-breds. His record of $3,485,398 was broken by Kentucky Derby winner Unbridled.

Hooper has had a great influence on the national and the state industry, although at first he was not as fiercely patriotic toward the state industry as some others were. Hooper did things his own way, bucked criticism, refused to be daunted by traditional roadblocks, and was aggressively independent. He is thus the perfect emblem of the Florida breeder.

Born in 1898 and raised in Cleveland, Georgia, Fred Hooper was one of eight children. His father, Thomas Hooper, like most of his neighbors, made his living farming, plowing, hoeing, and wood chopping. These chores became second nature to one very ambitious boy. Never content with the simple things in life, Hooper dutifully plowed by day but after practicing on his brothers' hair, he worked evenings cutting his neighbors' hair. It was not long before his burning ambition led him to pack his bags for Atlanta, where he attended the Molar Barber College and earned his license. He went to work in Crawford's Barber Shop, where he rapidly advanced toward the head chair.

During World War I, Hooper tried to serve overseas but was turned down. When he was not yet eighteen, he moved to Alabama where he worked in the steel mills and also boxed. Boxing was his favorite sport. When Hooper knocked out the local bully in the ring in Muscle Shoals, Alabama, he was declared heavyweight champion of Alabama.

But the great outdoors was calling, and he remembered a real estate man who had come through Georgia talking about how one could get rich growing potatoes and cabbage in Florida. Potatoes were selling for $18 a barrel, and one could count on seventy barrels to an acre. Hooper moved to Florida, borrowed money to buy forty acres west of Palatka at $200 an acre, and then went into debt to seed and fertilizer suppliers. For three years he cleared his land, built a house, raked, hoed, worked eighteen-hour days, and bought more and more land until he owned 230 acres. In 1923, when a potato blight hit the entire State of Florida, Hooper was ruined in four days. He was $20,000 in debt, and he quit farming.

He went back to barbering in Bunnell, Florida, near Daytona Beach. About this time the double-track Florida East Coast Railroad (the part called the Moultrice Cutoff) was being built. Many of the workers were Hooper's customers at the barbershop. When he heard of a contractor who could not pay for his trucks or complete his contract, Hooper hung up his scissors for the last time and entered the construction business.

All did not go well at first. With the help and hire of many other blight-stricken farmers, he cut the required hundred-foot swath through swamp and hammock, thus earning his nickname, "the Swamp Rabbit." "That's just the way I am," Hooper would later explain in one of many interviews. "In the construction business they used to call me the Swamp Rabbit because I'd go and build roads where no one else would go. That's how I breed too. No one taught me bloodlines. I taught myself. And I do it my own way."

From this construction job, he pocketed a few dollars. In 1923, Hooper ran for Flagler County Commissioner and won. However, politics was not as appealing as it had originally appeared, so he resigned and went back into construction. His next big job was the twenty-three mile stretch of Ocean Shore Boulevard, which is part of U.S. 1. Difficulties developed in obtaining the proper rock for the base, and he was $75,000 in debt before he finally began laying the road. He completed that massive job with a mere $12,000 profit.

His seed and fertilizer creditors came calling, and once again he was forced to start from scratch.

In those early years of getting started, Hooper dashed from town to town, bid on jobs, deposited money in one bank, and asked for credit in the next with a referral from the former. He worked in the blazing sun all day and by floodlights into the night. In this way, he began building not only funds, but credit. From these modest beginnings began Hooper Construction Company, which eventually developed into the South's biggest contractor. Later, the company became the multimillion-dollar General Development Corporation, which provided major construction work in seven southeastern states.

While he was doing roadwork in Alabama, Hooper became aware of cotton farmers who were going broke. He was thus able to add to his real estate holdings by purchasing about sixteen farms (some 5,000 acres). After accumulating all this land, Hooper naturally needed to do something with it. In the 1930s, he began raising shorthorn cattle on his Palatka, Florida, ranch. By the mid-1940s, he had the largest herd of prize shorthorn cattle in the entire Southeast on his Circle H Stock Farm in Alabama.

Hooper's love of horses began with the farm animals he had worked with as a child. Always in the back of his mind was the thought that someday he would get a "real" horse. His dream finally came true with his first buy, a filly named Seminole Lady, which he purchased from Jimmy Bright. She won many match races for Hooper in Florida, Georgia, and South Carolina. He purchased his next horse because he needed a good cow pony. He bought a crossbred gelding, Prince, from Carl Rose; Prince was supposed to be good at herding cattle. But Hooper couldn't resist trying his new acquisition out against the locals and discovered that the horse had a little speed. In the mid to late 1930s, Hooper matched Prince against any comer. The gelding started fifty-five times and won forty-nine of those starts, most of them on half-mile tracks and against thoroughbreds. This is a record that Hooper's later champions, Kentucky Derby winner, and millionaires could not better. Based on his performances, the horse, whose owner would recall him forty years later as the best horse he ever owned, was appropriately redubbed "Royal Prince." But Prince had served his purpose: Hooper was hooked.

With the onset of World War II, however, Hooper was not able to pursue his newest passion. By 1943, he was head of a major construction company, with headquarters in Montgomery, Alabama; he was running the largest stock farms in the Southeast; and he had other offices and homes in Jacksonville and Coral Gables, Florida, where he enjoyed playing golf occasionally with his friend Sam Snead. But that minor relaxation was not enough to offset the price Hooper had paid to get where he was. He had worked so hard that he was on the verge of a nervous breakdown. Hooper's doctors advised him take a rest from business for awhile. He went to a cottage in North Carolina to rest. But for a man like Hooper, rest only means doing something different. While at the cottage, he read about the upcoming yearling sales held at the Keeneland sales pavilion in Lexington, Kentucky. Hooper's rest was cut short, and he was off to the sales.

In Lexington, Hooper ran into an old friend in the Lafayette Hotel, the contractor Warfield Rogers. When Rogers asked what he was doing there, Hooper said he had come to buy a horse. Rogers thought that Hooper probably knew nothing about horses, so he introduced him to the short gentleman with him. "This is Ivan Parke," he said. "He can help you find a horse."

The story of Hooper's first horse purchase at the yearling sales is a well-known Cinderella story. He had decided he wanted to breed thoroughbreds, so he wanted fillies. Some studies that he had read convinced him that he particularly wanted *Sir Gallahad III fillies. A *Sir Gallahad III colt caught his eye first. "He had a sharp style of walking," Hooper would later explain to me, using expressive arm motions. The man who wanted to start out by breeding fillies bought the colt for $10,200.

Hoop, Jr., one of 6,427 foals born in 1942, started five times as a two-year-old, won twice, was second three times, and inspired his rookie owner to insist that the following year his *Sir Gallahad III colt would win the Kentucky Derby. Everyone laughed. For the next forty-five years, Hooper never cared who laughed. He did things his own way. In 1945, Hoop, Jr. won the Kentucky Derby. No one was laughing anymore. Hoop, Jr. bowed (to bow is to injure the tendon or tendon sheath; the injury often renders the horse unraceable) in the Preakness and retired to stand at Ridgewood Farm in Kentucky.

During that first year at the sales, 1943, Hooper bought six yearlings, for a total of $56,900. In addition to Hoop, Jr., he also purchased Pry for $17,500 and Alabama for $17,000; both went on to become good racehorses for Hooper. It might have been beginner's luck, but if so, it stayed with him for the next forty-five years.

In 1944, Hooper went back to the sales and bought ten horses for $101,300. In 1945, his stable earned $126,120. In 1945, he bought five horses for $66,100. One horse in that lot, Education (Ariel–Faculty, by *Swift and Sure), went on to become the highest-earning two-year-old in the nation in 1946: $164,473. Education was multiple stakes winner, was voted two-year-old champion for the year, would later stand in Florida at Red Vines's Wake Robin Farm, and ended his career with total earnings of $188,698. Hooper made further national impact in 1947 when he imported *Quibu (=Meadow–=Querendona, by =Diadochos) from South America. He purchased *Quibu for the highest price ever paid for a horse in Argentine history: $20,000. Hooper was one of the first persons to purchase a stallion in South America for racing and breeding in the U.S. This later became a fairly common practice.

One of his greatest contributions to the Florida industry occurred when Hooper bought Olympia (*Heliopolis–Miss Dolphin, by Stimulus), a month-old weanling colt, from his trainer, Ivan Parke. (Hooper did not want his new trainer to have his own horses.) Miss Dolphin, a stakes-winning mare, had been trained by Parke and had beaten four track records. *Heliopolis, sired by Hyperion, had won several stakes races in Europe, then was imported to stand at Coldstream Stud in Kentucky for a fee of $300. The farm was having little success getting any mares to him. Hooper was already attracted to the Hyperion bloodline, so he was happy to relieve his trainer of his *Heliopolis colt. As a two-year-old, Olympia earned $76,633.

On January 5, 1949, Hooper accepted a challenge that excited the thoroughbred world. Quintas I. Roberts of Palatka, Florida, was the owner of a champion quarter-horse racing mare, Stella Moore. Rogers challenged Hooper's Olympia to a match race. To resolve the question of which was better at a quarter mile, the quarter horse or the thoroughbred, Tropical Park scheduled the special race between regular races. One-quarter mile was carefully measured. Each side put up $25,000, winner take all. Olympia burst to the front first, to the surprise of everyone, and held on to the wire, winning by a nose in :22 4/5.

Olympia was not as fortunate in the Kentucky Derby. He went into the 1949 season as the winter book favorite for the Derby but

Fred Hooper (far right) got to know all the track people (Eugene Mori, Jr. and Sr.) when his horses started winning a lot of purses. Here they are attending horse sales. Photo by Leo Frutkoff (by permission of *The Florida Horse*).

was beaten by Ponder, an animal that would play a role later in Florida history as the sire of the Florida-bred, Needles. Olympia ended his career as a multiple stakes winner with a record of fifteen wins, twelve seconds, four thirds, and $365,632 in purses.

Olympia was *Heliopolis's best racehorse son. He became Hooper's foundation sire and an important sire not only for the Florida industry but nationally, as well. Olympia would be the leading brood mare sire in 1974. His influence would later be found in many of Hooper's homebred (Florida-bred) stars as well as in the pedigrees of countless stakes horses all over the country: Crozier, Tri Jet, Pia Star, Susan's Girl, Decathlon, Smart Angle, Cafe Prince, Sensitive Prince, Darby Creek Road, and Creme Dela Creme, to name only a few.

Hooper also influenced the Florida breeding industry by trying to beat it. When the Florida Thoroughbred Breeders' Association was first formed, the rule for Florida-bred status was very lenient. Hence, Hooper shipped his Alabama-based mares across the border just long enough to foal, then returned them to Alabama. Because

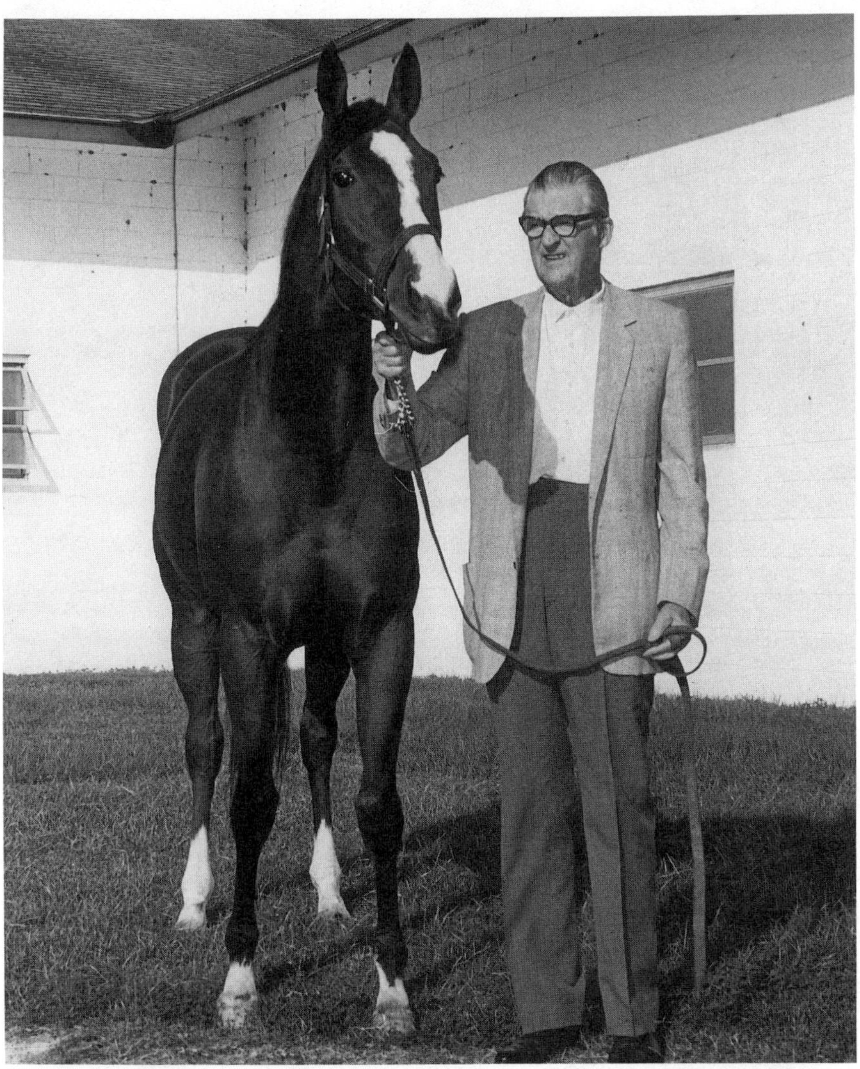

Fred and his millionaire girl, Susan's Girl. Photo by Arthur Kunkel (by permission of the FTBA).

he had such good fortune at the tracks, he was winning many of the breeders' awards and restricted races. The Florida breeders decided that if they couldn't beat him, they had better force him to join them. Hence, they changed the domicile rule so that nondomiciled mares had to remain in Florida at least long enough to be bred back to Florida stallions. For a while, Hooper still resisted; he gave some of his mares to friends in the Sunshine State in exchange for

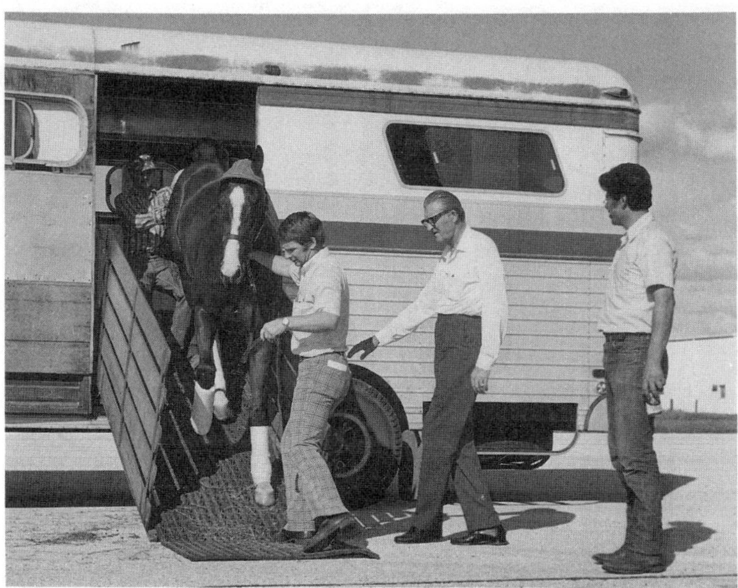

Even to this day well into his nineties, Fred Hooper oversees every aspect of his thoroughbred operation. Here in 1972 he carefully watches Susan's Girl disembark from a van. Photo by Arthur Kunkel (by permission of the FTBA).

Fred Hooper and his son Fred Hooper, Jr. (left) receive FTBA awards from editor of *The Florida Horse* Chuck Tilley for champion and Florida-bred Horse of the Year, Susan's Girl. Photo by Turfotos (by permission of the FTBA).

Fred Hooper roughhousing with one of his stallions Crozier, a very successful and important stallion to the Florida industry. Photo by Louise Reinagel (by permission of Louise Reinagel).

Florida-bred foals. But in 1966, he decided it was time to buy a farm in Ocala. He has been very influential in the Florida thoroughbred industry ever since.

Other contributions Hooper made to the breeding industry included the formation in 1958 of the American Thoroughbred Owners' Association, of which he was the first president. The association maintained public respect; attracted newcomers to horse racing; and improved, developed, and protected racing. In 1961, this organization merged with the Thoroughbred Breeders' Association to form the present-day Thoroughbred Owners' and Breeders' Association. Hooper also became well versed in racetrack construction, particularly that of turf courses. He was responsible for the turf courses at Santa Anita, Keeneland, and Gulfstream Park. Hooper built the Gulfstream turf course in 1958, prompting that park's new advertising slogan: "The Turf by the Surf!"

In October 1987, Fred Hooper celebrated his ninetieth birthday in the presence of some 300 relatives and special friends from all over the United States. They gathered to celebrate a man who believed in heart and to clap as he danced the jitterbug with his second wife, Wanda. At that time, Hooper still owned about eighty-five brood mares, had approximately fifty foals born each year, trained about thirty-five new two-year-olds to race each spring, and was standing several stallions (including a nationally leading sire, Tri Jet, and his millionaire sprint champion, Precisionist). Hooper is the epitome of Samuel Riddle's aphorism: "A man will never die as long as he has a promising two-year-old."

14

Cracker Thoroughbreds

In 1946, Florida-breds won $66,810. Thirty-two foals were born in Florida in 1946, with over fifty expected for 1947. Six new breeding farms were started in 1946, and several more were planned. By early 1947, there were twenty-two thoroughbred farms in Florida, most still in the south. About eighty Florida-breds were campaigning at the nation's tracks.

The Florida Thoroughbred Breeders' Association held a business meeting in Ocala for the first time on June 22, 1947, at the Marion Hotel; Carl Rose was honored for the outstanding contributions he had made to the industry. Two items of business worth noting were proper registration of Florida-breds and making requests to the three major tracks to hold restricted stakes races. Bright said on June 22, 1947, in an article by Bob Hayes in the *Orlando Sunday Sentinel Star*, "The people of this state have not yet been able to grasp the magnitude of the importance of our thoroughbred breeding, but we are rapidly coming to the front with a business." He predicted that in another fifteen years, Florida breeders would be breeding 1,000 thoroughbreds annually. (Nineteen eight-six saw 4,230 thoroughbreds foaled and registered as Florida-breds. Since every breeder does not bother to record horses with the state registry, the numbers were doubtless even greater.)

The first yearbook of the association (a publishing tradition that was unfortunately short-lived) came out in 1947. The farms were described and illustrated, and ten sires and eighty mares were listed as domiciled in the state. Charles Gregg was editor of the *Florida Thoroughbred*, a magazine independent of the breeders' organization that stimulated the publication of *The Florida Horse*. (No one has ever liked the title of the latter journal, since it connotes breeds other than thoroughbreds, but the prime name had been claimed.)

By this time, Carl Rose was recognized as the largest individual breeder in the Southeast. The first Florida-bred ever sold at public auction was a yearling filly of Rose's at the Keeneland (Kentucky)

Fall Yearling Sales. She brought $3,000 and according to the local Lexington paper, looked better than most of the other yearlings at the sale. By May 1947, Rosemere was the home of two stallions, eighteen mares, and eight yearlings, with Jacinth the pride of the farm and firmly established as the foundation mare. Rose was then advised that he had been approved for the German remount stallion *Samurai.

*Samurai was one of a group of stallions assembled by Adolf Hitler to create a race of superhorses. He was a prize of war taken by the U.S. Remount Service during World War II. When that agency was abolished, the horse was turned over to the Department of Agriculture, which contacted Rose. Everett Clay, a sportswriter in Miami, confirmed that the magazine *British Race Course* called *Samurai's bloodlines "the finest in Germany." *Life* magazine ran a story and pictures on this stakes-winning stallion the previous year, when he had been imported into the United States. *Samurai (=Oleander–=Sonnenwende, by =Nuage) was considered one of the greatest German horses ever imported. Rose was thus quite honored to acquire the stallion. However, because breeding records were lost during the war, The Jockey Club refused to approve *Samurai's bloodlines for registration. Not until 1950 would the horse be allowed to breed at all. When *Samurai's first progeny reached the races in 1953, they were registered "for racing purposes only"; this statement appeared at the bottom of the race program.

The first offspring to reach the races was Heubeck's homebred out of Leonardtown, Wolf Gal. She promptly proved her lineage by winning the 1953 Florida Breeders' Stakes, then raced on to win more stakes races, to set a track record, and to earn over $64,000. The Jockey Club finally eliminated the blemish on *Samurai's record halfway through 1953 when his progeny continued to prove the worth of his bloodlines. *Samurai went on to become a leading juvenile sire that year.

Meanwhile, Ramel, Rose's only nonwinner to date, finally won his first race October 10, 1947, and made Rose a 100 percent breeder of winners at the track. By this time, Rosemere-bred horses had earned over $100,000. By the fall of 1948, Carl Rose had been dubbed by the turf writers as "the man who brought Kentucky to Florida." The media frequently noted how much Rosemere's rolling hills and neat wooden fences looked like a Kentucky farm. So many visitors would stop when driving down State Road 200, attracted by the fields and horses, that one local wit suggested putting bleachers along the roadside.

In one of many interviews, Elmer Heubeck explained that horses were boarded for $50 a month and trained for $5 a day. He also explained that it took $1,500 to raise a foal to a two-year-old, including upkeep of the mare and the training itself. In another interview in early 1949, Heubeck was quoted as predicting that soon most of the big stables would begin shipping their stock to Florida to train because the weather was so favorable. His prediction came true that fall when four of the five divisional champions of the nation were expected to winter at Hialeah: A. G. Vanderbilt's Bed o' Roses, the 1949 champion two-year-old filly; Calumet's Two Lea, the 1949 champion three-year-old filly; Greentree Farm's Capot, the 1949 three-year-old champion and Horse of the Year; and Coaltown, the 1948 sprint champion, 1949 Handicap champion and 1949 Horse of the Year. (In those days, independent decisions were made by the different voting bodies; hence two Horses of the Year. Today, the sole voting body is a combination of the *Daily Racing Form*, the National Turf Writers' Association, and the Thoroughbred Racing Association.)

With the help of Werwolf, Florida-breds earned $66,165 and won twenty-three races in the first five months of 1949. But 1950 was the great year for what were becoming known as "Cracker thoroughbreds." By May, Florida-bred juveniles (two-year-olds) alone had already won fifteen races, five of which were stakes, a percentage unequaled by any other breeding state. Florida-breds had already broken $100,000 in earnings for the first time, and the year was not half over.

On March 22, Liberty Rab set a track record at Gulfstream Park in the Cuba-Florida invitational, the Rivalry Purse. In doing so, he defeated another talented Florida-bred, J. J. Starling's Fair Game (Ariel Game–Lady Fanar, by *Fanar: bred by Rosemere). A Florida-bred, Mr. A. B., ran third, while the best the Cubans could get was fourth. Fair Game next won the Bay State Kindergarten at Suffolk Downs (a track also owned by J. J. Starling of Clearwater, Florida) on May 13. In this race, the youngster defeated other juveniles by such heavyweight sires as Bull Lea (leading sire five times and leading brood mare sire four times), Jamestown (champion two-year-old), *Princequillo (leading sire two times and leading brood mare sire seven times), and Blue Swords (multiple stakes winner and often at the top of the leading sire lists).

The first division of the Hialeah Juvenile (a race is divided when there are enough entries in a single race to warrant or demand it be split into two races) was won by a popular, so far unbeaten colt,

Fair Game wins the James Connors Memorial at Narragansett Park in 1950.

Battlefield (War Relic–Dark Display, by Display). Liberty Rab (Doublrab–Lady Liberty, by Liberty Limited), a colt bred by Mrs. T. Christopher, won the second division of the Hialeah Juvenile. In New York's Youthful Stakes at Jamaica track, Liberty Rab dared to face Battlefield, the king, but the king maintained his unblemished record. Liberty Rab ran third, after Battlefield and Count Turf. This performance was shortly followed by the first major upset by a

Florida-bred in a nationally prominent stakes. Five days later, Liberty Rab turned the tables and in the biggest upset of the racing year, pulled away from the undefeated Battlefield in the Belmont Juvenile. The shrieks of joy from Florida breeders may have been heard all the way up the East Coast. The son of Doublrab had beaten the sons of proven sires Revoked, War Relic, Tiger, and Chance Sun. One Florida newspaper jubilantly announced: "A year ago there were less than eighty mares in all of Florida and ten stallions. Of thirty-four registered foals, twenty-four had raced, eight won, five stakes wins. Liberty Rab is now the world's leading money-winning juvenile for 1950 with $33,312."

This earnings record did not stand past Battlefield's next start. The son of War Relic would finish the year as the national two-year-old champion. Battlefield would also break the record for male juvenile earnings with a total for the year of $198,677. Only the champion fillies Top Flight, Bewitch, and Bed o' Roses had ever earned more as two-year-olds. The facts that he had wintered in Florida as both a two- and a three-year-old and had held his form throughout the racing season would be pointed out by experts ready to admit that winter racing was working. Battlefield later retired with total earnings of $474,727, a fortune in those days. His talent only made the upset by Liberty Rab that much sweeter.

Fair Game and Liberty Rab were not the only baby Crackers making headlines in 1950. Rosemere-bred Maid of Hearts won an unprecedented four straight at the Gulfstream meet. Then a historic double occurred when two Florida-breds, Ariel's Mark and Game Belle, both won on the same afternoon and on the same card in Maryland.

The industry was beginning to look more attractive to outsiders. After watching the success of Rosemere-breds and inspecting the farm itself, trainer Tommy Bonham shipped five of the best-bred horses in Argentina for their owner (a Miami Springs doctor) to Rosemere for training under Heubeck. Heubeck was "gaining wide recognition for his success," according to one turf writer.

In 1950, Rose persuaded four more breeders to purchase land near Rosemere. They built barns and homes and erected the neat, white, board fences that contrasted so well with the rich green fields and contributed even more to the look of a Kentucky horse farm.

One of the newcomers was J. E. Hardy, a Miami electrical company executive and for many years a breeder of walking horses. He bought 650 acres, which he named Oak Lane Farm. He planned to raise cattle and show horses. The farm later became one of the showplaces of the area. R. G. Heine had been running a shorthorn farm in Dade County before he purchased 140 acres in Marion County. R. G. Hardy (unrelated to J. E. Hardy) of Miami Beach bought 300 acres at Summerfield. He planted eighty acres in Southland oats, a new cultivar developed by the University of Florida.

The fourth person to set up a horse farm in Marion County at this time was a Miami contractor William E. Leach. Leach had owned a racing stable for many years and participated in management at Gulfstream Park. He was now shifting his headquarters to Marion County. He purchased 153 acres of choice, unimproved land, originally owned by Carl Rose. However, Leach purchased it from Martin Anderson, owner of the *Orlando Sentinel*. By August, a beautiful, new barn had been built and another was under construction. He named his new farm Dickey Stables in honor of his wife, whose maiden name was Dickey. This farm, like Rose's, was so thick with Pensacola Bahia and pangola grasses that Leach had to turn cattle out on it to keep it mowed. Like Rose, Leach also kept cattle with the horses to calm the high-strung thoroughbreds.

Leach's whitewashed fences went up quickly, and the three-eighths mile track was soon under construction. Jack Little, former manager of Christopher Ranch, was brought north to run Dickey Stables. There were eighteen horses on the farm, including the stallions Fly Away (*Blenheim II–Themesong, by High Time); El Mono, hero of the 1948 Widener, who held the record for one-and-one-quarter miles at Hialeah; King's Stride (Coldstream–Royal Sandal, by *Royal Minstrel); and Liberty Franc (Liberty Limited–Francaise, by Black Toney). Before the year was out, Leach began to rival Rose as having the largest training operation in the county. Both farms were open to the public for boarding, breeding, and training; they also handled their own stock.

At this point, the Florida Thoroughbred Breeders' Association began sponsoring tours of the three farms together: Rosemere, Dickey Stables, and Oak Lane Farm. Rose viewed this growth with satisfaction and said to Milton Plumb, in an article that appeared in the *Tampa Sunday Tribune* on August 20, 1950, "A few more like these and the Bluegrass won't have a thing on Marion County." When coyly asked the part he played as realtor in getting Leach and J. E. Hardy to Marion County, Rose happily answered, "I wanted them here. It will do Marion County a lot of good. It leaves me with 750 acres on Rosemere Farm and that's good enough for me!"

Rose purchased three mares at the 1950 breeding stock sales in Kentucky, raising his total to twenty-two. He had thirteen foals in 1950 and sixteen yearlings. Rosemere now was the site of four modern barns with another twenty-stall training barn planned for the following spring. The training barn would be considered the finest in the country. Like all the barns on the farm, this one would run east to west to take advantage of the breezes. New, modern homes for the trainer and grooms were also built. In 1954, Rose became the first person in the country to use black board horse fencing (the black metal paint came from Alabama ore mines) because he found that the horses thoroughly disliked the taste. Little did he know at the time that the trend he started would become standard. It was first used in Ocala and, eventually made its way to Kentucky. The traditional white board fencing fell to black boards, which were easier to maintain.

By 1955, Rose's now 600-acre farm contained 90 percent improved grasses. He had discovered these grasses with the help of the University of Florida; they withstood winter frosts best. His fields were so lush that hay was baled from pangola, Pensacola Bahia, and Alyce clover. He also grew Southland oats and experimented with Coastal Bermuda. Never again would the equine industry in the Sunshine State suffer from lack of knowledge about adequate feeding in the southern climate and soil. At this point, land that Rose had purchased for $20 to $30 an acre was selling for an amazing $600 an acre.

Tourists came to the farm by the busload. One bus spotted motoring through Ocala sported a large banner on its side proclaiming, "Orlando Visits Carl Rose." The tourists told a local reporter they were on their way to visit the "world-famous Rosemere Farm." The farm was well worth the trip. Besides the usual horses and neat patchwork of fences, the modern farm was graced with ancient oak, camphor, and mulberry trees native to the county. A limerock cave with a sparkling spring was an important stop on the tour. Here Rose would disembark to feed the fish from a bag of stale bread. A visitor to the "Green Grass County of Florida" remarked unabashedly to Woody Thompson of the *Orlando Sunday Sentinel Star* on April 22, 1951, that he was amazed at the size of the Florida weanlings and yearlings. He guessed them to average twenty-five pounds more than their Kentucky counterparts. This observation would last until the modern day. Although Kentucky supporters counter that by adulthood, horses raised from any state seem to average out about the same, the mild winters and early outdoor exercise do seem to benefit the early growth of the Florida youngster. The age of runty thoroughbreds was long past.

In November 1950, Rose shipped twenty-two horses to Hialeah for training and racing. An established price for yearlings on the farm was $5,000, but by the time this crop was shipped to the track, they were valued at as much as $10,000. Of $282,075 earned by Florida-breds in 1950, Rosemere horses accounted for $102,652. Five of the top ten Florida-breds for 1950 came from Rosemere. Rosemere's success seemed limitless. By 1954, Rose had twenty-five yearlings to ship to Hialeah. But the track had finally put a lid on, and he was allotted only sixteen stalls. Still, Rose did not worry. Rosemere horses sold so quickly that he only had to keep filling the stalls as they emptied.

By early 1951, Rosemere was beginning to look like a modern-day stallion station. Besides *Samurai and Ariel Game, new stallions started shipping in from various ports outside of Florida: Noble Hero (*Heliopolis–Boat, by Man o' War), winner of the Choice Stakes in 1948 and sired by the leading sire of 1950 and 1954, *Heliopolis; and Sir Sprite (Ariel–Southern Beauty, by *Light Brigade), winner of the 1949 Michigan Mile. In 1952, the popular *Laico (=Petrarca–=La Gloire, by =Babar Shah) from Argentina and winner of the 1950 Chicago Handicap joined the group. In 1953, Rinaldo (Challenger II–Trumps, by *Teddy), foaled by Heubeck in Maryland several years previously, retired to Rosemere.

In 1951, a new plan for regional vice presidents was set up by the Thoroughbred Club of America. When Grant Dorland of Kentucky stepped down from his positions of vice-president and treasurer, Carl Rose was elected eastern regional vice-president. Further accolades came in 1952 when Rose was appointed to an executive committee to negotiate the merger of the National Association of Thoroughbred Breeders and the American Thoroughbred Breeders' Association. In 1953, he was made a lifetime member of the Florida Thoroughbred Breeders' Association. Rose was also elected president of the National Association of Thoroughbred Breeders, thus gaining national recognition for Florida. By this time, his farm had produced six stakes horses since 1949: Werwolf, Fair Game, White Cliffs, Game Gene, Wolf Gal, and Oclirock.

The first Florida-bred to enter the winner's circle in 1952 was Game Gene, a Rosemere-bred who won by seven lengths. The horse was then promptly purchased for $20,000, a new record for a Florida-bred. In the February 15, 1952, *Daily Racing Form,* Nelson

Dunstan wrote that not only was $20,000 a good price for a Florida-bred, but "it is a good price anywhere for a horse that has won only one race and never gone beyond three furlongs. . . . They are not raising world-beaters down there, or even American champions, but the fact remains that Florida has been sending out some good horses and that a few of them go on to perform well against the best campaigning on the east coast."

Game Gene was sold to Don Raymond Mitchell's Do-Ra-Mi Stables; the horse then won the Florida Breeders' Stakes. Early in 1953, the promising colt was nominated to a $100,000 stakes race. Sadly, he died of a heart attack during a morning workout before the race.

Oclirock (Nelson Dunstan–Yasum, by Black Servant) was another horse with a story behind him. As Elmer Heubeck recalled:.

> He was named after Ocala Limerock (Rose's limerock company). Mr. Rose used to like to feed his horses corn on the cob because he thought it helped their teeth and gums. Well, this yearling colt swallowed this cob and it lodged in his throat and before I could get to him he drank half a bucket of water and had gotten it on his lungs.
>
> He was in bad shape and Dr. Joe Powers [still an equine veterinarian in Ocala in 1989], our vet, had just come by and I asked him what we could do about it. The colt was in training and looked like he was going to be pretty nice. I thought we were going to lose him. But Doc Powers said, "Don't worry about it, get a rope."
>
> Well, we got a big old soft cotton rope and knotted it around the horse's hind pasterns and we pulled that horse right up into a tree and drained every bit of water out of him. I never saw anything like it in my life. I thought he'd pull every muscle in his body but it didn't hurt a thing. I asked Doc later how often he'd done that trick and he said never, he just thought it was the only thing left to do!

Oclirock went on to win the Bay State Kindergarten Stakes and to place second in the Florida Breeders' Stakes. He was sold for $30,000, again a record price for a Florida-bred at the time, and continued to be a stakes winner for his new owner, Peter Fuller of Rhode Island. Rosemere Farm had come a long way since it sold its first horse for $275. Since so much attention was focused on the farm in the center of the state, the management of Gulfstream Park made a fourteen-minute movie devoted to Rosemere.

As if his thoroughbred activities weren't enough, Rose was now president of Ocala Limerock Corporation, Marion Construction

The FTBA began to hold a "baby show" beginning in 1952 and continuing well into the 1960s when it was incorporated into the two-year-old-in-training sales. This photo is of the 1959 show when Bonnie Heath's colt (far left) Pio was selected Best of Show and Carl Rose's filly Noble Heroine won Best Filly. Rose is in the center flanked on the right by J. J. Weipert, co-judge of the show, and Lou Doherty, senior judge. Bonnie Heath is at far left. They stand in the Hialeah walking ring. Photo by Leo Frutkoff (by permission of *The Florida Horse*).

Showing the "babies" in 1963 at Hialeah. Photo by Joe Migon (by permission of the FTBA).

At yet another baby show, Liz Whitney Tippett holds a yearling while judge Dr. James G. Catlett, who first talked Rose into breeding thoroughbreds, holds the awards. Photo by Turfotos (by permission of *The Florida Horse*).

Company, Marion Motor Company, Ocala Insurance and Investment Company, Marimere Corporation, the Marion County Chamber of Commerce, and the Ocala Rotary Club. For twelve years, he was the chairperson of the Harry Anna Crippled Children's Home.

The first "baby show" for yearlings in Florida was held on January 6, 1952, at Hialeah. It became an annual event, judged by some of the best horsemen and horsewomen of the times: Horatio Luro, James Fitzsimmons, Sherrill Ward, Ben Jones, George M. Odom, and Mrs. Richard Lunn, among others. The first baby show was judged by Lexington trainer Preston Burch. The best yearling colt was Jimmy Bright's Florida Flash, while Rosemere's Ari Gold took best filly. The second year of the show, Rosemere captured all three classes, taking best colt or gelding, best filly, and best of show.

Prompted by the county's growing reputation, more interested horse owners and businesspersons began coming to Marion County to purchase farms: Howard Reinemann, prominent Chicago businessperson and owner of the 1,250-acre Crown Crest Farm in Kentucky; Tom Mooney, mayor of Lexington; and Neville Dunn, managing editor of the *Thoroughbred Record*. They visited Rosemere and the surrounding countryside. Seven yearlings were sent to Rosemere from Kentucky to train during the 1951 to 1952 winter season. This continuing trend would later escalate into an industry of its own; Ocala would be recognized worldwide as a major training center.

By 1952, Ocala had 12,000 inhabitants. The principle industries of the county were livestock, lumber, naval stores, tung oil, fruits, and vegetables. With an annual production of 1,500,000 cattle, Marion County was a leading livestock center of the Southeast. Ocala is still the world's largest producer of Brahman cattle. Silver Springs (adjacent to Ocala), Rainbow Springs (a short drive to the west), and the Ocala National Forest (the eastern border of Ocala and Silver Springs) had become major tourist attractions. Silver Springs is reputed to be one of the greatest natural springs in the world; it produces 800,000,000 gallons of fresh, cold water daily. The glass-bottomed boat originated there. People still come from all over the world to view underwater wildlife and flora in some of the clearest water to be found. Ocala was the junction for three U.S. highways and four state roads, making it an overnight stopover for more visitors than any other city in the state.

The first "Ocala Week" (later to become a traditional part of the breeding stock sales held in Ocala every October and including parties, meetings, and stallion shows) could well have been held at Rosemere Farm. In 1954, the Florida Thoroughbred Breeders' Association and Rose collaborated on an invitation to Kentuckians coming to Gainesville for the big University of Kentucky–University of Florida football clash. A dinner was planned for Friday, October

15, in conjunction with a meeting of Florida horsemen. The following morning, the visitors toured Rosemere and Dickey Stables. A cocktail party was scheduled for 10:00 A.M. at Dickey. The visitors were back in Gainesville, forty-five miles to the north, in time for the kickoff.

In December 1955, Rose became the first breeder of a Florida-bred to win over $100,000. Marked Game (Ariel Game–Simplemark, by Invermark), a six-year-old gelding trained and part-owned by Wilma Kennedy, won an allowance race at Tropical Park on December 17 and boosted his lifetime earnings to $100,430. On December 26, he won the Christmas Handicap and raised his earnings to $108,225, a triumphant finish to the year for the Florida thoroughbred industry. Nobody suspected its biggest year was coming up.

Part Three

Needles in the Bahiastack

Marion County, Florida
Throughbred Horse Farms, 1957–58

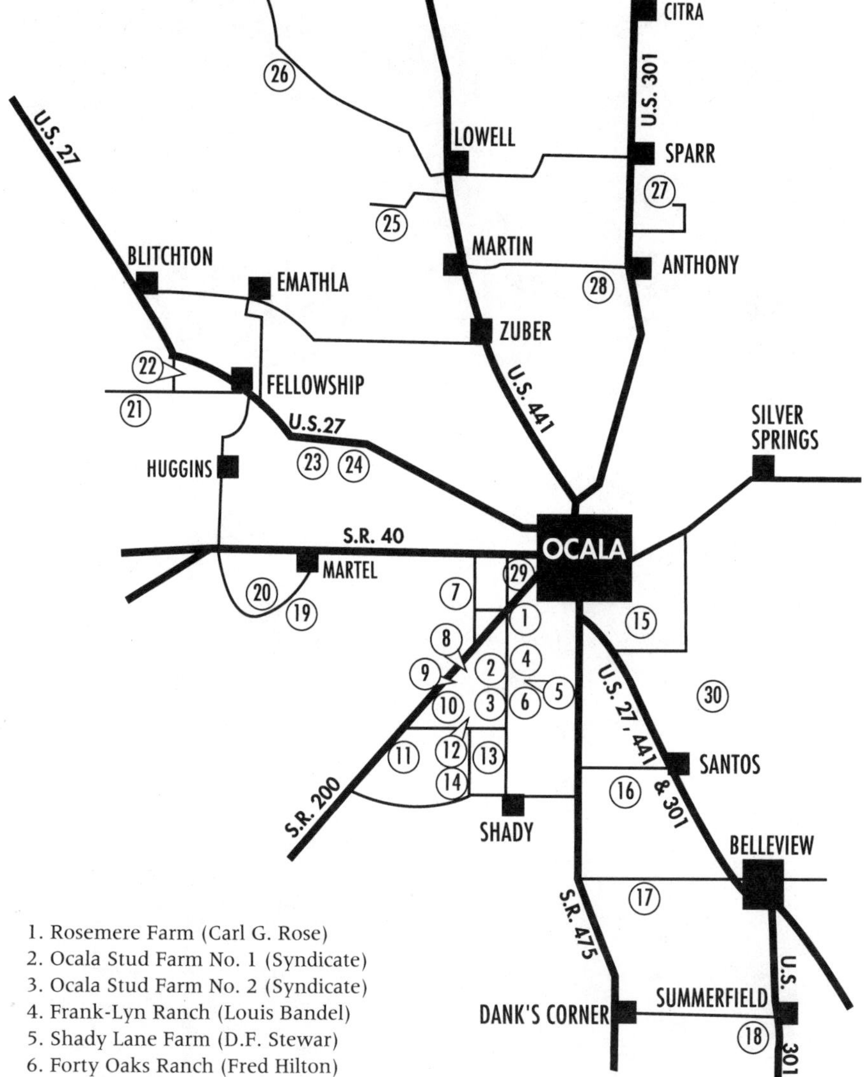

1. Rosemere Farm (Carl G. Rose)
2. Ocala Stud Farm No. 1 (Syndicate)
3. Ocala Stud Farm No. 2 (Syndicate)
4. Frank-Lyn Ranch (Louis Bandel)
5. Shady Lane Farm (D.F. Stewar)
6. Forty Oaks Ranch (Fred Hilton)
7. Meadowbrook Farm (William M. Lynch)
8. Dr. J.J. Colando Farm
9. Bonnie Heath Farm
10. J.C. Dudley Farm
11. A.J. Leeward Farm
12. L.L. Hollandsworth Farm
13. Bellows Ranch (Harry Bermon)
14. J.E. Romlo Farm
15. John Clardy Farm
16. Roseland Farm (Grant A. Dorland)
17. Sunshine Stud, Inc. (Dan Chappell)
18. Willow Lake Farm (V.L. Creal)
19. Horne Brothers Farm
20. P.A.B. Widener III Farm
21. Pine Crest Farm (G. Cavanaugh, Jr.)
22. A.G. Goebel Farm
23. Broadmoor Farm (Tom Daniels)
24. Castro Ranch (Bernard Castro)
25. Wake Robin Farm (W.C. & H. J. Vines)
26. Quails Roost (Elmer Heubeck)
27. Barry Farm (Harry Trotsek)
28. Rosewood Farm (James E. Wood)
29. Bell Rock Farm
30. Belynada Farm (Nat Tooker)

15

Threading the Needle

It is said that Needles sold more real estate in Marion County than any realtor. There were twenty-two thoroughbred farms in the entire state early in 1956; only four of those were in Marion County according to the *Florida Thoroughbred*. There were 33 stallions and 199 mares in the state. In 1955, 74 two-year-olds were registered with the state breeders' organization, and Florida-breds won seventy-two races.

In 1955, James D. Norris bought 180 acres southwest of Miami. He moved all his stock there from Spring Hill Farm near Paris, Kentucky, including the stallions Crowfoot (Blue Larkspur–*Ann Earn, by =Bridge of Earn) and Grey Wing (Halcyon–War Grey, by Man o' War). Elkcam Stable, located in Highlands County near Sebring, included stock brought in by the brothers Elliott, Frank, and Bob Mackle from their Kentucky farm three years earlier. V. L. "Country" Creal, a trainer, moved from Chicago to establish Willow Lake Farm near Summerfield, about five miles south of Ocala. In 1955, he purchased 284 acres, 172 acres of which he developed into a horse farm. By late 1956, he had a concrete twenty-stall barn; his stallion Sedgemoor (*Blenheim II–Ladana, by Lucullite) and thirteen other horses were in residence. A training track, residence, and more barns were under construction.

One of the four farms in Marion County was Shady Lane Farm. In 1954, Douglas T. and Margaret Stewart bought an eighty-six acre farm south of Rosemere. Stewart, who had dabbled in horses in Indiana, was the owner of a huge tool and die company in Indianapolis. He spent his summers in Marion County, Indiana, and his winter months in Marion County, Florida, a practice that later explained why he named a colt that he bred by El Mono "Marion County." John Shropshire managed the Stewarts' farm, which by 1956 supported nineteen horses. The farm buildings were of a special fireproof fiberboard. Stewart was already beginning to fear the

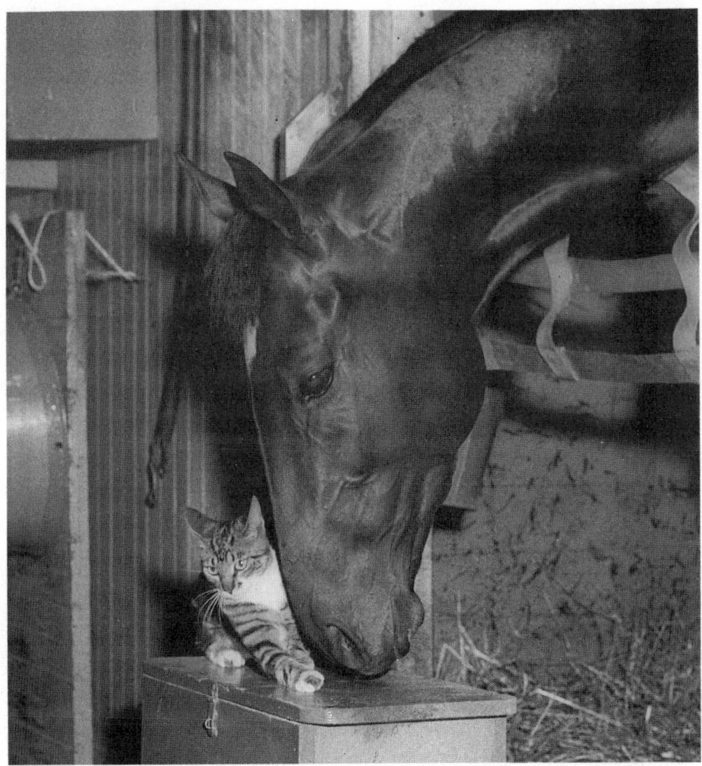

Needles with a friend. Photo by Mike Sirico (by permission of Scott Dudley).

Elkcam Farm, owned by the Mackle brothers, Elliott, Frank, and Bob, was located in Highlands County beginning in 1952 (by permission of *The Florida Horse*).

Elliott Mackle in the early 1960s (by permission of the FTBA).

Mr. and Mrs. Douglas T. Stewart, owners of Shady Lane Farm. Photo by Leo Frutkoff (by permission of *The Florida Horse*).

encroachment of big industry on the horse farms in Ocala, something that had steered him clear of Lexington, Kentucky.

Meanwhile, by 1956, Rosemere had expanded to forty mares and five stallions. However, Dickey Stables was growing into an operation second in the Southeast only to Rosemere. In October 1953, Mr. and Mrs. Leach sent their first homebreds to the track. They were received with excitement and anticipation because of their bloodlines, appearance, and condition. Joe McLaughlin visited the farm in 1954 to view the horses about to be shipped south. He remarked that the two-year-olds looked great, but that the best-looking animal was still a year away from the races. In the October 28, 1953, *Miami Herald*, McLaughlin wrote that "there is a youngster with which to ponder and he happens to be a son of the great Ponder." But in 1954, the prize possession of the farm was El Mono (Head Play–Hand Organ, by *Strolling Player). He had been the winner of the 1948 Widener, in which he set a new stakes record for the one and one-quarter mile distance. Porter Roberts, who squired him to victory that day, became the Leaches' trainer.

By 1955, more acreage had been added. The farm was now separated into three tracts of 40, 150, and 634 acres. Facilities included a six-furlong training track with a seven-furlong chute and an eight-stall regulation starting gate. There was also a smaller three-eighths mile track. Four new barns accommodated 150 horses, and four houses were being built for the personnel. The owner's residence was last on the list to be built. Mrs. Leach, the former Mary Madeline Dickey, often conducted tours. She took great pride in showing off the facilities, which included spotless barns and a modern laboratory in the stud barn.

As at Rosemere, the grasses on this farm grew so thick that they were mowed for use as bedding in the stalls. Visitors learned that the famous Kentucky bluegrass simply was not hardy enough for Florida. However, the green grass of Florida flourished thick and sweet, and the healthy, blooming stock was a credit to the environment.

Once their animals hit the track, Dickey Stables' reputation soon rivaled that of Rosemere. By 1955, Dickey Stables had already gained wide recognition for its stakes winners, Menolene (not actually a Florida-bred, since she had arrived at the farm at three weeks of age), First Cadet, and Smooth Stride. The story behind the success of Dickey Stables began in 1945 when Samuel Feinberg, owner of a large furniture store in Wilmington, Delaware and a small racing stable, purchased three fillies of moderate breeding and proceeded to race them. In 1949, because of failing eyesight, he decided to get out of active participation in racing.

Feinberg entered into an agreement with W. Rhodes Estill, an octogenarian friend of John Madden's, regarding the three mares. Estill would board them at his own farm, support and cover their expenses, and also share in any profits they might bring in. Somewhat belatedly, he realized the potential of profit was not very high on these three. He wanted to get out of the deal and to get the mares off his farm. In the spring of 1952, Dan Chappell heard about the mares and informed Bill Leach that they might be worth looking into. Leach telephoned a friend, Paul Little, in Lexington, and asked him to check the mares out. Little did so, then transferred them to his own Palmeadow Farms, which he and his brother, Kellar, ran in Lexington.

Little and Leach would own the mares as partners, and Feinberg would get the third foal of each mare. By the time this deal was consummated, it was late in the breeding season and Little had to move fast to get his new charges booked (contracted to go to a particular stallion for mating). Quickly, he arranged for Carol Lee (*Benagi–Sweepsora, by Sweep) to go to The Doge (*Bull Dog–My Auntie, by Busy American) and for Sis Brier (Bull Brier–Pinky's Sister, by Desperate Desmond) to be sent to Model Cadet (Requested–Hadepine, by Hadagal).

Little then stopped by Calumet Farm, because he had heard that the 1949 Kentucky Derby winner Ponder (Pensive–Miss Rushin, by *Blenheim II) had just been retired. Little knew that Calumet Farm would not have time to get a full book this year. He secured a season (the right to breed to a stallion) for the third mare, Noodle Soup (Jack High–Supromene, by Supremus). Thus the Jack High mare, winner of only one race, had the luck to join the court of a major racehorse, earner in those times of $541,275. Noodle Soup became the dam of one of only four foals by Ponder in the United States the following year. A fifth was born to a mare exported to Venezuela. That mare's foal, Poder, became to Venezuela what Needles would become to America.

Although Needles came from a modest bottom line, he could hardly have asked for a better top line. Ponder was the first stakes winner from his sire Pensive's first small crop. Pensive, who died right after Ponder's Kentucky Derby win, had won the same classic in 1944. Needles therefore would be the third Kentucky Derby winner, the fifth derby winner (=Gainsborough and =Hyperion

Sis Brier was included in the package of three mares Leach purchased. Here she is shown with her 1956 colt by Fly Away with Roy Yates at her head. Sis Brier is also the dam of First Cadet who went on to win the Florida Breeders' Stakes and over $25,000 in earnings (by permission of Roy Yates).

won the Epsom Derby), and the sixth in his male line to be the best horse of his classic (three-year-old) year.

Following many telephone conversations, Leach became more and more insistent that the foals of the three mares be dropped in Florida. Little wanted nothing to do with that, so he stepped out of the deal. In the summer of 1952, Little shipped the three mares and their offspring to Dickey Stables in Ocala, Florida. No one would have been able to guess the future value of that vanload of horses. Sis Brier was carrying the future Youthful Stakes winner First Cadet. Carol Lee, in foal to The Doge, had a suckling filly at her side by Super Duper and a yearling filly named Carolling, which became a better than average winner. Noodle Soup had a suckling filly, Menolene, by Bull Brier at her side. Menolene would become a multiple-stakes winner of $43,750 as a two-year-old when she was the third best two-year-old filly in the country. Early in 1955, she would be sold at auction for an incredible $75,000 to Circle M Farm in Lexington. At the time, Noodle Soup was carrying Needles.

These two stakes winners, Noodle Soup's first two foals, were the first class introduced in her line for two generations. Not until her third dam was there any evidence of previous class. The third dam was *Golden Harp, who produced =Harpsichord. =Harpsichord became the dam of *Hairan, another horse that would figure in Dickey Stables' history.

Noodle Soup's own race record provided little to indicate her future role in history. She could not stay sound long enough to race much. She attained one win and ended her career in $3,000 claiming races, with a total bankroll of $1,975. On April 29, 1953, Noodle Soup foaled a bay colt with a white star and short white stockings on his left foreleg and his right hind leg. When he was five weeks old, the bay colt contracted equine pneumonia, an often fatal disease. For weeks he ran a high fever, and his chance of survival was slim. Roy Yates was at the farm then; he had been a horseman since he ran away from home to get involved in the horse business. He worked in Kentucky under Colonel E. R. Bradley, was a jockey for a time, and trained a public stable (open to the public as opposed to training for a private client or two). In 1953, he came to Florida to work for the Leaches. He arrived when Needles was a very sick baby.

Yates, Madeline Leach, a trained nurse, and Dr. W. Reuben Brawner, the farm veterinarian, worked around the clock giving the colt injections and oxygen to save his life. Mrs. Leach hated to stick him with yet another needle. Because of the number of injections the colt received, the suggestion was made to call him Needles. "But he could just as easily have been called Oxygen!" Yates reflected.

Of course, Needles survived. Roy Yates became his trainer on the farm and Yates's son, Frank David "Buddy," was the sixteen-year-old gallop boy for the good-looking colt. "I believe we broke twenty to twenty-five head that year [the winter of 1954–55]," Yates recalled. "That was a big operation back then. There were just the two farms training, Rosemere and us, so it didn't take much to be big! We had just the short track then. When we breezed, we'd work from the post to the tree. That was three furlongs. The only way to get them slowed down was to turn them into the deep sand."

"Needles was just an average colt then," Buddy Yates said. "I had to kick him in the belly sometimes to make him go, but we never had problems with him like they had later. We thought he'd be a decent horse, but we sure didn't think he'd turn out the way he

Noodle Soup with a young Needles at her side. Photo by Harold R. Piel (by permission of Scott Dudley).

did. He didn't start to wake up until about December of his yearling year. We just started to see something then."

When he was ready, Needles, along with the rest of the year's crop, was shipped to trainer Elmo Shropshire at the track. Like Rosemere, Dickey Stables was a commercial operation; racing-to-sell was the farm's goal. But before racing, there was the annual Florida Breeders' Baby Show to enter. The judge, well-known trainer Sherrill Ward, pinned the blue on Needles. It was to be the first of many honors this horse would receive. At the Florida Breeders' Baby Show, Bonnie McCoy Heath, Jackson Curtis Dudley, and Hugh Fontaine bought Needles. Heath (then thirty-eight years old) and Dudley (then forty-three years old) were successful oilmen who had struck it rich in Oklahoma with their Dudley-Heath Drilling Company of Stillwater, Oklahoma (Dudley's home). In 1950, Dudley was still running the drilling operation and spending a few months each winter at Heath's home in Ft. Lauderdale, where the two men frequently went deep-sea fishing. In

December 1952, Heath called Dudley and told him that he had met a horse trainer.

Dudley told the story of their start in racing. "I was getting tired of fishing and racing sounded interesting. But we didn't know anything about horses." Heath had discovered Hugh Fontaine, an ex-trainer who had trained Ladysman to beat Equipoise in the Suburban and had won a championship with Brookmeade Stable's filly, Handcuff. But he was having hard times and was selling yachts in Ft. Lauderdale. Dudley and Heath were intrigued with the sport of racing and, sure enough, Fontaine just happened to know where he could get his hands on some useful horses. Dudley went on:

> We went to the baby show that spring. We figured we'd buy one horse and race it through the season then sell it. So we picked out a little filly. Well, she was awful fat and a long way from a race, so Fontaine said "Let's get another that's a little closer to a race." So we picked out a colt. Well, he was a just turned two-year-old like all of them so we were probably going to have to wait a while on that one too. So Fontaine said, "Well let's get one racing right now so he can buy the oats for these two." So before we were done, we were going to buy one horse and we ended up with a whole bunch of them!"

Phyllis Dudley and Opal Heath, the men's wives, picked out the racing silks: Texas orange and North Carolina blue. The D & H Stables were ready to hit the racetrack. Business was not great, however. "We won a few small races but they didn't cover many oats," Dudley remembered ruefully. "By 1955 we were ready to get out of it. We almost didn't buy Needles." Elmo Shropshire talked them into coming up to Dickey Farm to look at a Ponder colt he had for sale. "We went to look at him three different times and we liked him so well, we tried to talk everyone we knew into buying him," Dudley said. "We wanted to get out of the business. He was an awful nice looking colt, but the price was $20,000 and that was pretty steep, especially for a Florida-bred."

The partners watched Needles win the Baby Show. "If you won't buy him," Fontaine pleaded, "will you loan me the money to buy him? I'll give you a mortgage on everything I own but my wife."

"Do you really have that much faith in the horse?" they asked.

"I have that much faith in the horse," Fontaine declared unhesitatingly.

Shropshire talked them into watching Needles work going three-eighths. "We all had stopwatches that morning," Dudley said. "He was by himself and he did it so easy, under a good hold." He broke

Needles' family: (left to right) Bonnie McCoy Heath, Opal Heath, Phyllis Dudley, and Jackson Curtis Dudley (by permission of Scott Dudley).

the track record in that breeze for three furlongs. Dudley and Heath finally bought the Ponder colt.

"For the son of a horse which was slow to catch fire and a mare which never caught fire," as one turf writer put it, Needles was a very precocious two-year-old. He began his career on March 29, 1955, at Gulfstream Park under Canadian rider John Choquette. His first three starts were in four and one-half furlong sprints. He won his first by five lengths, missing the track record by two-fifths. He then ran in his first stakes race, the Gulfstream Park Dinner Stakes. He hung in the beginning, then ran wide all the way, finishing fourth to Getthere Jack, Swoon's Son, and Flying Teddy. In his next start, an allowance, he won by three and shaved one fifth off the track record, running the four and one-half furlongs at Gulfstream in :52 2/5. On June 22, he ran five furlongs at Monmouth Park, one tick short of the track record. Once again he entered a stakes, the Tyro, on July 4 but was squeezed out of a move, finishing fourth to Decathlon, Nan's Mink, and Beau Fond. Finally, on August 8, Needles got his stakes win. In the Sapling, at Monmouth Park, New Jersey, he was pitted against two unbeaten colts, each giving him eight pounds. Decathlon and Polly's Jet ran each other out, and Needles came on to win by two over Decathlon. In the Hopeful Stakes at Saratoga on August 27, Needles was four lengths ahead at the eighth pole and coasted home easily over another late runner, Career Boy.

The only other jockey to ride Needles as a two-year-old was Eddie Arcaro in the World's Playground Stakes at Atlantic City, on September 10. Needles moved too slowly, finishing third to Busher Fantasy and Espea, beaten by a length. Eddie Arcaro remembers the ride. "I put him in position on the turn for home, and when I did, he kind of backed up, he just didn't fire. Heath took me off and put another rider up and he won. I never rode again! That's the way it goes!"

On October 15, following a $10,000 supplemental entry fee, Needles won the Garden State Stakes at Monmouth Park, coming from last place and setting a track record of 1:37 1/5 for the mile over a sloppy track. On October 29, Needles finished third to Prince John and Career Boy, a defeat which may have cost him unanimous choice as the topweight for the year. He finished his season with six wins and two thirds in ten starts, earnings of $129,805, and two track records to his credit.

On the Experimental Free Handicap (a theoretical year-end evaluation of the year's top racehorses compiled by The Jockey Club committee; the assignment of a handicap weight ranks the horses relative to each other) Needles was weighted even with Nail at 125 pounds, one pound below topweight Career Boy. Many considered this bad handicapping, particularly when Nail did nothing in 1956 and Career Boy fulfilled handicapper Frank E. Kilroe's expectations only once, nowhere near matching the later status of Needles. However, Needles was voted champion two-year-old of 1955, thus becoming Florida's first national champion. But it was as a three-year-old that he would make his real impact on the Florida thoroughbred industry.

Needles, the first Florida thoroughbred to win the Kentucky Derby (1956), at Bonnie Heath Farm in 1982. Needles also won the Belmont Stakes that year. Photo by Kerry Heubeck.

Post parade at Gulfstream Park from paddock. Photo courtesy of Joe Tannenbaum, Gulfstream Park.

Calder Race Course. Photo by Charlene R. Johnson.

Carry Back, the second Florida thoroughbred to win the Kentucky Derby (1961). Carry Back also won the Preakness that year. Photo by Kerry Heubeck at Dorchester Farm in 1979.

Reverie Knoll Farm. Photo by Charlene R. Johnson.

Slew o' Gold in paddock, Wooden Horse Stud Farm, Marion County. Photo by Charlene R. Johnson.

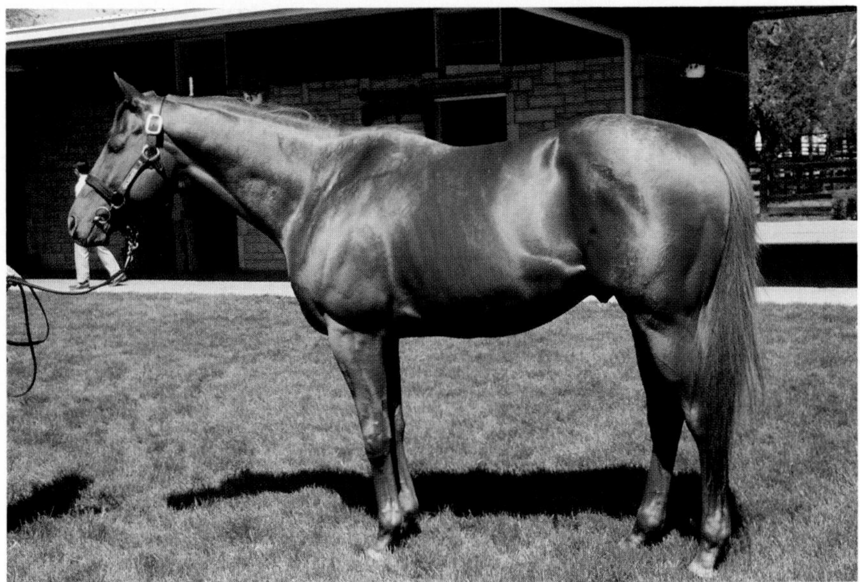

Affirmed, the first Florida thoroughbred to win the Triple Crown: Kentucky Derby, Preakness, and Belmont Stakes (1978). Photo by Charlene R. Johnson at Spendthrift Farm, Kentucky.

One of many signposts pointing the way to Marion County thoroughbred farms. This one originally appeared at the intersection of U.S. Route 27 and State Road 225A, Marion County. Photo by Charlene R. Johnson.

Fred Hooper, who has won more awards than any other breeder nationally, with one of his millionaire champions, Susan's Girl. Photo by Charlene R. Johnson at his Marion County farm in 1983.

The flamingo fountain at Hialeah. Hialeah became famous for the first captive breeding flock of flamingos. They are still the trademark for the track. Photo by Kerry Heubeck.

Hialeah sales ring during a two-year-old sale. The first two-year-old sales held in the United States were in Florida in 1957. Photo by Kerry Heubeck.

Hialeah backside. Photo by Kerry Heubeck.

16

May 3, 1956: Needles Sews It Up

In January 1956, Needles became the first thoroughbred ever to receive an accolade from a university: he was made an honorary member of the Letterman's Club of Oklahoma A & M, Bonnie Heath's alma mater. At about the same time, Jackson Dudley and Heath purchased the 572-acre CY Cattle Ranch on Highway 200 for $200,000 from Mr. and Mrs. Richard Salsbury. Dudley and Heath planned to turn it into a major horse farm. Heath would move onto the farm, Elmo Shropshire was named manager, and Dudley would remain in Oklahoma with the oil business a little longer.

It was also in January that Bill and Dickey Leach sold their farm due to Bill's failing health. Dickey Stables was purchased by a syndicate headed by Bruce Campbell of Towson, Maryland. Joseph O'Farrell, also of Maryland, was named farm manager. At first, it was thought that the new farm name would be Ken-Mar because the principals of the syndicate were all from Kentucky and Maryland. Instead, the farm became Ocala Stud Farms.

With these purchases, there were nearly 2,000 acres devoted to the raising of thoroughbreds in Marion County. All this acreage was located west of Highway 441. Carl Rose was ebullient after these last two significant purchases. He predicted that the future trend would be toward smaller farms, since access to other tracks and facilities would not necessitate full-facility farms such as Rosemere had been. "They told me the country around here would never amount to anything for breeding and training horses when I started nearly twenty years ago," Rose exulted. "Now with these two big sales of the last few days, there's no telling how big the business might become."

At this point, there were a few farms in North Georgia and around Point Clear, Alabama, but no area in the Deep South had reached the development of Ocala. Still, they could have said back then, "You ain't seen nuthin' yet." Following the success of

Needles, Ocala would blossom as a breeding center at a rate that has never, before or since, been matched anywhere in the world.

Although the Leaches were forced to leave the business, their impact continued to be felt. Another Dickey Farm-bred, King Hairan, began making news in 1956, adding to the sudden fame of the Sunshine State. King Hairan was descended from one of the few remaining "American" female lines, meaning that a nineteenth century descendant, an unnamed Top Gallant mare, could not be traced back to the British stud books. Leach bought Lady Hairan (*Hairan–Lady Menifee, by Menifee) at the fall sales for $5,500. She was then in foal to Devil Diver. He bought King's Stride from an estate sale for $15,000 and began breeding him in 1950. One year after Needles won the best-in-show at the Baby Show, Leach again took the top blue for King Hairan. This time, the judge was trainer Ben A. Jones. Two days later, the "King" scored a five-length victory in a three-furlong race at Hialeah, equaling the :32 2/5 track record.

King Hairan was promptly sold to Leo Edwards, former chairperson of the Florida Racing Commission, and Harry B. Massey of Pittsburgh, owner of Grandview Stable, for $35,000. King Hairan then won the Florida Breeders' Stakes for them. Then followed victories in the Hialeah Juvenile Stakes and the Gulfstream Park Dinner Stakes. King Hairan came within one-fifth second of the record both times. He then popped a splint (a common bony growth on the shin, usually the result of stress) and was laid off. When King Hairan came back, he ran second to Bold Ruler (who would be champion three-year-old and Horse of the Year in 1957, champion sprinter in 1958, and a leading sire eight times) twice in a row. He then won five straight. King Hairan's best race was the Hopeful Stakes, in which he beat Nearctic (later the sire of the greatest sire in the modern-day world, Northern Dancer), who finished fourth, and Cohoes. This was the second year in a row that a Florida-bred had captured this stakes. King Hairan popped a splint again and was again laid off to await his three-year-old season. At the end of the year, with eight added-money events to his credit and earnings of $191,575, he was weighted on the Experimental at 122, four pounds below Barbizon and three pounds below Bold Ruler and Federal Hill.

Ecstatic Florida breeders had two top quality racehorses to watch in 1956: a two-year-old and a three-year-old. But it was Needles who took the limelight, and he did so with more than just talent.

Needles on the track before the Flamingo Stakes, Dave Erb up (by permission of Scott Dudley).

He won the hearts of his fans with more character than a horse is expected to have. After his precocious speed as a two-year-old, Needles now changed his style to that of an off-the-pace runner. It was as though he knew he had earned the right to do things his own way. Needles handlers soon learned that he had a mind of his own. Once Needles made up his mind, it was very difficult to change it, even if this meant the difference between winning and losing.

Needles began his three-year-old campaign under a new jockey, Dave Erb. Their first event together was on February 6 in a five-furlong race against co-weight Nail. Nail finished next to last, and Needles trailed the field, just rallying in time to finish second, behind Call Me Lucky.

On February 25, thanks to the Florida-bred concession, Needles carried 117 pounds compared to 122 on the fourteen others entered in the Flamingo Stakes. Prior to the Flamingo, largely due to the success of Needles and at the request of the Florida breeders, the Florida Racing Commission voted to amend the five-pound allowance rule for Florida-breds to apply only to overnight races (ones for which entries close only three days or less before the program; these are generally claiming and allowance races, rather than stakes). Since this change would begin with the 1956 to 1957 season, Needles was still allowed the advantage. Nevertheless, Maine Chance Farm's entry of Gun Shot and Busher's Idol were the favorites. The Flamingo was still considered a difficult race for a Florida-bred. Again Needles lagged at the beginning, although he was never quite last, allowing Nail and Busher's Idol to set the pace. Needles' running style might have appeared brilliant but for the times. Many critics contended that he won only because the rest of the field stopped. This would be a criticism heard throughout the rest of Needles' career, despite the fact that he set three track records and equaled a fourth. But he won the Flamingo; he was the first Florida-bred to win an important prep for the classic races.

Needles vindicated himself in the Florida Derby. Once again, there were fourteen entries, and this time, Needles was favored. He broke dead last and was about twelve lengths behind the pace set by Pintor Lea and Golf Ace. Halfway around the last turn, he was up to five lengths behind the leaders, but they did not come back. Instead, they picked up speed. Erb took his horse to the outside, and in a thrilling stretch run that took the last three furlongs in little more than thirty-six seconds, he drove on to win, lowering the track record by one-fifth, to 1:48 3/5. Needles had triumphed in the first $100,000 race ever won by a Florida-bred. It was one of three races he would win in 1956. He was firmly established as the favorite for the Kentucky Derby, an incredible feat for a Florida-bred.

At this point in his career, Needles was developing some very strong quirks. His antics provided amusing reading for his fans and some moments of grim anxiety for his owners, breeder, trainers, handlers, and jockeys: "NEEDLES—Sharp Without Sharpening," was the way the cover of the May 12, 1956, *Blood Horse* accurately summed up his oddities. Needles hated morning workouts. Following the Florida Derby, trainer Hugh Fontaine plotted a course that included no more races until the "Run for the Roses" six weeks later. This notion alone left many hardboots aghast. Needles then helped to assure that his trainer would be "needled" by consenting to work only four times in those six weeks.

Although he had shown his distaste for working before, Needles' dislike approached an art form when he reached Louisville. Rarely

Needles wins the Florida Derby (by permission of Scott Dudley).

Needles exhibits his characteristic displeasure during a morning workout at Churchill Downs (by permission of Scott Dudley).

has any trainer received as much advice on how to handle a horse as did Fontaine. But Fontaine had character of his own. As a member of Eddie Rickenbacker's "Flying Circus" in World War I, he became America's first aviation ace from below the Mason-Dixon line. He was not above theatrics to obtain his goals. Fontaine was probably the only trainer for Needles. After the Derby, and after all the criticism and skepticism, Raleigh Burroughs would write on May 11, 1956, in the *Chronicle of the Horse*, "It's just possible the man knows what he is doing!"

Needles definitely did not believe in wasting energy. Almost any time of day when visitors came around, it was quite possible that they would find the equine star sprawled inelegantly in his stall, fast asleep, his faithful groom, Joe Rutter, standing guard. "Nothing phases Needles," Fontaine admitted unabashedly to the *Blood-Horse* on May 12, 1956. "You could start a motorcycle behind him and he wouldn't care. But he won't take abuse, won't stand for it. He'll work all right, when *he* wants to." Fontaine was generous in his credit to Needles' groom, Joe Rutter, who had been with Needles since his yearling days on the farm. To Rutter often fell the task of getting Needles to his task. Gleefully, the press recorded with pen and camera many a training session with Rutter frantically flapping a lead shank or a blanket at a blankly staring Needles, while Dave Erb pounded the horse's sides relentlessly with his heels.

Occasionally, the pleading and prodding of his handlers would encourage Needles to finally break into a cumbersome lope onto the track. About halfway around, he would stop again. Rutter ran across so many infields with the weapon of the day that he probably logged more miles than Needles did. Occasionally, Rutter would prod him in the ribs with Fontaine's walking stick or slap his old slouch hat across the royal equine derriere; such tactics would finally convince Needles to work or fake a workout. "It was against his principles to waste his energy when there was nothing at stake but exercise," one turf writer happily wrote in "Needles," in *American Race Horses*, by Joe Estes.

Erb could usually tell when Needles was in a mood to work. Eight days before the Kentucky Derby, he knew it and begged Fontaine to let him work the horse. But Fontaine had promised the press a last workout the following morning and he would not break his word. The next day, journalists, photographers, fans, and clockers lined the backstretch railing, waiting to see their hero's final prep for the derby. But Needles was not in the mood. For a full

Trainer Hugh Fontaine. Photo by Leo Frutkoff (by permission of *The Florida Horse*).

thirty minutes, Fontaine, Rutter, and Erb pleaded, coaxed, pushed, pulled, and finally resorted to throwing dirt clods and curses. Finally, Needles decided to move, very slowly. It was perhaps the slowest prep in the history of the Derby. The Derby distance of one and one-quarter miles was covered in the unconvincing time of 2:09.

No one who was connected with the horse worried. "He stays in better shape than almost any horse I ever saw," Rutter stated confidently in the May 12 "The Week's Racing" column in the *Blood-Horse*. "You just can't train this horse like any other," Fontaine added, unperturbed. "He doesn't need a race. He'll do all right."

Still, skepticism and bad luck seemed to follow Needles on the Derby trail. Five days before the Derby, Dave Erb came down with a bad cold and was bedridden right up until the day of the race. No horse with an "N" name had ever won the Derby; neither the jockey, trainer, nor owners had never come close to winning one; and as everyone knew, no Florida-bred had even competed in the king of races before. The critics figured that the race was stacked against Needles. But the horse had won the heart of the public, and he went to the post the morning of the big day as the favorite against sixteen comers. His breeder, William Leach, was forced to cancel plans to attend when he was stricken with a bad attack of gout. But Dudley and Heath made up for his absence by playing host to some 100 friends and neighbors, many of them other Florida breeders.

The track was very fast on Derby Day. Two records were set in earlier races for four and one-half furlongs and for five furlongs. There were 78,322 fans on hand to witness the annual renewal of America's greatest race. Before the Run for the Roses, however, Florida breeders had the stage set for them in the Debutante Stakes two races earlier. Delamar (Wine List–Myfirstoday, by Tiger), a Florida-bred that was never actually registered in the state registry and therefore is often missed in the historical accounts, not only won that prestigious stakes, but also set a track record, to the glee of the Florida breeders on hand.

In the big race, Needles, seeming ready to prove his critics right, got off to a poor start. On the backstretch, he actually spit the bit out, causing jockey Erb's heart to nearly fail. But then Needles seemed to realize this was the real thing and took hold again. He was second to last, more than twenty lengths off the leaders at the half-mile pole when he started to roll. By the top of the stretch he was in seventh place. The orange and blue silks were flying in hot pursuit of the devil-red and blue silks of Calumet's Fabius. Some said that it was the strongest stretch run in the eighty-two year history of the Derby. Others, who attempted to compute Needles' every running step, said that it was the most even tempo ever run. They contended that the win occurred because the front runners came back so fast. Theories didn't matter. The telephone lines to

Needles wins the Kentucky Derby, May 3, 1956 (by permission of Scott Dudley).

Florida sang. A Florida-bred had won the hardboots' classic. The Sunshine State and the national thoroughbred industry would never be the same.

During the jubilation on the reviewing stand, a U.S. marshall elbowed his way to Fontaine and served him with an attachment on his winnings for $2,000 owed in back income taxes. "That don't bother me, boy," Fontaine said, grinning broadly, according to the *Blood-Horse*. "Not today!"

But the pressure was not over. Fontaine, who felt Needles did best with long rests between his races, had to face the Preakness in two weeks. Since Needles was the first Florida-bred to have a chance at the Triple Crown, Fontaine could hardly say no. He was not surprised when his charge failed to overtake Fabius despite a tremendous charge, again from about twenty lengths off the pace. The distance was quickly closing, but it ran out too soon. Needles finished second. Charles Hatton, writing in the *American Racing Manual*, was eloquently impressed with Needles' show that day despite his loss. "He must have been all of twenty lengths off the leaders with the end of the backstretch looming. The disadvantage

Needles wins the Belmont Stakes, 1956 (by permission of Scott Dudley).

simply was too great. Needles responded generously entering the final turn, moving courageously between horses where there appeared to be insufficient room. His rush had such impetus he seemed to explode the field as he charged at Fabius . . . he gripped the bit between his teeth and his head shook with each stride as he hit the ground."

Three weeks later everyone in the industry was at Belmont Park in New York for the final and longest leg of the Triple Crown races. In the post parade before the race, Needles pulled one of his famous stunts and stopped dead on the backside. "He just stood there," Dudley remembered, "The outriders, grooms, starters—everybody was out there pushing, tugging, trying to do anything to get him to move. Thousands of people in the grandstand and this horse doesn't want to move. That was very embarrassing. We didn't know what we were going to do." Finally, Needles apparently decided it was the real thing and happily moved off to load into the gate.

Seemingly intent upon keeping his owners and fans in suspense, Needles did not get back out of the gate any too quickly, however.

Once again, he was last by twenty-two lengths and did not make his move until the half-mile pole. By the quarter pole, Fabius had a seven-length lead over Career Boy, Ricci Tavi, and Needles. With one of his fabulous and seemingly hopeless stretch runs, Needles charged past them all to win by a neck over Career Boy. Fabius was fading fast. A Florida-bred had won two legs of America's Triple Crown series.

In his next race, a prep for the American Derby, Needles never got out of last place after being topweighted at 120 pounds, although he was the only three-year-old in the field. He then finished fifth over the turf in the American Derby, his late-running style leaving him too far behind for too long. Even so, he was beaten by only two and three-quarter lengths. Needles was injured in that race, necessitating his retirement for the season. Some thought he simply disliked the grass. Nonetheless, his glamor image was somewhat damaged. Needles was taken out of training for a rest, finished the year with earnings of $440,850 and was declared champion three-year-old for the year.

A song was composed by some Florida "good ole boys" to be sung to the tune of "We Are the Boys from Old Florida":

He is the champ from Old Florida;
  Needles!
Where the bass are the longest
The 'shine is the strongest
Of any old state down our way.

We are all strong for
  Needles!
Down where the old Gators play,
In any old weather
We'll all stick together
  for Needles!

17

Needles Country

The impact Needles had on Florida was immediate. He finished 1956 as the leading money-winning horse of the year, while King Hairan was the leading stakes winning two-year-old of the year. In 1956, 145 Florida-breds won 363 races. Four Florida-breds were weighted on the Experimental Handicap: Needles was second highest weighted in the nation at 125, First Cadet and Smooth Stride were both weighted at 111, and Avis was 108. In 1957, King Hairan was listed at 122 and Delamar at 110.

For the first time, Florida-breds went over the million-dollar mark; they earned $1,459,791, almost double the previous year's earnings. Meanwhile Kentuckians, jealous of Needles' reputation, attempted to lay claim to him by virtue of his conception in Kentucky. Up to now, there had been little reason to monitor the state in which a horse was bred, as most of the good ones were from Kentucky. Now, gleeful Floridians pointed out that The Jockey Club ruling stated very clearly that a horse is "bred" in the state in which it is dropped, not conceived.

Suddenly tourists were coming to Ocala, not to see Silver Springs or the Ocala National Forest, but to see the winner of the Kentucky Derby. Billboards outside Ocala proclaimed the city to be the home of Needles and gave directions to his farm. By October 1956, Heath and Dudley had decided to form two separate farms. The Bonnie Heath Farm would still house most of their jointly owned horses, some fifty-five head. Since Jack Dudley still did not feel pressed into moving to Florida, he took the side of the farm that was not yet developed. His wife's parents would move onto and manage the property in the late 1950s. It was actually one of Dudley's sons, Scott, who would move onto the property in the 1960s and begin monitoring more seriously the horses that were stabled there. Dudley moved there in 1972. In the 1950s, Dudley Farm was still in the process of being cleared.

Major horse farms around the country began sending their

Left to right: Jack Dudley, Joseph O'Farrell, and Bonnie Heath (by permission of Scott Dudley).

Commendations kept coming in. In 1974, Jack Dudley shows Needles yet another one from the State of Florida. Photo by Art Kunkel (by permission of Scott Dudley).

young stock to the Ocala area to train. Ocala Stud, bursting with well-bred animals and possessing a separate trainer for each of its three barns, boasted thirty-six head of Elmendorf Farm's (Widener's Kentucky farm) young stock. The Jan Burke Stable of New York, Justin Funkhauser of Maryland, Darby Dan Farm of Ohio and Kentucky, John E. Hughes of Chicago, James Roberts of Houston, and many more had their horses trained and boarded at Ocala-area farms.

Needles' popularity did not stop with the horsey set. During half-time of the big game in Gainesville between the University of Florida and the University of Miami, Needles pranced onto the field, complete with jockey Dave Erb in racing silks, coincidentally the same colors as the University of Florida's: blue and orange. In November, the Ocala Chamber of Commerce made Needles an honorary member, citing both Needles and King Hairan as major boosts to the industry. Needles was the first four-legged member to be inducted into Florida's Sports Hall of Fame.

Ocala Stud was now the owner of Noodle Soup, her yearling filly by Fly Away, and her weanling colt by Bull Brier. Following The Jockey Club's rejection of a number of names for Needles' half brother by Jack High, Ocala Stud decided to hold a contest to name him. The winner would receive a large portrait of Needles winning the Derby. The letters poured in by the thousands, proof of the popularity of Needles in the Sunshine State. A Miami schoolgirl won the contest with the name Sky High. But Needles was not through yet. As a four-year-old, he started only three times. But in his final race at Gulfstream Park in the Ft. Lauderdale Handicap going one and one-sixteenth miles and conceding eight to eighteen pounds to his rivals, he went out in a typical blaze of glory, equaling the track record. He finished his career with a record of twenty-one starts, eleven wins, three seconds, and three thirds. Needles' total earnings were $600,355.

"He was always a very generous horse," Bonnie Heath remembered. "He was considered by a few jealous detractors to be a plodder in his time, but he always gave 200 percent. I've never seen a horse with more heart and courage than he had." To end once and for all the idea that Needles was anything but a fast racehorse, Heath plotted all Needles' own fractions in the Kentucky Derby. "He ran the first half in :52 flat, the third quarter in :22 4/5, the fourth quarter in :23 flat, and the final quarter in :25 3/5. So he ran the final three quarters of a mile in 1:11 2/5. That's hardly the time of a plodder!"

Owners Dudley and Heath went through serious soul-searching when it came time to stand Needles. Their dedication to the Florida industry was as great a donation as was Needles' spirit. Needles became the first champion to stand outside of Kentucky. "We were invited to stand him at Spendthrift and Claiborne," Heath said. "It was a very attractive proposition, but we were interested in the Florida program. That's why we bought the land. From the horse's viewpoint, there's no question he would have been more successful as a stud if he'd gone to Kentucky.

"But he accelerated the Florida breeding program by years. People from all over the world realized for the first time that we could produce good horses in Florida. That was worth it to us."

When Needles first retired in 1958, Dudley and Heath attempted to syndicate him. Shares were priced at $25,000 each, sixteen to be sold, sixteen to keep. When they could get firm commitments for only about six shares, they decided to forget about syndication and keep the horse themselves. Despite the odds, Needles was no shirk at stud. He sired twenty crops and averaged fifteen foals a year. Of 317 foals, 294 got to the races and 233 were winners. Thirteen percent (twenty-one) were stakes winners. Needles' best was Irish Rebellion, who won the Pan American Handicap and placed in fifteen stakes. Needles was a leading juvenile sire in 1964, with twelve winners of nineteen races, four of them stakes horses. He stood for $5,000. Four of his progeny were listed on the Experimental in the same year Bold Ruler and Prince John each had five. One son, Ishkooda, was considered good enough for an attempt at the Kentucky Derby. Many years later, in 1984, a yearling filly would sell at the Keeneland Summer Sales for $3,750,000. She was by the popular sire of the time, Seattle Slew, out of the mare Fine Prospect; her third dam was Noodle Soup.

Needles had unbelievable longevity. Elmer Vickers of Calder Race Course couldn't believe it. In a promotional film for Calder in 1977, he intoned sadly, "Needles is gone now." He was quickly informed of his mistake. Years later, when Needles was thirty-one years old, Ocala Mayor Wayne Rubinas declared April 13, 1984, "Needles and Carry Back Day." The latter star, Carry Back, just missed his special day; he had died only a week or so earlier. Needles was the oldest living winner of the Kentucky Derby or the Belmont. He was in fact the second oldest winner of the Derby; only Count Fleet, who died at thirty-three, had lived longer.

The old stallion loved visitors. Needles would "ham it up" any time a camera clicked and hang forlornly over the gate when his visitors left. A favorite trick was to offer his tongue to be tugged and played with. Then, ever so casually, he would draw his tongue back into his mouth until fingers were within nipping distance.

Always one to take care of himself, Needles more or less retired himself from breeding in 1978, thereafter living life at a leisurely pace until his death on October 15, 1984. He was buried at the Ocala Breeders' Sales complex, where a monument was erected.

Rarely has an animal had as much impact on an industry as this horse did on the thoroughbred industry in Florida. Not everyone was pleased with this success, however. Kentuckians' respect for the Florida industry was given as grudgingly as ever. The year Needles won the Derby, Ocala Stud attempted to book Noodle Soup back to Ponder, who stood at Calumet. Calumet's Fabius, of course, had been beaten in the Derby. Ponder was strangely unavailable for a booking for Noodle Soup.

In a press interview in Miami, Governor LeRoy Collins stated, "I am confident we will see extensive investments here in Florida by leading thoroughbred stables soon. Large scale racing stables are a substantial investment in themselves, but they also bring large additions to the state's total payroll and focus national attention on us as well." In November 1956, the governor made a trip to New York specifically to invite the nation's best racehorse owners to move their stables to Florida. He attended the annual meeting of top stable owners at the Waldorf-Astoria, where he presented his proposal. Eugene Mori, Sr. of Hialeah accompanied him. This kind of support from the governor's office was very welcome. Unfortunately, it was not indicative of lasting goodwill between the thoroughbred industry and state government.

Heath actively worked to promote the industry as well. In an address to the Ocala Rotary in October 1957, he offered figures to support the benefits of racing to the state. He stated that Florida racing produced almost $25,000,000, with about $175,000 distributed to each county. He then gave a breakdown of what was done with each handicapping dollar. Besides the return to handicappers on their $2 investments, the track took 14¢ for operating costs.

> But you will be interested in what the state of Florida did with the seventeen cents it received in taxes. . . . Eleven and a half cents were used to help the old folks of Florida, for housing, food and other necessities. . . . Your other six cents is paying for everything from a tuba to a veterinarian. . . . Sixty-one counties used all or part for

A farm tour in Ocala includes (left to right) Eugene Mori, Sr., Fred Hooper, Jack Dudley, trainer Jimmy Jones, Everett Clay, and Eugene Mori, Jr. (by permission of *The Florida Horse*).

> schools. . . . In six other units all of your racing tax was spent for highways and bridges.
>
> Twenty-one counties appropriate part of their parimutuel money for county health units. Six counties have built hospitals with the assistance of racing funds . . . and some [money went] for high school band instruments . . . and to pay the salary of a county veterinarian.

Heath also cited pest control, libraries, harbor improvements, canals, and drainage as more beneficiaries of the state's portion of the take.

Meanwhile, the industry was growing rapidly in "The Kingdom of the Sun," as Marion County became known. Ocala was a booming city of 15,000 inhabitants. The limestone vein running through the heart of sunshine land was declared by the Department of Agriculture to be the best in the United States.

At the beginning of 1957, there were seven thoroughbred farms in Marion County; by the end of the year, there were twenty-one, an incredible leap in what was rapidly becoming a very important industry for Florida. Some 8,446 acres were being used for breeding and training thoroughbreds. Within the state, there were fifty-five farms in thirteen counties, 59 stallions, and 477 mares, according to a report by the Florida Thoroughbred Breeders' Association. The FTBA's membership had grown to eighty-five.

Four of the seven early farms, boasting some two-hundred horses in training among them, were Rosemere, Ocala Stud, Shady Lane, and Bonnie Heath Farm. Heath's farm had grown to 700 acres, with ninety horses on the farm, twenty-five of which belonged to Dudley and Heath. A number of horses boarded on the farm were owned by Pete Widener. New concrete-block barns were the latest in design. A path cut through the woods provided access to Ocala Stud's training track a half-mile away. Recognizing the need for established sires in Florida, Heath arranged to lease Curandero (Brazado–Ciencia, by *Cohort), a product of the carefully developed breeding program of the famous King Ranch. He stood the 1958 breeding season for $500. The other three farms included the 250-acre Brazito Stud Farm, owned by R. C. "Roy" Howard of South Carolina. This farm was the home of stallions Attention Mark (Attention–Night Market, by *Man O'Night) and Sir Goya (*Goya II–Gallonia, by *Sir Gallahad III). Willow Lake and a third farm developed by Joe Komlo, a midwestern horseman, rounded out the group. There was also Dudley's partially developed acreage and a seventeen acre plot across the road purchased by Fontaine. The reporters could not keep up with the new and speculative farms.

Tom M. Daniels sold his Lexington farm, Broadmoor, to Henry H. Knight of Almahurst Farm in Kentucky and was just closing a deal on 190 acres northwest of Ocala on Highway 27 for $63,000. He planned to move his breeding stock, fifteen mares, eight yearlings, and his stallions, Ace Destroyer and Jet Ace, to his new Florida farm (also named Broadmoor) following the foaling and breeding season. Daniels, a manufacturer of metal furniture with his business headquarters in Birmingham, Alabama, spent $80,000 on special steel fencing for his new farm. Plans included a thirty-stall training barn, a six-stall stud barn, and a twenty-four-stall mare barn. He told local reporters that he had moved his operations from Kentucky to Florida for three reasons: Lexington was becoming too industrialized, Marion County limestone grew such excellent bone, and training could be conducted year-round.

The largest farm in Marion County was a 3,500-acre cattle farm, Finley Farm. The farm was purchased by a syndicate from Miami, which planned to divide and sell it as six horse farms. Instead, syn-

Shady Lane Farm, yearlings and training horses (by permission of Roy Yates).

Forty Oaks Farm in 1962. Photo by Art Kunkel (by permission of *The Florida Horse*).

dicate members sold it to Bernard Castro of Castro Convertibles, who then turned part of it into a thoroughbred farm. Today, Castro Farms is a major stop on the southeastern horse show circuit.

As 1957 progressed, P. A. B. Widener III, grandson of Hialeah's Joseph Widener, purchased 6,700 acres that would gradually be developed into Live Oak Plantation. By the mid-1960s, he had built a house and barns reminiscent of the châteaux in France. At that time, he moved his stables from Kentucky to Florida. His name in Ocala did a great deal for the area's credibility as a horse-breeding region. Others who now came into the area included Harry Trotsek, who was clearing 106 acres near Anthony; Dr. Joseph J. Colando, who moved from Yardley, Pennsylvania, and purchased the shorthorn farm Hiland Acres to start Point-A-View Farm; James Woods, who developed the 80-acre Rosewood Farm near Anthony; Nat Tooker, who owned the 70-acre Belynada Farm and who stood the stallion Watch Toy (Bull Brier–Day Toy, by Quince King); M. T. and Jack Horne, who owned the 300-acre Horne Brothers Ranch; Fred Hilton, who owned the 40-acre Forty Oaks Farm, which he soon sold to Charles Kieser; and W. C. Vines, who owned the 80-acre Wake Robin Farm.

Wesley C. "Red" Vines was the southern sales manager for the Bucyrus-Erie Company, which had offices in Atlanta and Lowell, Florida. Through that construction business, he became acquainted with Carl Rose, whom he described as his best friend. That friendship got him his farm in Florida for $90 an acre. Today that farm is Mabar Farm, but for fourteen years, it was Wake Robin. Vines had been a horseplayer for many years before he got into the breeding game. Before his farm was finished in 1957, he was at the Fairgrounds Race Track in New Orleans where he saw, to his horror, Fair Game, the good stakes horse bred by Carl Rose, entered in a $2,000 claiming race. The seven-year-old broke down at the end of the stretch. Red Vines went to visit the trainer, Clayton Prickett, the next morning. When Vines learned that the horse's racing career was over, Vines purchased him for $2,000 and sent him home to Rosemere until his own farm was completed. Fair Game thus became the first Florida-bred stallion to stand in his home state (although by breeding season in 1958, Needles would also be retired). He retired with a career record of fifty-eight starts, sixteen wins, fifteen seconds, twelve thirds, and earnings of $51,467.

After his own farm was completed, Vines ran a very successful racing stable, Cross-Vines Stable. His partner, James P. Cross, was a Louisiana racing commissioner. Their entry of Fair Phina by Fair Game and Cab Stan by First Cabin in the Florida Breeders' Futurity in 1963 became the only entry to run first and second in the history of the race. In 1962, Red Vines and Cot Campbell started the Georgia Thoroughbred Breeders' Association with Vines as president. At the time, Vines felt that the proximity of Georgia to the highly successful breeding center of Ocala would guarantee similar success for Georgia. Vines was also great friends with Fred Hooper and stood his stallion Education alongside Fair Game. Hooper would later name a horse Red Vines in honor of the man; it was a good stakes horse. Vines took five of Hooper's mares in exchange for giving him back five Florida-bred foals.

George Cavanaugh started Pinecrest Farm and stood the good stallion Prince Quest (Requested–Teddys Queen, by *Teddy). He became heavily involved in promotion and support of the industry.

Grant Dorland moved from Kentucky to start Roseland Farm in 1957. This farm was somewhat south of most of the other farms in what was then the "boondocks." This was Roseland #3; the first two were located in Kentucky. When this famous hardboot breeder

Fair Game, a good stakes winner, retired to his home state, taking up stud duties first at Rosemere, then at Wake Robin Farm (by permission of W. Vines).

Riders at Sunshine Stud (by permission of Dorothy Davis).

decided to relocate in Ocala, he sold his northern farm and most of his stock, bringing with him only one mare. He fell in love with Ocala. "A well-ordered thoroughbred farm in this area actually looks more like a park," he said in an interview in *The Florida Horse*. Dorland was in the process of the syndication of Correlation (Free America–*Braydore, by Roidore), the 1954 winner of the Florida Derby and the Wood Memorial and holder of a world's record. The stallion was to stand at Bonnie Heath Farm. Indicative of an industry possibly still ahead of its time was the fact that although Correlation had earned over $300,000, Dorland had to struggle to sell shares in him at $1,000. (When a stallion is syndicated, usually 40 to 50 shares are sold. The shares give the owner lifetime breeding rights, which he can either use or sell annually as a "season.") Dorland planned extensive rebuilding of the farm he bought, with new fencing, a twelve-stall barn, and remodeling of the main residence and the farm manager's cottage. He was famous for giving all his colts Indian names and naming all his fillies after perfumes. Today, Roseland Farm is Fitzpatrick Farm and one of many more in the same area.

In late 1957, Dan Chappell of southern Florida fame and a partner, Abe Mersky, started Sunshine Stud. The property then was 480 acres purchased from Martin Anderson, owner of the *Orlando Sentinel*, who had called it Maverick Farm when it was his cattle ranch. Chappell stood King Bruce II (Fair Trial–*Spider's Web, by Bois Roussel) and My Banker (Sun Again–Goose Cry, by *Royal Minstrel). Sunshine Stud would later become Lasater Farm and today is Southland Farm.

By the end of 1957, it had become apparent that Ocala-Marion County had experienced a change of course in its history. The thoroughbred industry from this point forward was the most important thing to happen to the heart of the Sunshine State.

Part Four

Kingdom of the Sun

Marion County, Florida
Throughbred Horse Farms, 1961

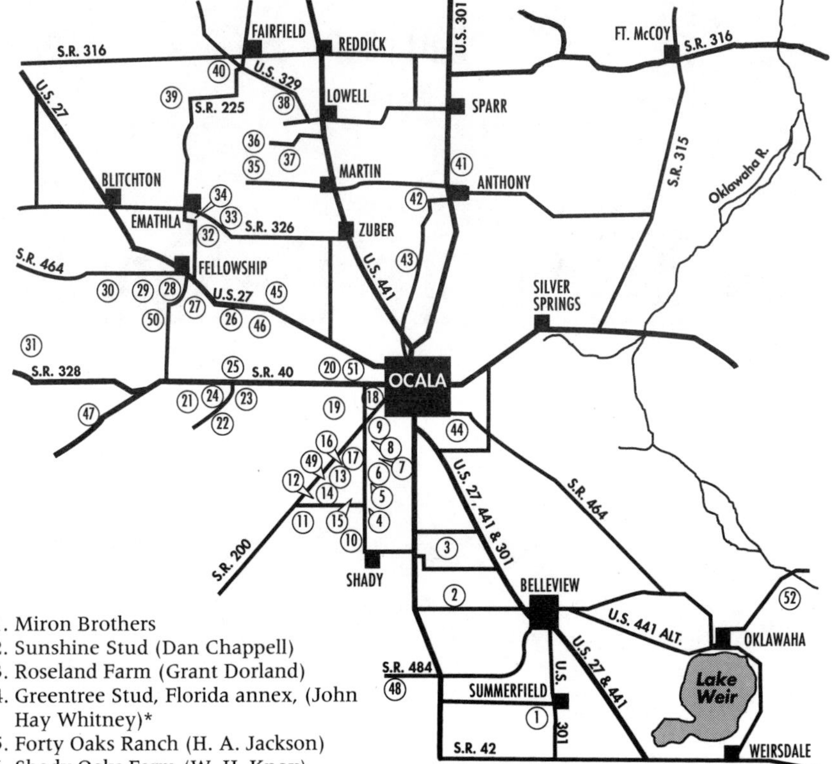

1. Miron Brothers
2. Sunshine Stud (Dan Chappell)
3. Roseland Farm (Grant Dorland)
4. Greentree Stud, Florida annex, (John Hay Whitney)*
5. Forty Oaks Ranch (H. A. Jackson)
6. Shady Oaks Farm (W. H. Knox)
7. Frank Lynn Ranch (Louis Bandel)
8. Shady Lane Farm (D. F.Stewart)
9. Rosemere Farm (Rosemere Stud Inc., Lessee)
10. Bellows Ranch (Harry Berman)
11. Leeward Farms (A. J. Leeward)
12. Jack C. Dudley Farm
13. Bonnie M. Heath Farm
14. Tartan Farms, W. L. McKnight
15. Messana Farm (Steve Messana)
16. Florida Horse & Florida Breeders' Sales Association
17. Ocala Stud Farms, Inc. (Joe O'Farrell)
18. Bell Rock Farm (E. S. Rockefeller
19. Meadowbrook Farms, Inc.
20. 3 "B's" Farm
21. P.A.B. Widener III
22. Horne Brothers
23. Sylvester Adair
24. Joe Schneider*
25. Dario Farms (B. A. Dario)
26. Castro Farms
27. Broadmoor Farm (T. M. Daniels)
28. Harbor View Farm (Louis Wolfson)
29. Pinecrest Farm (George Cavanaugh)
30. Norton Farm*
31. Early Bird Farms
32. Leslie Combs II*
33. Ralph Wilson*
34. Sam Pancoast*
35. James A. Bohannon*
36. Brookfield Farm (Harry Isaacs & Jennie Bardwell)*
37. Wake Robin Farm (W. C. Vines)
38. Quail's Roost (Elmer Heubeck)
39. Jack Dreyfus*
40. Starlite Trading, Ltd.
41. Barry Farm (Harry Trotsek)
42. Ryder Farm
43. Powers Farm
44. John Clardy
45. Mary El Farm (Harry B. Matthews)
46. Double L Ranch (L. L. Hollandsworth)
47. West Wind Ranch (J. Nadler)
48. Furrow Farm (Wade H. Furrow)*
49. Springfield Farm (leased by Mrs. Louisa d'A Carpenter)
50. Emerald Farm (E. R. Goodale)
51. Swamp Angel Ranch (P. N. Prewitt)
52. Schwahn's Lake Fey Horse Farm (A. Schwahn)

* Under development

18

Joe and Mr. Bruce

"I came to Ocala with Joe O'Farrell the second time he ever came down here," said Karl Koontz, present-day manager of Lin-Drake Farm in Ocala, who remembered that 1956 trip very well. Koontz said:

> He wouldn't fly in those days so we had to drive. He'd been here once before and he was so busy talking and showing me with great excitement the rolling hills and the grass and making sure that I didn't miss anything that we ran out of gas!
>
> We flagged down a truck driver who gave us a ride into town. So my first sight of Ocala was from a semi. We spent the first night at the Rock Court Motor Inn which is now the Ocala Lumber Company. We had dinner for the first time at the Marion Lunch across from the old Libby plant. It was horrible!

With such an unlikely beginning, it must have been hard to realize that a new chapter in the history of the Florida thoroughbred breeding industry was about to begin. What one man had started, another man was about to develop into an art form. Enter Joseph Michael O'Farrell. But the reason Joe O'Farrell came to Ocala in the first place was Bruce S. Campbell.

Bruce S. Campbell was born and raised in Maryland, where his first introduction to anything equine came in the form of a one-eyed mule that pulled wagons loaded with rock from a quarry operated by his father, H. T. Campbell. From those quarries would develop a business later inherited by the son: H. T. Campbell and Sons Company, later to become a part of Flinkote Corporation. The man who would eventually be known as "Mr. Bruce" in Florida thoroughbred circles became enamored of racing following the "gift" of two racehorses that he received on an unpaid debt. He acquired a few good ones, such as Barbara Childs, a top race mare, and his Kentucky Derby starter, Ram O'War. He began a life-style of breeding horses in Maryland and wintering in Miami.

Bruce Campbell (left), master of Ocala Stud, and Dan Chappell in later years. Photo by Turfotos (by permission of *The Florida Horse*).

One day, while Campbell was in a doctor's office in Miami, he picked up a brochure listing a horse farm for sale in Ocala, Florida. According to *This is Horse Racing* by Chuck Tilley, Campbell would later tell friends, "I didn't know where Ocala was but those were sure pretty pictures of pretty horses." On January 15, 1956, he called his son, McLean (Mack), and a friend, Joe O'Farrell, and asked them to meet him at the Dickey Stables in Ocala. It was snowing in Maryland when O'Farrell left that first time. He reached Ocala at 11:00 A.M. on the 16th after a train ride through undeveloped Florida forest. By 11:00 P.M. the same day, Campbell had been to a bank, called some friends, and the farm was purchased. "I took one look at those rolling hills, the green grass and live oak and all the wonderful bloom on those broodmares and foals and I was sold right away on Florida as a place to raise thoroughbreds," Joe would later recall. "I called my wife Nancy and told her to pack up, we were moving to Florida." O'Farrell was forty-nine years old.

He was born on February 5, 1907, and raised at Windy Hills Farm in Westminster, Maryland. He and his brother Tom were "born hus-

Tom O'Farrell (by permission of *The Florida Horse*).

tling," according to Koontz, a friend of the family. The brothers worked in fruit-packing canneries for 16¢ an hour, pushed "Georgia buggies" filled with liquid cement on construction gangs, rode show horses, and helped their mother run their farm after their father died. In college, Joe pitched baseball and played half-back for Mt. St. Mary's in Emmitsburg, Maryland, and for Western Maryland in Westminster, Maryland. Somewhere along the line, he managed to get a degree from George Washington University in Washington, D.C.

Joe and Tom bought their first brood mare in 1936 for $125. They purchased La Canter for fox hunting from Dr. I. W. Frock, who lived twelve miles away, and took turns riding her home. They bred her to the best stallion they could find, Wave On, by Upset. The stallion's owner, Janon Fisher, Jr., was a family friend. The boys slept in hammocks over the foaling stalls every foaling season, even in subzero weather. The result of their first breeding effort was Prince Canter. Prince Canter would earn $22,568 from 152 starts over eight years of racing; he had eleven wins, twenty-one seconds, and seventeen thirds. The brothers acquired an Allis-Chalmers Farm Equipment franchise in 1943, then a Kaiser-Fraser dealership, and then a Pontiac dealership in Westminster. By the time he was forty two years old, Joe had been breeding horses for fifteen years, selling automobiles and farm machinery by day, and working the farm in the afternoons and evenings.

Dickey Stables, on the market because of the failing health of Bill Leach, was purchased for $700,000 by a nine-person syndicate headed by Campbell. The syndicate was composed of Campbell and his son, R. McLean (of Towson, Maryland); Joe and Tom O'Farrell (of Westminster, Maryland); William Veeneman (of Louisville, Kentucky); William Reynolds (also of Louisville); George Obrecht and John Hampshire (of Baltimore, Maryland); and Thomas E. Wood, Sr. (of Cincinnati, Ohio).

William Veeneman was for years the head of Frankfort Distilleries. He owned and operated the thousand-acre Spring Hill Ranch near Louisville with his three sons and was chairperson of the board of directors of Churchill Downs. He acted as a roving ambassador for the Kentucky Derby, visiting England, France, Australia, New Zealand, Italy, Egypt, Greece, Turkey, Lebanon, and the Soviet Union. Thomas E. Wood, Sr. was a real estate and insurance broker. He owned Tumblewood Stables in Cincinnati. After his death, his son, Thomas Wood, would take over his father's share of the operation. Bruce Campbell was named president of the syndicate, and Joe O'Farrell was elected vice-president and farm manager. R. McLean was secretary-treasurer. Reynolds, Obrecht, and Hampshire were investors.

There were a few problems to be straightened out. Following the original decision not to call the farm Ken-Mar because owners were from Kentucky and Maryland, but rather Ocala Stud Farms, Inc., the syndicate immediately ran into difficulties. The name did not clearly establish the identity of the farm. Horsemen from other parts of the country too often took the name to mean all of the farms around Ocala. Ambiguities arose concerning the shipment of horses to the proper location (to which of the Ocala farms?) and in advertising, as well. Consequently, by July 1957, the name was formally shortened to Ocala Stud.

At the time of purchase, Dickey Stables, now Ocala Stud Farms, Inc., consisted of two separate farms totaling 800 acres. A third piece purchased from Carl Rose was then incorporated, for a total of 993 acres. There were facilities for two-hundred fifty horses. Included in the farm purchase were all of Leach's twenty-one head of stock: six-

Thomas E. Wood, Sr. (by permsission of *The Florida Horse*).

teen brood mares including Noodle Soup (who was about to become famous) and Iltis by War Relic (who would also become famous), both of them dams of future champions. More horses began arriving, until there were sixty mares on the farm. In June, there were four stallions on the farm: King's Stride (Coldstream–Royal Sandal, by *Royal Minstrel); Fly Away (*Blenheim II–Themesong, by High Time), and Bull Brier (*Bull Dog–Rose Eternal, by Eternal), which were all included with the Dickey Farm purchase, and Rough 'n Tumble (Free for All–Roused, by *Bull Dog), which came down for the one season from Maryland with O'Farrell. By 1958, Ocala Stud was a major stallion station with ten stallions.

The training horses quickly filled the four training barns as well, each barn falling under the supervision of a different trainer. Roy Yates of Needles fame had one barn. Famous people who would train in these barns would be Colonel W. Randolph Tayloe, another Marylander who was a retired army officer and whose forefather, John Tayloe III, was the breeder of Sir Archy back in 1805; Jim Barker, who filled his barn with Elmendorf Farm horses; and Russell Downs and Frank Lamoureux, who would train for the Reynolds brothers' 4R Stable. All the barns would eventually be named for famous horses trained and raised at Ocala Stud: Leather Button, Wayward Bird, Needles, and King Hairan. Noodle Soup, of course, was the main brood mare barn.

Joe O'Farrell was the ringleader of the entire operations. One of the first moves O'Farrell made for the new organization was to hire the *Chronicle*'s (now the *Chronicle of the Horse*) racing editor, Karl Koontz, another Marylander, as the farm's business manager and publicity director. "Joe was the eternal optimist, a marvelous person to be around," Koontz said. "I'd spend a little time with Joe and always felt like I was walking a few inches higher than I had before. If he believed in something he was so optimistic and enthusiastic about it, it was awfully hard to disagree with him."

As often heard in interviews with others as well as from Koontz, the enthusiasm and infectious excitement were probably the most visible and remembered traits of the outspoken O'Farrell. Bonnie Heath knew him as long as he was in Ocala. "I knew Joe slightly before we moved to Ocala," he corrected.

> By total coincidence we moved from south Florida and he moved from Maryland within thirty days of each other. His place was only partially developed and mine was a cattle ranch. That was when Needles was about to start as a three-year-old.
>
> Back then there were only about six of us trying to make things go; Carl Rose, Doug Stewart, George Cavanaugh, Grant Dorland, Joe and myself. Anytime we had a problem, a new disease, political problem or anything, the group would get together to try to do something about it. But Joe was the driving force. He just *knew* that Ocala would become what it is today. He was an incurable optimist, always saw the bright side of things. He never saw limits to where we were going. We've come a long way from where we were then, and a lot of it is because of Joe.

Chuck Tilley, a writer and former director of the FTBA, had this to say about Joe O'Farrell:

> He hit the ground running and he never stopped. I never knew a man with so much zest for life. It infected everyone around him.
>
> The first time I ever saw him was at the Keeneland sales in his big old broad-brimmed hat and shirt sleeves. He would talk to anyone that would stop long enough to listen, trying to get people to send their horses to Florida to train. As soon as someone bought a horse, he was right there trying to get them to send their horses down. And a lot of them did.
>
> The first time I ever came to Ocala was in 1961. I was working in Lexington for the *Thoroughbred Record* and we'd heard of Ocala—had written some ads and a few little bits about the new industry there.

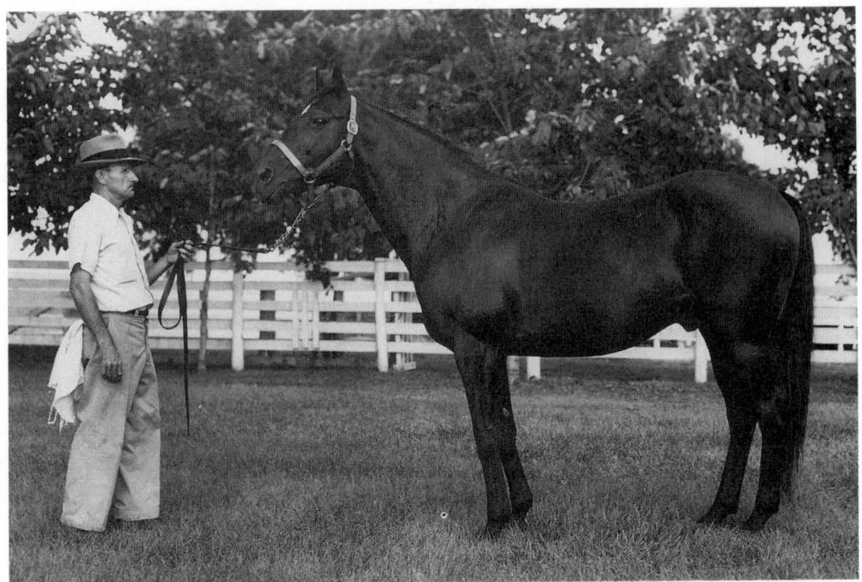

Bull Brier stood first for Dickey Stables, then for Ocala Stud Farms. Roy Yates stands him up (by permission of Roy Yates).

Left to right: Karl Koontz, Joe O'Farrell, and Roy Yates watch training horses at Ocala Stud (by permission of Roy Yates).

> He called me and asked if I'd come down and have a look at the place. So we did.
>
> We sat in the Ocala Stud clubhouse talking to people—Mr. Rose, Bonnie Heath—and finally Joe said, "Come on let's go look at the farms." I thought there'd be a bunch of them.
>
> Well, Joe was a very fast driver—he was the only man I knew who could make Miami in three, three and a half hours, when he didn't have so many points on his license he couldn't drive—and he always smoked these big black cigars so the smoke would be boiling inside the car. And the roads were mostly dirt back then. He'd go wheeling around with the dust and the smoke boiling and say "Here's that one, here's this one." I couldn't see a thing!
>
> Joe was an individual. He was the right man in the right place at the right time if ever Florida was going to get anywhere in the breeding industry. Joe was the catalyst.

Tilley was neither the first nor the last person Joe O'Farrell ever drove around in his car, trying to sell Florida. O'Farrell spent hours helping people find farms or set up operations. "I don't think there's anyone who built a farm through the 1960s or 1970s who didn't come into contact with Joe," his son, Michael, present-day owner of Ocala Stud, remembered. "They had a clubhouse up there where the mall is now. There was an open door policy and anybody that came to town to buy property or had a farm but no place to stay, they all stayed at our farm and there was always free whiskey. They were wined and dined, and you'd have to say my father played a big role in promoting the area."

O'Farrell was also one of the hardest-working persons in the industry, applying that same enthusiasm to his work. He gave free advice and also gave free services to his stallions. While he was kindhearted, open, and unselfish, he was also opinionated, stubborn, and had a one-track mind. While many came to Florida because of the influence of Joe O'Farrell, there were others who were unappreciative of his constant badgering. But no one ever doubted his motivations: he truly believed Florida was the best state for raising and training thoroughbred horses. Joe once offered a description of himself: "I don't claim to be the most intelligent man in this business, but I haven't met a man yet I couldn't outwork. I'm always in a hurry. I hate anything that forces me to sit around and do nothing. You know how it is with horses; some settle right down and others are always wound up. I think the same thing applies to people; I'm the type that never unwinds."

O'Farrell first began the practice of borrowing money from a bank to buy horses when he borrowed $50,000 in 1956. Today,

Yearlings in training in 1956: (left to right) W. Scamen on Romeme, later to become a winner of $1,290; A. Penny on Toong Soong, stakes-placed earner of $22,504; Frank Yates on Shuu, winner of $22,935; S. Calloway on Paradise Peak, winner of $17,115; and L. Dusang on Charmador, winner of $34,775. Photo by Harold R. Piel (by permission of Roy Yates).

Ocala's bankers often accept horses as a form of collateral. O'Farrell also proved to be an innovator when he experienced difficulties getting the proper kinds of feed and hay for his horses. "He was an innovator in the use of lab analysis," Dr. Ronald Chak, resident veterinarian at Ocala Stud from 1965 to 1972, said in a 1983 interview that appeared in *The Florida Horse*, "He had consultants come in from the state lab in Kissimmee to tell us what was missing in the soil. He had Dr. [Jefferson] Flowers test blood, urine, and hair to determine the condition of his horses." O'Farrell discovered the idea of testing hair when he read about Napoleon, whose exhumed body was studied by analysis of his hair. O'Farrell kept careful track of the condition of his training horses, noting which broke down and which did not; he then altered the program to better the results. He maintained a staff of specialists in research and nutrition and used his data when he started developing his feed. The sweet feed (a mix of grains including molasses as a sweetener) used in the Ocala area today is the result of Joe O'Farrell's study and experiments.

The first official starter for Ocala Stud was Toong-Soong (Fly Away–Susan Dear, by Eight Thirty), who started in January 1957 and finished second. She would later become stakes placed. The first crop of horses foaled and raised by Ocala Stud (two-year-olds of 1958) included twelve winners of twenty-seven races, a record

Frank Yates in 1956 on Toong Soong who became the first official starter for Ocala Stud. She would later become stakes placed when she ran third in La Centinela Stakes in 1958. Horse in background is Alpha with rider A. C. Penny partially visible (by permission of Roy Yates).

Hot walking at Ocala Stud (by permission of Roy Yates).

that earned Ocala Stud the status of one of the best breeders of juveniles in the nation. By August 1958, Ocala Stud was already advertising one hundred four winners broken and trained at the farm, including eight stakes winners and eleven stakes-placed winners (counting both boarders and O'Farrell's own horses), an incredible start by anyone's standards.

Ocala Stud jumped to the top of the Florida lists, ranking as the largest and most successful in the state by 1959. During that year, with only two crops to race, the farm's homebreds earned $436,985, which landed Ocala Stud on the breeders' lists ahead of such established breeders as Leslie Combs II, Elmendorf Farm, F. W. Hooper, Maine Chance Farm, Jonabell Farm, J. W. Galbreath, and many other Kentucky greats. Nationally recognized by the media as the "General Motors of thoroughbred breeding," Ocala Stud bred or sold winners of over $1 million in its first three years of business. By 1960, the farm was tenth on the list of leading breeders but was the leading "commercial" breeder in the nation. This was a distinction Ocala Stud enjoyed, for it put the farm ahead of many Kentucky-based breeders who bred strictly for the sale ring. In 1960, Ocala Stud earned its ranking with 56 winners, 134 wins, 130 seconds, 118 thirds, and $655,075 in earnings. Florida was now a state to be reckoned with in the thoroughbred industry. But Joe was not done yet.

19

The Sale Where the Buyer Gets a Break

The arrival of Ocala Stud and Joe O'Farrell on the Florida breeding scene marked the advent of a new commercialism for the industry. O'Farrell could see the potential of the industry in a climate and on land such as Ocala offered, but he could also see the drawback of pedigrees that could not compete in the Keeneland and Saratoga yearling sales, at which the best blooded stock in the world was offered. Holding yearling sales in Florida would result in little profit for the same reason. The idea of holding public thoroughbred auctions in Florida was not an original one. O'Farrell had to come up with a better idea.

Humphrey S. Finney was president of the New York-based Fasig-Tipton Company; in the 1950s, it was the older of two thoroughbred sales companies in the country. The professional auction house had been established in 1898 and quickly had become a monopoly, thus leading to the introduction of the Keeneland sales and soon of the Florida sales companies. Most of the selling at that time was of the "mixed sales" format: broodmares, weanlings, yearlings, stallions, and stallion shares. The yearling sales held in the fall of the year in Lexington and Saratoga represented the cream of the crop; these sales paced the rise and fall of thoroughbred values, a trend which would continue up to the present. Fasig-Tipton was, therefore, an important part of the thoroughbred industry in the United States.

Its president was also an oft-quoted writer. In a 1943 article that Finney contributed to the *Blood Horse,* he predicted Florida's potential future as a great breeding area. "The post-war shortage of horses and surplus of ready cash led to some wonderful thoroughbred sales in Florida," he added. In a December 1958 article in *The Florida Horse,* entitled "Florida Reminiscences," Finney remembered the first public sale of thoroughbreds ever held in Florida. The sale was a quickly conceived idea conducted by several men who simply wanted to sell horses. It took place at Tropical Park "long before the war. Standing on a patrol judge's stand high in the air, I recall two tiny 2-year-olds not fourteen hands which we sold. They were so small, they ducked under the rope rail we used to outline the sales ring and everyone had a grand time cracking jokes about their appearances." Finney and Jimmy Ross sold stock of all ages that day.

Finney was with the U.S. Coast Guard's Seventh Naval District Mounted Beach Patrol and was stationed on the Florida beaches during the war. In 1944, he presided over sales in Del Ray, Fort Pierce, and St. Augustine and sold some 1,000 of the Coast Guard's patrol horses. He got to know some of the Florida breeders in the process and often attended the quarter-horse races held at Rosemere.

In February 1945, Robert Sterling Clark, a major racehorse owner at the time, retired from racing and shipped his entire stable from Belmont to Hialeah to sell at auction in the warmer climate. The horses were on the grounds showing for a week, while buyers came from Cuba, California, Canada, and New York. Fasig-Tipton would conduct the sale, its first sale in the Sunshine State. George Swinebroad wielded the gavel and Finney was the announcer. Bell-The-Cat, by Jamestown, was the sales topper at $20,000; the horse was purchased by Emil Schwartzhaupt. The Clark dispersal marked the beginning of an annual horses in training sale conducted by Fasig-Tipton at Hialeah. This sale would continue up to the present at Calder in association with the two-year-old sales. Also in his December 1958 article in *The Florida Horse*, Finney wrote, "A cold West wind had the horses really on their toes and what a sale that was! Just 80 percent above estimates and expectations. From that day to this, Florida has been the best spot in the U.S.A. to hold a sale of racehorses.

"The reason is obvious. Only in Florida does one find in one area the stables from New England, New York, New Jersey, Maryland, Michigan and Chicago. If you have a good horse to offer, you'll have a buyer."

On January 25 and 26, 1956, Fasig-Tipton held a special sale at Hialeah for Dickey Stables and several other consignors (A. H. Bowen, Frank L. de Paolo, W. Arnold Hangar, William L. McKnight, and the estate of Dorothy Palmer) who wanted a sale of racehorses that included two-year-olds. Because of William Leach's failing health, the Leaches had decided to sell their farm and disperse their livestock through this sale. The catalog listed fifteen head in the Dickey segment, of which ten were sold. King Hairan was entered in this sale but was scratched after he was sold privately.

Carl Rose had been one of the first breeders in the industry to be known as a "commercial" breeder, one who bred strictly to sell as opposed to racing his own stock. In April 1956 he gave a public explanation of his method of raising his horses to two-year-olds and taking them to the track broken, trained, and ready to race. "There are no thoroughbred yearling auctions in Florida, so we are forced to take our yearlings to the track to sell them. The auctions will come later," he predicted in an article by George Krehbiel that appeared on April 16, 1956, in the *Brooksville Sun*. Joe O'Farrell was quick to see the need and the potential, and he rushed in. In 1957, before Ocala Stud was even a year old, he rounded up a batch of two-year-olds and hosted the first two-year-old-in-training sale. Fasig-Tipton conducted the auction on February 25.

At this time within the state, some factionalism was evident. With the removal of the Florida Thoroughbred Breeders' Association from South Florida, animosity between the southern and Ocala-based breeders was growing. When O'Farrell decided to have his sale, his only support came from northern breeders, who at that time numbered only a handful. Carl Rose, Elmer Heubeck, and Douglas Stewart were the only other consignors. At the last minute, Rose scratched his entries for unknown reasons. The sale was held in Hialeah's walking ring on a balmy tropical night. The stately palms swayed in the breeze; strings of bright lights competed with the stars above; and the nervous, prancing thoroughbreds added their own magic to the event. A dark cloud blotted out some of the stars and threatened to ruin everything just as the sale was about to start, but Joe O'Farrell was not to be denied. After only a sprinkle, the rain passed on.

A total of thirty-seven head were sold, most of them Ocala Stud's. One of the biggest draws was a half sister of Needles, Blenomene. But the sales topper was a colt named Four Fives (King's Stride–Tea Deb, by Carrier Pigeon) consigned by Ocala Stud and sold to Mrs. H. B. Massey for $15,200. This colt was one of several to come out of that first sale and to go on to become a stakes winner. Another was Ragtime Cowboy (Rough'n Tumble–Softie, by Flares), who would go on to become a champion stakes winner over the hurdles. He was purchased for $12,000 from Ocala Stud by trainer Morris

Needles' half-sister Blenomene with Roy Yates at Ocala Stud in 1956 (by permission of Roy Yates).

Dixon for C. M. Kline. In a year in which the record price for a yearling at Saratoga was $87,000 and the record at Keeneland was $86,000, these prices for Florida-breds far exceeded all expectations. In all, the thirty-seven head grossed $171,500 and averaged $4,824. The Ocala Stud stock averaged $7,166.

After that resounding success, it was obvious that O'Farrell had stumbled onto an exciting new way to market the newest Florida product. Breeders were offering the potential buyer a shortcut by selling horses ready to run. Training rates on the farms were at least $8 a day back then. Just as they do today, the two-year-olds-in-training sales offered a very real savings to new owners in terms of money, time, and possible injuries avoided. Buyers were also given the chance to purchase a horse that looked like it could run, as opposed to gambling on breeding to get a racehorse. When discussion of the next sale came up, O'Farrell ran into a snag. Eugene Mori refused to allow the sale to be held at Hialeah Park. "If I let one breeder hold a sale here to get rid of his stock, every breeder is

Frank Yates up on Four Fives at Hialeah. He was the first two-year-old sales topper in 1957 and would become a stakes winner. He was consigned by Ocala Stud and sold to Mrs. H. B. Massey for $15,200 (by permission of Roy Yates).

going to want to do the same thing," Humphrey Finney, Jr., a bid spotter, remembered Mori saying. Mori assumed, not without reason, that it was really only Ocala Stud's stock going on the block.

In November 1957, O'Farrell, Rose, Heath, and Stewart organized the Florida Breeders' Sales Association. According to their own written policy, their primary function was to meet the need for an effective sales organization with more aggressive advertising and promotions. They hoped to develop and produce a better thoroughbred, promote expansion of thoroughbred breeding farms in Florida, improve racing conditions, develop better press coverage, and attract public interest. Two different classes of membership were set up: voting members at $500 plus $50 annual dues and associate members at $50 annual dues. There were six charter members of the Florida Breeders' Sales Association: Joseph O'Farrell was named president; Doug Stewart, vice-president; Bonnie Heath, vice-president; Karl Koontz, secretary-treasurer; Carl Rose, Elmo Shropshire, and Karl Koontz, board of directors. Only the first four were voting members. In 1958, Grant Dorland became a voting member. He was followed by George Cavanaugh and Bruce Campbell. No one ever joined as an associate member.

"It was all a sham," Finney explained. "Joe *did* just want to sell

Bruce Campbell on the right with famous Kentucky breeder Harry Isaacs, breeder of Intentionally. Photo by Turfotos (by permission of *The Florida Horse*).

his own horses and wanted to be able to do it at Hialeah. Later on, of course, when the sale really took off, then the others were coming in and it all looked like a wonderful idea." At first, only members of the Florida Breeders' Sales Association were permitted to consign to the sale. For the second sale (the first held under the auspices of the Florida Breeders' Sales Association), consignors included Heath, Rose, and Stewart; of the sixty head sold, forty were owned by Ocala Stud.

The sale was held on February 3, 1958, at the Hialeah Municipal Auditorium, several blocks north of the track on Palm Avenue. There was no pavilion at the track; the promoters remembered the threat of rain the previous year and wanted to be under cover just in case. The weather did indeed become a factor during the sale. Temperatures dropped suddenly, mocking the water-proof building. Buyers who had not thought to bring their topcoats to a Florida sale marched briskly about to keep warm instead of concentrating on buying two-year-olds. In spite of the weather, the sale was a success.

A number of horses from the previous year's sale had won stakes by this time. Leather Button, winner of the 1957 edition of the Arlington Futurity, had passed through the ring for a paltry $5,400.

The successes of Four Fives and Ragtime Cowboy also assured good attendance for the 1958 sale. One of the colts consigned to the 1958 sale, Cri de Guerre, was already a winner.

Bonnie Heath's Count Amore (Count Flame–Amore Mia, Sun Again) brought the top price of $30,000. A total of sixty head sold for $294,700, an average of $4,911. On the following day, the estate of Samuel D. Riddle sold as a Horses of Racing Age Sale (a sale not restricted to two-year-olds but including older racehorses as well).

Joe O'Farrell would later tell reporters in an article that appeared in the *Orlando Sentinel* on November 23, 1961, "We had to prove our horses. We proved they were sound and could stand training." O'Farrell had accomplished his goals; Ocala Stud's opportunities seemed limitless. By May 14, 1958, ten graduates of the 1958 sales had won races and several had been second; eight had been bred and sold by Ocala Stud. By December 1958, graduates from the first two sales had earned over $600,000. Of seventy Ocala Stud juveniles sold over these two years, 88.5 percent had started and 68 percent of those had won. They had earned over $500,000, averaging $8,559 per starter and $12,631 per winner, an astounding record for the time. Both Ocala Stud and the new juvenile sale format had arrived. "It is the only event of its kind in the country where breeders sell their homebreds trained and ready to run. The only time buyers have an opportunity to rival this, is in a dispersal sale of a racing stable which seldom comes along," the December 15, 1958, *Morning Telegraph* reported.

For the January 26, 1959, sale, a new 100-foot by 60-foot fireproof building was installed as a sales pavilion at the northeast corner of the Hialeah track through the generosity of Eugene Mori and Walter Donovan. Consignors now had increased to include Walter M. Pierce and George Cavanaugh. The annual Baby Show had been incorporated into the sales, and Bonnie Heath's Best in Show winner, a Fly Away colt, was the sales topper for 1959; he was purchased for $20,600. Joseph LaCroix was listed as the leading buyer at this sale. In January 1960, Finney remarked in a *Daily Racing Form* interview that breeders in Florida were making great strides in attempting to upgrade the quality of their mares and stallions. He added, "I doubt that this sale will ever get much larger in number of horses sold (fifty-six this year), but the quality of the consignments has risen markedly and the stock is winning races in open competition."

During the early years, stabling for the sales horses was in makeshift barns at Tropical and Gulfstream and with various trainers at Hialeah. There was little room in the regular barns for the racehorses. The result was confusion for buyers and sellers alike when they attempted to view or show horses prior to the sale. The first sales barn was built at Tropical Park in 1961. When it became necessary for the sales company members to pay for such improvements, the association was changed into a stock company and incorporated in 1962 under the name "Florida Breeders' Sales Company" (FBSC). When Carl Rose had to drop out due to failing health, his $500 membership was refunded; there were then only six stockholders.

Of fifty-six horses sold in 1960, only five failed to reach the starting gate by November 1961. The fifty-one starters won seventy races and an average of $8,121, compared with the national average of $2,493 for two-year-olds' earnings.

In January 1961, Joe O'Farrell said, "They claimed we were crazy. Maybe we were . . . but nobody holds that opinion now. We've come from nowhere to a position as the fourth largest thoroughbred sale in the United States." Saratoga, Keeneland, and Del Mar in California were the only sales that surpassed the FBSC sale, and they were the prime yearling sales. Florida still boasted the only two-year-old sales in the country.

Tommy Devine interviewed Ralph Retler, an eight-year veteran Fasig-Tipton auctioneer, for the January 26, 1961, *Miami News* at the same time as he interviewed O'Farrell. "The consignments offered elsewhere have fancier bloodlines, but in no case have the horses sold been more successful," he stated. "A higher percentage of stakes winners comes out of the Florida sale than any other auction in the United States."

Proof of growth became apparent in 1962 when, for the first time, the sale required two sessions. The sale had become a highlight of the winter racing season. The Florida Breeders' Sales Company and Fasig-Tipton agreed to share equally the costs of building an 850-seat pavilion at Hialeah. The 94-foot by 94-foot octagonal structure was the largest sales pavilion in the country when it went up.

By 1962, a number of horses were being left out of the selection process for the big two-year-old sale. Therefore Fasig-Tipton, which had been selling many of these excess horses in its Horses of Racing Age sale, decided to conduct an open two-year-old sale following the Florida Breeders' Sales Company select sale. It was also in 1962,

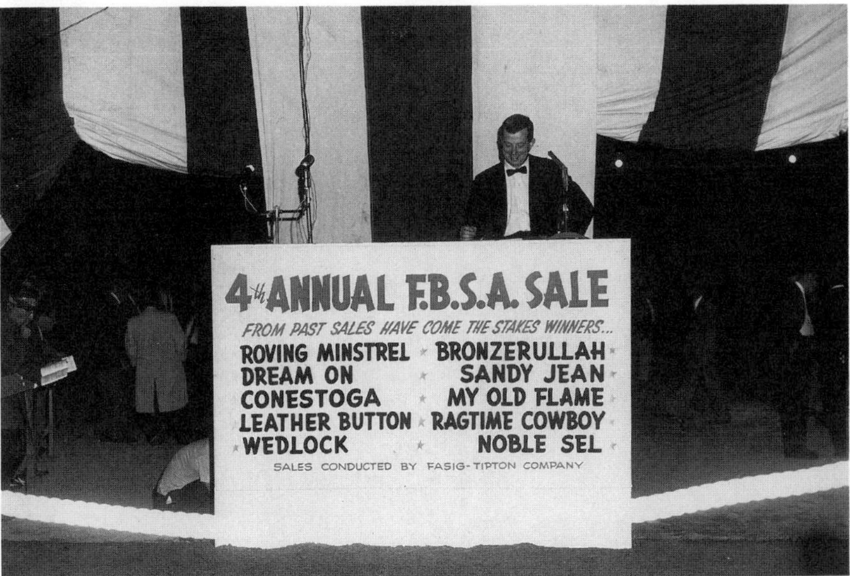

In 1961 a sign outside the "tent pavilion" advertises successful stakes horses sold out of the sale. Photo by Leo Frutkoff (by permission of *The Florida Horse*).

The bidding is hot and heavy inside the tent, 1962 (by permission of *The Florida Horse*).

on October 12, that the Florida Breeders' Sales Company held its first sale in Ocala, under a tent at Ocala Stud. The sale was soon to become an annual mixed event. The previous day, a farm tour was offered. The sale and the tour were the beginnings of the events that would grow to become "Ocala Week." Fasig-Tipton had nothing to do with these sales; instead, Tom O'Farrell was the auctioneer and Chuck Tilley, new editor of *The Florida Horse*, was the announcer. Sixty-seven mares, stallions, and yearlings sold for a gross of $210,950, an average of $3,148. The sales topper at $25,000 was a sixteen-year-old bay mare, Turkish Delight. She was by Count Fleet and in foal to Restless Wind.

This sale was a little slower to take hold, prompting O'Farrell to say that first year, "There's not as much money here as in the poorhouse!" It was a success, however, and the next year the sale was moved to the Southeastern Livestock Pavilion, where 116 head were cataloged. The next step was the conversion of an old cattle facility into the Doyle Conner Pavilion. In 1966, the Florida Thoroughbred Breeders' Association moved its annual elections to "Ocala Weekend," because so many members were in town then. This was also the first year of the annual Stallion Parade hosted by the Florida Thoroughbred Breeders' Association, which continues today as part of the Ocala Week festivities. By 1972, the Florida Breeders' Sales Company had eight voting members: Joseph LaCroix, Richard D. Irwin, Martin Anderson, Bruce Campbell, Grant Dorland, Louisa d'A. Carpenter, Jeri Stewart, and Ocala Stud.

One innovation started by the Florida Breeders' Sales Company would have a major impact on sales companies everywhere. Instead of assigning the best nights of a sale to special customers, as was the tradition, the FBSC chose a letter (which happened to be "K") the first year and cataloged the horses alphabetically for the whole sale by the names of the dams. Each year, the FBSC moved ahead a few letters, thereby assuring everyone an equal opportunity for a good position. This practice has now been adopted by most sales companies. In the early years, there was some flexibility, however, in that consignors were allowed to move their horses around within a single night. If they preferred to have their best horse sell first instead of late at night, where it might fall alphabetically, consignors could swap the best horse's position with that of their lesser horse, but only among their own horses and on the same night. Hence, the old sales catalogs occasionally showed dams

Joe O'Farrell showing off Ocala Stud stock to James Donn, Sr. and James Donn, Jr. in front of a new barn at Gulfstream Park. Photo by Turfotos (by permission of Gulfstream Park).

listed out of order. This practice stopped as the sale grew larger and the alphabetical scheme spread throughout the country.

Since promotion was a major aim of the company, it appeared logical to begin a magazine focusing on Florida-bred horses. Karl Koontz was around for that, too.

> When we [Ocala Stud] first came down here, we started putting out our own little farm newsletter in 1957 and 1958 and called it the *Ocala Stud Farm News*, then changed it to the *Ocala Stud Gazette* in 1959. I was the office manager for Ocala Stud, and we reported foals arriving and what was happening; it became quite popular in the area. Mr. Carl Rose, Bonnie Heath, Doug Stewart, Elmer Heubeck and a couple of others all thought it was a nice idea and decided to make it into a magazine.
>
> They wanted to call it the *Florida Thoroughbred* but right at that time another magazine came out with that name [published monthly out of North Miami; first issue, July 1957; Michael Abrams, editor]. It

lasted only two issues, but we were stuck with the name *The Florida Horse*.

The first issue of *The Florida Horse* came out in June 1958. A picture of Hubcap (Boodle–Rub-A-Dub, by Pensive) winning the Swift Stakes was on the cover. Hubcap, the second leading money-winning Florida-bred of 1957, was bred and raised by the brothers Frank, Robert, and Elliott Mackle; they were Miami contractors and raced under the name Elkcam Stable. Boodle (*Mahmoud–Boojiana, by Boojum) stood at their Elkcam Farm at Lake Placid. *The Florida Horse* began publication under the auspices of the Florida Breeders' Sales Company. O'Farrell was the president, Stewart and Heath were vice-presidents, and Koontz was both the secretary-treasurer and the editor of the magazine. The first issue listed the aims and purpose of the company, then proceeded to list the magazine's own aims: "The purpose of this magazine is to disseminate information of interest to Thoroughbred breeders, particularly in the state of Florida. . . . [Its business] will be conducted in an aggressive intelligent fashion and in a manner to bring credit upon the thoroughbred breeding interests in Florida."

The Florida Horse began as a bimonthly because the printer took nearly a month to print it. When Chuck Tilley became editor, he found a new printer and the magazine became a monthly. Covering the fledgling industry was not always an easy task, as Koontz recalled: "Back then there weren't too many Florida-breds, so the ones that were running well were big news. Our biggest problem came in an issue when we had to write our feature story about two horses who came in second! Indian Maid was beat a nose in the Beverly Handicap at Arlington Park and My Dear Girl was beat a neck in the Arlington Lassie Stakes in Chicago. Although they were seconds, it was still great news!"

In 1974, after the Florida Breeders' Sales Company had had a virtual monopoly on sales in Florida for sixteen years, Joe O'Farrell was again a part of a group that formed a rival sales company. The Ocala Breeders' Sales Company (OBS) became one of the largest mixed-sale companies in the world. It was not until 1984, when it bought out the Florida Breeders' Sales Company and became a monopoly itself, that the OBS began conducting two-year-old sales in South Florida.

Just before the merger of the two Florida-based companies, Fasig-Tipton split from the Florida Breeders' Sales Company and decided to conduct its own two-year-old sale at Calder Race

Ground breaking for the Ocala Breeders' Sales Company's pavilion in July 1974. Left to right: Bob Gaudio, George Onett, Joe O'Farrell, Doyle Conner (Florida Secretary of Agriculture), Roy Kennedy, and Governor Reuben Askew. Photo by Art Kunkel (by permission of the FTBA).

Course. The Ocala Breeders' Sales Company attempted to secure the Hialeah pavilion for its two-year-old sales, but Hialeah management was uncooperative. Beginning in 1986, the premium two-year-old sales traditionally held in South Florida and conducted by the Ocala Breeders' Sales Company were, like Fasig-Tipton's sale, held at Calder Race Course.

Although factionalism, discontent, and monopolistic practices have been problems for the thoroughbred industry over the years, there is no doubt that Florida is still the greatest place in the world to buy a ready-to-race two-year-old. The Florida-based two-year-old sales are recognized as market places for good value as opposed to Kentucky sales, where top-line pedigrees too often go for inflated prices. But Marion County's success required more than just Joe O'Farrell, the Florida Breeders' Sales Company, or *The Florida Horse*. It also needed good horses—and it had them.

20

Rough'n Tough Ladies

On December 29, 1958, the following excerpt appeared at the end of the *Daily Racing Form*'s Florida breeding column: "Just in Passing . . . Mr. and Mrs. Harold Genter of Minneapolis, Minnesota will be racing a two-year-old Florida-bred daughter of their former stakes winner Rough'n Tumble in 1959. The chestnut filly out of Iltis by War Relic, a half-sister to Is Proud, has been named My Dear Girl."

From the late 1950s to the early 1960s, the rest of the nation was very aware of the impact Florida-bred and -raised horses were making in the racing wars. There simply could be no faulting the way these horses ran: consistent, competitive, able to run with the best in the nation, and very speedy. When the first Florida-bred was foaled in 1936, Kentucky had already established superiority as a major breeding center for the past 100 years. From 1938 to 1958, the combined earnings of Florida-breds totaled $7,046,120. In that twenty-year period, only 645 Florida-breds were registered; their average earnings were $10,924.20, an astounding figure for the times.

Over 19,000 foals were registered with The Jockey Club in 1956 and 1957. Florida produced only 176 foals in those two years, yet of those two crops, there were ten two- and three-year-olds listed in the Experimental for 1959. The state ranked ninth in the nation in producing thoroughbreds, but fourth in producing stakes winners, behind only Kentucky, California, and Virginia. One racing wag was heard to say, "Florida can't raise all the horses, so they just raise the good ones."

Marion County in particular was rapidly becoming the solid center of Florida's breeding industry. The increasing number of stakes horses emerging from that county dominated the few Florida-bred races. In 1959, the first four spots in both the Florida Breeders' Stakes and the Florida Breeders' Futurity were taken by horses bred in Marion County. No one could deny the racing ability

Frances and Harold Genter. Photo by Turfotos (by permission of *The Florida Horse*).

of these horses, but still they were praised grudgingly. They were often said to be "outrunning their pedigrees," a phrase which would haunt Florida breeders for the next thirty years in their struggle to upgrade and improve the bloodlines of their stock. Even so, the Florida-bred was occasionally coveted. In a record transaction for Florida, Doug Stewart sold his eighty-six-day-old Needles colt to Mrs. Louisa d'A. Carpenter. She raced in the name of Springfield Stable and maintained a breeding farm by that name in Maryland. The record price for this weanling half brother to stakes winner Hoosier Honey was $15,000.

The arrival of Ocala Stud and the growth of the Florida marketplace, as well as the taunts of outsiders, stimulated Florida breeders to upgrade the quality of their horses' pedigrees. Serious efforts were made to get better mares and stallions into the state. Bonnie Heath was one of the first to attempt to bring good stallions to stand in the Sunshine State. He leased the well-bred Curandero (Brazado–Ciencia, by *Cohort) from the King Ranch for a season. He brought in Preakness winner Alsab (Good Goods–Winds Chant, by Wildair) to stand for $2,000, a stud fee second in the state only to Needles' $2,500 fee. Doug Stewart brought south the brilliant two-year-old race horse *Stella Aurata (=Arctic Star–=My Aid, by =Knight of the Garter). Carl Rose stood champion sprinter Sheila's Reward (Reaping Reward–Smart Sheila, by Jamestown).

During the 1959 season, King Hairan became the first good, retired Florida-bred to stand in Kentucky at Warner Jones's Hermitage Farm in Goshen. This $35,000, two-year-old purchase retired with total earnings of $237,837 and twelve wins. He brought Florida a great deal of honor because this rival state so coveted him.

Ocala Stud quickly entered the stallion station business. In 1960, the farm imported *Luminary II (=Fair Trial–=Luciebella, by Rodosto), the only other horse to stand for as much as $2,000. This stallion was the first proven sire to be imported from abroad to stand in Florida. He was a leading juvenile and sprint sire in England and Ireland before he came to the Sunshine State.

A few stallions had made enough impact on the breeding business to be recognized outside the state: *Samurai, Ariel Game, Noble Hero, and King's Stride. But the stallion that has gone down in history as Florida's foundation sire is Rough'n Tumble. This stallion, along with some "ladies" with whom his name is inevitably linked, has had more influence on establishing a "Florida bloodline" than any other horse. Everyone knows the two ladies: My Dear Girl and Mrs. Frances Genter.

Rough'n Tumble (Free For All–Roused, by *Bull Dog) was bred by Dr. Charles E. Hagyard, a Kentucky veterinarian. The bay colt was foaled March 23, 1948, at Greenridge Farm on Paris Pike near Lexington, Kentucky. "Rough," as he was later known at Ocala Stud, was from Free For All's first crop and became his first stakes winner. He was to become his sire's best offspring. The Genters entered racing in 1939 with the acquisition of a few racehorses who did little to make their name known. Rough'n Tumble was purchased privately for $3,400 for Harold and Frances Genter by their trainer, Melvin "Sunshine" Calvert. As a two-year-old in 1950, Rough'n Tumble debuted in a $7,000 claimer on June 20, at Arlington Park. He easily won by four and one-half lengths, assuring that he would never run in the claiming ranks again.

Rough'n Tumble's second start was in the Primer Stakes, where he broke the five-race win streak of King's Hope. Then in both the Futurity Trial and the Futurity, he finished third behind the great Battlefield. He added a pair of seconds in the Garden State Stakes in which he lost by a short head to Iswas; and the Remsen, in which he finished behind Repetoire. As a two-year-old, Rough'n Tumble was rated fifth highweight at 119 pounds at the Experimental Free Handicap. Not only was he the best horse the Genters had had to this point, he was his trainer's first stakes horse.

As a three-year-old, Rough'n Tumble's speed was further demonstrated when he won his greatest race, the Santa Anita Derby. In 1986, the great lady of racing, Mrs. Frances Genter, said, "Over the years I have been asked the same question by many people: 'What is the biggest thrill you ever had in racing?' It is really a difficult question to answer because I have been in the business a good many years and have had many thrills. Up until now I have always answered, 'Rough'n Tumble winning the Santa Anita Derby in 1951'." Not until the 1986 Breeders' Cup Series of races (when her homebred, Smile, won the Breeders' Cup Sprint, also at Santa Anita), could she think of a bigger thrill than her first big stakes victory with Rough'n Tumble. Because of his Santa Anita Derby win, handicappers and turf writers of the West Coast gave Rough'n Tumble the vote for the title Best Three-Year-Old of the 1951 Santa Anita meeting. He was now a primary candidate for the Kentucky Derby, but a recurring splint prevented him from starting in that race. He ended his three-year-old season as fifth highweight on the Experimental Free Handicap and fourth highweight on the Blood-Horse Handicap. Rough'n Tumble was retired with earnings of $120,480. The Genters attempted to find someone to stand him in Kentucky, but no one was interested. He did not have a bottom line to boast of, since he was the first major stakes winner for many generations on his distaff side.

The O'Farrell brothers heard about Rough'n Tumble, went to see

Rough'n Tumble in training at Santa Anita (by permission of Karl Koontz).

him in Kentucky, and promptly purchased an interest in him. They took him home to their Windy Hills Farm in Maryland to stand the 1954 season. He stood for $250, less if the breeder just could not afford the price. His first small crop arrived in 1955. When O'Farrell came to Ocala, he brought Rough'n Tumble with him to stand the 1956 season, then sent him back to Maryland for the 1957 breeding season. At the first two-year-old sale in 1957, the four Rough'n Tumble offspring offered for sale averaged $8,875. The first foal he ever sired, Tara Tella, sold in this lot to L. C. Rothermal. She became her sire's first winner on March 6, 1957, and would later become stakes placed. By the end of June 1957, with his first crop at the races, Rough'n Tumble stood eleventh by amount of earnings and eighth by number of wins on the nation's leading juvenile sire lists, with only four starters, three of them winners of seven races.

The first stakes winner ever bred by either of the O'Farrells was a hurdler from Rough'n Tumble's first crop, champion stakes winner over jumps Ragtime Cowboy. By 1959, Rough'n Tumble offspring averaged $10,133 at sales. In 1957, when he was fourth leading sire of two-year-olds in the nation, Ocala Stud purchased the stallion outright and brought him back to Florida, where he would remain for the rest of his life. The only way the Genters agreed to let him go, however, was with one stipulation: that they get first pick of his 1957 Florida-bred crop.

The Genters and trainer Calvert made several inspections of the 1957 weanlings. They had always raced colts, a fact that O'Farrell and Ocala Stud were banking on. But the final cut included two colts and one filly. The filly was out of a good race mare named Iltis. Iltis had won $19,425 in four years of racing and showed enough talent to be tried in stakes races. She was a half sister to the stakes winner Is Proud and had produced one good winner so far, Tiswar, by Prince Quest. The Genters liked Iltis's filly's conformation, breeding, and attitude, but they had never raced a filly before.

There was a final clincher: the filly had been born on Frances Genter's birthday: February 17. Finally, one evening at dinner, Harold Genter said, "You know, Sunshine, a man ought to have room for a little sentiment in this game. Let's take the filly." Genter, a retired manufacturer of electrical equipment from Minneapolis, had a fond habit of saying to his wife, "Now my dear girl." Hence, one great lady was named after another. The two colts not chosen were Conestoga out of Ruddy Belle by Errard, who became a stakes winner of over $100,000; and the stakes-placed Carollton out of the Vincentive mare Old Bess. The Genters knew a good horse when they saw one. And they were right about the filly, too.

Meanwhile, Rough'n Tumble was wasting no time making his mark. Wedlock, a full sister to Ragtime Cowboy and a $4,500 purchase in the 1958 sale, became the first registered Florida-bred filly to win a classic when she won the Kentucky Oaks in 1959. That particular race was of great interest to Florida breeders. Wedlock was one of three Florida-bred fillies entered in the split race. New Star by *Stella Aurata finished fourth to Wedlock, while Indian Maid ran second in her division. The three Florida-breds took 40 percent of the purses in the two divisions.

My Dear Girl began her racing career at the hands of trainer George Seabo, since Calvert was in Maryland at the time. She had a tough time learning her gate manners and acted so badly in her first start that she was unplaced. Her next start was in the Florida Breeders' Stakes on February 25, 1959, when she entered the gate at odds of 179 to 5. Most thought she had justified that lack of faith when she broke through the stall, banging jockey Manuel N. Gonzalez's head on the top of the gate. She was quickly taken in hand and reloaded. This time when she broke, she demonstrated some of her inherent talent by leading the cavalry charge of twenty-five two-year-olds for the three-furlong distance. She won by two lengths.

My Dear Girl was then sent north to Sunshine Calvert, who took her to Chicago with his string. He took plenty of time to retrain her in the gate, babied her with sugar, and stood her in the stalls for hours. "My Dear Girl was the first filly we ever raced," Frances Genter remembered well. "She always has had a special place in my heart, but she definitely had a mind of her own. She always wanted her own way. Yet I could walk into her stall, feed her carrots or sugar and she was as gentle and calm as could be. I fell completely in love with her."

Early in June, she dashed off to a five-length victory in the Miss Chicago Stakes, running the five and one-half furlongs in track-record time of 1:03 1/5. Calvert's next destination was the Arlington Lassie, but he wanted a prep race first. Every one he entered failed to fill. By the day of the big stakes, his charge had not run in fifty days and she was ready to buck her shins (shins are said to "buck" when the periosteum—the membrane of the connective tissue covering the shinbone—splits or becomes inflamed, usually because of stress). She finished a courageous second on sore legs.

Nineteen fifty-nine was very similar to 1956 when King Hairan, a great racehorse, ran in the shadow of the even greater Needles. This was the fate of the extremely talented Indian Maid, a three-year-old who would be overshadowed by the exploits of My Dear Girl. *The Florida Horse* reported My Dear Girl's second in the Arlington Lassie in the same issue in which it reported Indian Maid's (Rinaldo–Bold Verse, by Bold and Bad) second in the Beverly Handicap. Indian Maid had been the best two-year-old Florida-bred of 1958. She was sold to Mary Keim by breeder Elmer Heubeck. Indian Maid ran the fastest mile of any filly or mare in the history of Churchill Downs and shared with Honeys Gem the honor of running the fastest mile of any filly or mare in North America when she ran second in the Beverly Handicap. She also ran the fastest seven furlongs of any filly or mare at Churchill Downs when she won the Enchantment Purse. Keim was so pleased with her filly that she went back to Heubeck in 1960 and purchased Indian Maid's yearling half sister. By the end of 1959, Indian Maid, racing in the shadow of My Dear Girl, earned $71,495 for the season to

The charge of twenty-five juveniles in the Florida Breeders' Stakes stretches across Hialeah's Nursery Course. Photo by Jerry and Leo Frutkoff (by permission of *The Florida Horse*).

My Dear Girl surges to the fore with Niequest and Algenib in second and third spots. Photo by Jerry and Leo Frutkoff (by permission of *The Florida Horse*).

become only the second Florida-bred filly to earn over $100,000. She would eventually earn a bankroll of $303,457 and set a track record at Sportsman's Park.

But My Dear Girl did better. She came back from her rest to win a race at Aqueduct in the slop (usually during or right after a downpour; track conditions at such times are terrible) by five lengths, then won the mile and one-sixteenth Gardenia Stakes by five lengths. With the two-year-old filly championship plainly in view, the Genters took their star back to New York for the Frizette. For the first time in her life, My Dear Girl went off as the favorite. She earned her laurels with the grit and determination of a true champion. Coming from off the pace, she had to grind down Irish Jay in the long stretch run and got her nose in front just in time.

She ended 1959 with five wins and one second in seven starts. She was the leading money-winning Florida-bred two-year-old, with total earnings of $185,622. Florida had its second champion, this one bred, conceived, born, and raised in the Sunshine State. No one could doubt that sunshine ran in her veins.

By the end of 1959, Florida had its place in the sun. Florida breeders had produced the champion two-year-old filly, a top handicap mare, and Florida-breds had won or placed in thirty-four open stakes races. Florida had an unprecedented ten horses listed in the Experimental. Rough'n Tumble was fourth on the nation's leading sire list of juvenile winners. From three small crops to race, he now had sired the best hurdler of his year, Ragtime Cowboy; Kentucky Oaks winner Wedlock; top handicapper Yes You Will; and champion My Dear Girl. The dams had been low-quality mares; Iltis had been the best sent to Rough'n Tumble during those first three years. His $250 stud fee had gone up to $750 in 1958, and to $1,000 in 1959. In 1960, his stud fee made a dramatic leap to $5,000 to far surpass the next highest in the state, that of Needles.

Just prior to the announcement of My Dear Girl's championship, plans for syndication of the stallion were completed. There were thirty-two shares in the syndicate, and Ocala Stud retained seventeen. Members of the syndicate included Harold Genter, Barclay Stable, John McShain, Bieber-Jacobs Stable, Bruce Campbell, Bonnie Heath, George Cavanaugh, Sr., George Cavanaugh, Jr., Meadowbrook Farms, Inc., William Veeneman, John Hampshire, J. Sargeant Reynolds, and Ralph Wilson, Jr.

In July 1960, another Rough'n Tumble offspring, a colt named Conestoga, set a track record of 1:36 at Delaware Park when he fin-

Ocala Stud in 1960. Today much of the land is Paddock Park Shopping Mall and Central Florida Community College. Photos by Kunkel Aerial Surveys (by permission of *The Florida Horse*).

ished twelve lengths to the fore in a one-mile race. Conestoga had been sold through the Florida Breeders' Sales Association two-year-old sales for $14,000. In 1960, Yes You Will won Maryland's richest race, the John Campbell Handicap, and was hailed as the all-time great Maryland-bred. In 1961, Conestoga won the same race, the second Rough'n Tumble horse to do so. This feat prompted Snowden Carter of the *Maryland Horse* to write that Rough'n Tumble was the greatest horse to have stood in Maryland since *Challenger II; Carter ranked him above Native Dancer and Discovery.

A half sister of My Dear Girl went through the two-year-old sales with a $20,000 reserve. When an announcement was made about partial paralysis of her respiratory system, no bids were forthcoming, and she went back to Ocala Stud. Mrs. Bruce Campbell, who raced under her own stable name of Tally Ho Stable, then purchased the filly privately. My Old Flame became the first horse to capture both the Florida Breeders' Stakes and the Florida Breeders' Futurity. Unfortunately, she later died of a cerebral hemorrhage.

On March 14, 1960, another record was set when Mrs. Richard C. duPont purchased the bay suckling filly, a full sister to My Dear Girl, for $40,000. She was sold at the tender age of 192 hours. This was probably a record for a foal that age anywhere, not just in Florida.

Tumble Turbie, O'Calaway, Gunflint, and Flag Raiser would be later stakes horses sired by the prolific Rough'n Tumble. The somewhat shaky sire line of Questionnaire was probably saved by this little stallion in Florida. Not only his sons but his daughters and granddaughters as well would carry on the line with honor.

The potency of the Rough'n Tumble line was significant because the horse made his mark without the availability of exceptional mares. He sired thirty-five stakes performers by October 1969. He died at the age of twenty, in April 1968, at a time when his stud fee was at $10,000. Ocala Stud, which had already built Rough'n Tumble a large swimming pool because of a foundered condition he had fought for years, now built a cemetery dedicated to him. Around him would later be buried Iltis; Tarantella, dam of Swinging Mood; Noodle Soup; Roman Zephyr, dam of Roman Brother; and Ruddy Belle, dam of Conestoga. By the time of his death, Rough'n Tumble's progeny had earned over $5 million. In 1968, his son Dr. Fager would bring him his greatest honor yet: that colt was declared champion sprinter, champion grass horse, champion

Rough'n Tumble's swimming pool at Ocala Stud (by permission of *The Florida Horse*).

handicap horse and the second Florida-bred to become national Horse of the Year (Roman Brother was the first, in 1965). The polls had never before recorded so many championships for the same horse in the same year.

Meanwhile, the Genters, who had always had a home in South Florida and never owned a farm, became greatly influential in the Florida breeding program with their support, first of Ocala Stud, and then of Tartan Farms. The Genters retired My Dear Girl with total earnings of $209,739. My Dear Girl was to become the strongest foundation mare in Florida. By 1983, she had produced no less than thirteen winners from fifteen foals, eight of those stakes horses, four of them stakes producers. Her last foal, My Dear Lady, won the Princess Stakes at Ak-Sar-Ben on July 1, 1983, to become her dam's seventh stakes winner. My Dear Girl died on January 11, 1988.

My Dear Girl was the granddam of Dr. Carter, a major stakes winner who earned $890,562 in the 1980s. But her greatest gift to the industry was her second foal, In Reality. At the time of In

My Dear Girl with her Intentionally foal of 1964, In Reality. Photo by Allen Brewer (by permission of *The Florida Horse*).

Reality's stakes prowess, My Dear Girl was hailed as the youngest queen ever to produce a major stakes winner. (Because many producers who were successful runners did not produce their best horses until later in life, it had been thought that successful racing took energy out of a horse, energy that required a few years to be built back up. The theory is unproven.) In Reality was another Campbell Handicap winner; he amassed total earnings of $795,824 and won many of the best stakes in the country including the Sapling, the Florida Derby, the Jersey Derby, and the Metropolitan Handicap, among many others.

"When she produced In Reality and he won his first start, we were ecstatic. He too, gave us many thrills," Frances Genter said of another of her favorites. In Reality would later sire Smile, the winner of the Breeders' Cup Sprint and another national champion. In Reality's greatest influence was as a sire. By 1984, his $80,000 stud fee was the highest in the state. By 1986, he had been beaten in price only by his barn mate, Fappiano, an outrageously hot and successful sire out of a Dr. Fager mare.

Both these stallions have achieved worldwide recognition and respect, which occasionally escape Florida-based stallions. Those that do make it big in Florida generally are shipped to Kentucky, where they command higher fees and attract a better class of mare. In Reality and Fappiano were rarities: they remained in the state. (When the great Tartan Farms stable was dispersed in 1988, both of these stallions were finally shipped to Kentucky.)

Frances and Harold Genter are to be thanked. Together with Tartan Farms, they assured that the thoroughbred breeding industry in Florida would become so strong that the early dreams of Jimmy Bright and Carl Rose would become fulfilled. Their faith in the industry has provided some of the most thrilling moments in racing history.

21

The Ocala Era

In 1941, the *American Racing Manual* reported only two thoroughbred farms in Florida. In 1960, fifty-two were listed. The manual charts the undeniable growth: from 10 mares and 2 stallions to 600 mares and 56 stallions. In 1960, Florida ranked tenth in thoroughbred production but third in the number of stakes winners bred; only Kentucky and California produced more winners. In 1960, the Florida-bred earned an average of $8,161 compared to the national average of $2,493.

Events from 1957 through 1960 clinched the course of Marion County's future: the championship of Needles, the advent of Ocala Stud, the birth of the Florida-based sales company, and the second championship of My Dear Girl. Never again would the area be known as just the home of Silver Springs and the citrus industry. Marion County was a ninety-minute flight from Miami and easily reached by bus or train. Like the spokes of a wheel, all the main roads in Florida led to Ocala. The Chamber of Commerce joined in recognition of the economic importance of horse breeding and began to advertise the industry. In 1959, the Florida Department of Agriculture published a sixty-page booklet on the growth of thoroughbred racing and breeding in the state; it included a directory of all horse farms and listed owners, managers, and principal farm facilities.

In the southern end of the peninsula, the breeding industry was dying out. The Christophers abandoned breeding, sold their entire herd of thirty-three horses to William Scottie McDade of Maryland, and put their farm up for lease. The future of Pine Island was in doubt when Charlie O'Neil died. A few hardy souls, determined to keep the spirit alive, set up new farms: Louis Schlosser's, James D. Norris's, and Nancy N. Greene's farms were newcomers to South Florida in the early to mid-1950s. Schlosser Farm gave up in the late 1950s and was leased to Freeman Keyes of Reverie Knoll Farm. Keyes planned to continue the operation of his 700-acre farm in

Danville, Kentucky, but he shipped his yearlings to South Florida to be raised and trained. This trend continued up to the present; training in South Florida could still survive. But while the southern breeders had their successes, they did not have a chance against the "Kingdom of the Sun," as Marion County was being dubbed.

There the farms were going stronger than ever. In the summer of 1958, William M. Lynch, a Central Florida developer (he owned American Land Development Corporation of Orlando), purchased R. C. Howard's 172-acre farm off Route 200 and developed it into a showplace, Meadowbrook Farm. Joe Considine, past trainer of Oclirock, was the general farm manager and trainer. Lynch stood his stallion, The Hammer (*My Babu–*Dark Rose II, by =Nearco), and immediately purchased four well-bred yearlings at the summer sales in Kentucky. He did not plan to begin breeding actively, but his racehorses were to be handled by John Nerud of Hollywood, Florida, when they reached the track. The farm was beautifully outfitted with concrete block barns, a three-quarter-mile training track, dormitories, and farm kitchen. A year later, Lynch changed his mind about the whole affair.

In mid-1959, Meadowbrook Farm was sold to a syndicate out of Miami headed by C. H. Lovely. One of the most active members of the syndicate was Joseph LaCroix. Under the new ownership, Meadowbrook rapidly began making an impact by purchasing and bringing to the area some excellent brood mares. By 1960, the farm had grown to nearly 400 acres and stood the stallion Ambehaving (*Ambiorix–Dentifrice, by Reaping Reward). By March 1961, Bruno Ferrari, a Latrobe, Pennsylvania, construction magnate, acquired a one-third interest in Meadowbrook from the partnership of LaCroix and Israel Nasher. Later, LaCroix would become sole owner of the Meadowbrook Farm.

From the 1958 to 1959 season, the state received over $14.5 million in direct revenue from the racing industry. Universities and colleges in the state received over $600,000. Yet the state did not support thoroughbred breeding to the extent that other major breeding states did. There was no real breeders' awards program other than the $250 that the Florida State Racing Commission ruled the southern tracks had to pay for wins; $500 for stakes, and $100 at Sunshine Park. Attempts to pass a breeders' program through the legislature had so far failed. Thus, when gubernatorial candidate Farris Bryant came out in support of the industry, citing it as one of Florida's greatest tourist attractions, the state breeders backed his candidacy vigorously. In a speech given in April 1960

Joseph and Barbara LaCroix of Meadowbrook Farm. Photo by Turfotos (by permission of the FTBA).

Left to right: Grant Dorland of Roseland Farm, Farris Bryant advertising Floridabreds on his lapel, and Bonnie Heath. Photo by Leo Frutkoff (by permission of *The Florida Horse*).

and reported in the April/May 1960 issue of *The Florida Horse,* Bryant pointed out the many benefits the breeding industry had brought the state in terms of increased property values and national recognition:

> Its potential has been but scratched. Florida has yet to recognize the future this unique endeavor holds for the state and its progress has resulted almost entirely from the efforts of the enthusiastic individuals who have pioneered this new agricultural interest. This is an oversight we must certainly correct.
>
> Although the growth of thoroughbred breeding has been remarkable in Florida it would have progressed even further was it not for a problem which has virtually stopped expansion of thoroughbred breeding in our state. Other areas, including Puerto Rico and such states as Illinois, Maryland, California and Michigan, have devoted large purses to races limited to homebred horses, and breeding within those states has been encouraged as the result.
>
> While breeders in other states are extremely interested in Florida as a new area for investment in breeding farms, they have delayed immigration due to the comparatively small purses made available to Florida-breds by Florida tracks. Puerto-Rico-breds, as a comparison, now run for $1,250,000 annually while Florida-breds are eligible for less than $100,000 in purses and breeders' awards limited to them, even though these two areas are practically identical in number of animals produced.

Farris Bryant was elected in November 1960 with the breeders' support. Senate Bill 601, passed in the first legislative session, was a landmark bill for the Marion County breeders, who were now assured a proving ground for their stock. The bill implemented a preferred program: one race per day was to be written at each track at which Florida-breds were preferred as entries. The first Florida breeders' program became effective in May 1961.

"It was the best of its kind at the time," Karl Koontz remembered. "We didn't want closed races, we just wanted an opportunity to run. The program was so successful that other states—Maryland and Illinois—requested help in setting up similar programs." In 1963, the law was expanded to include breeders' awards that equaled 10 percent of the race purse. In 1977, it was further amended to include stallion awards and to increase the breeders' awards to 15 percent of the purse. Until June 4, 1980, the awards came off the top from a percentage of the track's handle. After that date, the awards were taken out of breakage and uncashed tickets, called "escheats." But back in 1961, when the law first passed, it could not have come at a better time because Florida was about to get its next national champion.

Jack Price, stocky and smiling, was known as a hustler. His reputation began when, as a boy, he worked as a "candy butcher," selling candy on the rails of the Cleveland train station. But it was not long before the lure of the racetrack attracted the gambler within him and he began walking hots, cooling out hot horses after exercise. To help make ends meet Price also worked as a Western Union messenger.

Later, he founded Winslow Manufacturing Company, a highly successful machine-tool company, which he eventually sold to his brothers. With the proceeds from the sale of Winslow, Price at last gave in totally to the passion that he had indulged only sporadically: horses.

In the early 1950s, he and his wife, Katherine, purchased a farm in Kirtland, Ohio, which they named after the street on which they had lived in Cleveland, Dorchester Farm. Here they bred a few mares while Jack learned the ropes and became a trainer. They boarded a few mares, including one named Joppy. When the board bill reached $150, her owner suggested that Price take the mare for another $150 since he could not pay his bill. Thus, the Prices acquired what was then a cheap mare.

In 1956, the Prices decided to give the sun a chance to help their young horses; they shipped their yearlings to Ocala Stud to be broken and trained. Two stakes horses came from that group: Stay Smoochie, who earned close to $100,000, and Bang Up, winner of the Dinner Stakes. Pleased with those successes, the Prices decided to escape the cold themselves. In 1957, they moved to Coral Gables and made arrangements to ship their mares to Ocala Stud to foal.

Three mares made up the first group sent south. They were shipped by the long route, through Maryland. At Country Life Farm outside of Baltimore, the mares were bred to a stallion named Saggy. Saggy had been a decent, fast racehorse. He had won several stakes including the Ral Parr, the Eastern Shore, the Wakefield, and the E. R. Bradley Memorial. He set a world record of :51 4/5 in the four and one-half furlong Aberdeen Stakes and established a new Gulfstream Park three-furlong mark of :34. His biggest claim to fame was that he was the only horse to beat Citation as a three-year-old; Citation started twenty times that year. But, like Onion (one of only a few horses to ever beat Secretariat), Saggy, doomed by his name, "got no respect." As a stud, the stallion was as mediocre as his breeding (although there was some good blood there: Equipoise, Gainsborough, Hyperion, and Blandford). Saggy produced only one filly of some account, Outer Space. But Price liked the horse's sprinting abilities and hoped only for a moderate runner that would earn a few dollars. Price made a deal to breed all three mares to the $500 stud for a package price of $1,200. Two of the resulting foals never won a race.

Joppy was the dam of the third foal. She was by Star Blen and as a racehorse had achieved a reputation of unruliness in the gate. Joppy was ruled off the track several times for refusing to break. Her pedigree was even less noteworthy than Saggy's. Price would later say, with a twinkle in his slanted eyes, that he had abided by the greatest rule of breeding: "Breed the best to the best." As he explained many times, "I bred the best that I had to the best I could afford."

Two years after Needles won the Derby, a small, brown horse was born on April 16, 1958, the day after income tax day. Carry Back was named for a tax loophole. Joe O'Farrell would later explain to reporters in an article by Jim Moorhead that appeared on November 19, 1961, in the *Ocala Star Banner:* "The Prices were losing so much money on their racehorses, they decided if this new one turned into a winner, they'd take the winnings and carry them back on their losses!" The son of Saggy and Joppy was so petite and slow to grow that as a yearling he was only thirteen hands high. When full grown, he was only 15.1 hands high and weighed less than 1,000 pounds. One day, when he was inspecting his yearlings in training at Ocala Stud, Price expressed disappointment in the dark brown colt. "He'll have to do a lot of growing if he's going to win any races," he was quoted—also in Moorhead's article of November 19, 1961.

O'Farrell agreed. "As a yearling," he would later tell reporters, "Carry Back showed a lot of determination. . . . He always showed a lot of aggressiveness and individualism. He was different. But I honestly didn't think he'd make a good race horse, much less a great one."

Joppy's first foal was Beautiful A.M., a two-year-old winner. Price was simply hoping for another winner from the mare's second foal. He never minced words about why he was in the racing business: to make money. Price thought that the small colt's only shot to give him some return on his investment would be to get Carry

Jack Price and Carry Back (by permission of Jack Price).

Carry Back in training (by permission of Jack Price).

Back out early and run him a lot. Price therefore decided to start him as an early two-year-old. On November 21, 1959, Carry Back and another yearling, Could Mean Luck, arrived at Tropical Park. It was against the track's rules to stable yearlings there since no two-year-old races would be run until after January, so Price smuggled Carry Back in using another horse's name.

About this time, Price asked O'Farrell's advice about paying $600 to nominate the colt to a stakes race. O'Farrell would often relate the story while chuckling at himself. "Save your money," was his advice. Luckily, Price decided to take a chance anyway. Carry Back debuted on January 29, 1960. He finished tenth after a bad break from the gate, leaving the Prices with the nightmarish thought that he had inherited his mother's racing genes. But Carry Back won his second start, and for a few more starts, he swung from good to mediocre and back again. But occasionally, he flashed brilliance. In his second win, an allowance at Gulfstream, Carry Back reduced the track record for five furlongs by one full second.

That sort of demonstration earned him a trip to New York, where he promptly won the Cowdin Stakes over Harbor View's Roving Minstrel and Bronzerullah, both Ocala Stud-bred and -trained graduates. Two weeks later Carry Back again hung in the gate in the Champagne Stakes, giving Roving Minstrel his chance for the stakes win. Two weeks later, Carry Back breezed home in front in the world's richest race, the $288,000 Garden State Stakes. The Remsen was added to his victories, and first race callers and then the media, specifically the *Ocala Star Banner* on January 21, 1961, began talking about "the little brown colt from the wrong side of the tracks." Carry Back ended his two-year-old season with an incredible record of twenty-one starts, five wins, four seconds, and four thirds. With total earnings of $286,299, he was now the leading money-winning two-year-old in Florida history.

At this point, Carry Back's racing style was set. He always broke from the back of the pack and appeared to have little shot at ever catching the front-runners. He then would shift into high gear and roar past the stands. Time after time, he provided heart-stopping thrills by accomplishing the impossible. Even the supposedly unperturbable Price was heard to say excitedly one day, "Did you see him in the stretch? He looks like he's mad at everything in front of him, like he's supposed to be in front . . . like he had every cent he owned on the race."

Carry Back, Bronzerullah, and Roving Minstrel helped Florida gain solid prestige on the national level. In 1958, 277 foals were born in Florida, 2,934 in Kentucky and 1,560 in California. In spite of the overwhelming odds against them, there were no fewer than five Florida-breds among the 128 from that crop listed in the 1960 Experimental Free Handicap for two-year-olds. Hail to Reason was the top two-year-old, followed by Carry Back, with Louis Wolfson's Roving Minstrel in fifth place. But the nation had not heard the last from the plucky, little, dark brown colt with the long tail.

22

Carry Back, The People's Choice

In his first start as a three-year-old, Carry Back met Fred Hooper's Crozier for the first time. Long before Affirmed and Alydar were a gleam in their grandfathers' eyes, the duels between Carry Back and Crozier gave racing fans unsurpassed thrills. But the Aqueduct Handicap was one of only two times Crozier would get his short nose ahead of Carry Back at the finish line. He finished second; Carry Back was in fourth place.

The Everglades was the first of a long string of spectacular victories. Consistently, Crozier would be out front flying while Carry Back would trail, appearing to be too far back to be a contender; then as if he had sprouted wings, down the homestretch he would come, to get his nose barely up in front of Crozier's. Everyone, except Fred Hooper, loved the show. Carry Back became known as "the people's choice." The little brown colt with the long tail was the epitome of the rags-to-riches story. Although he may have been the people's choice, he drove his handlers crazy. Unlike his predecessor, Needles, this little colt could not stand still. He was constantly looking for something to do, and biting was a favorite pastime. His grooms hated giving him a bath; they often took one with him.

Carry Back became only the second Florida-bred to win the next two prestigious races. In the Flamingo, Carry Back defeated Crozier by a head. In the Florida Derby, during a cloudburst, Crozier swerved suddenly, nearly putting Carry Back out of contention, but the game little colt came on a second time and edged his nose across the wire first. Llangollen's Game broke down in that grueling race.

Two days after the Florida Derby, Joppy was killed in a paddock accident. She left behind a yearling and a weanling, both by Eds Day (Bull Lea–Still Blue, by Blue Larkspur), a stallion Price owned that stood at Ocala Stud. In typical laconic fashion, Price covered his pain with practicality. "Better her than Carry Back," he told one reporter.

In his New York debut, Carry Back lost narrowly in the Wood

Presentation of trophy for Carry Back's win in the Flamingo Stakes. Left to right: Eugene Mori, Sr., Johnny Sellers, Jack Price, Katherine Price, and Walter Donovan. Photo by Leo Frutkoff (by permission of *The Florida Horse*).

Memorial to Leonard Sasso's Globemaster, a yearling purchased at the Saratoga yearling sales for a then-record price of $80,000. By Kentucky Derby time, Carry Back was firmly ensconced as the favorite by the betting public. A special train carried 175 people from Marion County, Florida, to Churchill Downs to see the Sunshine State's second starter in the Run for the Roses. Bryan Field, popular race caller for the Kentucky Derby, would forever remember his famous words as the 1961 field left the gate. No one would ever let him forget. At the break, Carry Back was in eleventh position, Crozier in third. "Carry Back is too far back to make it . . . he can't unless he hurries." Field announced hopelessly. Field would soon learn what jockey Braulio Baeza would later state, "You never think you have any race won as long as Carry Back is behind you."

Carry Back obligingly hurried, with a stretch run even more impressive than Needles' run because he had even more ground to make up. Relentlessly, he pursued Fred Hooper's chance for a second Kentucky Derby win. With all the grit of a hero, he pounded the dirt and seemed to cover with each stride twice as much ground as did the other horses. Once again, Crozier and the other competitors were no match. Carry Back pulled ahead by an easy—for him—

Carry Back at Dorchester Farm in 1979 (photo by Kerry Heubeck).

three-quarters of a length. Florida became the only state ever to have two winners for two starters in the Kentucky Derby.

Back home, a new tradition pealed the news to Ocala all through the night. A 700-pound, brass-clappered bell, taken off the recently decommissioned battleship the USS *Kentucky*, had just been hung from a tower at Ocala Stud the day before. It swung over a one-ton chunk of symbolic limestone. Nancy O'Farrell began ringing the bell when Carry Back crossed the finish line, thus starting a tradition that would last for years. Every time a Florida-bred crossed the finish line first in a stakes race, the bell was rung. This tradition formed the basis for an award that would be established in 1984. To honor the sales horse of the year, the Florida Thoroughbred Breeders' Association and *The Florida Horse* commissioned a statuette of the bell; it was to be given to the owners of the best performing two-year-old sold through the juvenile sales in Florida for the year.

Carry Back then won the Preakness, his fourth $100,000 race in a row. In that race, Globemaster, a familiar rival, set the pace for the $700 colt. Katherine Price's blue and white silks became the first to ride a Florida-bred to victory in the second leg of the Triple Crown series. By winning the Preakness, Carry Back moved into thirteenth position on the all-time earnings list. His victory made

Joe O'Farrell stands beneath the bell at Ocala Stud which was rung whenever a Florida-bred won a stakes race. Beneath it is a symbolic chunk of limestone (by permission of *The Florida Horse*).

Florida only the fourth state to produce a winner of that race; only Kentucky, Maryland, and Virginia had produced horses that came home first in earlier years.

Turf writer Joe Kolb of the *Ft. Lauderdale News* described Carry Back on June 2, 1961: "Carry Back isn't exceptionally fast, but somehow he manages to get the job done with a whirlwind finish. . . . Carry Back is a router, a colt that lags behind while the sprinters battle for the lead. But in the final quarter mile, Carry Back appears to be assisted by a jet." Charles Hatton wrote in the *American Racing Manual*, "Carry Back had color, character, personal dignity and honor." As the Kentucky Derby continued to elude him for the next twenty-five years, Fred Hooper would reminisce how much money Crozier could have made if only Carry Back had been born in a different year.

Florida's hopes were riding on the little brown colt in the Belmont, the state's first shot to win the Triple Crown. It was not to be. He injured an ankle in that race and finished a disappointing seventh. But Carry Back was not yet through for the year. It was common knowledge that Jack Price wanted his charge to earn $1 million. Following a two-month layoff, Carry Back came back to win an allowance, then promptly beat Sherluck, winner of the Belmont, in the Jerome Handicap, clinching his championship status for the year. Now Carry Back was seventh on the all-time earnings list. He fell into line right behind the big boys: Round Table, Nashua, Citation, Swoon's Son, Stymie—and with earnings of $851,648, he was just a few dollars ahead of Swaps. He was the richest horse still racing when he was declared the three-year-old champion of 1961.

The fallout was contagious. Carry Back made certain that the boom Needles had started did not slacken. In 1956, about $2 million worth of property in Florida was devoted to the raising of horses; by 1961, land devoted to the raising of thoroughbreds had increased, in value as well as volume, to about $15 million. When the price of the horses was also counted, the industry was worth $35 million. Ocala Stud was America's leading commercial breeder for 1960, with $655,075 in earnings. In 1961, the farm handled 400 to 450 horses, including 300 boarders for seventy-five owners, and broke 166 yearlings. At the height of the training season, Ocala Stud had 133 employees.

Just after Carry Back won the Derby in May, six new breeding farms were purchased in quick succession. John Hay Whitney, owner and publisher of the New York *Herald Tribune*, purchased 266 acres. Liz Tippet (Whitney's former wife) of Llangollen Farm—one of the best-known names in thoroughbred breeding and racing—leased acreage from Leeward Farms on Route 200 and shipped four stallions, twenty-five mares, and twenty weanlings from her Virginia home to the Florida station. Harry Isaacs and Mrs. Robert Bardwell established their new Wolf Run Farm fifteen miles northwest of Ocala after a beltway bisected their Lexington, Kentucky, property. Together they had been responsible for breeding many good stakes horses, including Intentionally, who would later figure prominently in Florida breeding. Louis Wolfson, owner of Roving Minstrel, bought 575 acres (which rapidly grew to 1,500 acres) called Harbor View Farm, a name that would lead the breeders' lists in 1970. He was responsible for the racing of Raise a Native, Exclusive Native, and Roman Brother (who was soon to be a Florida champion). Robert Marks, former owner of a Madison Avenue advertising and public relations firm, first bought 509 acres west of Ocala at 50¢ an acre in 1951. In 1961, he finally turned the acreage into Robin's Nest Farm. To this showplace farm he attracted the stallions *Noholme II, Bold Reason, and Ridan, all destined to

A stallion parade in the 1960s held at the Golden Hills Country Club (by permission of *The Florida Horse*).

become important stallions on a national level. The farm produced numerous stakes winners, including future champion Shecky Greene. (Robin's Nest Farm would later become Kinsman Farm and Double Diamond Farm.) Joe Kolb, sports editor of the *Ft. Lauderdale News*, wrote in a January 1, 1962, article: "Thoroughbred breeding farms in Marion County no longer are operated by eccentrics."

Carry Back's influence went beyond Florida. Saggy, back in Maryland, was sold to a syndicate with thirty-two shares priced at $5,000 each, thus placing a $160,000 value on Stanley Sagner's $4,200 yearling purchase. He was moved to stand at Larry McPhail's Glenangus Farm in Maryland. Johnny Sellers, the leading rider in 1961 with 328 winners, was Carry Back's regular rider. Crozier, who might have become a millionaire himself but for Carry Back, retired in 1963 with earnings of $641,733. He, too, would figure prominently in Florida pedigrees after he retired to Hooper Farm.

In South Florida, Florida-breds had finally earned enough respect from track managers that on January 14, 1962, Pat Farrell, field secretary for the Florida Thoroughbred Breeders' Association at

Tropical Park, began to brand programs with a circled "F" to designate Florida-breds. These were the first programs of any state to do so; other states soon copied this practice.

Not only physical manifestations but mental attitudes as well, began to change. Suddenly, Florida was a thoroughbred force capable of inciting fear, resentment, and admiration. With the outspoken support of Joe O'Farrell, Florida could develop class horses regardless of pedigree. O'Farrell was quoted in many articles, one of which was by Bob Balfe in the *Palm Beach Times* on June 2, 1961. O'Farrell said: "Breeding is helped best by environment. And the best kind of environment found anywhere is found in Florida's green grass country with its magical sunshine, healthy limestone soil and water, protective shade trees, muscle-building topography and year-round mild climate." To further incite war cries among the blue bloods he added, "Sociologists long ago proved the strong influence of environment in raising children, so why should it be any different in animals?" Following an upset victory by yet another "ill-bred" Florida-bred, another observer remarked, in an article that appeared on May 15, 1961, in the *Cocoa Tribune*, "It sure isn't the blood, so it must be the soil!"

The Kentucky Thoroughbred Breeders' Association was chartered in June 1961 to promote Kentucky's thoroughbred industry. Columnist Bud Wallace of the *Lexington Herald* and the *Thoroughbred Record* explained it this way to Paul Ferguson of the *Orlando Sentinel* on June 20, 1961: "It is simply a matter of self-preservation. Florida, Maryland, Virginia and California have made such inroads into the breeding picture that we have got to start promoting the Kentucky-bred thoroughbred." He cited the occurrence of Ocala Stud Farms near the top of the nation's breeding lists, the first non-Kentucky farm in history to rise so high.

Another response to the seeming defensiveness of Kentuckians appeared in the Louisville *Courier Journal* on June 1, 1961. Earl Ruby noted that Kentucky had discovered that Florida had surpassed the West Coast in rate of increase of farms, horses, and acreage. He further pointed out that while Kentucky-bred horses had a 65 percent conception rate, the warm climate of Florida tended to produce a 75 percent rate, which could mean a difference of $20,000 a year to a breeder.

Some of the response was pure admiration. Correspondent Bob Horwood, writing from Bowie, Maryland, answered this question: If he could go to any stud with a fee of $1,000 or less, who would he pick? "Send her to any stud you can for that fee who is standing in Ocala, Florida," was his answer. "I don't know whether it's a question of climate . . . or the good limestone soil in that area, but it seems that you have a good chance of getting a stakes winner, or at least a decent sort of horse, by breeding to almost any Central Florida stud."

Meanwhile, Carry Back continued to do his part. "Buster," as groom Matt Reddy called Carry Back, was only the second horse to be given an honorary membership in the Marion County Chamber of Commerce. On "Carry Back Day" he was given a special blanket labeled "Carry Back, From the Kingdom of the Sun, Marion County, Florida." He was also presented with a feed pail and a key to the city.

By the end of 1961, Price had turned down offers of over $1 million for his homebred. But the "carrybacks" on his income taxes were no longer working, and because of the great demands by the IRS on Carry Back's earnings, Price was forced to consider syndication. He even went so far as to scratch his horse from the Roamer because "he would just be running for the collector of internal revenue anyway." With Carry Back's credentials in hand, Price went proudly to the Kentucky hardboots to offer his prize. He was rejected and insulted by the bluegrass horsemen; there was no blue blood in Carry Back's pedigree. Price, well-known for his quick comebacks, both humorous and otherwise, quickly alienated himself from the traditionalists in the bluegrass. Insulted and angry, by February 1962 he finally struck a deal with young Tom Gentry. Carry Back would stand at the two-year-old Tom Gentry Farm in Lexington. Thirty-three shares were offered at $35,000 each, valuing the son of Saggy at $1,225,000, one of the highest syndication prices to date for a stallion. But by March, the deal had fallen through. Potential buyers were warned off the stallion by their bluegrass advisors, and the shares were not selling. But while the hardboots may have blackballed Carry Back's stud career, the people still loved him. The filmmakers knew a winner when they saw one. Dick Powell's Four Star Productions began a movie about Carry Back; the script was written by Academy Award winner Douglas Morrow.

As a four-year-old, Carry Back had it a little tougher. He went up against champion sprinter Intentionally in his first start back. First in the Palm Beach, then in the Seminole, Intentionally, trained by John Nerud and owned by Tartan Farm, narrowly beat Carry Back.

Jack Price and Chuck Tilley, editor of *The Florida Horse*. Photo by Mason, Inc. (by permission of the FTBA).

But he was not dishonored in his losses. Intentionally held the world record for a mile with Swaps. Following the Seminole, Intentionally retired to become the second most influential horse (in terms of offspring) to stand in Florida after Rough'n Tumble. He would later sire Florida's greatest sire to date, In Reality, when mated to My Dear Girl.

After three seconds and two third-place finishes, Price, hoping for a change, switched jockeys, fired Sellers, and hired Manuel Ycaza. Finally, Carry Back won the Marriage Purse, only an allowance race, but the win put him in fifth spot and ahead of Stymie on the all-time earnings list. Then, with his old style, on May 30, 1962, with Johnny Rotz up, Carry Back won the Metropolitan, defeating two-time Horse of the Year Kelso, and equaling the track record to become Florida's first racehorse to earn $1 million. Now Carry Back was behind only Round Table, Nashua, and Citation for most earnings ever. Because of an outstanding victory in the Whitney in which Carry Back carried 130 pounds to Crozier's 111, Price shipped his charge to France for a chance at

Carry Back in 1980 at Dorchester Farm. Photo by Louise Reinagel (by permission of Louise Reinagel).

the Prix de l' Arc de Triomphe. But Carry Back disappointed there, finishing eleventh over the unfamiliar turf course.

Carry Back retired at the end of his four-year-old season because Price thought he was tired of racing. He retired perfectly sound with thirteen stakes wins and eighteen stakes places. He serviced thirty mares in 1963 while his owner kept him in light training at Ocala Stud. From that first crop came sixteen foals, of which twelve were starters, and two were stakes winners. In 1963, following his breeding season, he was sent back to the races. On August 17, he finished second in the Buckeye Handicap and later finished third in the United Nations Handicap. He finished unplaced in his next two starts and was reported to be lame. Price was criticized for subjecting his horse to the racing wars again. But Carry Back vindicated his owner's faith by defeating Mongo in the Trenton Handicap. At that point, Price really called it quits. The people's choice retired with total earnings of $1,241,165 and a record of sixty-one starts, twenty-one wins, eleven seconds, and eleven thirds.

From the earnings, Price built his Dorchester Equine Preparatory

School, sometimes referred to as the "Princeton of the South." Begun in 1965 on 120 acres of land, this farm would train some sixty head a year, taking weanlings through all their basic schooling and conditioning. The colts' barn was called Carry Back Hall, the fillies' was Regret Hall, and the brood mare barn was Expectation Hall.

Carry Back died on March 24, 1983, only two weeks before a special "Needles and Carry Back Day" scheduled by the Florida Thoroughbred Breeders' Association to honor "the two oldest living Derby horses," as the program read. During the ceremonies, which featured clips of Carry Back's races and brought goose bumps to the arms of modern-day breeders, Jack Price said emotionally, "He was our son, a member of our family. He introduced us to the top people in the racing industry including the top sports writers of the era. They became friends of ours and we would never have gotten to know them if not for Carry Back. He was a terrific competitor and taught us the meaning of gameness. He might have been a great horse if I had managed his racing and stud career a little better." On May 5, 1985, Carry Back's ashes were buried at the new Kentucky Derby Museum in Louisville under a headstone that reads "The People's Choice."

23

Lexington of the South

In November 1960, the same month in which Farris Bryant was elected governor, a new farm started up. It was destined to have an impact on the Florida breeding industry internationally at least as much as had Ocala Stud. William L. McKnight purchased 320 acres of Bonnie Heath's farm, and Tartan Farms was born.

McKnight, chairperson of the board of Minnesota Mining and Manufacturing (3M), was one of America's wealthiest persons and a leading industrialist. Three M's new product, Scotch Tape, was becoming very popular. The tartan on the dispenser was the plaid of the McKnight clan and would become the racing silks of Tartan Stables. McKnight enjoyed dabbling in horses. In 1957, when his office in St. Paul, Minnesota, collected $6,500 to buy something for his seventieth birthday present, a company executive, Mr. Weyand, went shopping for a horse. The best he could find for the money was a three-year-old filly by Better Self out of Tilly Rose by Bull Brier. The filly had earnings of only $5,115, all she would ever make. By the time McKnight received her, she had two broken knees. She was named Aspidistra. One of Aspidistra's future foals would be named Weyand in appreciation, but in 1957 the only appreciation forthcoming was for a thoughtful gift. No one knew then what she would produce.

McKnight raced in a small way with a partner, W. C. Webster, who was manager of McKnight's Miami interests. McKnight later bought Webster out and raced strictly in the name of Tartan Stables. In 1959, he met the man who would change his direction and that of the Florida breeding program.

McKnight won the 1958 edition of the $75,000 Hialeah Turf Cup with his Chilean-bred stallion *Meeting (=Brick–=Eos, by =Strip the Willow). Everett Clay, publicity director for Hialeah, informed a trainer, John Nerud, that he thought McKnight was ready to get into thoroughbreds in a big way. At first Nerud wasn't interested. In an interview he said, "I told Ev I didn't need anybody who didn't have any money," Nerud recalled. "I already had Ralph Lowe and Joseph Roebling whose cable company built the Brooklyn Bridge. I told Ralph Lowe about it and Ralph Lowe called me back in about an hour and laughed and said, 'Now you *are* working on a bankroll,' so I took him!"

Nerud met with McKnight in 1959; they were to form what was to become one of the world's greatest breeding farms and racing stables. At the time John Nerud was the renowned trainer of *Gallant Man. The story is a famous one. Ralph Lowe, owner of *Gallant Man, had a dream the night before the Derby that jockey John Choquette misjudged the finish line and pulled *Gallant Man up too soon. Nerud in particular got a good laugh over that one, since he had already replaced Choquette with the fresh young William Shoemaker. "So you have nothing to worry about," he told the owner.

In the 1957 Kentucky Derby, *Gallant Man was leading when young Shoemaker misjudged the finish line and stood up in the irons too soon, allowing Iron Liege to win by a nose. Nerud, forty-four years old at the time, cried like a baby, as did several others. He later insisted that this mishap was not the cause of his refusal to nominate his horses to the Kentucky Derby. Instead, he declared that the world produces very few Kentucky Derby potentials and that most owners are kidding themselves to nominate, a premise that is hard to fault.

Nerud was born in Minatare, Nebraska, in 1913 and was raised on a ranch, one of nine children. At the age of thirteen, he left home to ride the rodeo circuit, earning $3 a head for riding Brahman bulls. He upgraded when he learned he could earn $5 for riding horses as a jockey on the bush tracks in Wyoming, North and South Dakota, Nebraska, and Montana. He was soon begging jobs at Jefferson Park, already hungry for the track and the horses. By eighteen, he was an owner and trainer with a license in Nebraska. His first horse was a foal born in 1930 named Dr. Coogle (Actuary–Catonia, by Rock View). He traded a $40 draft mare for the horse and won many races with him at the bush tracks.

After the war, in which he served as a U.S. Navy signaler, he moved to Florida and went to work at Hialeah for Woolford Farms, for which he trained the sprint champion Delegate. By 1952, Nerud was on his own, with a string of horses in New England. He also worked at whatever job he could find on the tracks, including jockey's agent. A horse named Switch On came into his charge, and

John Nerud (by permission of *The Florida Horse*).

once again he was riding high with victories in the Tropical Inaugural, the Palm Beach Handicap, and the McLennan. That last victory brought him his Texas client, Ralph Lowe. One of some twelve to fourteen horses Lowe sent him was a $25,000 Aga Khan cull with bad ankles. The little colt earned a mediocre $7,075 as a two-year-old. That was in 1956.

In 1957, the same well-bred, imported colt, *Gallant Man, equaled the Tropical Park record of six furlongs in 1:09 2/5. When he won the Hibiscus Stakes, beating the winter book Derby favorite General Duke, Nerud knew he was on his way again. In spite of the hard-luck Derby, *Gallant Man was a remarkable racehorse. When he won the Belmont, he set a track record that would not be broken until Secretariat came along in 1973. In later years, he would also become fifth leading sire and fifth leading brood mare sire in North America.

In 1959, Nerud began working for McKnight. "I told him then that the money was in breeding horses," Nerud explained. "He asked me where he should buy a farm and I told him there were only two places to raise thoroughbreds, Kentucky and Florida. He said his home was in Florida now [Miami] so he told me to buy him a farm here." Nerud later admitted,"Actually, I was hoping that he would say Kentucky because that's where all the good stallions were. But I've never regretted being in Florida." Not a man to act on impulse, McKnight first hired a lawyer and an accountant, who traveled the United States for one year and compiled a dossier on Nerud "two and a half inches thick," Nerud said.

In November 1960, Nerud purchased some of the Heath acreage, on which were already located two twenty-four-stall training barns and a three-quarter-mile track with a starting gate and a lake in the center. Nerud was made president of Tartan Farm Corporation; he owned one-quarter of the business, which included all the racing stock; Tartan Stables; breeding interests; and the farm, Tartan Farms. Nerud's first move was to locate the Irish trainer working at Thistle Downs, John Hartigan, and invite him to manage the farm. Hartigan and his wife, "Sandy," the former Mildred Riddle, accepted the offer and would later become well-known with their own farm, Cashel Stud.

The first improvements to the perimeter-fenced property of the new Tartan Farms were four more miles of fencing and the construction of a brood mare barn. This $50,000, twenty-four-stall barn with laboratory was considered the most modern and elabo-

The Tartan Farm management team (left to right): John Hartigan, John Nerud, Charlotte Nerud, and Sandy Hartigan. Photo by Turfotos (by permission of *The Florida Horse.*)

rate structure on any farm anywhere. It was prepared for full occupancy by 1962. The other two barns were converted to a weanling and a yearling barn. A manager's house was put under immediate construction. That first breeding season, 1960 to 1961, Tartan Farms stood one stallion, McKnight's *Meeting. That was as small as Tartan Farms would ever be, for it grew immediately and spectacularly. With Hartigan managing the corporation's farm, Nerud was free to pursue his training of the farm's horses in New York. One of his first goals was to find a good stallion to stand at Tartan Farms. The horse had to meet his criteria: soundness, speed, conformation, and four black legs.

Intentionally (Intent–My Recipe, by Discovery) met those qualifications, and Nerud spent $750,000 of McKnight's money to purchase him from Harry Isaacs, a breeder with connections to Florida. (Isaacs gave all his horses names that started with the letter I.) Intentionally, from the bloodline of Fair Play, retired in February of 1962 after running three times under Nerud. Nerud's talent resulted in Intentionally's first wins over a distance of ground (races over a mile long). "The biggest reason I wanted to run him was to get McKnight's picture in the winner's circle with him and a trophy. That meant more when the horse would retire," Nerud explained.

Intentionally retired with total earnings of $652,258 and a career record of eighteen wins in thirty-four starts. He was a co-world-record holder with Swaps for a mile in 1:33 1/5, a time that was set in the Warren Wright Memorial Stakes. Counted among his wins are the Withers and Jerome handicaps and the Delaware Valley Stakes. He was voted Champion Sprinter of 1959 and was syndicated for $750,000.

Nerud followed the breeding patterns of three people he highly respected, Fred Hooper, Ada Rice, and Harry Isaacs, "because they raised and raced their own horses and they were successful. I also read every book I could find about breeding," he said. Nerud bred speed to speed and liked big, strong mares that could run. One of the mares Nerud begged to breed to Intentionally was My Dear Girl, who went to the stud in 1963, his second year of service. He was impressed with this mare's delicate beauty as well as her racing ability. This was the beginning of what would grow to become one of the most important racing and breeding associations within the industry: Frances Genter and Tartan Farms.

The result of the mating was a small bay colt, foaled in 1964, with a three-by-three cross to War Relic. In Reality, like Indian Maid and King Hairan before him, was born the second best Florida-bred in his crop. He was a great racehorse, finishing his career with a total of $795,824 and a career record of fourteen wins, nine seconds, and two thirds.

The Florida-bred that In Reality raced against on several occasions, who always finished just ahead of him, Dr. Fager, was the result of the mating of Rough'n Tumble and McKnight's gift horse Aspidistra, who was turning into a very nice gift after all. By 1967, she would be the dam of six foals, all winners, three of them stakes winners. But her colt, as well as In Reality and two other Rough'n Tumble colts (who would later be named Minnesota Mac, for McKnight, and Ruffled Feathers), were playmates growing up in 1964. They would come to represent one of the strongest single crops of any farm.

While these four youngsters were gamboling in the Florida sunshine, John Nerud suffered a serious injury because of a runaway on the Belmont track. The injury left him with blinding headaches and amnesia. His wife finally took him to a neurosurgeon, who removed a blood clot from his brain. In gratitude, Nerud named the tall, leggy, clubfooted bay colt out of Aspidistra, Dr. Fager, after the surgeon. As late as 1986, after many great racehorses and championships, Nerud still insisted, "I only trained one horse that could

Dr. Fager wins the Arlington Classic in the slop way off by himself. His owner William McKnight accepts the trophy (by permission of Tartan Farms).

really run. Dr. Fager was the only horse I ever had in forty-seven years of racing that could do it all. He was the fastest horse that ever lived; that ever raced on the North American continent. The rest are impostors!"

As two-year-olds, Dr. Fager was second highweight on the Experimental Free Handicap and In Reality was fourth. Nineteen fifty-seven had often been used as a barometer of good racing years, for that was when Round Table, Bold Ruler, and *Gallant Man competed. Those horses also became great sires. But 1967 was the same kind of year, for that was the three-year-old year of Damascus, Dr. Fager, and In Reality, another group that would prove to be great sires in years to come. Damascus would just barely nose out his rivals for Horse of the Year, but Dr. Fager would be named Sprint Champion of 1967.

In appearance, the two Florida-breds, In Reality and Dr. Fager, were as different as two horses could be. Dr. Fager was tall, 16.3 hands at three years of age, angular, and long-striding: poetry in motion. In Reality was small, tough, and his heart showed in the many strides he took to match the speed of his competitor. While he never actually got his nose in front, he drove Dr. Fager to some of his best races. In the New Hampshire Sweepstakes Classic, Dr. Fager had to set a track record of 1:59 4/5 for the mile and one-quarter to beat the second-placed In Reality by just over a length.

By the end of 1968, Dr. Fager had earned honors that have yet to be matched. He was voted Champion Sprinter, Champion Grass Horse, Champion Handicap Horse, and Horse of the Year. Even Secretariat in 1973 would earn only three titles. Dr. Fager retired with total earnings of $1,002,642 and a career record of eighteen wins, two seconds, and one third in twenty-two starts. He had set three records and equaled a fourth. Five shares were sold for $100,000. The farm kept every other share, of which ten were Nerud's. When Dr. Fager was a three-year-old, Nerud sold his one-quarter interest in Tartan Farm Corporation back to McKnight. Included in the deal were Nerud's ten shares of Dr. Fager.

In Reality and Dr. Fager both retired to Tartan Farms in 1969, and at stud both would prove successful sires of champions. In Reality got the edge in this career, partially because by 1987 he was still alive, while Dr. Fager unfortunately died early. Dr. Fager, however, proved to be an excellent brood mare sire. Both horses became the most important sires to influence Florida breeding, even as Tartan Farms itself became an important farm. Today the sons and grand-

Left to right: John Nerud, Secretary of Agriculture Doyle Conner, Bruce Campbell of Ocala Stud, and Thomas Wood, Jr., who replaced his father at Ocala Stud. Photo by Turfotos (by permission of *The Florida Horse*).

sons (as well as the daughters and granddaughters) of Dr. Fager and In Reality include some of the most important horses in racing. Frances Genter's Smile, by In Reality, won the 1986 Breeders' Cup Sprint. Nerud's Fappiano, a grandson of Dr. Fager, was one of the hottest sires in the world in the late 1980s, was a leading freshman and juvenile sire his first year at stud in 1985, and a leading juvenile sire in 1986. His son Tasso earned a national juvenile championship in 1985.

While Florida was becoming recognized as a commercial marketing and breeding area, Tartan Farms brought in the quality and the upper class of pedigree without which Florida would have been considered a fluke breeding state in which "horses outran their pedigrees." With the influence of Tartan Farms and more breeders who would follow its example, the pedigrees finally began to match the racing records. The faith that McKnight showed in allowing his president to have total control of his farm was carried on at McKnight's death by his daughter and son-in-law, James H. and Virginia Binger. By 1986, Tartan Farms had been at the top of the nation's leading breeders' lists for eighteen years. In 1987, due to Mr. Binger's failing health, Tartan Farms was dispersed.

Nerud would be one of the prime movers behind the Breeders' Cup Series, which debuted in 1984. By 1986, Florida-breds had won seven of the twenty-one Breeders' Cup races that had been run in three years, a phenomenal 33 percent of what is considered the best racing in the world. "Kentucky will always be the breeding center of the world because they have the stallions," Nerud admitted. "But Florida breeds a tougher, better horse than Kentucky. I've never figured that one out. They're tough and they can run, but I don't know why!"

24

The End of the Beginning

In 1961, Ocala Stud sent a small, ceramic statuette to every owner of new foals born at the farm. This five-inch statuette came in five different colors and poses and around its neck hung a sterling silver map of the State of Florida with the inscription, "I'm a Florida-bred," as well as the foaling date, color, sex, dam, and sire of the new foal it was announcing. Shipped with the statuette was a poem:

> Hello, my birthplace is Ocala Stud
> and I'm a thoroughbred;
> So watch my speed as I grow up
> 'cause I'm a Florida-bred.

Over eighty of these statuettes were shipped out during the 1961 foaling season, representing only a small fraction of the $50,000 Joe O'Farrell claimed to spend on advertising each year. The word was out about Ocala Stud. In June 1961, Bud Wallace, author of a *Lexington Herald* article joked, "O'Farrell would have his unsuspecting farm buyers believe that Ponce de Leon was looking for an Ocala horse breeding site and not the Fountain of Youth!"

In the spring of 1963, Louis Wolfson of Harbor View Farm purchased one of the Ocala Stud two-year-olds for $23,500 at the Florida Breeders' Sales Company sale. This tiny gelding, which would never stand any higher than 15.1 hands, was by Third Brother out of Roman Zephyr by Roman. Very quickly, Roman Brother proved that size is of little consequence. By the time he won the Champagne Stakes, he was four-for-four, undefeated. Throughout 1964 and 1965, Roman Brother continued one of the toughest racing careers any modern-day horse has endured. He appeared to thrive on work and gained weight after races. By the end of 1965, Roman Brother was voted the Handicap Champion and Horse of the Year; he was Florida's fourth national champion

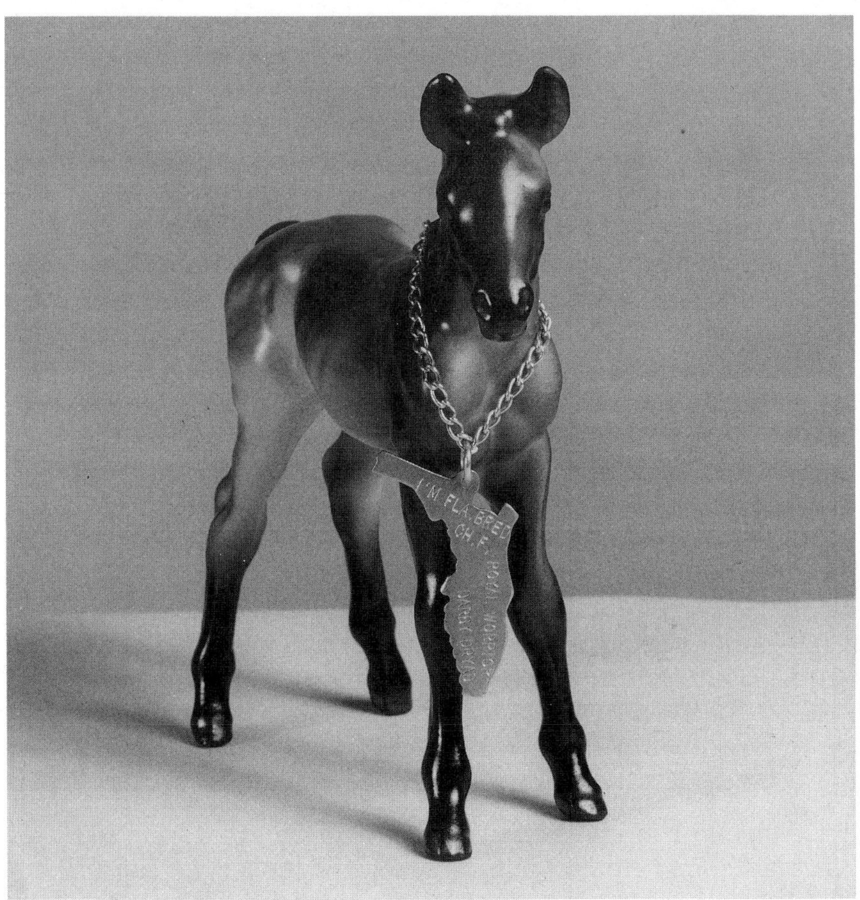

Ocala Stud's unique birth announcement for foals. Photo by Tierney & Killingsworth, Inc. (by permission of *The Florida Horse*).

and the state's first Horse of the Year. By that time, Roman Brother had earned $935,200 and was the richest horse and the biggest bargain ever purchased at public auction. He was also the first horse sold at public auction to make it as far as Horse of the Year. Ocala Stud, the Florida Breeders' Sales Company, and the Florida breeding program could have asked for no better advertisement.

In November 1961, Ocala Stud broke 158 yearlings, the largest group in training at a single farm in the United States. The same farm now stood 17 stallions, with some 300 mares going to them each breeding season, and 120 foals born in the spring of 1962. Ocala Stud was second only to Spendthrift Farm in Lexington as a U.S. stallion station; Ocala Stud encompassed 1,067 acres by 1962.

Roman Brother, Florida's first Horse of the Year and fourth national champion (by permission of *The Florida Horse*).

This was a far cry from the days in which the farm's owners had purchased twenty-one horses from Dickey Stables in order to enter the breeding business. The business had, in fact, grown too large for some of the owners, and in 1962, Ocala Stud was up for sale. "My partners are men getting up in years," O'Farrell explained to Tommy Devine of the *Miami Daily News*, in an article that appeared on May 31, 1962. "They have reached a point in life where they believe an operation of this size and type is too much worry for them."

The asking price was $2,500,000. All the prospective buyers wanted O'Farrell to stay on as manager; he owned 29 percent of the stock and had no desire to get out of the business. For over a year, bids and expressions of interest were fielded as the owners tried to sort out what they really wanted to do. By the end of 1963, the Ocala Stud syndicate was reorganized so that controlling interest went to Thomas E. Wood, Jr., his sister Dorothy (Bunny) Wood Price, and Joe O'Farrell. Wood, a twenty-nine-year-old Cincinnati real estate and insurance broker whose father was one of the original Ocala Stud founders, was named president. O'Farrell was made executive vice-president and general manager; Albert

Cash, an attorney, was voted secretary, and Bill Sena, an investment broker, became treasurer. William Veeneman was chairperson of the board; the board members were Mrs. Price, Bruce Campbell, Sr., and Tom O'Farrell.

In 1956, when Ocala Stud first came into existence, there were four breeding farms in the county. By 1964, there were thirty-four. Racing was the state's largest source of tax revenue: in 1962, $13,647,365 come in from horse racing alone. In less than thirty years, from 1936 to 1964, Florida had leaped to third place in the nation in quantity of thoroughbred foals produced. Only Kentucky and California continued to produce more.

Carl Rose watched this phenomenal growth with obvious satisfaction and remarked in a *Daily Racing Form* article by Joe Hirsch, February 3, 1958, that in spite of there being about twenty-eight farms in the county, "there are still fifteen to twenty good sites available for farms." He predicted that those lots would be snapped up in a couple of years; then breeders would have to go outside Marion County to buy farms. He remembered when he bought this land for $10 to $12 per acre twenty-five years earlier and marveled that it was now hard to find farmland for $1,000 an acre.

That year, Rose helped his beloved farm manager find a farm of his own. "He told us he was going to have to get out of Rosemere soon," Elmer Heubeck said. "He'd had his first heart attack and he was worried about us. He wanted us settled before all the land was gone, so he looked until he found just the right farm for us." In 1958, Elmer and Harriet Heubeck acquired Quail Roost Farm; it was one of the first farms in the northern part of the county, which was a relatively undeveloped area. It was soon to be followed by Hobeau Farm.

As Ocala Stud was starting a new chapter in the Florida breeding industry, sadly, an old chapter was about to end. Few people have had as much impact on a state as Carl Rose did on Florida. Rosemere was responsible for a large number of stakes winners: Werwolf, Fair Game, Game Gene, White Cliffs, Wolf Gal, Oclirock, Merriwolf, Marked Game, Noble Sel, Heroshogala, Benell, and, the great Indian Maid. Rose's original 5,000 to 6,000 acres of land were now Ocala Stud, Bonnie Heath Farm, Tartan Farms, and Shady Lane Farm. Even as late as 1961, Rose was still making important public statements about thoroughbred racing. He had been appointed once again to the Florida State Racing Commission.

Joe O'Farrell and Tom Wood, Jr. Photo by Turfotos (by permission of *The Florida Horse*).

Joe O'Farrell with Francis S., a stallion that became an important broodmare sire (by permission of *The Florida Horse*).

Because of failing health, he resigned in June 1961, but not before he had taken a public stand regarding that political body. He advocated that commissioners' jobs become full-time ones complete with decent salaries; that the title "Director of Racing" be abolished; and that two or three division heads be named, one each to monitor dog racing, jai alai, and horse racing. At the time, commissioners were paid a total of $13,200 to oversee pari-mutuel interests; these interests attracted $6,328,535 in paid admissions for the fiscal year ending June 30, 1961. The mutuel handle for the same time period was $344,173,946. "It is time to face the fact that parimutuels are big business," Rose stated simply to Tommy Devine of the *Miami Daily News*. He did not live to see Governor Reuben Askew, a governor unsympathetic to the breeding and racing industry, abolish the entire racing commission several years later.

In 1961, in an unusual transaction, Nelson Bunker Hunt, acting through trainer Tommy Root, purchased three two-year-olds privately from Rose: a half brother of Indian Maid that had won the best of show in the Baby Show of 1961, a full brother of Noble Sel, and a half sister of stakes winner Heroshogala. These horses represented the best of Rosemere's 1961 two-year-old crop. Root, who was about to help Hunt expand his racing interests, was very excited about the acquisition of these three well-bred horses. These puchases marked the beginning of the end of Rosemere. In March 1961, Rose announced that he had just closed a deal to sell all breeding stock at Rosemere to a group of Virginia horsemen headed by Tyson Gilpin and his brother Kenneth Gilpin, Jr. Included in the transaction were thirty-three mares, four stallions, and twenty-seven yearlings. The Virginia group also got a two-year lease on 250 acres, which included the training facilities on Rosemere, until they could purchase their own land.

"This land is worth $1,500 an acre for development purposes," Rose said to Paul Ferguson, in an article in the *Orlando Sentinel* in January 1961. "They'd be fools to pay that kind of money for a horse farm."

The group, incorporated in Virginia as Rosemere Stud, Inc., planned to sell the stock at a dispersal and planned to become involved in the Florida industry. Colonel Randolph Tayloe was to assume the post of resident manager. Tyson Gilpin was owner of Kentmere Stable in Boyce, Virginia. He was treasurer of the Fasig-Tipton Company, which his father had founded. In a statement to the *Orlando Sentinel* on March 10, 1961, he announced, "We couldn't

Elmer and Harriet Heubeck at their own farm in 1986. Photo by Kerry Heubeck.

Colonel Randolph Tayloe talking with Tyson Gilpin (by permission of *The Florida Horse*).

Orlando Sentinel on March 10, 1961, he announced, "We couldn't beat the Florida breeders so we decided to join them."

"That winter was the last year we had horses at Hialeah," Heubeck said. "That's when we knew we wouldn't be going back to Rosemere. When we came back, we rented a little house in town." It was also the year Heubeck met up with Jack Dreyfuss of Dreyfuss Mutual Funds on a recommendation from Rose:

> They came by to see me the last week at Hialeah. I was real busy trying to sell the last five two-year-olds we had so I didn't give him much time of day. So they decided to come up to Rosemere the following weekend. When they got there it was pouring down rain and I had some sick horses so I turned them over to Graham [Rose] who was into real estate since they wanted to buy a farm. They hardly got out of the car all day.
>
> Well, before taking them to the airport I took them by Quail Roost because I had to check on some horses. About then the sun came out and he fell in love with the hilly country up there.

They were standing on what was Bo-Bett Farm when Dreyfuss asked if he could buy this farm. Since he did not really know his potential client, Heubeck's novel answer was, "You don't have enough money to buy this farm!" Huebeck continued, "Of course, then he told me to buy it. When I found $100,000 wired into my bank account, I knew he was serious." Instead of purchasing Bo-Bett, Dreyfuss and Heubeck bought a 1,250-acre cattle and feed lot for $250 an acre, more land than Heubeck really felt they should have. The property was a mile wide with four miles of road frontage.

Hobeau Farm became the only other farm Heubeck would ever work on besides his own. In the beginning, he had some familiar help in developing the farm. Karl Koontz resigned as editor of *The Florida Horse* to become pedigree adviser and office manager for Hobeau, but his wasn't the only familiar face. "After he sold his horses Mr. Rose didn't have anything to do so he'd come up to Hobeau and tell me [Heubeck] how to do my job there. He continued to get up before 6:00 every day to come watch the horses train on the track. He was even beginning to put a few mares together again."

In a special ceremony on March 26, 1962, State Road 200, a road that Carl Rose had built in 1935, was named Carl Rose Highway. Unveiled at the dedication was a concrete road marker bearing a

Carl Rose (left) at the dedication of the new interstate highway at MacClenny on May 23, 1962 (by permission of Carl Rose, Jr.).

bronze plaque whose text began "To know Carl Rose is to love him." John Hammer, chairperson of the Florida Turnpike Authority, credited Rose with national influence in road building because of his use of limestone as a road-building material. In 1961, Rose had obtained a turnpike extension from Ft. Pierce to Wildwood. Hammer also reminded the crowd of the sixty thoroughbred farms within the state and their land value of $15 million. "No citizen has done more for the state," he concluded in an article in the *Orlando Sentinel* on March 26, 1962, written by Paul Ferguson.

With Rose at the dedication were his wife Ann, his sons and their wives (Graham and Ann Hope, Donald and Pat, Carl, Jr. and Carolyn), and four grandchildren. Only daughter Ann was missing. Across the road from the marker was the original Rose farm, where the first thoroughbred was foaled in Marion County.

In 1962, the Virginia syndicate turned Rosemere back to Rose, and he then leased it to Freeman Keyes, who leased the farm with the option of buying it. On February 26, 1963, at the age of seventy, Carl Rose died of a heart attack. "He was here at Hobeau watching me train that day," Heubeck recalls. "He followed me around all day. Then he went home, sat down in his chair, went to sleep and never woke up. He still had his boots on." In an article in the *Orlando Sentinel,* Governor Farris Bryant expressed the shock and sorrow of many: "The loss of Carl Rose will be felt by our entire state." Carl Rose was a lucky man: he had seen his dreams come true.

Part Five

Appendixes

CONTENTS

Breeding and Racing Facts and Figures

Breeding and Racing Organizations

Florida Racetracks: Facts and Figures

Historic Florida Races

Florida Stallion Stakes Races

BREEDING AND RACING FACTS AND FIGURES

Historical Events in Florida and in Horseracing

1494 Christopher Columbus brought 12 mares and 2 horses to Haiti.

1497 Amerigo Vespucci discovered the coast of America–Florida.

1513 Juan Ponce de León named La Florida; possibly brought horses but none survived.

1527 Cabeza de Vaca landed in Florida with 42 horses, but all died.

1528 Panfílo de Narvaez landed near Tampa Bay with 80 horses and 600 men, the first white men to see the Province of Ocali. No horses survived.

1539 Hernando de Soto landed near Tampa Bay with 1,000 men and 225 horses. These horses escaped and formed the basis for the wild herds that later roamed the North America continent. De Soto was the first to conduct horse races and horse breeding on the continent.

1562 First colony in Florida founded by the French near the St. Johns River, destroyed by the Spaniards.

1565 St. Augustine, the oldest town on the North American continent, founded by Spain.

1724 First known thoroughbred, "Fortune," imported by way of Virginia.

1776 Formal race meets held in Philadelphia.

1821 United States bought Florida from Spain for $5 million.

1832 Tallahassee Jockey Club formed; the first race meet held in Florida on December 19 at Tallahassee.

1834 Mary Doubleday—noted as a Florida-bred—was also a winner!

1841 Three known race tracks in Florida: Calhoun Course near St. Joseph, Marianne Course near Tallahassee, and Franklin Track near Apalachicola.

1845 Florida became a state with Marion County among the first officially named counties.

1846 Plans begun for a new county seat to be named Ocala.

1868 Town of Ocala incorporated; official county population 10,804. First volume of *American Stud Book* came out.

1907 James Bright moved to Miami area.

1908 Marion County Fair began conducting racing.

1909 One-mile course opened at Tampa, featuring Thanksgiving Day Handicap. Moncrief Park also opened in Jacksonville. Pensacola only other area with racing at this time.

1911 Florida passed anti-betting law. No more racing until 1916.

1915 James Donn moved to Miami and opened a flower shop, Exotic Gardens.

1916 Carl Rose moved to Florida and discovered limestone.

1918 Rose began buying land in Ocala; Rosemere Farm was established.

1919 An unsuccessful legislative attempt was made to negate anti-gambling law.

1-15-1925 Miami Jockey Club opened inaugural meet at Hialeah.

1925 Four major tracks in the state: St. Johns Park, Pompano, Tampa Downs, and Hialeah. Dan Chappell moved to Florida, became city attorney of Hialeah.

1926 Newly built Tampa Downs inaugurated the Florida Derby, then closed down before the scheduled end of the meet.

1929 State Representative Chappell tried unsuccessfully to get parimutuel passed in Florida.

1930 Widener bought Hialeah and renamed it Hialeah Park.

6-16-1931 Parimutuel made legal in Florida.

6-27-1931 First Racing Commission installed by Governor Carlton.

12-26-1931 Tropical Park, converted from dog track, operated first day of legal parimutuel in Florida. First fight over racing dates.

1-14-1932 Hialeah held its first "legal" race day. Newfangled Parimutuel Machines installed.

1932 Faireno first horse to campaign in Florida in the winter, then go on to win a classic race.

1933 Introduction at Hialeah of photo-finish camera, saliva test, and the first turf race held in America. Rose appointed to the State Racing Commission, served until 1936.

1936 Martha's Queen, first thoroughbred registered in Florida, foaled at Martha Bright Ranch.

1939 Martha's Queen became first registered Florida-bred winner. Rosemere Rose was the first Florida-bred foaled in Marion County.

2-1-1939 Gulfstream Park opened but only for four days.

1-28-1939 First turf stakes race in America, the Miami Beach Handicap, held at Hialeah.

3-30-1940 First thoroughbred stallion to stand, Green Melon, arrived in Marion County.

1943 Rosemere Farm and Marion County had their first winner when Gornil won at Tropical Park.

12-1-1944 Gulfstream Park reopened under the leadership of James Donn, Stefan Zachar, Harold Clark, and William Leach.

1945 Elmer Heubeck moved to Ocala to manage Rosemere Farm.

9-11-1945 Florida Thoroughbred Breeders' Association formed in Miami.

1-21-1946 First Florida-bred race—Maiden 2-year-old event—held at Hialeah.

1946 Donna's Ace became first Florida-bred to win a stakes race when she took the $10,000-added Ponce de Leon Handicap.

1-23-1947 Old Tampa Downs reopened as "Sunshine Park."

2-6-1948 First Florida-bred stakes race, Florida Breeders' Stakes at Hialeah.

1948 Cuba-Florida series of races began.
1950 William Leach started Dickey Stables in Ocala, the third farm in the county.
3-17-1950 Liberty Rab won the Belmont Juvenile, defeating unbeaten Battlefield, the first major upset by a Florida-bred and was, for awhile, the world's leading money-winning juvenile.
5-13-1950 Fair Game won Bay State Kindergarten at Suffolk Downs, beating Bull Lea, *Princequillo, and Blue Swords.
1952 Game Gene sold privately for $20,000, a record for a Florida-bred.
1-6-1952 The first Baby Show was held at Hialeah.
1954 Eugene Mori purchased control of Hialeah
1955 Needles became Florida's first national champion by winning the 2-year-old championship
12-17-1955 Marked Game became the first Florida-bred to win over the $100,000 mark.
1-15-1956 Dickey Stables purchased by a nine-man syndicate, became Ocala Stud.
1956 Needles won the first $100,000 stakes for a Florida-bred when he captured the Florida Derby. He then won the Kentucky Derby and the Belmont and earned the 3-year-old championship.
2-25-1957 First 2-year-old sale held at Hialeah by Ocala Stud.
2-3-1958 First 2-year-old sale held by the newly formed Florida Breeders' Sales Association.
3-15-1958 First Florida Breeders' Futurity at Sunshine Park.
1958 *The Florida Horse* started as part of FBSA.
1959 My Dear Girl won the 2-year-old filly championship.
12-30-1959 Only time a race decision was reversed: Saul Silberman at Tropical Park based a decision on a wet print of a photo finish but changed it after the print dried and was reexamined.
1960 Carry Back the leading Florida-bred 2-year-old ever with earnings of $286,299. McKnight purchased Tartan Farms in Ocala.
1961 Legislature passed the first breeders' bill. FTBA headquarters moved to Ocala. Carry Back won the Kentucky Derby and the Preakness and was 3-year-old champion. Rose leased Rosemere to a Virginia syndicate headed by Tyson Gilpin.
5-30-1962 Carry Back became Florida's first millionaire.
1962 The first mixed sale held in Ocala by FBSC under a tent at Ocala Stud.
1963 Ocala Stud resyndicated. Carl Rose died.
1964 Dr. Fager, In Reality, Minnesota Mac, and Ruffled Feathers all born on Tartan Farm.
1965 Summer racing authorized by state legislature. Roman Brother became handicap champion and Florida's first Horse of the Year.
1966 A new synthetic track built inside dirt track at Tropical Park.
1967 Dr. Fager was Sprint Champion.
1968 Dr. Fager was Sprint, 3-year-old, and handicap champion and Horse of the Year.

1969 In Reality and Dr. Fager retired to Tartan Farms.

1-8-1969 A caiman (a type of alligator) sunned himself during the races on the track homestretch at Tropical Park, making the racehorses jump over him!

5-6-1971 Calder held its first meet.

1-15-1972 Tropical Park held its last race day at its own location.

1974 Ocala Breeders' Sales Company started.

1980 Sunshine Park renamed Tampa Bay Downs when George Steinbrenner bought into the ownership.

Innovations Begun in Florida

1933: at Hialeah—photo-finish camera, saliva test, the tote board, Parimutuel Totalisator machines, first turf racing in the United States.

1933–34 (winter): NASRC formed in Miami.

1939: first turf stakes race, the Miami Beach Handicap, in the United States.

1957: first 2-year-old sales held in the United States.

1961: alphabetizing of first dams in sales catalogues.

Jan. 15, 1969: Barbara Jo Rubin had permission to ride Stoneland at Tropical Park, but thirteen jockeys refused to ride against her. She won her first race near Nassau at Hobby Horse Hall on Bryan Webb's Fly Away, January 28, 1969.

Feb. 7, 1969: Diane Crump, the first female jockey licensed in the United States, received her permit from Hialeah stewards and was scheduled to ride on this day. The horse also was on the eligible list but did not run.

Other firsts initiated in Florida: urinalysis tests; ringer-proof system of the photo i.d; breakdown of prejudice against winter racing; American Horse Council patterned after Florida Horse Council; first state to allow nondomiciled mares to drop foals in the state as Florida-breds if bred back to a Florida stallion—other states copied; first flamingoes hatched in captivity at Hialeah, which now has largest domestic flock in world; first parimutuel plan where every county received an allotted share from racing revenue; richest match race in history to date was match race between Stella Moore and Olympia; first racetrack chaplain, Dr. Arthur Vansant, Hialeah.

Early Florida-breds: The South Florida Industry

Note: This is not considered a full list but is the most complete available.

1928–35 Noreaster'24 (North Star III-Bunchy, by Llangwn)
Several foals born and raised in this time period; most sold for polo ponies.

	Breeder	Foals
1936	James H. Bright	Martha's Queen (Full Dress-Rocky Day)
		Lady Florida (Full Dress-Hillsaint)
	William M. Fry	Miami Maid (Full Dress-Saxon Lady)
1937	James H. Bright	Lou Bright (Full Dress-Betty Niles)
		Seminole Lady (Full Dress-Sweepstone)
		Formal Dress (Full Dress-Hillsaint)
		Florida Chief (Full Dress-Rocky Day)
	William M. Fry	Judfry (Full Dress-Saxon Lady)
1938	James H. Bright	Evening Dress (Full Dress-Bold Flirt)
		Day Dress (Full Dress-Rocky Day)
1939	Carl G. Rose	Rosemere Rose (Full Dress-Jacinth)
	E. A. Waters	Half Dress (Full Dress-Hillsaint)
1940	James H. Bright	Chorsie (Sun Arena-Sweepstone) [Bing Crosby may have claimed this horse!]
		Marjorie K. (Sun Arena-Betty Niles)
	Dan Chappell	Miami Sun (Sun Arena-Miss Capers)
1941	Carl G. Rose	Gornil (Green Melon-Jacinth)
	James H. Bright	Florida Storm (Stormscud-Betty Niles)
	John G. DuPuis, Jr.	Golden Flash (Stormscud-Transverse)
	E. Z. Waters	Tropical Storm (Stormscud-Hillsaint)
	Fred W. Hooper	Lady Melon (Green Melon-Seminole Lady)
1942	M/M Stefan H. Zachar	Smooth Gallop (Stormscud-Cendrillon)
	Charles A. O'Neil, Jr.	Buck Thirteen (Stormscud-Ok Polly)
	Carl G. Rose	Lucy S. (Green Melon-Jacinth)
	James H. Bright	Florida Breeze (Stormscud-Betty Niles)
	Charles O'Neil, Jr.	Chorsie Storm (Stormscud-Pekaki)
	E. Z. Waters	Royal Jack (Stormscud-Hillsaint)
	James H. Bright	Florida Whirl (Stormscud-Masked Pleasure)
1943	Mrs. Tilyou Christopher	Sammies Image (Sammie-Connie Plaut)
	Collins & Humphries	Florida Prince (Port Au Prince-Polipatta)
	Collins & Humphries	Winter Storms (Stormscud-Winter Sea)

Sources of Racing Dollars, 1931–1950

Year	Hialeah alone	All other horse tracks	Dog tracks	Jai-alai
1931–32	258,772.23	145,099.42	333,429.05	—
1932–33	318,991.16	98,515.50	358,068.09	—
1933–34	432,267.98	193,028.61	447,052.63	—
1934–35	498,710.65	282,504.57	572,205.08	—
1935–36	505,888.39	313,648.53	570,239.39	18,429.19
1936–37	677,912.96	396,114.51	706,061.39	30,411.98
1937–38	772,544.04	413,975.87	718,449.68	33,564.62
1938–39	756,790.98	457,492.32	721,454.38	32,902.62
1939–40	894,919.78	532,876.36	792,523.24	49,406.69
1940–41	876,345.59	587,214.61	883,746.76	55,497.23
1941–42	2,148,086.26	1,332,436.03	826,190.70	61,952.69
1942–43	Closed by war	246,854.49	756,494.13	41,808.92
1943–44	3,285,376.43	1,737,756.26	1,672,837.28	98,366.82
1944–45	Closed by war	962,226.72	824,847.11	195,629.33
1945–46	4,741,625.23	4,856,400.04	4,675,609.53	260,365.63
1946–47	4,329,810.34	5,337,177.71	4,669,618.70	291,873.51
1947–48	4,024,579.17	4,722,188.04	4,433,914.69	310,236.07
1948–49	3,807,330.23	4,414,237.19	4,668,733.87	278,047.56
1949–50	3,910,878.88	4,353,334.67	4,569,704.62	234,160.72
Totals	32,240,830.30	31,383,076.45	33,201,180.32	1,992,653.58

Kentucky Derby Winners Trained in Florida*

1938	Lawrin	1956	Needles
1941	Whirlaway	1957	Iron Liege
1942	Shut Out	1958	Tim Tam
1944	Pensive	1960	Venetian Way
1945	Hoop, Jr.	1961	Carry Back
1948	Citation	1962	Decidedly
1949	Ponder	1963	Chateaugay
1951	Count Turf	1964	Northern Dancer
1953	Dark Star		

*Through 1964

Jacinth: Pedigree and Produce

Jacinth (1936)	*Jacopo •••	=Sansovino •••	=Swynford
			=Gondolette
		=Black Ray •••	=Black Jester
			=Lady Brilliant
	Calycanthus •••	Brown Bud •••	*Brown Prince II
			June Rose
		*Pacify •••	=Sunstar
			*Conciliate

YOB	Foal	Sex, sire	Years raced	Starts	Wins	Earnings
1939	Rosemere Rose	f, Full Dress	6	122	18	$10,712
1941	Gornil	f, Green Melon	5	95	6	4,060
1942	Lucy S.	f, Green Melon	4	58	6	15,095
1943	Rosemere Dee	f, Green Melon	5	75	7	20,075
1945	Cao Jr.	c, Suffern	4	38	4	7,775
1946	Ann Rose	f, Suffern	4	87	14	17,260
1947	Suffinth	c, Suffern	4	80	4	7,602
1948	Norcal	c, Suffern	3	73	3	15,720
1949	Rosemere Cindy	f, Ariel Game	3	25	4	7,850
1950	Rosemere Zoe	f, Ariel Game	4	51	2	3,170
1953	Cindyam	f, Noble Hero	4	52	3	7,840
1954	Show Hero	c, Noble Hero	4	53	1	1,818
1955	Saminth	f, *Samurai	5	62	6	5,965
1957	Thyminth	f, Thymus	6	77	8	21,541

The Florida Industry in 1947

(Ten stallions and 55-80 broodmares)

Mucho Gusto (Marvin May-Sweetheart Time, by Hanbridge)
Golden Shoe Farm
Doublrab (*Sherab-Double Shamrock, by *Double Entendre)
Christopher Ranch
Sammie (Man o' War-*Thread, by =Gainesborough)
Christopher Ranch
Suffern (Sweepster-Saffron, by Marathon)
Rosemere Farm
Ariel Game (Ariel-Play Dis, by Display)
Rosemere Farm
Liberty Franc (Liberty Limited-Francaise, by Black Toney)
Hunter Lyon
Don Bruce (Don Leon-Kitty Bruce, by Whisk Broom II)
Martha Bright Ranch
Rosewell (*Boswell-Pan of Roses, by Peter Pan)
Martha Bright Ranch
On Location (*Teddy-Cinema, by Sweep)
C & H Farm (near Jacksonville)
Al-Tram (Transmute-Miss Alert, by *Challenger II)
H. H. Horne Farm

Stakes Winners and Wins, 1947–1957

1947 Donna's Ace (Ponce de Leon at Tropical Park)
1948 Rablim (Florida Breeders' at Hialeah).
1949 Werwolf (Florida Breeders' at Hialeah).
1950 Mr. A. B. (Florida Breeders' at Hialeah), Liberty Rab (Juvenile at Hialeah, Juvenile at Belmont Park), Fair Game (Bay State Kindergarten at Suffolk Downs).

1951 Jolisam (Florida Breeders' at Hialeah), Fair Game (Ohio Championship at Beulah Park).

1952 Game Gene (Florida Breeders' at Hialeah), Fair Game (Governor's at Suffolk Downs), White Cliffs (Narragansett Nursery at Narragansett Park), Air Pine (Newport at Narragansett Park, Coral Gables at Tropical Park).

1953 Wolf Gal (Florida Breeders at Hialeah, Juvenile at Hialeah), Oclirock (Bay State Kindergarten at Suffolk Downs).

1954 Wolf Gal (Imperial Handicap at Thistledown), Merriwolf (Florida Breeders at Hialeah), Marked Game (Mountain State at Waterford Park).

1955 First Cadet (Florida Breeders' at Hialeah), Smooth Stride (Youthful at Jamaica), Avis (Old Colony Juvenile at Lincoln Downs), Marked Game (Christmas H. at Tropical Park), Needles (Sapling at Monmouth, Hopeful at Saratoga).

1956 Needles (Flamingo at Hialeah, Florida Derby at Gulfstream Park, Kentucky Derby at Churchill Downs, Belmont S. at Belmont), Delamar (Debutante at Churchill Downs, Miss Chicago at Balmoral, Joliet at Balmoral), King Hairan (Florida Breeders at Hialeah, Juvenile at Hialeah, Dinner Stakes at Gulfstream Park, Tremont at Jamaica, Great American at Jamaica, Sapling at Monmouth, Hopeful at Saratoga).

1957 Hubcap (Florida Breeders at Hialeah, Christiana at Delaware, and Dade County at Tropical), King Hairan (Swift at Jamaica, Delaware Valley at Garden State), Needles (Fort Lauderdale at Gulfstream).

Foals Registered in Florida in 1949

Marion County, 18; Dade County, 9; Broward County, 7; Duval County, 2

Rosemere Farm
   6 colts, 6 fillies by Ariel Game
   2 colts, 3 fillies by Jakajones
Christopher Farm
   2 colts, 4 fillies by Doublrab
   2 colts by Sammie
Golden Shoe
   2 fillies by *Hamilton II
   1 colt, 1 filly by Mucho Gusto
Keeneland Farm (W. B. Keene)
   1 colt, 1 filly by *Saguenay II
Fred Hooper
   1 colt by Education
      (foaled at Hialeah Park!)
Pine Island Ranch
   1 filly by Rosewell
Dr. G. E. Woollard
   1 colt by Doublrab
Martha Bright Farm
   1 colt by Rosewell

Leading Florida-bred Winners for 1950

Horse	Breeder	Winnings
Liberty Rab	Mrs. T. Christopher	$33,587
Uncle Edgar	F. C. Peters	20,195
Mr. A.B.	Mrs. T. Christopher	13,030
Ariel's Mark	C. G. Rose	11,450
Maid of Hearts	C. G. Rose	10,525
Suffki	C. A. O'Neil	9,265
Gay Liberty	B. L. Whitten	9,005
Librab	Mrs. T. Christopher	8,365
Fair Game	C. G. Rose	8,325
Suffazon	C. A. O'Neil	7,956

Florida-bred Winners, Winter Season, 1950

Breeder	Horse	Track	Date	Sire
Carl G. Rose	Maid of Hearts	TP	Dec. 16	Seven Hearts
	Tedson	"	Dec. 16	Jakajones
	Maid of Hearts	"	Jan. 3	Seven Hearts
	Tedson	H	Jan. 25	Jakajones
	Norcal	"	Jan. 30	Suffern
	Ariel's Mark	"	Feb. 14	Ariel Game
	Dalpark	"	Feb. 19	Suffern
	Fair Game	"	Feb. 26	Ariel Game
	Rosemere Chick	GP	Mar. 9	Jakajones
	Rosemere Cindy	"	Apr. 16	Ariel Game
	Game Lady	"	Apr. 17	"
	Game Flower	"	Apr. 20	"
Golden Shoe	Bow Compass	SP	Jan. 30	Mucho Gusto
	Ruling Pen	"	Feb. 20	"
	"	"	Mar. 10	"
	Sand Paper	"	Mar. 14	"
	Ruling Pen	GP	Apr. 21	"
Mrs. T. Christopher	Connie Rab	HP	Jan. 30	Doublrab
	Jolisam	"	Feb. 7	Sammie
	Bundlrab	"	Feb. 25	Doublrab
	Miss Rab	SP	Mar. 5	"
Dr. C. C. Collins	Can Locate	TP	Jan. 10	On Location
	LoCate	HP	Jan. 23	"
	Can Locate	GP	Apr. 21	"
Mrs. G. L. Larkin	Glaemel	TP	Jan. 11	Green Melon
	"	HP	Feb. 2	"
	"	GP	Mar. 27	"
E. D. Proctor	Ariel Streak	SP	Feb. 20	Ariel Game
	"	"	Feb. 27	"
	"	"	Mar. 13	"
M. I. Brooks	Sunny South	"	Feb. 22	Sammie
	"	"	Mar. 9	"
Collins & Humphries	Local Band	TP	Dec. 22	On Location
	"	"	Jan. 11	"
Hunter Lyon	Feefifofum	GP	Mar. 23	Yellow Tulip
	Franc's Cracker	"	Apr. 7	Liberty Franc
B. Fisher	Galloping Pass	SP	Feb. 16	Pass Out
Elmer Heubeck	She Wolf	GP	Apr. 20	Ariel Game
J. J. Starling	Sunshine Rose	"	Apr. 20	"
E. Z. Waters	Clabbering Jim	HP	Feb. 16	Old Colony
Dr. G. Woollard	Picadelia	GP	Apr. 18	Pictor

Thirty Top Stallions of 1952 in the U.S. *

	1952					1951					Two-Year
	Crop	Winners	Races	Amount	Average	Crop	Winners	Races	Amount	Average	Average
Rosemont	5	2	5	68,835	13,776	4	4	5	11,850	2,962	8,965
Polynesian	26	12	28	309,375	11,896	19	6	12	72,995	3,482	8,497
Errand	19	10	27	199,320	10,491	20	10	28	67,283	3,364	6,811
Spy Song	15	4	7	120,720	8,048						
*Heliopolis	20	10	22	120,943	6,409	26	10	14	27,605	1,062	3,229
Alquest	11	5	15	67,676	6,152	16	5	11	18,070	1,130	3,176
Easy Mon	20	8	14	107,600	5,380	24	12	25	49,649	2,068	3,545
Hampden	11	6	11	60,615	5,511	13	3	6	9,615	740	2,483
Ariel Game **	16	9	28	74,265	4,641	14	6	10	14,995	1,071	2,975
Education **	5	3	10	21,700	4,340	4	2	6	9,465	2,714	3,460
Bimelech	24	14	23	95,955	3,989	27	8	13	26,750	990	2,330
Menow	14	4	11	51,380	3,670	24	6	13	222,835	9,285	7,216
*Mahmoud	18	11	21	62,930	3,496	23	5	14	34,450	1,500	2,730
Brookfield	21	11	23	70,950	3,379	14	7	13	32,375	2,310	2,961
Count Fleet	32	9	15	101,172	3,160	39	10	19	75,815	1,944	2,460
Psychic Bid	12	6	12	96,020	3,002	7	3	3	4,000	571	2,106
*Princequillo	26	10	15	77,085	2,969	22	8	9	12,180	620	1,859
Grand Admiral	26	11	28	71,110	2,738	23	14	28	41,265	1,794	2,285
With Regards	25	10	23	66,840	2,624	24	14	22	50,470	2,150	2,394
Bull Lea	29	8	16	81,600	2,814	28	4	10	79.870	2,852	2,833
Requested	22	8	17	68,075	3,094	16	5	8	24,400	1,625	2,433
Depth Charge	15	6	13	39,161	2,611	9	6	13	11,301	1,256	2,103
*Royal Gem II	17	6	11	41,167	2,480						
War Jeep	21	9	22	51,675	2,461	11	5	7	20,272	1,843	2,248
Mighty Story	23	12	26	56,194	2,443						
Revoked	24	13	23	58,369	2,432	23	8	16	49,367	2,147	2,292
War Admiral	22	8	12	52,250	2,375	25	8	9	18,625	745	1,508
Jamestown	9	5	11	20,975	2,331	8	4	5	7,410	926	1,905
Pictor	7	4	7	15,405	2,200	5	1	2	4,550	910	1,663
Silver Horde	9	4	13	19,280	2,142	12	4	10	18,200	1,517	1,785

* On the basis of average earnings of registered two-year-olds. Asterisk before horse's name indicates import from foreign country.

** Florida -bred.

Ariel Game: Pedigree and Racing Record

Ariel Game

Ariel •••
Eternal •••
Sweep
Hazel Burke
=Adana •••
*Adam
=Mannie Himyar

Play Dis •••
Display •••
Fair Play
*Cicuta
Gavotte •••
*Light Brigade
Toddle

Racing Record

Year	First	Second	Third	Unplaced	Winnings
1943	3	3	2	3	$ 6,765.00
1944	3	3	0	4	10,360.00
Total	6	6	2	7	$17,125.00

Suffern: Pedigree and Racing Record

Suffern

Sweepster •••
Sweep •••
Ben Brush
Pink Domino
Oktibenna •••
*Rock Sand
Octoroon

Saffron •••
Marathon •••
=Martagoon
Ondulee II
Yellow Sally •••
Star Shoot
Frances McClelland

Racing Record

Year	First	Second	Third	Fourth	Winnings
1937	1	0	0	1	$4,480
1938	3	1	1	2	1,960
1939	4	2	4	2	5,920
1940	3	0	0	2	2,475
1941	3	1	3	2	3,705
1942	0	0	0	1	80
Total	14	4	8	10	$18,620

Florida Farms and Stallions, 1955

Bar One Seventeen Ranch, South Miami; Ralph Yero; Samuel Warden, manager; 52 acres; 6 mares; about 5/8-mile banked track.

Christopher Ranch, Rt. l, Miami; Mr. and Mrs. Tilyou Christopher; Jimmy Knowles, manager; 150 acres; seven-furlong track.

Contented Stables, Hallandale; owned and managed by Joseph S. Binstock; 80 acres; 3 mares; one-half-mile straightaway track.

Dickey Stables, Ocala; owned and managed by W. E. Leach; 833 acres; 18 mares; stallions: King's Stride, Bull Brier, Fly Away, El Mono, Liberty Franc.

Elkcam Farm, Lake Placid; Mackle Brothers; W. C. Osborn, manager; 116 acres; 10 mares; stallions: Boodle, Eternal City.

Fuentes Farm, Tampa; 110 acres; Elliott Fuentes and D. C. Stearns; Elliott Fuentes, manager; 110 acres; 3 mares.

Gladeview Farm, Miami; A. J. Della-Pietra; John Della-Pietra, manager; 2 mares; quarter-mile track; stallion: Count-A-Bit.

Golden Shoe Farm, Broward County west of Davie; Mr. and Mrs. Stefan H. Zachar; Gerald A. Dooley, manager; 108 acres; 10 mares; quarter-mile grass track; stallions: Foot Saver, Panheim.

Gulfstream Ranch, Hollywood; owned and managed by E. T. McMahony; 5 acres.

H. H. Horn Breeding Farm, Hialeah; owned and managed by H. H. Horn; 70 acres; 16 mares; half-mile track; stallions: Dashing Ted, Pouter, Brier Cerria.

Horne Brothers Ranch, Ocala; T. J. Jack and Ray Horn; Leslie L. Horn, manager; 300 acres; 6 mares; 3/8-mile track.

Keeneland Farm, Jacksonville; owned and managed by W. H. Keene, Jr.; 20 acres; 4 mares; 3/8-mile track; stallion: Reaping Sickle.

McLean Farm, Pompano Beach; owned and managed by W. K. McLean; 30 acres; 2 mares.

Nani La Hale Ranch, Hallandale; owned and managed by Dr. George E. Woollard; 30 acres; 3 mares; 5/8-mile track.

0. G. Ranch, Broward County west of Davie; Mr. and Mrs. Oscar Garrigues; Richard Lopez, manager; 50 acres; 12 mares; half-mile track; stallion: In Suspense.

Pine Island Ranch, Broward County west of Davie; Charles A. O'Neil, Jr.; Milton Wurster, manager; 160 acres; 13 mares; half-mile track; stallions: Ariel Game, Harvest Reward.

Pleasant Acres Farm, Perrine; George J. Landon, manager; stallion: Admiral's Pride.

Prince Quest Stud Farm, Davie; F. R. Peroni; Norman Friend, manager; 40 acres; 9 mares; half-mile track; stallion: Prince Quest.

Rosemere Farm, Ocala; Carl G. Rose; Elmer Heubeck, Jr., manager; 600 acres; 44 mares; half-mile track; stallions: *Samurai, Noble Hero, *Laico, Rinaldo.

S & N Stables, Oldsmar; C. A. Napper and J. J. Starling; J. J. Starling, manager; 20 acres; stallions: Good Egg, Lautenberg.

Schlosser's Farm, west of Ft. Lauderdale; owned and managed by Louis Schlosser; 120 acres; 4 mares; 600-foot straightaway track; stallions: New Dough, Poo Bah.

Six D. Stock Farm, South Miami; Mrs. D. R. Sena; C. E. Howard, manager; 10 acres; 5 mares; one-fifth-mile track; stallion: Eternal Road.

Smith Stables, Inc., Hialeah; Norman B. Smith; Don J. Ramsay, manager; 15 acres; 9 mares; 3/8-mile track; stallion: Balu Mike.

Stewart Farm, Ocala; Mr. and Mrs. D. F. Stewart; John Shropshire, manager; 86 acres; 9 mares; stallion: *Stella Aurata.

White Star Farms, Clearwater; W. S. Wightman; Norman Walker, manager; 35 acres; 6 mares; 3/8-mile track; stallions: Uncle Ace, Platform.

Needles: Pedigree and Racing Record

Needles	Ponder •••	Pensive •••	=Hyperion
			*Penicuik II
		Miss Rushin •••	*Blenheim II
			Lady Erne
	Noodle Soup •••	Jack High •••	John P. Grier
			Priscilla
		Supromene •••	Supremus
			*Melpomene

Racing Record

Year	Starts	First	Second	Third	Winnings
1955	10	6	0	2	$129,805
1956	8	4	2	0	440,850
1957	3	1	1	1	29,700
Totals	21	11	3	3	$600,355

Racing Record 1956

Date	Track	Race	Dist	Wt.	Fin.	Odds
2-6	HP	Golden Glades	7/8	112	2	3 1/4-1
2-25	HP	Flamingo S.	1 1/8	117	1	2 3/4-1
3-24	GP	Florida D.	1 1/8	117	1	8-5
5-5	CD	Kentucky D.	1 1/4	126	1	8-5
5-19	PIM	Preakness S.	1 3/16	126	2	3-5
6-16	BP	Belmont S.	1 1/2	126	1	2-3
8-4	WP	Orpheus H.	3/4	120	8	5 1/4-1
8-18	WP	American D.	1 3/16	126	5	1-1

Leading Florida-breds of 1957

Name	1957 Earnings	Age	Breeding	Breeder
King Hairan	$44,950	3	King's Stride-Lady Hairan	W. E. Leach
Hubcap	40,200	2	Boodle-Rub-Adub-Dub	Elkcam Farm
Oclirock	33,045	6	Nelson Dunstan-Yasum	Carl G. Rose
Needles	29,700	4	Ponder-Noodle Soup	W. E. Leach
Floral Girl	22,085	3	Noble Hero-Brown Flower	Carl G. Rose
Air Wonder	19,440	3	Ariel Game-Wanderment	C. A. O'Neil, Jr.
Sweet Mandy	18,231	2	Prince Quest-Magnolia	Jacob Sher
Harry Husman	16,605	4	*Hunters Moon IV-Pomventure	Harry Husman, Lyle Phillips
Home Boy	15,300	6	Kings Blue-Magnolia	Jacob Sher
Sun King	14,150	2	In Suspense-Trans Egret	Oscar Garrigues
Blenfly	13,730	6	Fly Away-Noodles	W. E. Leach
Byroon	13,315	3	Noble Hero-Brown Miss	Carl G. Rose, Elmer Heubeck,Jr.
Eternal Flame	12,930	3	Fly Away-Eternal Miss	W. E. Leach
Four Fives	12,680	2	King's Stride-Tea Deb	Dickey Stables
Mighty Bout	12,215	5	Mighty Story-Boutefeu	Carl G. Rose
Devil's Image	11,000	5	Devil Diver-Lady Hairan	W. E. Leach
Game Conqueror	10,975	2	Fair Game-Rose Morse	White Star Farms
Helsa	10,800	2	*Samurai-Helpit	Carl G. Rose
Silver Rab	10,325	5	Doublrab-Silver Drift	Mrs. T. Christopher

Florida Breeders' Sales Association

Charter members
- Carl G. Rose
- Douglas F. Stewart
- Bonnie M. Heath
- Elmo Shropshire
- Karl Koontz
- Joseph M. O'Farrell

Officers in 1958
- Joseph M. O'Farrell, president
- Douglas F. Stewart, vice president
- Bonnie Heath, vice president
- Karl Koontz, secretary-treasurer

FBSC Sales

Year	No. horses sold	Total receipts	Average
2-year-old sales			
1958	60	$294,700	$ 4,911
1959	55	292,300	5,314
1960	56	286,600	5,117
1961	63	528,600	8,390
1962	103	910,000	8,835
1963	96	796,000	8,291
1964	145	1,538,500	10,610
1965	210	2,534,200	12,067
1966	231	3,298,200	14,278
1967	291	*3,325,000	11,426
1968	213	*3,000,000	14,085
1969	231	*3,500,000	15,152
Mixed sales			
1962	67	*200,000	2,985
1963	102	*180,000	1,765
1964	121	*250,000	2,066
1965	129	*500,000	3,876
1966	369	*1,100,000	2,981
1967	295	*1,000,000	3,390
1968	331	*1,300,000	3,927
1969	440	1,755,800	3,990
1970	476	1,368,700	2,875
1971	473	1,602,000	3,387
1972	551	2,209,800	4,011
1973	843	3,347,100	3,970
1974	702	2,569,300	3,660

*Only rounded-off figures available.

Leading Florida-breds of 1959

Earnings	Horse	Breeder
$185,622	My Dear Girl	Ocala Stud Farms, Inc.
71,495	Indian Maid	Elmer Heubeck, Jr.
44,641	Net Ball	Elmer Heubeck, Jr
34,427	Noble Sel	Carl G. Rose
28,755	Geechee Lou	Mrs. J. A. Prather
26,423	Wedlock	Ocala Stud Farms, Inc.
24,882	Betty Linn	Carl G. Rose
24,817	Coltrane	Louis Schlosser
18,671	Confuse	F. W. Hooper
18,664	Good Joy	Eric Ericson & Ben Calderone
18,585	Dark Legacy	Ocala Stud Farms, Inc.
18,580	Running Wolf	Carl G. Rose & Elmer Heubeck
17,987	Conestoga	Ocala Stud Farms, Inc.
17,590	Bokaris	Louis Schlosser
17,005	Sound'n Fury	Ocala Stud Farms, Inc.
16,600	King's Image	Dickey Stable
15,775	Pryson	F. W. Hooper
15,727	Hubcap	Elkcam Farm
14,360	Niequest	Graham E. Rose
14,182	Benell	Carl G. Rose
13,805	Sun King	Mr. & Mrs. O. Garrigues
13,070	Cable King	Jackson Dudley & Bonnie Heath
12,835	Idle Time	Douglas F. Stewart
12,760	Raven Wing	Ocala Stud Farms, Inc.
12,760	Great Orbit	Elkcam Farm
12,330	Head Way	Douglas F. Stewart
12,160	Mal-Don-D	W. V. McCall
11,915	Oclirock	Carl G. Rose
11,750	Chendzod	Mr. & Mrs. S. H. Zachar
11,214	New Star	Douglas F. Stewart
11,195	Ednez	Roscoe T. O'Neil
11,050	Postal	Vera S. Bragg
10,780	Cri De Guerre	Ocala Stud Farms, Inc.

Ocala Stud-bred Stakes Winners

1959
Conestoga
My Dear Girl
Wedlock

1960
Bronzerullah
Conestoga
My Old Flame
Roving Minstrel

1961
Conestoga

1962
Do Declare
O'Calaway

1963
Roman Brother
Put On Airs

1964
Roman Brother
Bright Object

1965
Bright Object
Flame Tree
Roman Brother
Rorque

1966
Bright Object
Florida Value
Ring Frances
Swinging Mood
Treasure Chest
Wagon Dance

1967
Florida Value
Light of Freedom
Sir Winzalot
Swinging Mood

1968
Alley Fighter
Sir Winzalot

1969
Elect the Ruler
Office Queen
Royal Saxon

1970
Arrolane
Kilts n Kapers
Office Queen

1971
Chevron Flight
Fireside Chat
Meadow Mint
Office Queen

1972
Chevron Flight
Prince of Truth

1973
French Fable
King's Reel
Prince of Truth
Verkade
Wittgenstein

1974
Miss Musket
Prince of Truth
Wittgenstein

1975
Festive Mood
With Distinction

1976
Festive Mood
Hail Liberty

1977
Extravagant
Festive Mood
Galimore
Jet Diplomacy
Patriot's Dream

1978
Cherry Pop
Country Queen
Galimore
La Soufriere[a]

1979
Cherry Pop
Country Queen
Jet Diplomacy
La Soufriere

1980
Cherry Pop
Country Queen
Smilin' Sara

1981
Diverse Dude

1982
Bold Finesse[b]
Explosive Bid[c]
Victorious
Widad

1983
Majestic Flag[b]

1984
Covert Operation
Explosive Bid
Mighty Appealing
Queen Alexandra

1985
Covert Operation
Tough Talk
True Silver
Wising Up[b]

1986
Bolshoi Boy
Dessa
Don's Diplomacy
Gun Carriage
Harwin Drive
Oxford Star
Queen Alexandra
Proudest Duke[d]

1987
Bolshoi Boy
Medieval Victory
Proudest Duke
Queen Alexandra
Russian Diplomacy

1988
On to Royalty[d]
Twice Too Many

1989
Dessa
Ocalarado

1990
Garden Gal
Medieval Victory
Wedding Bank

a. Bred in partnership with Neal Swanson.
b. Bred in partnership with J. Michael O'Farrell and Dr. Ed Wiest.
c. Bred in partnership with Angie Greiner and J. Wilkerson.
d. Bred in partnership with J. Michael O'Farrell, Scott Dudley, and Dr. Ed Wiest.

Florida–breds in Money in 1960 Stakes

Indian Maid
First in Yo Tambien at Hawthorne
First in Hawthorne Inaugural at Hawthorne
First in Los Angeles at Santa Anita
First in Modesty at Washington Park
First in Beverly at Washington Park
First in Falls City H. at Churchill Downs
Second in New Castle at Delaware
Second in Santa Margarita at Santa Anita
Second in Interborough at Aqueduct
Third in Las Flores at Santa Anita
Third in Santa Monica at Santa Anita
Third in Santa Maria at Santa Anita

Carry Back
First in Garden State Stakes at Garden State
First in Cowdin at Aqueduct
First in Remsen at Aqueduct
Second in Dover at Delaware
Second in Christiana at Delaware
Second in Florida Breeders' at Hialeah
Third in Tyro at Monmouth
Third in Great American at Aqueduct
Third in Sapling at Monmouth

Bronzerullah
First in Saratoga Special at Saratoga
Second in The Tremont at Aqueduct
Second in Great American at Aqueduct
Second in Hopeful at Saratoga
Third in Champagne Stakes at Belmont

Conestoga
First in Ventnor at Atlantic City
First in Atlantic City Handicap at Atlantic City
First in King Neptune at Atlantic City
Second in Turf Cap at Laurel
Third in Select at Delaware
Third in Leonard Richards at Delaware

Roving Minstrel
First in Champagne at Belmont

Confuse
First in Jasmine at Hialeah
Second in Miss Woodford at Monmouth
Third in Misty Isle at Washington Park
Third in Margate (2nd Div.) at Atlantic City

Dream On
First in Rancocas at Garden State
Second in Colleen at Monmouth

Heroshogala
First in Illinois Owners at Hawthorne
First in Charles W. Bidwill at Hawthorne
Second in Hawthorne Gold Cup at Hawthorne
Second in Chicagoan at Washington Park
Second in Christmas Day Handicap at Tropical Park
Third in Wright Memorial at Washington Park
Third in American Derby at Washington Park
Third in Chicago Handicap at Hawthorne

Geechee Lou
First in Puritan at Suffolk Downs
Second in Turf Handicap at Suffolk Downs
Third in Delaware Handicap
Third in Miss America at Atlantic City

My Dear Girl
Second in Interborough at Aqueduct
Second in The Las Flores at Santa Anita
Third in Gallorette at Pimlico

My Old Flame
First in Florida Breeders' at Hialeah
First in Florida Breeders' Futurity at Sunshine park
Second in Rancocas at Garden State

Nobel Sel
First in Bougainvillea at Hialeah
Second in New Orleans Handicap at the Fairgrounds
Second in Canadian Championship at Woodbine

Prompt Hero
First in Fair Play at Ft. Erie
Third in Canadian Championship at Woodbine
Third in Jockey Club Cup Handicap at Woodbine

Sandyjean
First in Florida Breeders' Championship at Tropical Park
Second in Mermaid at Atlantic City
Third in Blue Hen at Delaware

Princess Leeyan
Second in Sorority at Monmouth

Fire Trail
Second in Ohio Owner's Stakes at Randall Park

Arbol Grande
Third in Ak-Sar-Ben Juvenile Stakes (lst Div.) at Ak-Sar-Ben
Third in Florida Breeders' Futurity at Sunshine Park

Florida Thoroughbred Farms in 1960

(Broodmares include farm-owned and boarders.)

Anthony Farm, Hialeah; 5 acres; Mrs. A.L. Constantino; 4 broodmares; stallion: Apollo.

Barry Farm, Anthony; 300 acres; R.H. Caple and Harry Trotsek; 18 broodmares; stallion: Admirals Pride.

Bellows Ranch, Ocala; 640 acres; Harry Berman; 8 broodmares.

Bell Rock Farm, Ocala; 115 acres; Mr. and Mrs. E.S. Rockefeller; 1 broodmare.

Belynada Farm, Silver Springs; 10 acres; Nat Tooker; 3 broodmares.

Butterfield Farm, Ft. Pierce; 25 acres; Ray Johnson, Jr.; 2 broodmares; stallion: Pamheim.

Bonnie Heath Farm, Ocala; 750 acres; B.M. Heath; 55 broodmares; stallions: Needles, First Cabin Alsab, Sir Mango, Shines Bright, *Meeting Ever More.

Broadmoor Farm, Ocala; 280 acres; Mr. and Mrs. T.M. Daniel; 12 broodmares; stallions: Ace Destroyer, Jet Ace, Buck 'n Gee.

Christopher Ranch, Miami; 125 acres; Mr. and Mrs. Tilyou Christopher; 1 broodmare.

Circle Palm Ranch, Homestead; 18 acres; Sumner L. Eddy, Jr.; 2 broodmares.

Colonial Acres Stable, Lake Worth; 35 acres; Mrs. Ruth Ann Gosser; 5 broodmares; stallion: Ariel Game.

Contented Stable, Hallandale; 86 acres; Joe Binstock; 4 broodmares.

Crowder Farm, Brooksville; 40 acres; H. Crowder; 1 broodmare.

D-Bit Farm, Fairfield; 15 acres; Mr. and Mrs. A.E. Dodson; 1 broodmare.

Dery Stable, Lake Worth; 10 acres; Blanche and Bud Dery; 2 broodmares.

Diamond W Ranch, Davie, Ft. Lauderdale; 80 acres; Myron M. Weiss; 6 broodmares.

Don-Lee Farm, Davie, Ft. Lauderdale; Mr. and Mrs. E. D. Withnell, 3 broodmares.

Double L Ranch, Ocala; 75 acres; L.L. Hollandsworth; 3 broodmares.

Elkcam Farm, Lake Placid; 116 acres; Robert F., Elliott J., and Frank E. Mackle; 15 broodmares; stallions: Ifabody, Atoll.

Everglades Farm, Davie, Ft. Lauderdale; 20 acres; Hilton A. Dabson; 7 broodmares; stallions: Nance's Lad, Trajan, Star O'Destiny.

Florida Stud Farm, Lake Worth; 20 acres; Thomas E. (Ted) David and Sam David; 5 broodmares; stallions: Foot Saver, Knight Baker.

Forty Oaks Ranch, Ocala; 38 acres; H.A. Jackson; 4 broodmares.

Frank Lynn Ranch, Ocala; 103 acres; Louis Bandel and Joseph Rabin; 6 broodmares.

Golden Shoe Farm, Davie, Ft. Lauderdale; 87 acres; Mr. and Mrs. Stefan Zachar; 1 broodmare.

Hayman Ranch, Odessa; 40 acres; S.L. Hayman and Elliott Fuentes; 5 broodmares; stallion: Attention Mark.

H.H. Horn Breeding Farm, Lake Placid; 400 acres; H.H. Horn; 6 broodmares; stallions: *Pactole, Sneak Preview.

Horne Brothers Farm, Ocala; 400 acres; M.T., Jack, and Ray Horne; 6 broodmares.

J.C. Dudley Farm, Ocala; 140 acres; .Mr. and Mrs. J.C. Dudley; 24 broodmares.

John Clardy Farm, Ocala; 300 acres; John Clardy; 2 broodmares.

J.W. Wunsch Farm, Lake Worth; 10 acres; J.W. Wunsch; 2 broodmares.

Lake Magdalene Farm, Lutz; 200 acres; Thomas, Jack, Ignacio, and Nelson P. Zambito; 16 broodmares; stallions: Good Egg, Platform.

Lazy H Ranch, Tampa; 100 acres; M.J. Hulsey, Jr.; 10 broodmares; stallions: Samson D., Coastal Gold.

Leeward Farms, Ocala; 1,100 acres; Mr. and Mrs. Albert J. Leeward.

Lily Ann Farm, West Hollywood; John J. Dordan.

Little Moon Lake Ranch, New Port Richey; 325 acres; Meredith E. Dobry.

Live Oak Plantation, Ocala; 500 acres; P.A.B. Widener; 10 broodmares.

Meadowbrook Farms, Inc., Ocala; 372 acres; Meadowbrook Farms, Inc., 23 broodmares; stallions: Ambehaving, *Petare.

Meffert Farm, Lowell; 1,105 acres; 802 Corporation; 8 broodmares; stallion: Attention Mark.

Mitchell Brothers Ranch, Elfers; 300 acres; Jim and Jack Mitchell; 14 broodmares; stallions: First Glance, Alcova, Thither.

Nob Hill Ranch, Davie, Ft. Lauderdale; A.B. McCarty.

Ocala Stud, Ocala; 1,060 acres; Ocala Stud Farms, Inc.; 183 broodmares; stallions: Rough'n Tumble, *Luminarv II, Arrogate, Count Flame, Fly Away.

Pinecrest Farm, Ocala; 250 acres; George Cavanaugh, Jr.; 21 broodmares.

Powers Farm, Ocala; 15 acres; Joseph C. Powers, D.V.M.; 2 broodmares.

Prince Quest Stud Farm, Greenacres City; 200 acres; P.R. Peroni; stallions: The Pimpernel, Prince Quest, Royal Pen, *Rowdy, *Royal Ferry.

Quail Roost, Lowell; 270 acres; Elmer Heubeck; 11 broodmares.

R & M Ranch, Monticello; 200 acres; C. Ballard and R. Gosser; 5 broodmares.

Roseland Farm, Ocala; 120 acres; Grant A. Dorland; 16 broodmares; stallion: Correlation.

Rosemere Farm, Ocala; 600 acres; Rosemere Farm, Inc., Carl G. Rose, Sr., president; 51 broodmares; stallions: Noble Hero, Hilarious, Thymus, Sheilas Reward, Half Time II, Ham Bone.

Ryder Farm, Anthony; 170 acres; Mr. and Mrs. Robert J. Ryder; 7 broodmares.

Shady Lane Farm, Ocala; 100 acres; Douglas F. Stewart; 30 broodmares: stallion: *Stella Aurata.

Spring Hill Farms, Kendall; 180 acres; Spring Hill Farms, Inc., James D. Norris, president; 4 broodmares; stallions: Dr. Stanley, Octopus.

Stephen A. Calder's Farm, Delray; 134 acres; Stephen A. Calder; 15 broodmares; stallions: *Cascanuez, *Cid Campeador, Naval Salute, Gone Native.

St. Lucie Park, Indiantown; 400 acres; St. Lucie Horsemen's Association, Inc.

Sunny Knoll Farm, Ocala; 75 acres; Steve and Kitty Messana; 15 broodmares; stallions: Count-A-Bit, Homely Duke.

Sunset Acres, Miami; 8 acres; Benoita Corporation.

Sunshine Stud, Ocala; 350 acres; Sunshine Stud, Inc.; 19 broodmares; stallions: On Course, My Banker.

Swamp Angel Ranch, Ocala; 40 acres; P. N. Prewitt and C. G. Rodes, Sr.

Tampa Thoroughbred Breeding Farm, Limona; 40 acres; Charles J. and Sarah L. Higginbotham; 6 broodmares; stallions: Lord Bull, Mad War.

3 B's Farm, Ocala; 40 acres; C.L. and H.G. Butler; 3 broodmares; stallion: Prudy's Boy.

Trade Winds Farm, Pomano Beach; 50 acres; Mr. and Mrs. W.K. McLean; 8 broodmares; stallion: *Hasty Prince.

Vaughan Thoroughbred Farm, Brooksville; 140 acres; Jane and John Vaughan; 80 broodmares.

Wake Robin Farm, Lowell; 80 acres; W.C. Vines; 11 broodmares; stallion: Fair Game.

William MacDonald Jr. Farm, Delray; William B. MacDonald, Jr. Corporation; 12 broodmares; stallion: Count Trim.

Florida Stallion Roster, November 1960.

The list below has all the stallions on whom a current report was received who stood in Florida during the 1961 season.

Ace Destroyer, strawberry roan, 1950; by Grand Admiral–Ghazni, by *Mahmoud (Mr. and Mrs. T.M. Daniel); Broadmoor Farm; fee: $500.

Admirals Pride, chestnut, 1947; by War Admiral–Balanza, by Equipoise (H.R. Caple); Barry Farm; fee: $500.

Alcova, bay, 1952; by Gray Dream–Admiral Girl, by War Jeep (Mitchell Brothers); Mitchell Brothers Ranch; fee: $250.

Alsab, bay, 1939; by Good Goods–Winds Chant, by Wildair (Alsab Syndicate); Bonnie Heath Farm; fee: $2,000 live foal.

Ambehaving, brown, 1954; by *Ambiorix–Dentifrice, by Reaping Reward (Meadowbrook Farms, Inc.); Meadowbrook Farms; fee: $750 live foal.

Apollo, chestnut, 1952; by Mr. Busher–Jeanne's Poise, by Equipoise (Elkcam Farm); Anthony Farm; fee: $500 live foal.

Ariel Game, brown, 1941; by Ariel–Play Dis, by Display (Mrs. Ruth Ann Gosser); Colonial Acres Stable, Heritage Farms; fee: $500.

Arrogate, chestnut, 1951; by *Goya II–Hug Again, by Stimulus (Ocala Stud Farms, Inc., and Elmendorf Farm); Ocala Stud; fee: $750 live foal.

Ashenden, brown, 1951; by Spy Song–Driven Snow, by Ariel (Leon Murkison); Circle A. Ranch; fee: private contract.

Atoll, brown, 1956; *Flushing II–Coral Island, by Errand (Elkcam Farm); Elkcam Farm; fee: $1,500.

Attention Mark, chestnut, 1949; by Attention–Night Market, by *Man o'Night (R.C. Howard, Sr.); Meffert Farm.

Bolivar II, bay, 1948; by Birikan–Book Debt, by Buchan (S. David Shor); Pinecrest Farm; fee: $500 live foal.

Buck 'n Gee, chestnut, 1950; by The Rhymer–Pansy's First, by Phalaros (Mr. and Mrs. T.M. Daniel); Broadmoor Farm; fee: $250.

By Five, bay, 1948; by Teddy's Comet–Sleepytime Gal, by Questionnaire (W.F. Carpenter, Jr.); Carpenter's Farm; fee: $300.

Cascanuez, bay, 1948; by =Partab–=Vuelta al Pago, by =Ipe (Edna Allen and Stephen A. Calder); Stephen A. Calder's Farm; fee: $500.

*Cid Campeador II, chestnut, 1954; by Make Tracks–=Collette, by =Diadoque (Stephen A. Calder); Stephen A. Calder's Farm; fee: $500.

Coastal Gold, dark bay, 1951; by *Coastal Traffic–Jonquil, by *Isolater (M.J. Hulsey, Jr.); Lazy H. Ranch; fee: private contract.

Combat Boots, bay, 1948; by Our Boots–Miss Dodo, by Man o'War (Ocala Stud Farms, Inc.); Ocala Stud; fee: $500 live foal.

Correlation, bay, 1951; by Free America–*Braydore, by =Roidore (Correlation Syndicate); Roseland Farm; fee: not available.

Count-A-bit, bay, 1946; by Count Fleet–Hugabit, by Chance Play (Stephen Messana); Stephen Messana Farm; fee: $500.

Count Flame, chestnut, 1949; by Count Fleet–Morning, by American Flag (Ocala Stud Farms, Inc.); Ocala Stud; fee: book full.

Count Trim, chestnut, 1950; by Count Fleet–Decor, by Ariel (William B. MacDonald, Jr. Corporation); William B. MacDonald, Jr. Farm.

Dr. Stanley, light bay, 1950; by Crowfoot–Breaking Point, by Danger Point (James D. Norris); Spring Hill Farm; fee: $500.

Eds Day, dark bay, 1951; by Bull Lea–Still Blue, by Blue Larkspur (J.A. Price); Ocala Stud; fee: $500 live foal.

Esmero, bay, 1949; by =British Empire–=Sin Gracia, by =Parkgate (D.W. Creal); Willow Lake Farm; fee: $500.

Ever More, bay, 1953; by *Nasrullah–*Highway Code, by =Hyperion (Brae Burn Farm); Bonnie Heath Farm; fee: private.

Fair Game, brown, 1948; by Ariel Game–Lady Fanar, by *Fanar (W.C. Vines); Wake Robin Farm; fee: private contract.

Fair Ruler, bay, 1952; by *Nasrullah–Fair Weather, by Sickle (Fair Ruler Syndicate); Ocala Stud; fee: book full.

First Cabin, chestnut, 1952; by Sun Again–Whirling Girl, by Whirlaway (M.B. Armer, Jr., J.H. Nail and D and H Stable); Bonnie Heath Farm; fee: $500 live foal.

First Glance, brown, 1947; by Discovery–Bride Elect, by High Time (Mitchell Brothers); Mitchell Brothers Ranch; fee: $500.

Fly Away, chestnut, 1945; by *Blenheim II–Themesong, by High Time (Ocala Stud Farms, Inc.); Ocala Stud; fee: $500 live foal.

Gone Native, bay, 1956; by Native Dancer–Wise Scholar, by High Lea (Stephen A. Calder); Stephen A. Calder's Farm.

Good Egg, bay, 1946; by Discovery–Ovalette, by *Chicle (Lake Magdalene Farm); Lake Magdalene Farm; fee: $350.

Gulf Stream, chestnut, 1950; by Wait a Bit–Lapis Lazuli, by Equistone (R.A. Parachek and Vaughan Thoroughbred Farm); Vaughan Thoroughbred Farm; fee: $500 live foal.

*Half Time II, chestnut, 1955; by =Denturius–=Interval, by =Jamaica Inn (Rosemere Farm, Inc.); Rosemere Farm; fee: $250.

Ham Bone, bay, 1948; by Anibras–Loustel, by Sweeping Light (Rosemere Farm, Inc.); Rosemere Farm; fee: $500.

*Hasty Prince, bay, 1949; by =Hyperion–=Princess Asturias, by =Asterus (Mr. and Mrs. W.K. McLean); Trade Winds Farm; fee: $350 live foal.

Hilarious, bay, 1950; by Bimelech–Laughter, by Johnstown (Rosemere Farm, Inc.); Rosemere Farm; fee: $500.

Homely Duke, bay, 1948; by Gallant Duke–Hi-Home, by Hi-Jack (Stephen Messana); Stephen Messana Farm; fee: $250.

Ifabody, bay, 1951; by Brookfield–Itsabet, by *Heliopolis (Elkcam Farm); Elkcam Farm; fee: $750.

Inyureye, brown, 1949; by Brookfield–Liz F, by Bubbling Over (Brookfield Farms); Ocala Stud; fee: $500 live foal.

Jet Ace, bay, 1949; by Jet Pilot–Alyearn, by Blue Larkspur (Mr. and Mrs. T.M. Daniel); Broadmoor Farm; fee: $500.

*Luminary II, chestnut, 1946; by =Fair Trial–=Luciebella, by =Rodosto (Luminary II Syndicate); Ocala Stud; fee: $2,000 live foal.

*Meeting, chestnut, 1953; by Brick–Eos, by-Strip the Willow (Tartan Stable); Tartan Farm; fee: $500 live foal.

My Banker, dark bay, 1950; by Sun Again–Goose Cry, by *Royal Minstrel (Sunshine Stud, Inc.); Sunshine Stud.

My Request, chestnut, 1945; by Requested–Sugapud by *Sickle (Mrs. B.F. Whitaker, Leslie Combs II and Ocala Stud Farms, Inc.); Ocala Stud; fee: $750 live foal.

Nance's Lad, bay, 1952; by Slide Rule–Nance's Ace, by Case Ace (Nance's Lad Syndicate); Everglades Farm.

Naval Salute, bay 1955; by Crafty Admiral–Bizonia, by Jamestown (Stephen A. Calder); Stephen A. Calder's Farm; fee: $300.

Needles, bay, 1953; by Ponder–Noodle Soup, by Jack High (Jackson Dudley and Bonnie Heath); Bonnie Heath Farm; fee: $2,500 live foal.

Noble Hero, bay, 1945; by *Heliopolis–Boat, by Man o'War (Rosemere Farm, Inc.); Rosemere Farm; fee: $1,000.

Octopus, bay, 1956; by Johns Joy–Red Fleet, by Count Fleet (James D. Norris); Spring Hill Farm; fee: $2,000.

Oh Johnny, bay, 1953; by Johns Joy–Saracen Flirt, by Pilate (Wallace Gilroy and Meadowbrook Farms, Inc.); Meadowbrook Farms, Inc.; fee: $750 live foal.

On Course, chestnut, 1954; by *Alibhai–True Bearing, by *Sir Gallahad III (Dan Chappell); Sunshine Stud.

*Pactole, brown, 1943; by Fair Copy–=Linda Rubia, by *Stefan the Great (H.H. Horn); H.H. Horn Breeding Farm; fee: $300.

*Petare, bay, 1951; by =Moslem–=Collette, by =Diadoque (Meadowbrook Farms, Inc.); Meadowbrook Farms; fee: $750 live foal.

Platform, chestnut, 1947; by Our Boots–Blue Lu, by Blue Larkspur (Lake Magdalene Farm); Lake Magdalene Farm; fee: $350.

Prince Quest, chestnut, 1946; by Requested–Teddys Queen, by *Teddy (P.R. Peroni); Prince Quest Stud Farm.

Rough'n Tumble, bay, 1948; by Free For All–Roused, by *Bull Dog (Rough'n Tumble Syndicate); Ocala Stud; fee: $5,000 live foal—full book.

Rowdy, bay, 1948; by =Parlanchin–=Rustom's Legend, by =Rustom Pasha Prince Quest Stud Farm.

*Royal Ferry, bay, 1953; by *Royal Charger–=Dover Ferry, by =Furrokh Siyar; Prince Quest Stud Farm.

Royal Pen, bay, 1954; by *Princequillo–Princess Lea, by Bull Lea; Prince Quest Stud Farm.

Samson D., bay, 1949; by Polynesian–Darby Delilah, by *Sir Gallahad III (M.J. Hulsey, Jr.); Lazy H. Ranch; fee: private contract.

Sheilas Reward, bay, 1947; by Reaping Reward–Smart Sheila, by Jamestown (Rosemere Farm, Inc.); Rosemere Farm; fee: $500.

Shines Bright, bay, 1953; by Count Fleet–*Desert Sun II, by =Hyperion (Brae Burn Farm); Bonnie Heath Farm; fee: private.

Sir Mango, brown, 1950; by Gilded Knight–Marie Kantar, by Kantar (Harry N. Eads); Bonnie Heath Farm; fee: $750 live foal.

Sneak Preview, bay, 1954; by Lord Putnam–Cingalese, by Broadway Jones (H.H. Horn); H.H. Horn Breeding Farm; fee: $200.

Star O'Destiny, brown, 1953; by *Royal Gem II–Isolde by *Bull Dog (Sunshine Stud, Inc.); Sunshine Stud; fee: $500.

*Stella Aurata, bay, 1949; by =Arctic Star–=My Aid, by =Knight of the Garter (D.F. Stewart); Shady Lane Farm; fee: $1,000 live foal.

The Pimpernel, chestnut, 1949; by Pavot–Chalara, by *Challenger II (Charles Freidfertig); Prince Quest Stud Farm.

Thither, brown, 1951; by *Easton–Elsewhere, by *Alibhai (Mitchell Brothers); Mitchell Brothers Ranch; fee: $100.

Thymus, brown, 1949; by Questionnaire–Babys Breath, by *Sickle (Rosemere Farm, Inc.); Rosemere Farm; fee: $500.

Trajan, bay, 1952; by Roman–Search Me, by Menow (H.A. Dabson and C.J. Caithness); Everglades Farm; fee: private contract.

*Tharp, bay, 1955; by =Limekiln–=Mother Rectress, by =His Reverence (*Tharp Syndicate); Pinecrest Stable; fee: $1,000 live foal.

Tartan Farms–bred Stakes Winners

1964
A. Deck

1965
Grand Splendor

1966
Tequillo
Dr. Fager

1967
Tequillo
Dr. Fager
Chinatown
Minnesota Mac
Ruffled Feathers

1968
Dr. Fager

1969
Ruffled Feathers
Ta Wee

1970
Mountain Man
Ta Wee
Shelter Bay
Willmar

1971
Black Pipe
Lonesome River
Play Pretty
Shut Eye
Willmar
Arachne
Shelter Bay

1972
Actuality
Willmar

1973
Actuality
Lonetree
Willmar
Worldling

1974
Land Girl
Finery
Lonetree
Tastybit
Tin Goose
With Aplomb
Hunka Papa

1975
Heloise
Land Girl
Willmar
Tin Goose

1976
Imminence

1977
Great Above

1978
Dr. Patches
Great Above
Arachnoid
Kam Tam Kan
Magnificence
Quip

1979
Virilify
Arachnoid
Extra Shot
Kam Tam Kan
Open Gate
Tax Holiday
Tweak

1980
Codex
Great Neck
Idyll
Kam Tam Kan
Raisin Thunder
R. F. Dee

1981
Acaroid
Great Neck
Idyll
Muttering
Sepulveda
Tax Holiday

1982
Muttering
Great Hunter
Acaroid
Maudlin
Mezzo
Parcel
Raisin Thunder
Liturgism

1983
Acaroid
Maudlin
Liturgism

1984
Agacerie
Entropy
Eskimo
Rilial
Liturgism

1985
Ogygian
Equalize
Who's for Dinner
Agacerie
Important Business
Entropy

1986
Ogygian
Equalize
Ataentsic
Cintula
Important Business
Jeblar
Erstwhile
Jeblar
Lament
Mezzo
Final Reunion
Guyana
Hare Brain
Id Am Fac
Malchalstva

1987
Coup de Fusil
Feudal
Yaguda
Jeblar
Schism
Wakan Tanka
Kex
Malchalstus
Nyama
Pentelicus
Sciustre
Id Am Fac

1988
Ataentsic
Billie Osage
Purl One
Uene
Wakan Tanka
Zie World

1989
Primal
Surging
Ataentsic
Billie Osage
Coolawin
Equalize
Feudal
Izatys
Jane Scott
Kapulua
Pentelicus
Portage
Purl One
Unbridled
Urbanity

1990
Coolawin
Feudal
Heart of Joy
Jane Scott
Miner's Dream
Pentelicus
Primal
Portage
Purl One
Quiet American
Unbridled
Urbanity

FTBA Inaugural Hall of Fame

In 1968, the FTBA voted to open a Hall of Fame, honoring their only Horse of the Year, four divisional champions, five dams of champions, two top caliber race horses, and their leading sire. The unveiling took place on October 6, 1968, as part of Ocala Week. Following is the list of those first honored members.

Rough'n Tumble
Noodle Soup, dam of Needles
Iltis, dam of My Dear Girl
Joppy, dam of Carry Back
Roman Zephyr, dam of Horse of the Year, Roman Brother
Aspidistra, dam of Dr. Fager
Needles, champion at 2 and 3
Carry Back, champion at 3
My Dear Girl, champion filly at 2
Hail to All, winner of Belmont and Jersey Derby in a period of less than a week
Roman Brother, Horse of the Year
Dr. Fager, champion sprinter and leading candidate for Horse of the Year 1968
In Reality, near champion at 2, 3, and 4

Money Won by Early Florida-breds

1938	0
1939	$675
1940	$4,785
1941	$5,970
1942	$7,055
1943	$2,190
1944	$12,260
1945	$11,650
1946	$66,810
1947	$123,947
1948	$152,227
1949	$188,072
1950	$285,455
1951	$363,801
1952	$482,782
1953	$539,673
1954	$570,942
1955	$859,800
1956	$1,459,781
1957	$1,000,000+
1958	$1,033,230
1959	$1,662,418
1960	$2,620,717

Breeders, Owners, Trainers of the Florida Breeders' Futurity Winners

Year	Horse	Breeder	Owner	Trainer
1958	Indian Maid	Elmer Heubeck, Jr.	Mrs. Mary Keim	Elmer Huebeck, Jr.
1959	Benell	Carl G. Rose	Foster Stock Farm	Lila Phillips
1960	My Old Flame	Ocala Stud	Tally-Ho Stable	Melvin Calvert
1961	First Banker	Sunshine Stud	Sunshine Stud	L.P. Hebert
1962	Jewelry	George E. Allen, Jr.	C.S. Handelman	R. Bohn
1963	Fair Phina	W.C. Vines	James P. Cross & W.C. Vines	A.E. Dodson
1964	Golden Joey	Marion Frankel	Marion Frankel	Howard Jacobson
1965	Born Royal	Irving Gushen	Rovan Farms	Robert Van Worp, Jr.
1966	Wagon Dance	Ocala Stud	Neil Hellman	Howard Jacobson
1967	Fleet Swoon	William H. Floyd	Cambridge Grant Farm	Doug Dodson
1968	Gravy Bull	Elias Brothers Farm	Elias Brothers Farm	Carlos Mojena
1969	Call For Nat	D.E. Taylor	D.E. Taylor	Marvin Moncreif
1970	Dothan	Patrick Rowe	Thomas E. Wood, Jr.	Vincent Cincotta
1971	Clandustin	Mary Zimmerman	Mary Zimmerman	Joe P. Williamson
1972	Osage River (C)	William Harrod	Orangebrook Stable	C. Sanborn
1972	Kathlon (F)	Grosse Pointe Stock Farm	Clayton O'Quinn	L. Barbazon
1973	Barb's Charcoal (F)	Waldemar Farms, Inc.	Charro Stable	A. Dazinis
1973	Lizabeth Action (F)	Jim Paulk	Jim Paulk	Keith McKathan
1973	Golden Guinea (C)	Bennie Wayne Fesmire	Ralph Sessa	J.B. Sonnier
1974	Big Decision (C)	Norman Casse	Hokin House Farm	D. Sazer
1974	Track Fiddler (C)	E. Fuentes & L. Hayman	Fuentes & Hayman	Fuentes
1974	Mor Coup (F)	G.R. Sutton	G.R. Sutton	P.E. Johnson
1975	Invader's Baby (F)	Dr. Marvin Silver	H & W Stables	B. Webb
1975	So Magic (F)	Sam F. Davis	Brooksville Farm	P. Powell
1975	Seabreeze Jolly (C)	Tony Licata	Tony Licata	Loren Kress
1975	Worthy Opponent (C)	B.A. Dario	Stanley M. Ersoff	A.A. Scotti
1976	Steve's Friend (C)	Early Bird Stud	Kinship Stable	B. Hargrove
1976	Nasty Nancy (F)	Jerry M. Kroot	H. Bernstein	M. Riccardo
1976	Winner's Hit (C)	Lawrence Plante	Lawrence Plante	L.J. Barbazon

Note: (C) is Colt's Division; (F) is Filly's Division.

Florida-bred National and International Champions

Year	Champion	Horse	Breeder	Owner
1955	2-colt	Needles	Dickey Stables	D&H Stable
1956	3-colt	Needles	Dickey Stables	D&H Stable
1959	2-filly	My Dear Girl	Ocala Stud	Frances Genter
1961	3-colt	Carry Back	Jack Price	Katherine Price
1965	HoYear,* handicap	Roman Brother	Ocala Stud	Harbor View
1967	sprint	Dr. Fager	Tartan Farms	Tartan Stables
1968	2-colt	Top Knight	Steven Wilson	Steven Wilson
1968	HoYear, sprint, handicap, turf	Dr. Fager	Tartan Farms	Tartan Stables
1968	2-filly	Process Shot	Mrs. M. Tippett	Elberon Farm
1969	sprint	Ta Wee	Tartan Farms	Tartan Stables
1970	3-filly	Office Queen	Ocala Stud	Steven Calder
1970	2-filly	Forward Gal	Aisco Farm	A.I. Savin
1972	2-filly	Susan's Girl	Fred Hooper	Fred Hooper
1972	2-colt	Noble Decree (England)	Kinsman Stud	N. Bunker Hunt
1972	2-filly	Fiery Diplomat (Ireland)	Farnsworth Farms	Ms. R. Gallagher
1973	handicap-m**	Susan's Girl	Fred Hooper	Fred Hooper
1973	3-filly	Desert Vixen	Ms.Vanderbilt Adams	Harry Mangurian
1973	sprint	Shecky Greene	Joseph Kellman	Joseph Kellman
1974	handicap-m	Desert Vixen	Ms.Vanderbilt Adams	Harry Mangurian
1974	2-colt	Foolish Pleasure	Waldemar Farms	John Greer
1975	handicap-m	Susan's Girl	Fred Hooper	Fred Hooper
1975	2-filly	Dearly Precious	Jean Pancoast	R.E. Bailey
1975	2-colt	Honest Pleasure	Waldemar Farms	Bert Firestone
1977	2-colt	Affirmed	Harbor View	Harbor View
1978	3-colt	Affirmed	Harbor View	Harbor View
1978	HoYear	Affirmed	Harbor View	Harbor View
1978	2-filly	It's in the Air	Happy Valley	Harbor View
1978	turf	MacDiarmida	John Hartigan	Dr. J. Torsney
1978	sprint	Dr. Patches	Tartan Farms	Tartan Stables
1979	handicap	Affirmed	Harbor View	Harbor View
1979	HoYear	Affirmed	Harbor View	Harbor View
1981	3-filly	Wayward Lass	Horatio Luro	Flying Zee
1982	HoYear	Conquistador Cielo	Lewis Iandoli	Henryk de Kwiatkowski
1982	3-colt	Conquistador Cielo	Lesis Iandoli	Henryk de Kwiatkowski
1982	sprint	Gold Beauty	Mr. and Mrs. Phil Hoffman	Mr. and Mrs. Phil Hoffman
1984	sprint	Eillo	Ollie Cohen	Crown Stable
1985	sprint	Precisionist	Fred Hooper	Fred W. Hooper
1985	2-colt	Tasso	Tartan Farms	Tartan Stable
1985	turf	Cozzene	John Nerud	John Nerud
1986	2-filly	Brave Raj	Dr. W. Karutz	Dolly Green
1986	3-colt	Smile	Frances Genter	Frances Genter
1989	older filly	Proper Evidence (Canada)	Dr. Edward Wiest	Harry Gampel & Barry Schwartz
1989	HoYear	Mister Frisky (Puerto Rico)	Newchance Farm	Solymar Stud
1989	3	Bo Judged (Puerto Rico)	Richard Kane	—
1989	2-filly	Weepeat (Puerto Rico)	Old Mill Acres	—
1990	3-colt	Unbridled	Tartan Farms	Frances Genter
1990	2-filly	Meadow Star	Jaime Carrion	Carl Icahn
1990	turf	Itsallgreektome	Sugar Maple Farm	Jhayare Stables

* Horse of the year
** Handicap-mare

Florida State Champions

Year	Horse of Year	3-Year-Old Colt	3-Year-Old Filly	2-Year-Old Colt	2-Year-Old Filly	Turf Horse	Sprinter	Handicap Female	Handicap Male	Steeplechase Horse
1967	Dr. Fager	Dr. Fager	Treacherous	Subpet	Go Go Windy	Ruffled Feathers	Dr. Fager	Desert Trial	Dr. Fager	–
1968	Dr. Fager	–	–	Top Knight	Process Shot	Dr. Fager	Dr. Fager	–	Dr. Fager	–
1969	Ta Wee	Fast Hilarious	Process Shot	–	Office Queen	–	Ta Wee	Ta Wee	–	–
1970	Ta Wee	My Dad George	Office Queen	–	Forward Gal	–	Ta Wee	Ta Wee	Fast Hilarious	–
1971	Red Reality	Bold Reasoning	Forward Gal	Chevron Flight	Susan's Girl	Red Reality	Duck Dance	Process Shot	Fast Hilarious	–
1972	Susan's Girl	Freetex	Susan's Girl	Noble Decree	Natural Sound	–	Duck Dance	Convenience	Red Reality	–
1973	Desert Vixen	Linda's Chief	Desert Vixen	Wittgenstein	Irish Sonnet	Tentam	Shecky Greene	Susan's Girl	Tentam	–
1974	Foolish Pleasure	Destroyer	Quaze Quilt	Foolish Pleasure	Aunt Jin	London Company	Full Pocket	Desert Vixen	Arbees Boy	Augustus Bay
1975	Susan's Girl	Foolish Pleasure	Aunt Jin	Honest Pleasure	Dearly Precious	London Company	Step Nicely	Susan's Girl	Step Nicely	Augustus Bay
1976	Honest Pleasure	Honest Pleasure	Dearly Precious	For the Moment	Wavy Waves	Break Up The Game	Due Diligence	Yes Dear Maggy	Foolish Pleasure	Happy Intellectual
1977	Affirmed	Silver Series	Countess Fager	Affirmed	Stub	Lightning Thrust	Affiliate	Hail Hilarious	On The Sly	Happy Intellectual
1978	Affirmed	Affirmed	Country Queen	Jose Binn	It's in the Air	Mac Diarmida	Dr. Patches	Len's Determined	Dr. Patches	Happy Intellectual
1979	Affirmed	Crest of the Wave	It's in the Air	Gold Stage	Love Street	Country Queen	Whatsyourpleasure	Country Queen	Affirmed	–
1980	Codex	Codex	The Wheel Turns	Well Decorated	Carolina Command	Known Fact	Colonel Moran	It's in the Air	Tunerup	–
1981	Wayward Lass	Proud Appeal	Wayward Lass	Timely Writer	Skillful Joy	Great Neck	Fappiano	Honey Fox	Amber Pass	–
1982	Conquistador Cielo	Conquistador Cielo	Gold Beauty	Copelan	Crystal Rail	General Holme	Gold Beauty	Honey Fox	Pair of Deuces	–
1983	Island Whirl	World Appeal	Able Money	Dr. Carter	Minnieoso	Acaroid	Maudlin	Gold Beauty	Island Whirl	–
1984	Gate Dancer	Gate Dancer	Fashionably Late	Mighty Appealing	Diplomette	Roving Minstrel	Eillo	Sultry Sun	World Appeal	–
1985	Precisionist	Smile	Kamikaze Rick	Tasso	Twilight Ridge	Cozzene	Precisionist	Donstop Themusic	Precisionist	–
1986	Precisionist	Ogygian	Spirit of Fighter	Brevito	Brave Raj	Flying Pidgeon	Smile	Shocker T.	Precisionist	–
1987	Lost Code	Lost Code	Without Feathers	Firery Ensign	Flashy Runner	Talakeno	Banker's Jet	Coup de Fusil	Show Dancer	–
1988	Lost Code	Proper Reality	Maplejinsky	Fire Maker	Stocks Up	Equalize	Fire Plug	Tappiano	Lost Code	–
1989	Prized	Prized	Coolawin	Grand Canyon	Cheval Volant	Prized	On the Line	Aptostar	Proper Reality	Victorian Hill
1990	Unbridled	Unbridled	Charon	To Freedom	Meadow Star	Itsallgreektome	Prospectors Gamble	Buy The Firm	Quiet American	–
1991	Itsallgreektome	Jackie Wackie	Meadow Star	Tri to Watch	American Royale	Itsallgreektome	Shuttleman	Buy The Firm	Itsallgreektome	–

Florida-bred Classic Winners

Needles	1956	Kentucky Derby, Belmont Stakes
Carry Back	1961	Kentucky Derby, Preakness Stakes
Hail to All	1965	Belmont Stakes
High Echelon	1970	Belmont Stakes
Foolish Pleasure	1975	Kentucky Derby
Affirmed	1978	Triple Crown: Kentucky Derby, Preakness Stakes, Belmont Stakes
Codex	1980	Preakness Stakes
Aloma's Ruler	1982	Preakness Stakes
Conquistador Cielo	1982	Belmont Stakes
Gate Dancer	1984	Preakness Stakes
Unbridled	1990	Kentucky Derby

Performances of Florida Derby Competitors in the Triple Crown

Year	Horse	Fla. Derby	Ky. Derby	Preakness	Belmont
1986	Snow Chief	Won	llth	Won	
1986	Badger Land	2nd	5th		
1985	Stephan's Odyssey	6th	2nd		
1984	Swale	Won	Won		Won
1983	Caveat	10th			Won
1982	Laser Light	7th	2nd		
1981	Pleasant Colony	5th	Won	Won	3rd
1979	Spectacular Bid	Won	Won	Won	3rd
1978	Believe It	2nd	3rd	3rd	
1978	Alydar	Won	2nd	2nd	2nd
1976	Great Contractor	2nd			3rd
1976	Honest Pleasure	Won	2nd		
1975	Foolish Pleasure	3rd	Won	2nd	2nd
1974	Little Current	5th		Won	Won
1974	Cannonade	2nd	Won	3rd	3rd
1973	My Gallant	5th			3rd
1973	Our Native	4th	3rd	3rd	
1973	Twice A Prince	6th			2nd
1971	Jim French	3rd	2nd	3rd	2nd
1971	Eastern Fleet	Won	4th	2nd	
1970	My Dad George	Won	2nd	2nd	
1969	Arts and Letters	2nd	2nd	2nd	Won
1968	Forward Pass	Won	Won	Won	2nd
1967	Reason To Hail	3rd	4th	4th	
1967	Gentlemen James	5th			3rd
1967	In Reality	Won		2nd	
1966	Kauai King	5th	Won	Won	4th
1966	Blue Skyer	11th	3rd		
1965	Native Charger	Won	4th	4th	
1965	Hail To All	2nd		3rd	Won
1964	Roman Brother	4th	4th		2nd
1964	The Scoundrel	2nd	3rd	2nd	
1964	Northern Dancer	Won	Won	Won	3rd
1963	Candy Spots	Won	3rd	Won	2nd
1962	Admiral's Voyage	3rd			2nd
1962	Ridan	Won	3rd	2nd	
1961	Crozier	2nd	2nd	3rd	
1961	Carry Back	Won	Won	Won	
1960	Victoria Park	3rd	3rd	2nd	
1960	Venetian Way	2nd	Won		2nd
1960	Belly Ache	Won	2nd	Won	
1959	Sword Dancer	2nd	2nd	2nd	Won
1958	Lincoln Road	2nd	2nd	2nd	
1958	Tim Tam	Won	Won	Won	2nd
1957	Iron Leige	3rd	Won	2nd	
1957	Bold Ruler	2nd		Won	3rd
1956	Needles	Won	Won	2nd	Won
1955	Saratoga	9th		2nd	
1955	Nashua	Won	2nd	Won	Won
1954	Correlation	3rd		2nd	
1953	Dark Star	13th	Won		
1953	Jamie K.	3rd		2nd	2nd

Note: In 35 runnings of the Florida Derby, 35 thoroughbreds have gone on to victories in Triple Crown competition—14 Kentucky Derby winners, 13 Preakness, and 8 Belmont.

Florida-bred Breeders' Cup Winners

1984	Eillo	Sprint
1985	Precisionist	Sprint
	Cozzene	Mile
	Tasso	Juvenile
	Twilight Ridge	Juvenile Fillies
1986	Smile	Sprint
	Brave Raj	Juvenile Fillies
1989	Prized	Turf
1990	Meadow Star	Juvenile Fillies
	Unbridled	Classic

Florida-Bred Millionaires
(as of December 31, 1991)

+ Unbridled	$4,489,475
Precisionist	$3,485,398
Gate Dancer	$2,501,705
Affirmed	$2,393,818
Prized	$2,262,555
Lost Code	$2,085,396
+ Itsallgreektome	$1,947,998
Proper Reality	$1,701,650
Smile	$1,664,027
Equalize	$1,455,298
Cutlass Reality	$1,405,660
+ Meadow Star	$1,394,950
Tappiano	$1,305,551
Susan's Girl	$1,251,668
Carry Back	$1,241,165
Foolish Pleasure	$1,216,705
Primal	$1,209,530
Tasso	$1,207,884
Flying Pidgeon	$1,154,337
Island Whirl	$1,144,010
On the Line	$1,125,810
Judy's Red Shoes	$1,085,668
Richman	$1,064,579
Bolshoi Boy	$1,039,542
Grand Canyon	$1,019,540
Clabber Girl	$1,006,261
Dr. Fager	$1,002,642
Forever Silver	$1,001,974

+Still racing.

Florida-based Winners of Eclipse Awards

1974	Dan Lasater, Outstanding Owner of the Year
1975	Dan Lasater, Outstanding Owner of the Year
1975	Fred Hooper, Outstanding Breeder of the Year
1976	Dan Lasater, Outstanding Owner of the Year
1978	Harbor View, Outstanding Owner of the Year
1978	Harbor View, Outstanding Breeder of the Year
1979	Harbor View, Outstanding Owner of the Year
1982	Fred Hooper, Outstanding Breeder of the Year
1991	Fred Hooper, Award of Merit

Florida-based Owners and Breeders on the National Lists

Florida owners on the leading owner lists by money won

1967	Hobeau Farm (J.J. Dreyfus, Jr.)	$1,120,149
1973	Dan R. Lasater	1,498,785
1974	Dan R. Lasater	*3,022,960
1975	Dan R. Lasater	2,894,726
1976	Dan R. Lasater	2,894,074
1978	Harbor View Farm	2,097,443
1979	Harbor View Farm	2,701,741
1980	Harbor View Farm	2,207,576

* New North American earnings record.

Florida owners on the leading owner lists by races won

1974	Dan R. Lasater	$3,022,960	494
1975	Dan R. Lasater	2,894,726	459
1976	Dan R. Lasater	2,894,074	404
1977	Dan R. Lasater	1,647,107	263

Florida breeders on the leading breeder lists by money won

		Starts	1st	2nd	3rd	
1970	Harbor View Farm	2,856	366	342	323	$1,515,861
1971	Harbor View Farm	3,160	394	348	358	1,739,214
1990	Tartan Farms	1,081	170	145	113	*6,030,043

* New North American earnings record.

Florida breeders on the leading breeder lists by races won

1970	Harbor View Farm	366
1971	Harbor View Farm	394
1972	Harbor View Farm	326

Number of Registered Florida-breds*

1950	53	1971	2,084
1951	50	1972	1,900
1952	69	1973	2,458
1953	79	1974	2,100
1954	90	1975	2,200
1955	115	1976	2,200
1956	133	1977	2,220
1957	237	1978	2,400
1958	277	1979	2,368
1959	312	1980	2,812
1960	336	1981	3,350
1961**	372	1982	3,897
1962	582	1983	3,928
1963	709	1984	4,217
1964	882	1985	4,314
1965	1,117	1986	4,300
1966	1,284	1987	4,172
1967	1,422	1988	3,797
1968	1,655	1989	3,583
1969	1,603	1990	3,504
1970	1,794	1991	3,101

*As of May 22, 1991

**The Breeders' Incentive program began in 1961.

FTBA Breeders' and Stallion Owners' Awards

1947 $250 paid by the tracks to all breeders of Florida-bred winners.

1961*	$32,350	1977	$822,740
1962	24,650	1978	1,409,415
1963	44,400	1979	1,655,327
1964	57,175	1980	1,800,775
1965	69,500	1981	2,674,899
1966	97,930	1982	2,779,544
1967	115,495	1983	2,909,860
1968	127,448	1984	3,440,668
1969	168,345	1985	2,635,801
1970	200,535	1986	3,123,500
1971	311,545	1987	3,181,790
1972	498,910	1988	3,354,301
1973	495,575	1989	3,338,395
1974	557,930	1990	3,290,984
1975	625,920	1991	3,180,315
1976	836,335		

*The Breeders' Awards program began in 1961.

Ocala-Marion County Turf Writers' Award Winners *

Year	Feature		News	
1965	Jobie Arnold	*Thoroughbred Record*		
1966	–		Peter Chew	*National Observer*
1967	Joe Agrella	*Chicago Sun-Times*	Ed Bowen	*The Blood-Horse*
1968	Bob Horwood	*The Florida Horse*	David Alexander	*The Thoroughbred Record*
1969	Gerald Strine	*Washington Post*	Bill Surface	*New York Times*
1970	Russ Harris	*Thoroughbred Record*	Jim Bolus	*Louisville Courier-Journal*
1971	Russ Harris	*Philadelphia Inquirer*	Bill Clark	*Orlando Sentinel*
1972	Furman Bisher	*Atlanta Journal*	Steve Cady	*New York Times*
1973	Edwin Pope	*Miami Herald*	Leon Rasmussen	*The Thoroughbred Record*
1974	Jack Mann	*The Horseman's Journal*	Richard White	*Tampa Times*
1975	Furman Bisher	*Atlanta Journal*	Sy Burick	*Dayton Daily*
1976	Joe Hirsch	*Daily Racing Form*	Tom McEwen	*Tampa Tribune*
1977	Larry Guest	*Orlando Sentinel*	Jim Bolus	*Louisville Courier-Journal*
1978	Whitney Tower	*Classic Magazine*	Billy Reed	*Louisville Courier-Journal*
1979	Jim Bolus	*Louisville Times*	Joseph P. Pons	*The Blood-Horse*
1980	Norm Froscher	*Gainesville Sun*	Julie H. Turner	*The Florida Horse*
1981	Dave Goldman	*The Florida Horse*	Merry Farrington	*The Florida Horse*
1982	Charlene R. Johnson	*The Horseman's Journal*	Bernie Dickman	*Ocala Star-Banner*
1983	Jim Bolus	*Louisville Times*	Eve H. Koier	*The Blood-Horse*
1984	Dave Feldman	*Chicago Sun-Times*	Luther Evans	*Miami Herald*
1985	Charlene R. Johnson	*Spur Magazine*	Gene Stevens	*Post-Time, U.S.A.*
1986	Norm Froscher	*Gainesville Sun*	Bernie Dickman	*Ocala Star-Banner*
1987	Bill Giaque	*The Florida Horse*	Dave Joseph/Fran LaBelle	*Ft. Lauderdale Sun-Sentinel*
1988	Charlene R. Johnson	*Thoroughbred Record*	Mike Bernos	*The Florida Horse*
1989	David Heckerman	*Thoroughbred Times*	JoAnn Guidry	*The Florida Horse*
1990	David Heckerman	*Thoroughbred Times*	Eric Mitchell	*Ocala Star-Banner*

*An FTBA-sponsored contest for the best articles covering the Florida industry over the previous year.

Florida Turf Writers' Award Winners*

Year	Trainers	Jockeys	Owners
1956-57	*Carl G. Rose, Horseman of the Year*		
1958	Sunny Jim Fitzsimmons	William Hartack	Calumet Farm Carl G. Rose
1959	Ben A. Jones Jimmy Jones	Sam Boulmetis	Calumet Farm Mrs. Elizabeth Graham Michael G. Phipps
1960	Arnold Winick	Robert Ussery	James D. Norris Bonnie Heath
1961	Jimmy Pitt	Manuel Ycaza	Louis Wolfson Capt. Harry Guggenheim
	Joseph O'Farrell, Horseman of the Year		
1962	Jack Price	John Sellers	Mrs. Jack Price
	Jack Price, Horseman of the Year		
1963	John Nerud	Walter Blum	William L. McKnight Irving Gushen
1964	H. Allen Jerkens	Walter Blum	Bohemia Stable
1965	Horatio Luro	Ray Broussard	E.P. Taylor Jack Dreyfus
1966	Doug Dodson	Bill Boland	Major Albert Warner
1967	Eddie Neloy	Braulio Baeza	Ogden Phipps William S. Miller
1968	Melvin Calvert	Jorge Velasquez	Frances A. Genter Mary D. Keim
1969	Al Scotti	Angel Cordero, Jr.	Calumet Farm Tartan Farm
1970	Frank Bonsal	Manuel Ycaza	Mrs. Laurel P. Wilson Albert Clay
1971	Arnold Winick Frank J. McManus	John L. Rotz	William L. McKnight Raymond M. Curtis
1972	Eddie Yowell	Jacinto Vasquez	Peter F. Kissel Celestino DiLibero
1973	Budd Lepman	Jacinto Vasquez	Maribel Blum Penny Tweedy
1974	W.A. Croll, Jr.	Walter Blum Gene St. Leon	A.I. Savin Joe Kellman
1975	Sherrill Ward Neal J. Winick Frank Gomez	Robert Woodhouse Ruben Hernandez	Mrs. E.H. Gerry Louis Wolfson
1976	Stanley Hough Frank Merrill	Marco Castaneda Gene St. Leon Jorge Salinas	Mrs. Roxie Gian Luther S. Remsberg
1977	Stanley Hough	Mickey Solomone Chuck Baltazar	Bertram Firestone Al Rosenberg Frank Ryan, Norman St. Leon
	Stanley Hough, Horseman of the Year		

1978	W.A. Croll, Jr. Stanley Hough	Mickey Solomone George Gomez	Tayhill Farm Carlos Rennert
	Warren A. (Jimmy) Croll, Horseman of the Year		
1979	Duke Davis Jimmy Bracken	Jorge Velasquez Izaac Jiminez	Calumet Farm Elmer Haack, Joel Sainer
	Louis E. Wolfson, Horseman of the Year		
1980	Bud Delp Frank Gomez	Jeffrey Fell Walter Guerra	Harry, Teresa, Tommy Meyerhoff William Harder, Dan Hickey
	Bud Delp, Horseman of the Year		
1981	Angel Penna, Sr. Jimmy Bracken	Angel Cordero, Jr. Walter Guerra	Ogden M. Phipps Alfred W. Smith Merritt Buxton, Mrs. Linda Spradlin Charles Largay
	Joseph and Barbara LaCroix, Horsemen of the Year		
1982	Woody Stephens Jose (Pepe) Mendez	Jean-Luc Samyn Alfredo Smith, Jr.	Dr. Jerome Torsney Mar-Deb-Ron Farm Nelson Gonzalez
	Woody Stephens, Horseman of the Year		
1983	Dominic Impresia Frank Gomez	Mary Russ Alfredo Smith, Jr.	Francis & Peter Martin Paula Tucker
	Fred W. Hooper, Horseman of the Year		
1984	Reynaldo Nobles Duke Davis	Alexis Solis Gene St. Leon	Ben F. Walden, Wells Hardesty Fred W. Wiersum
	Duke Davis, Horseman of the Year		
1985	Jimmy Bracken Woody Stephens	Alexis Solis Craig Perret	Frances Genter Claiborne Farm
	Woody Stephens, Horseman of the Year		
1986	Luis Olivares Jimmy Bracken	Jose Santos Jose Velez, Jr.	Star Crown Stable Thomasina Caporella
	James and Virginia Binger and John Nerud, Horsemen of the Year		
1987	Thomas W. Kelley John Tammaro	Julio Pezua Mike Gonzalez	Saron Stable Don Hurtak, Dennis Punches
	Robert Lester, Horseman of the Year		
1988	Luis Olivares Richard Lundy	Jorge Chavez Randy Romero	Arthur Appleton Harry Mangurian, Jr.
	John Tammaro, Horseman of the Year		

*Winners are based on vote on seasonal leaders. When there are two trainers or jockeys, one is for the winter season, one for the summer. Prior to 1956, Gene Markey and William Hartack had been named Horsemen of the Year, but the first dinner held in their honor was 1956. Horseman of the Year is an award given to the person who has contributed the most to the industry.

BREEDING AND RACING ORGANIZATIONS

Florida State Racing Commissioners

1931	L.D. Reagin, M.H. Mabry, R.L. Sweger, R.B. Burdine, R.N. Dosh
1932	R.B. Burdine, L.D. Reagin, M.H. Mabry, R.L. Sweger, R.N. Dosh
1933–34	Carl G. Rose, Walter H. Donovan (complete list unavailable)
1935	Walter H. Donovan, Thomas A. Johnson, R.R. Saunders, Roger H. West
1936–40	Joseph R. Stein, E.A. Williams, Frank P. Rogers, Samuel J. Hilburn, Parks Glover
1941	Alex M. Balfe, Louis J. Day, Samuel J. Hilburn, Joe L. Sharit, C.C. (Milo) Vega, Jr.
1942	Alex M. Balfe, Louis J. Day, Samuel J. Hilburn, Joe L. Sharit, Henry S. Baynard
1943	Alex M. Balfe, William C. Brooker, Samuel J. Hilburn, Joe L. Sharit, Henry S. Baynard
1944–45	Charles F. Baldwin, Emile Yde, William R. Watson, Jr., Thomas B. Swann, J.D. Johnson
1946	Charles F. Baldwin, Emile Yde, William R. Watson, Jr., Thomas B. Swann, J.D. Johnson, Charles E. Ware
1947	Charles F. Baldwin, Emile Yde, William R. Watson, Jr., Thomas B. Swann, J.D. Johnson
1948–49	Leo H. Edwards, R.L. Crum, P.O. Corbin, Roy L. Patience, B.P. Beville
1950	Leo H. Edwards, R.L. Crum, Roy L. Patience, B.P. Beville
1951	D.C. Jones, Carl Hanton, Charles S. Isler, Jr., Lawrence Rogers, G. Warren Sanchez
1952	Dr. Curtis A. Haggard, Robert Kloppel, Jr., J.K. Hayes, J.D. Johnson, J. Wesley Fry
1953	R.E. Dilg, M. Curruthers, Mildred G. Gilmore, Frank Wincell, Julian B. Lane, Robert Carton, Robert Kelly
1954	J. Saxon Lloyd, Clarence H. Ratliff, Warren H. Toole, Jr., J.D. Johnson, John R. Ring
1955–56	Clarence H. Ratliff, Warren H. Toole, Jr., J.D. Johnson, C. Sweet Smith, Jr., John R. Ring
1957–58	John R. Ring, Warren H. Toole, Jr., Roger J. Waybright, C. Sweet Smith, Jr., J. Dudley Johnson
1959	John R. Ring, Glenn Coryell, Walter L. Caldwell, J. Edwin Gay, C. Sweet Smith, Jr., J. Dudley Johnson

1960	Robert Morgan, Carl G. Rose, Jack Fiveash, John Torode, Joe Bill Rood
1961–62	Robert Morgan, Sam Pyle, Jack Fiveash, John Torode, Joe Bill Rood
1963	Robert Morgan, Sam Pyle, Jack Fiveash, John Torode, Joe Bill Rood, Knox Eldredge
1964	Judge Louis Bandel, James L. Lee, Sr., Sam Pyle, John A. Torode, Jack Fiveash, Frank Kappel
1965	Judge Louis Bandel, James L. Lee, Sr., Martin Segal, Robert C. Lechner, Jack Fiveash, Richard A. Kumble
1966	James W. Taylor, Judge Louis Bandel, James L. Lee, Sr., Martin Segal, L.B. Walker, Richard A. Kumble
1967	Larry B. Walker, Larry D. Plante, James W. Taylor, Judge Louis Bandel, James L. Lee, Sr., Martin Segal, George D. Johnson, Jr.
1968	Larry B. Walker, Larry D. Plante, James W. Taylor, Alfred S. Austin, Fred J. Ackel, D.D.S., George D. Johnson, Jr.
1969	Alfred S. Austin, Larry D. Plante, James W. Taylor, L.B. Walker, Fred J. Ackel, D.D.S., George D. Johnson, Jr.
1970	Alfred S. Austin, Fred J. Ackel, D.D.S., James W. Taylor, George E. Saunders, Pat Thomas, George D. Johnson, Jr.

Florida Division of Parimutuel Wagering*

1971	George D. Johnson, Jr., director
1972–75	H J. Patrick McCann, director
1976–77	Dan J. Bradley, director
1978	Gary Rutledge, director; Doug Morris, deputy director
1979–80	Gary Rutledge, director
1981	Robert M. Smith, Jr., director
1982	Robert M. Smith, Jr., director; Robert M. Rosenberg, deputy director
1983–84	Robert M. Rosenberg, director
1985	Robert M. Rosenberg, director; Robert M. Smith, Jr., deputy director
1986–88	William Vessels, director
1989–90	E. V. Jones, director
1991	Bill Tabor, director

*Replaced the Racing Commission in 1970

Florida Parimutuel Commission*

1978–81	Leon Van Wert, James Lewis, Stephen Abramson, Cope Newbem, William Vessels
1982–83	Stephen Abramson, Leon Van Wert, James Lewis, William Vessels, Theodore Couch

1984 Stephen Abramson, Mack Cleveland, James Lewis, Dr. M.S. Schofman, Theodore Couch
1985 Stephen Abramson, Dr. M.S. Schofman, Theodore Couch
1986 Joseph Priede-Rodriguez, L. Erich Braun, Berton Brown, Mack Cleveland, Armer E. White
1987–88 Joseph Priede-Rodriguez, L. Erich Braun, Berton Brown, James A. McGrath, Armer E. White
1989–90 Joseph Priede-Rodriguez, L. Erich Braun, Berton Brown, James A. McGrath, Armer E. White, William Vessels
1991 Sylvan Holtzman, Eddie C. Diaz, Janet Behnke, Berton Brown, Armer E. White

*Added in 1978.

Florida Thoroughbred Breeders' Association

1945 (September): James Bright, president; charter members: Dan Chappell, C.C. Collins, Hunter Lyon, Charles O'Neil, Jr., Tilyou Christopher, Carl Rose, B.L. Whitten, George Woollard, J.H. Yarborough, Stefan Zachar.

1947–48: James Bright, president; Carl Rose, vice president; Billie Zachar, secretary; Charles O'Neil, treasurer; Hunter Lyon, chairman.

1949–50: James Bright, president; Carl Rose, vice president; Tilyou Christopher, second vice president; Ev Clay, secretary; Charles O'Neil, treasurer; Hunter Lyon, chairman.

1951: Dan Chappell, president; Carl Rose, vice president; Tilyou Christopher, second vice president; Charles O'Neil, treasurer; Hunter Lyon, chairman.

1952: Dan Chappell, president; William E. Leach, vice president; George Woollard, second vice president; Ev Clay, secretary; Charles O'Neil, treasurer; Tilyou Christopher, chairman.

1953–54: Dan Chappell, president; Carl Rose, vice president; George Woollard, second vice president; Ev Clay, secretary; Jacob Sher, treasurer; Charles O'Neil, chairman.

1955: Dan Chappell, president; Carl Rose, vice president; William E. Leach, second vice president; Ev Clay, secretary; Jacob Sher, treasurer; Charles O'Neil, chairman.

1956–57: Dan Chappell, president; Carl Rose, vice president; Louis Bandel, second vice president; Ev Clay, secretary; Jacob Sher, treasurer; Carl Rose, chairman.

1958: Carl Rose, president; Roscoe O'Neil, vice president; Ev Clay, secretary; Bonnie Heath, treasurer; Carl Rose, chairman.

1959: Louis Bandel, president; Roscoe O'Neil, vice president; Ev Clay, secretary; Bonnie Heath, treasurer; Carl Rose, chairman.

1960: Bonnie Heath, president; Douglas Steward, vice president; Karl Koontz, secretary; Ev Clay, treasurer.

1961: Bonnie Heath, president; Douglas Stewart, vice president; Grant Dorland, secretary; Connie Geisinger, assistant secretary; Ev Clay, treasurer.

1962: Grant Dorland, president; Elmer Heubeck, vice president; Pat Farrell, secretary; Bonnie Heath, treasurer.

1963: Elmer Heubeck, president; Bonnie Heath, vice president; F. G. Farrell, secretary; Grant Dorland, treasurer.

1964: Bonnie Heath, president; Grant Dorland, vice president; Joe LaCroix, treasurer.

1965: Grant Dorland, president; Joe LaCroix, vice president; Elliott Mackle, secretary-treasurer; Charles Hechter, executive secretary.

1966: Elliott Mackle, president; Bonnie Heath, vice president; Robert Marks, secretary-treasurer.

1967–68: Elliott Mackle, president; H.O.H. Frelinghuysen, vice president; Robert Marks, secretary-treasurer; Jack Winterbotham, executive secretary.

1969–70: H.O.H. Frelinghuysen, president; Robert Marks, vice president; Buck Harris, secretary-treasurer; Joseph B. Moore, Jr., executive secretary.

1971: Fred Hooper, president ; Robert Marks, vice president; Buck Harris, secretary-treasurer; Ann H. Presley, executive secretary.

1972: Fred Hooper, president; Robert Marks, vice president; Buck Harris, secretary-treasurer; Charles Tilley, executive secretary.

1973–74: Fred Hooper, president; Peter Kissel, vice president; Norman Casse, secretary-treasurer; Charles Tilley, executive secretary.

1975: Fred Hooper, president; Joseph O'Farrell, vice president; Jack Price, secretary-treasurer; Charles Tilley, executive secretary.

1976–78: Fred Hooper, president; Jack Price, vice president; Philip Hofmann, secretary-treasurer; Charles Tilley, executive secretary.

1979: Philip Hofmann, president; Hilmer Schmidt, vice president; Joseph O'Farrell, secretary-treasurer; Charles Tilley, executive secretary; Charles Frentz, executive vice president.

1980–81: Philip Hofmann, president; Hilmer Schmidt, vice president; John Hartigan, second vice president; Gary Wolfson, secretary-treasurer; Charles Frentz, executive vice president.

1982: Hilmer Schmidt, president; John Hartigan, vice president; John Weber, second vice president; Gary Wolfson, secretary-treasurer; Charles Frentz, executive vice president.

1983: John Hartigan, president; John Weber, vice president; Lowell Hughes, second vice president; Gary Wolfson, secretary-treasurer; Charles Frentz, executive vice president.

1984: John Hartigan, president; John Weber, vice president; Lowell Hughes, second vice president; J. Michael O'Farrell, Jr., secretary-treasurer; Charles Frentz, executive vice president.

1985: John Hartigan, president; Lowell Hughes, vice president; J. Michael O'Farrell, Jr., second vice president; Scott Dudley, secretary-treasurer; Charles Frentz, executive vice president.

1986: Douglas Oswald, president; J. Michael O'Farrell, Jr., vice president; Greg Branch, second vice president; Scott Dudley, secretary-treasurer; Charles Frentz, executive vice president.

1987: Donald Dizney, president; J. Michael O'Farrell, Jr., vice president, Greg Branch, second vice president; Dennis Diaz, secretary; Scott Dudley, treasurer; Kettman Barber, executive vice president.

1988: Donald Dizney, president; J. Michael O'Farrell, Jr., vice president, Harry Mangurian, second vice president; Betty Lavery, secretary; Greg Branch, treasurer; Richard Hancock, executive vice president.

1989: George Steinbrenner, president; J. Michael O'Farrell, Jr., vice president; Harry Mangurian, second vice president; Betty Lavery, secretary; Greg Branch, treasurer; Richard Hancock, executive vice president.

1990: John Weber, president; Bryan Howlett, vice president; Bonnie Heath, second vice president; Betty Lavery, secretary; Greg Branch, treasurer; Richard Hancock, executive vice president.

Farm Managers' Club

1962 charter members

Vince Ellspermann
John Hartigan
Tom Murphy
Edsel Rohan
Roy Yates
Chuck Tilley
Robert Marks
Joseph O'Farrell
Elmer Heubeck
Douglas Oswald
Graham Rose
Dr. William R. Brawner
Frank Lamoreaux
Cyril Best

Presidents

1962–63	Vincent Ellspermann
1963–64	John Hartigan
1964–65	Howard Adair
1965–66	Vincent Ellspermann
1966–67	Bill Peterson
1967–68	Robert Marks
1968–69	Henry W. Smith
1969–70	Clayton O'Quinn
1970–71	Roy Yates
1971–72	Dr. Harold Gutteridge
1972–73	Norman Casse
1973–74	Jack Dunn
1974–75	John Hartigan
1975–76	Marion Lewis
1976–77	George May
1977–78	Sherman Armstrong
1978–79	Buddy Yates
1979–80	Buz Burke
1981–82	Mike Hovendon
1982–83	Ed Sauerbier
1983–84	Earl Pierpont
1984–85	Bill Read
1985–86	Bob Williams
1986–87	Don Giggle
1987–88	Bill Rainbow
1988–89	Brian Hartigan
1989–90	Dr. Tom Lane
1990–91	Dr. Tom Lane

Florida Thorobred Fillies

Ginny Mourar first had the idea of forming a group of women in the industry. In the spring of 1969 she persuaded the charter members to practice with her. The public was invited to watch for $2.50 at 7:30, March 18, at Golden Hills. John Hartigan was the announcer, and there were a floor show, dancing, and canapes. The organizers decided to prepare another for Ocala Week that year, and they practiced in Marge O'Quinn's barn. Marge and Theta Shipman were the hits that night as the Old Gray Mares. It was the beginning of yet another tradition of Ocala Week.

Charter Members

Margaret Adair
Mattie Alexander
Joan Baker
Vivian Best
Eunice Burgess
Ida Cherry
Jean Divine
Susu Dodson
Louise Dooley
Chris Ellspermann
Scottie Farley
Marie Gauthier
Connie Geisinger
Mobel Gettings
Doris Hall
Sandy Hartigan
Joe Hiler
Dot Holcomb
Leslie Horne
Julia Hudson
Mae Jolley
Georgia Kennon
Jean King
Ricky Kirby
LaVerne Lamoureux
Agnes Leathers
Selma Merritt
Manu Myall
Anne McCord
Advice McGrath
Nancy O'Farrell
Jeanne O'Toole
LaVerne Peterson
Sondra Powers
Jean Rodgers
Mabel Shanding
Fama Smith
Patsy Staletovich
Rebecca Tanner
Betty Tilley
Jackie Tortora
Louise Weigers
Kathleen Yates
Elinor Zoeller

Members Emerita

Ann Rose
Abby Holbert
Vivian Best
LaVerne Lamoureux
Louise Weigers
Virginia Mourar
Ida Cherry
Faye Schmidt

Presidents

Anne McCord	1962	Nada Kingwell	1976
Mattie Alexander	1963	Carol Yates	1977
Fama Smith	1964	Jean Burke	1978
Connie Geisinger	1965	Carol Heil	1979
Jeanne O'Toole	1965	Dottie Williams	1980
Vivian Best	1965	Dee Walther	1981
Virginia Mourar	1966	Kathy Prater	1982
Barbara King	1967	Louise Rector	1983
Joan Slater	1968	Donna Mobley	1984
Jackie Tortora	1969	Betty Lou Lee	1985
Marge O'Quinn	1970	Wendy Boyle	1986
Theta Shipman	1971	Eva Knowles	1987
Pat Nix	1972	Kathy Frank	1988
Marilyn Armstrong	1973	Helen Gardner	1989
Pam Peterson	1974	Linda Breakfield-Martin	1990
Faye Schmidt	1975	LaVerne Stinson	1991

Ocala Breeders' Sales Company, Inc.

Charter members, 1974

Original shareholders

Joseph M. O'Farrell
George L. Onett
Norman E. Casse
Roy A. Kennedy
Clayton O'Quinn
Hilmer C. Schmidt
Jack Winterbotham
D. E. Hunt
Buck Harris
Lee Gale
Noel Hickey
Jan Haller
Lois Myers
Arnold W. Willcox
Angelo Robert Gaudio
Ed Seedhouse
Jack Price
Dr. John Lee
Dr. John L. Peterson
Clyde E. Nix
Fred Elias
Charles Verheyden
Dr. Ronald Chak
John H. Hartigan
Richard D. Irwin

Presidents

Roy A. Kennedy
Norman E. Casse
Tom Chiota

Florida Thoroughbred Organizations

Florida Thoroughbred Breeders Association, 4727 N.W. 80th Avenue, Ocala, FL 34482, (904) 629-2160

Ocala Breeders' Sales Company, P.O. Box 99, Ocala, FL 32678, (904) 237-2154

Fasig-Tipton, Florida, Inc, Calder Race Course, (305) 625-1311, ext. 345; Box 36, Elmont, NY 11003, (516) 328-1800

Jockey Club Information, 4727 N.W. 80th Avenue, Ocala, FL 32675, (904) 629-0089

Farm Managers' Club, (904) 591-2604

Florida Thorobred Fillies, P.O. Box 937, Ocala, FL 32678

The Florida Horse, P.O. Box 2106, Ocala, FL 32678, (904) 629-8082

Calder Race Course, Inc., P.O. Box 1808, Carol City Branch, Opa Locka, FL 33055, (305) 625-1311

Gulfstream Park, 901 S. Federal Highway, Hallandale, FL 33009, (305) 944-1242

Hialeah Park, P.O. Box 158, Hialeah, FL 33011, (305) 885-8000

Tampa Bay Downs, Inc., P.O. Box E, Oldsmar, FL 33557, (813) 855-4401

FLORIDA RACETRACKS: FACTS AND FIGURES

Hialeah Averages

Year	Season	Total attendance	Total mutuels	Average attendance	Days
1944	Jan. 7–Mar. 4	430,124	36,786,127	8,602	50
1946	Jan. 17–Mar. 4	624,362	53,308,007	15,609	40
1947	Jan. 17–Mar. 4	631,160	48,271,317	15,799	40
1948	Jan. 16–Mar. 2	584,628	44,806,219	14,616	40
1949	Jan. 17–Mar. 3	577,077	42,662,025	14,427	40
1950	Jan. 17–Mar. 3	572,845	43,697,413	14,321	40
1951	Jan. 17–Mar. 3	601,753	52,055,908	15,044	40
1952	Jan. 17–Mar. 3	678,745	60,637,049	16,969	40
1953	Jan. 16–Mar. 3	701,157	62,084,596	17,529	40
1954	Jan. 16–Mar. 3	714,465	67,077,082	17,862	40
1955	Jan. 17–Mar. 3	693,571	68,413,252	17,339	40
1956	Jan. 17–Mar. 2	692,680	71,743,684	17,317	40
1957	Jan. 17–Mar. 4	659,716	70,790,024	16,492	40
1958	Jan. 17–Mar. 4	629,897	68,735,130	15,747	40
1959	Jan. 16–Mar. 3	624,250	68,407,045	15,606	40
1960	Jan. 16–Mar. 2	646,035	72,503,563	16,151	40
1961	Jan. 17–Mar. 3	605,660	68,008,796	15,141	40
1962	Jan. 17–Mar. 3	609,959	68,672,524	15,249	40
1963	Jan. 17–Mar. 4	604,386	71,421,319	15,110	40
1964	Jan. 17–Mar. 3	611,309	70,341,840	15,283	40
1965	Jan. 16–Mar. 3	625,690	75,770,975	15,642	40
1966	Jan. 17–Mar. 3	603,604	77,799,958	15,090	40
1967	Jan. 17–Mar. 3	577,463	73,108,007	14,436	40
1968	Jan. 18–Mar. 2	578,776	75,919,700	14,840	40
1969	Jan. 17–Mar. 4	594,153	82,682,903	14,854	40
1970	Jan. 16–Mar. 3	551,972	80,490,345	13,799	40
1971	Jan. 16–Mar. 3	519,327	76,311,677	12,983	40
1972	Mar. 3–Apr. 18	347,225	51,792,694	8,680	40
1973	Jan. 17–Mar. 3	482,544	69,705,152	12,064	40
1974	Mar. 5–Apr. 20	322,705	46,320,479	8,068	40
1975	Jan. 17–Mar. 4	500,393	66,767,960	12,510	40
1976	Jan. 15–Mar. 5	502,584	70,196,229	11,422	44
1977	Mar. 9–May 7	392,799	54,281,519	7,856	50
1978	Jan. 16–Mar. 4	468,517	70,432,178	11,155	42
1979	Mar. 7–May 12	737,676	65,472,325	7,474	50
1980	Jan. 15–Mar. 5	449,384	83,822,090	10,213	44
1981	Mar. 7–May 28	418,907	73,643,699	6,445	65
1982	Jan. 8–May 6	498,906	92,796,564	9,978	50
1983	Mar. 8–May 4	344,368	66,784,756	6,887	50
1984	Jan. 9–Mar. 6	442,920	95,664,782	8,858	50
1985	Mar. 7–May 3	439,706	71,485,620	6,694	5
1986	Mar. 7–May 3	408,543	67,983,461	*	50
	May 4–May 27	142,452	20,909,895	*	21
1987	Jan. 1–Mar. 6	539,116	101,577,793	*	50
	Nov. 11–Dec. 31	318,879	54,668,316	*	44
1988	Jan. 1–Jan. 7	64,534	12,964,874	*	6
1989	Mar. 8–May 28	537,827	86,686,428	*	71
	Nov. 18–Dec. 18	63,350	5,435,446	*	27
1990	No meet				

*Averages not available for 1986–1989.

Hialeah Park Presidents

Joseph Smoot	1924
Joseph Early Widener	1931
P. A. B. Widener II	1939
John Clinton Clark	1940
Eugene Mori	1954
Eugene Mori, Jr.	1962
John W. Galbreath	1974
John J. Brunetti	1978 to present

History of Hialeah Park

1924 Hialeah Park was conceived and headed by James H. Bright and Joseph Smoot, under the Miami Jockey Club.

1925 The first race was held January 15, 1925. General Manager Cassidy did not approve of women betting and tried to stop them at the mutuel windows, but the women were determined to make their wagers.

1926 Thoroughbred racing was held in the winter season, with a dog track and a Jai-Alai fronton.

1927 New installations on the backside barns.

1928 No racing was held.

1929 "Upset Lad" won the famed Flamingo Stakes.

1930 Certificates were used for payoffs instead of cash. Gambling was not yet legal in Florida.

1931 J. E. Widener became president. Gambling in Florida was legalized.

1932 Widener spent $2 million dollars renovating the racetrack, making Hialeah Park one of the most beautiful racetracks in the United States. He brought the first flamingos over from Cuba. New "tote-board" was installed. First filly to win the Flamingo Stakes was "Evening."

1933 First turf race was held. Hialeah Park was the first track in the United States to introduce the saliva test. The first photo-finish camera was introduced.

1934 Two new barns installed.

1935 Widener's horse "Black Helen" won the Flamingo Stakes.

1936 J. E. Widener changed the name of the Florida Derby to the Flamingo Stakes.

1937 The first flamingos were hatched in captivity, thirty babies in all.

1938 Two new barns erected.

1939 First turf stakes race in America was Miami Beach Handicap

1939 "Maeriel" won the Hialeah Turf Cup.

1940 John C. Clark named president.

1941 "Black Helen Handicap" was run for the first time, named after Widener's horse "Black Helen."

1942 Three new barns erected.

1943 No racing held because of war restrictions.
1944 Greentree Stable won the Widener Handicap for the second year in a row.
1945 No racing held because of the war.
1946 Winston Churchill visited Hialeah Park, calling it "extraordinary."
1947 "Armed," Calumet Farm, won the Widener Handicap two years in a row.
1948 "Citation" won the Flamingo Stakes, then went on to win the Triple Crown. He was the first horse to win $1 million in purse money.
1949 A 45 percent increase in overall space in the whole interior of the plant.
1950 Grandstand parking almost doubled with new outside lots. Tel-Autograph was added to speed payoffs.
1951 Construction costs passed $500,000 with installations of a 480-ton steel overhead structure.
1952 Film patrol introduced to Hialeah Park. Flamingo Stakes raised to $100,000.
1953 More escalators added. First year that the Flamingo Stakes was telecast.
1954 The old clubhouse was torn down, making way for the new structure, still in the Mediterranean style, at a cost of over $2.5 million. New escalators and elevators were added.
1955 "Nashua" won the Flamingo Stakes. Richest purse $104,600, for the Flamingo. Eugene Mori became president. Enlarged receiving barn.
1956 Largest attendance, 42,366, February 18. "Needles" won the Flamingo Stakes, first Florida-bred to do so. Highest daily average for the 1956 forty-day meet. Sky terrace was installed.
1957 Flamingo Plaza Fountain constructed in the grandstand. New mutuel windows and a new sprinkler system were installed. All horses started carrying the same weight in the Flamingo.
1958 New jockey quarters built, administrative building redesigned. Harry M. Stevens Co. took over the concessions. First time a horse was disqualified from the Flamingo. Tram trains were used for the public from the parking lots to the plant. Sprinkler system was installed in the clubhouse.
1959 New landscaping in the infield and grandstand. Bronze flamingos were added to the Flamingo Fountain.
1960 Permanent pari-mutuel windows installed and jockey quarters renovated.
1961 New "tote-board" installed. Lily pond put in behind the clubhouse. The entire paddock and Sidewalk Cafe redesigned. Highest daily-double pool. Relocation of more than eighty-five palm trees.
1962 New aviary and Shipwreck Aquarium built. "Carry-Back" won the Flamingo Stakes. Verandah level built in the clubhouse. Eugene Mori, Jr., assumed presidency.

1963 Two new dormitories installed, aluminum rails put up on the track. Sales Pavilion was constructed by Fasig-Tipton and Hialeah Park.

1964 New ceiling built to cover the entire grandstand. All the barns reroofed.

1965 New press box built, statue of Citation unveiled.

1966 Two new barns installed.

1967 A new receiving barn erected.

1968 New stable kitchen erected, two new barns added.

1969 Flamingo Terrace built. First woman, Diane Crump, to ride at a major racetrack.

1970 All barns updated and reconstructed.

1971 "Faneuil Hall" broke the American-world record for the distance of 5 1/2 furlongs, 1:02.5.

1972 Two new barns erected.

1973 Hialeah Park joined the Thoroughbred Racing Association.

1974 John Galbreath became president of Hialeah Park.

1975 "Foolish Pleasure" won the Flamingo Stakes.

1976 "Toonerville" broke the American-world record for the distance of 1 3/4 miles, 1:51.3. Hialeah Park's bicentennial year.

1977 John J. Brunetti purchased Hialeah Park and became president. "Seattle Slew" won the Flamingo Stakes. Rotation of the dates between Hialeah and Gulfstream began.

1978 Mediterranean Lounge added to the second floor of the clubhouse. The movie "The Champ" was filmed at Hialeah. Administrative building renovated.

1979 Hialeah Park became a national landmark. Grandstand floor was retiled. "Spectacular Bid" won the Flamingo Stakes. All snack bars updated.

1980 New Fountain Terrace built, clubhouse box seat area enlarged. Sprinkler system installed in the press box and clubhouse.

1981 Hialeah Park had its longest running meet, seventy-one days. Winners' Circle enlarged. New bar and lounge enlarged in the Food Factory.

1982 Highest one-day handle, $3,755,639, Flamingo Day, March, 6. Tel-a-bet was introduced, and Hialeah Park became the only racetrack in North America to have telephone wagering accounts. Pic-Six with Jackpot was innovated; the largest payoff was $382,344,80 on January 25. New Auto-Tote Mutuel equipment was installed with Bet-Cash windows. The Flamingo Stakes was raised to $250,000 guaranteed, the richest running stakes to be held in Florida.

1983 Complete new sewage system installed throughout the 200 acres. Two new dormitories with lavatories, recreation rooms, and laundry facilities and four new barns were constructed. Sidewalk Cafe was converted into a fast-food cafeteria. New Citation Terrace Bar on the first floor of the clubhouse. Mediterranean Lounge was expanded and the turf course reconditioned.

Tropical Park Meeting Yearly Leaders*

Trainers	Years	No. Wins	Jockeys	Years	No. Wins
Luis Olivares	1985–86	25	Marland Suckie**	1985–86	43
James Bracken	1984–85	18	Alexis Solis	1984–85	46
Joe Moos	1983–84	15	Jose Santos		46
Frank Gomez	1982–83	17	Gene St. Leon	1983–84	37
Antonio Arcodia	1981–82	20	Alexis Solis**	1982–83	50
Frank Gomez	1980–81	17	Mary Russ**	1981–82	49
Stan M. Hough	1979–80	20	J. D. Bailey	1980–81	36
Stan M. Hough	1978–79	35	Walter A. Guerra		36
Stan M. Hough	1977–78	25	Jacinto Vasquez		36
Stan M. Hough	1976–77	23	Jacinto Vasquez	1979–80	59
Neal J. Winick		23	J. D. Bailey	1978–79	47
Stan M. Hough	1975–76	18	J. D. Bailey	1977–78	43
Neal Winick	1974–75	21	Gene St. Leon	1976–77	44
A. N. Winick	1973–74	16	Charles Baltazar	1975–76	51
A. N. Winick	1972–73	16	Robert Woodhouse	1974–75	36
			Jacinto Vasquez	1973–74	50
			Jacinto Vasquez	1972–73	50
Most victories for a trainer, single meeting			Most victories for a jockey, single meeting:		
Stan M. Hough	1978–79	35	Charles Maffeo	1969–70	66

*Statistics for Tropical Park as of 1985.

**Apprentice.

Record Pools

Daily double pool (1-7-84)	156,352
Perfecta pool (1-5-85) 9th race	161,927
Trifecta pool (1-7-84) 8th race	129,817
Combined pool (1-13-79) 9th race	309,186

Record Mutuel Payoffs

Largest win payoff (12-31-75)	250.40
Smallest win payoff (12-18-72)	2.20
Largest daily double payoff (12-14-73)	7,907.80
Smallest daily double payoff (10-27-71)	9.20
Largest perfecta payoff (12-31-75)	5,208.00
Smallest perfecta payoff (12-18-72)	4.80
Largest trifecta payoff (1-6-79)	52,398.00
Smallest trifecta payoff (11-16-81)	21.20
Pic-six payoff (1–2–86) (1 ticket)	182,300.80

Record Mutuel Handle

January 5, 1985 2,434,490

Record Attendance

January 14, 1978 17,671

Top Five Mutuel Handles

2,434,490	1-5-85
2,432,856	1-7-84
2,366,782*	1-3-79
2,149,471	1-14-78
2,144,214	1-1-86

*Eleven races.

Top Five Attendances

17,671	1-14-78
17,620	1-13-79
17,158	1-10-76
16,331	1-3-76
16,011	11-18-67

Calder Averages

Year	Days*	Handle	Average	Attendance	Average/Day**
1971	120	55,163,398	459,694	859,870	6,667
1972	120	72,285,153	602,376	884,159	7,367
1973	120	85,864,255	715,535	968,353	8,070
1974	120	98,137,749	817,815	1,062,352	8,853
1975	120	102,413,622	853,446	1,113,017	9,275
1976	111	96,156,808	866,277	1,043,573	9,401
1977	120	106,659,833	888,831	1,104,536	9,204
1978	120	119,146,910	992,890	1,112,356	9,352
1979	119	125,049,506	1,042,079	1,102,313	9,185
1980	120	123,170,434	1,026,420	1,016,497	8,470
1981	120	123,596,909	1,029,974	995,767	8,298
1982	119	124,128,537	1,043,096	985,135	8,278
1983	120	128,763,857	1,073,032	964,409	8,037
1984	120	127,553,403	1,062,945	969,304	8,078
1985	120	137,074,542	1,142,288	978,614	8,155

(*continued*)

Calder Averages (*continued*)

Year		Days*	Handle	Average
1986	Jan. 1–Jan. 7	6	10,464,234	63,281
	May 30–Nov. 9	121	145,634,229	970,063
	Nov. 11–Dec. 31	44	54,946,839	353,244
1987	Jan. 1–Jan. 7	6	10,960,822	69,519
	May 30–Nov. 8	121	144,064,578	955,134
1988	Mar. 6–May 3	50	73,784,024	455,998
	May 4–May 27	21	22,850,631	163,171
	May 28–Nov. 9	121	139,404,969	946,505
	Nov. 11–Dec. 31	44	53,491,416	342,207
1989	Jan. 1–Jan. 7	6	10,319,281	56,307
	May 29–Nov. 18	122	136,985,510	948,223
	Nov. 19–Dec. 31	37	40,162,801	260,003
1990	Jan. 1–Jan. 14	12	18,212,644	104,479
	May 5–Nov. 16	143	160,213,002	1,131,240
	Nov. 17–Dec. 31	38	49,239,557	328,694

*Charity Days Not Included.

**Average/Day not available for 1986–1990.

Calder Statistics*

Highest mutuel handle, one day	2,095,376	June 9, 1984
Largest attendance, one day	17,564	Sept. 6, 1976
Highest mutuel handle, season (123 days)	127,522,912	1979
Largest attendance, season (123 days)	1,126,512	1979
Highest daily double pool	126,020	Sept. 4, 1978
Highest perfecta pool	114,437	Aug. 25, 1984
Highest trifecta pool	100,979	Aug. 27, 1983
Largest daily double payoff	2,671	July 2, 1976
Highest perfecta payoff	43,371	Oct. 3, 1984
Smallest perfecta payoff	4.20	June 12, 1974
Highest trifecta payoff	38,765.60	Nov. 9, 1982
Smallest trifecta payoff	20.20	June 17, 1980
Highest straight payoff	293.60	Sept. 17, 1973
Smallest straight payoff	2.10	June 12, 1974

*As of 1985.

Gulfstream Averages

Year	Season	Total attendance	Total mutuels	Average mutuels	Days
1944	Dec. 1-Dec. 23	90,686	5,638,050	281,902	20
1945	Dec. 1-Jan. 16	429,970	28,592,076	714,801	40
1947	Mar. 5-Apr. 19	442,945	29,507,761	737,644	40
1947	Dec. 1-Jan. 15	412,257	24,522,176	646,109	38
1949	Mar. 4-Apr. 19	439,643	26,692,985	667,324	40
1950	Mar. 4-Apr. 20	453,491	28,648,861	698,753	41
1951	Mar. 5-Apr. 21	484,808	34,390,900	818,831	42
1952	Mar. 4-Apr. 19	56,473	43,292,351	1,055,911	41
1953	Mar. 4-Apr. 21	601,682	47,906,175	1,140,623	42
1954	Mar. 4-Apr. 22	617,537	48,372,000	1,124,930	43
1955	Mar. 4-Apr. 22	608,942	48,619,498	1,130,686	43
1956	Mar. 3-Apr. 21	658,856	57,162,170	1,329,353	43
1957	Mar. 5-Apr. 23	647,449	54,481,161	1,267,004	43
1958	Mar. 5-Apr. 23	616,092	53,770,451	1,250,476	43
1959	Mar. 4-Apr. 21	599,555	52,966,703	1,231,784	43
1960	Mar. 3-Apr. 23	627,410	57,290,050	1,332,327	43
1961	Mar. 4-Apr. 24	615,303	52,937,708	1,231,109	43
1962	Mar. 5-Apr. 24	588,108	52,158,458	1,212,458	43
1963	Mar. 5-Apr. 24	543,877	49,297,474	1,146,453	43
1964	Mar. 4-Apr. 23	643,007	55,087,631	1,281,108	43
1965	Mar. 4-Apr. 23	620,420	56,439,593	1,312,549	43
1966	Mar. 4-Apr. 26	618,733	60,410,535	1,313,273	46
1967	Mar. 4-Apr. 24	584,313	58,468,425	1,359,731	43
1968	Mar. 4-Apr. 25	605,895	63,254,979	1,437,613	44
1969	Mar. 5-Apr. 26	587,245	64,170,439	1,492,336	43
1970	Mar. 4-Apr. 22	584,983	64,582,862	1,501,927	43
1971	Mar. 4-Apr. 22	557,629	58,536,766	1,361,320	43
1972	Jan. 17-Mar. 2	639,347	72,345,630	1,808,641	40
1973	Mar. 5-Apr. 30	551,057	60,980,112	1,270,419	48
1974	Jan. 17-Mar. 4	599,060	70,738,305	1,768,457	40
1975	Mar. 5-Apr. 30	568,013	58,059,942	1,184,896	49
1976	Mar. 6-May11	656,729	65,415,720	1,147,644	57
1977	Jan. 15-Mar. 7	633,776	71,292,175	1,620,277	44
1978	Mar. 6-May8	650,813	74,911,891	1,362,034	55
1979	Jan. 15-Mar. 6	683,241	94,568,590	2,149,285	44
1980	Mar. 6-May7	577,823	77,304,908	1,546,098	50
1981	Jan. 8-Mar. 6	714,803	103,531,722	2,070,634	50
1982	Mar. 8-May15	554,625	76,664,847	1,533,296	50
1983	Jan. 8-Mar. 7	696,551	104,049,307	2,080,986	50
1984	Mar. 7-May3	568,574	83,410,031	1,668,200	50
1985	Jan. 8-Mar. 6	695,375	114,940,056	2,298,801	50
1986	Jan. 8-Mar. 6	661,022	114,995,640	2,299,912	50
1987	Mar. 7-May 3	312,628	66,324,117	*	32
	May 5-May 28	580,541	96,304,797	*	50
1988	Jan. 8-Mar. 5	634,370	118,454,866	*	50
1989	Jan. 1-Mar. 7	664,960	122,700,270	*	50
	Nov. 3-Nov. 5	91,087	21,322,335	*	3
1990	Jan. 16-Mar. 4	968, 191	167,552,397	*	90

*Averages not available for 1987–1990

Gulfstream Presidents and Racing Secretaries

Presidents	Secretaries
James Donn, Sr., 1944	James P. Ross, Jr., 1944
James Donn, Jr., 1961	Edward C. McKinsey, Jr., 1971
Douglas Donn, 1978–	James Bell, Jr., 1979
	Thomas E. Trotter, 1981
	Terence Blair Meyocks, 1990–

Tampa Bay Downs

1947–65	Named "Sunshine Park."
1965	Bought and headed by Chester Ferguson; renamed Florida Downs and Turf Club.
1965–80	Sam Davis, president and general manager
1980	Stella Thayer, president; renamed Tampa Bay Downs.

Racing Secretaries		**Average Handle**		**Contributions to the State**	
1975	Bud Sears	1980-81	$358,513	1982-83	$148,588
1976-80	Jack Klucina	1981-82	370,763	1983-84	190,876
1980-84	Mel Chadwell	1982-83	384,763	1984-85	197,876
1984-85	Warren Wolf	1983-84	415,095		
1985-86	Robert Clark	1984-85	413,297		

HISTORIC FLORIDA RACES

Flamingo Stakes

1 1/8 miles, 3-years-olds, Hialeah Park, Hialeah

Year	First	Second	Third	Value	Time
1926	Torcher	Mary Kinkead	McTingle	4,450	1:57 1/5
1929	Upset Lad	Boris	Stand By	8,600	1:53 2/5
1930	Titus	Playfellow's Dream	Politen	9,900	1:52
1931	Lightning Bolt	Spanish Play	Mynheer	10,800	1:51 4/5
1932	Evening	Cathop	Trombone	9,725	1:50 4/5
1933	Charley O.	Jungle King	Inlander	10,475	1:49 3/5
1934	Time Clock	Agrarian	Boy Valet	10,075	1:49 1/5
1935	Black Helen	Mantagna	Roman Soldier	15,600	1:51
1936	Brevity	Dnieper	Bright Plumage	20,050	1:48 1/5
1937	Court Scandal	No Sir	Eli Yale	20,900	1:49 3/5
1938	Lawrin	Bourbon King	Pasteurized	20,100	1:50 4/5
1939	Technican	Volitant	Day Off	20,000	1:50 1/5
1940	Woof Woof	Prompt Pay	Red Dock	22,450	1:50 1/5
1941	Dispose	Curious Coin	The Rhymer	20,200	1:48 4/5
1942	Requested	Redthorn	Alsab	28,150	1:50 3/5
1944	Stir Up	Skytracer	Stymie	14,825	1:52 2/5
1946	Round View	Wee Admiral	Gay Moonbeam	29,600	1:52
1947	Faultless	Brabancon	Riskolater	49,500	1:49 3/5
1948	Citation	Big Dial	Saggy	43,500	1:48 4/5
1949	Olympia	Sneak	Reveille	48,500	1:48 4/5
1950	Oil Capitol	Lotowhite	Theory	44,800	1:48 1/5
1951	Yildiz	Timely Reward	Anyoldtime	50,000	1:51 1/5
1952	Blue Man	Jampol	Count Flame	47,450	1:50
	Charlie McAdam	Master Fiddle	Armageddon	47,450	1:50
1953	Straight Face	Royal Bay Gem	Tribe	116,400	1:49 2/5
1954	Turn-to	Black Metal	Maharajah	96,400	1:49 2/5
1955	Nashua	Saratoga	Cup Man	104,600	1:49 3/5
1956	Needles	Golf Ace	Fabius	111,600	1:49 2/5
1957	Bold Ruler	Gen. Duke	Iron Liege	94,200	1:47
1958	Tim Tam	Jewel's Reward	Talent Show	97,800	1:48 1/5
1959	Troilus	Open View	First Landing	86,070	1:49 1/5
1960	Bally Ache	Victoria Park	Keenation	90,800	1:48
1961	Carry Back	Crozier	Your Bill	84,370	1:50 3/5
1962	Prego	Ridan	Sunrise County	88,550	1:49
1963	Never Bend	King Toots	Royal Ascot	88,140	1:49 2/5
1964	Northern Dancer	Mr. Brick	Quadrangle	89,830	1:47 4/5
1965	Native Charger	Sparkling Johnny	Hail to All	93,340	1:50
1966	Buckpasser	Abe's Hope	Blue Skyer	88,660	1:50
1967	Reflected Glory	In Reality	Bold Monarch	93,990	1:48 3/5
1968	Wise Exchange	Iron Ruler	Subpet	89,050	1:48 1/5
1969	Top Knight	Arts and Letters	Beau Brummel	95,160	1:47 4/5
1970	My Dad George	Corn off the Cob	Burd Alane	104,910	1:48 3/5
1971	Executioner	Dynastic	Jim French	100,750	1:49 1/5
1972	Hold Your Peace	Upper Case	Tarboosh	86,190	1:48 2/5
1973	Our Native	My Gallant	Angle Light	91,520	1:48 1/5
1974	Bushongo	Hasty Flyer	Judger	83,720	1:49
1975	Foolish Pleasure	Prince Thou Art	Somethingfabulous	85,540	1:48 2/5
1976	Honest Pleasure	Inca Roca	Johnny Appleseed	85,605	1:46 1/5
1977	Seattle Slew	Giboulee	Fort Prevel	90,610	1:47 2/5
1978	Alydar	Noon Time Spender	Dr. Valeri	103,350	1:47
1979	Spectacular Bid	Strike The Main	Sir Ivor Again	96,850	1:48 2/5
1980	Superbity	Koluctoo Bay	Rockhill Native	107,850	1:51 1/5
1981	Tap Shoes	Well Decorated	Double Sonic	106,800	1:49 1/5
1982	Timely Writer	New Discovery	Le Danseur	150,000	1:49 3/5
1983	Current Hope	Chumming	Gen'l Practitioner	150,000	1:49 2/5
1984	Time for a Change	Dr. Carter	Rexson's Hope	210,000	1:47
1985	Chief's Crown	Proud Truth	Stephan's Odyssey	150,000	1:48 2/5
1986	Badger Land	Bolshoi Boy	Annapolis John	180,000	1:47
1987	Talinum	Cryptoclearance	Leo Castelli	270,000	1:50
1988	Cherokee Colony	Sorry About That	Cefis	150,000	1:49 4/5
1989	Awe Inspiring	Irish Actor	America's Friend	180,000	1:49 3/5

Note: Not run in 1927, 1928, 1943, or 1945. Run at Tampa in 1926. Run as Florida Derby prior to 1937. Run in two divisions in 1952. Top Bet finished third in the first division in 1952 but was disqualified and placed last. Jewel's Reward finished first in 1958 but was disqualified and placed second. Sunrise County finished first in 1962 but was disqualified and placed third. Iron Ruler finished first in 1968 but was disqualified and placed second. In 1985 Chief's Crown finished first but was disqualified and placed second; following an appeal, the original order of finish was restored.

Widener Cup Handicap

1 1/4 miles, 3-year-olds and upward, Hialeah Park, Hialeah

Year	First	Second	Third	Value	Time
1936	Matagna	Chance Ray	Sabin	10,150	2:01 4/5
1937	Columbiana	Finance	Dellor	52,000	2:01 4/5
1938	War Admiral	Zevson	War Minstrel	49,550	2:03 4/5
1939	Bull Lea	Sir Damion	Stagehand	46,450	2:02 2/5
1940	Many Stings	Big Pebble	Day Off		
			Supreme Sir	52,000	2:03
1941	Big Pebble	Get Off	Haltal	51,800	2:02 4/5
1942	The Rhymer	Best Seller	Olympus	53,950	2:05 1/5
1944	Four Freedoms	Sun Again	Alquest	29,350	2:04 3/5
1946	Armed	Concordian	Reply Paid	45,700	2:02 2/5
1947	Armed	Talon	Lets Dance	43,900	2:01 3/5
1948	El Mono	Stud Poker	Bug Juice	43,800	2:01
1949	Coaltown	Shy Guy	Faultless	42,300	2:02
1950	Royal Governor	Arise	Going Away	43,000	2:06
1951	Sunglow	Three Rings	County Delight	54,100	2:02 4/5
1952	Spartan Valor	Greek Ship	Pilaster	51,300	2:02 1/5
1953	Oil Capitol	Alerted	Battlefield	93,200	2:02 4/5
1954	Landlocked	Quiet Step	Andre	102,200	2:03 1/5
1955	Hasty Road	Capeador	Social Outcast	95,400	2:02 2/5
1956	Nashua	Social Outcast	Sailor	92,600	2:02
1957	Bardstown	Mr. First	Switch On	82,200	2:03
1958	Oligarchy	Iron Liege	Hoop Band	92,800	2:01 2/5
1959	Bardstown	Nadir	Bill's Sky Boy	87,240	2:01 1/5
1960	Bald Eagle	On-and-On	Talent Show	79,700	1:59 3/5
1961	Yorky	Never Give In	Bourbon Prince	81,770	2:01
1962	Yorky	Carry Back	Ambiopoise	87,620	2:02
1963	Beau Purple	Kelso	Heroshogala	83,460	2:01 4/5
1964	Mongo	Sunrise Flight	Admiral Vic	85,020	2:01 1/5
1965	Primordial II	Hot Dust	Your Alibhai	88,140	2:03 3/5
1966	Pia Star	Selari	Slystitch	87,620	2:01 3/5
1967	Ring Twice	Stanislas	Understanding	81,640	2:00 3/5
1968	Sette Bello	Bold Hour			
1968		Favorable Turn		92,950	2:01 3/5
1969	Yumbel	Funny Fellow	Mr. Brogann	89,180	2:03 1/5
1970	Never Bow	Beau Brummel	Ship Leave	86,970	2:01 3/5
1971	True North	Twogundan	Sunny Tim	96,850	2:03 4/5
1972	Good Counsel	His Majesty	Urgent Message	93,990	2:02 2/5
1973	Vertee	West Coast Scout	Triumphant	84,110	2:00 4/5
1974	Forego	True Knight	Play the Field	76,635	2:01 1/5
1975	Forego	Hat Full	Gold and Myrrh	81,055	2:01 4/5
1976	Hatchet Man	Toonerville	Hail the Pirates	78,975	2:02
1977	Yamanin	One More Jump	Mount Sterling	81,250	2:01 1/5
1978	Silver Series	Adriatico	Villador	96,688	2:02 1/5
1979	Jumping Hill	Sorry Lookin	Singleton	87,750	2:03
1980	Private Account	Lot O'Gold	Rivalero	90,900	2:03 1/5
1981	Land of Eire	Tunerup	Prince Valiant	93,450	2:01
1982	Lord Darnley	Joanie's Chief	Switcheroo	102,900	2:02 2/5
1983	Swing Till Dawn	Lord Darnley	Rivalero	89,250	2:01 1/5
1984	Mat Boy	Indian Lei	World Appeal	94,950	1:59 4/5
1985	Pine Circle	Dr. Carter	Selous Scout	98,250	2:00 4/5
1986	Turkoman	Darn That Alarm	Gate Dancer	136,200	1:58 3/5
1987	Launch a Pegasus	Creme Fraiche	Johns Treasure	120,000	2:01 3/5
1987	Personal Flag	Jade Hunter	Entitled To	120,000	2:01 4/5
1989	Cryptoclearance	Slew City Slew	Mi Selecto	120,000	1:49 2/5

Note: Run as Widener Challenge Cup Handicap prior to 1938. Day Off and Supreme Sir in a dead heat for third in 1940. Not run in 1943, 1945, or 1988. Hoop Band finished third in 1959 but was disqualified and placed fifth. Bold Hour and Favorable Turn in a dead heat for second in 1968. Romeo finished second in 1977 but was disqualified and placed seventh. Run in February and December in 1987.

Florida Breeders' Stakes

7/8 mile, 2-year-olds foaled in Florida, Hialeah Park, Hialeah

Year	First	Second	Third	Value	Time
1948	Rablim	Francs Cracker	Suffazon	3,940	:34 2/5
1949	Werwolf	Jolirab	Fan Lady	9,575	:34
1950	Mr. A.B.	Liberty Rab	Maid of Hearts	6,705	:34
1951	Jolisam	Brother March	Jones Brook	7,875	:35 3/5
1952	Game Gene	Ari Gold	Charier	9,750	:34
1953	Wolf Gal	Oclirock	Blenfly	15,575	:33 3/5
1954	Merriwolf	Royal Morse	Silver Rab	16,575	:34 1/5
1955	First Cadet	Smooth Stride	Game o' Hearts	15,925	:33 3/5
1956	King Hairan	Myla	Busy Harvest	14,850	:32 4/5
1957	Hubcap	Captina	Four Fives	14,500	:33
1958	Pryson	Marisa	Coltrane	16,075	:33 1/5
1959	My Dear Girl	Niequest	Algenib	17,327	:34 1/5
1960	My Old Flame	Carry Back	Julitta	15,345	:33 4/5
1961	Fair Gal	Scan the Sky	First Banker	16,380	:33 3/5
1962	Cavalanche	Flying Johnnie	Rough Note	12,480	1:24
1963	Taut Ship	Sun Native	Dirby Line	13,552	1:24 3/5
1964	He's a Gem	Greek Episode	A. Deck	16,250	1:24
1965	Golden Joey	Flag Raiser	Swift Stream	17,322	1:22 4/5
1966	Garry G.	Native Street	Handsome Boy	19,825	1:22 4/5
1967	Biller	In Reality	Crafty Look	21,190	1:23
1968	Laughing Bill	American Native	Conceited	20,442	1:22 4/5
1969	Royal Saxon	Immediacy	Shut Eye	19,695	1:22 4/5
1970	Joe Namath	Office Queen	Iron Warrior	20,442	1:24
1971	Pitching Wedge	Landing More	Brazen Brother	21,612	1:23 3/5
1972	Chevron Flight	Smiling Jack	Tentam	21,450	1:23 4/5
1973	Shecky Greene	Step Nicely	Jim Duncan	19,662	1:22 3/5
1974	Mark the Prince	Eric's Champ	The Grok	22,035	1:23 2/5
1975	Bilwyn	Fashion Sale	Patrick O'Hara	21,190	1:24 1/5
1976	Improve It	Controller Ike	Won't Yield	20,345	1:23 1/5
1977	Jonkiller	Jatski	My Budget	20,507	1:22 4/5
1978	Junction	Native Prancer	Gordie H.	21,320	1:22 1/5
1980	Creamette City	Sure Spry	Straight Strike	19,455	1:26

Note: Distance 3/8 mile for 2-year-olds prior to 1962. Conceited finished second in 1968 but was disqualified and placed third. Run as Florida Breeders' Handicap and Carl G. Rose Memorial prior to 1980. Not run in 1979.

Black Helen Handicap

1 1/8 miles (turf), 3-year-olds and up, fillies and mares, Hialeah Park, Hialeah

Year	First	Second	Third	Value	Time
1941	Sweet Willow	Silvestra	Up the Hill	4,810	1:23 2/5
1942	Pomayya	Silvestra	Dark Discovery	9,075	1:50 4/5
1944	Silvestra	Moon Maiden	Fiddlers Bit	4,130	1:52 1/5
1946	Adroit	Letmenow	Milcave	22,700	1:51 4/5
1947	Miss Grillo	Rytina	Sweet Caprice	19,400	1:49 4/5
1948	Shotsilk				
	Rampart		Afoxie	10,950	1:50
1949	Roman Candle	Brownian	Miss Mommy	16,850	1:49
1950	Bewitch	Roman Candle	Yoncalla	13,825	1:48
1951	Antagonism	Roman Miss	Ouija	15,050	1:51 3/5
1952	Roman Miss	Dinewisely	Drifting Maid	18,175	1:55 4/5
1953	Atalanta	Sunny Dale	No Score	23,600	1:49 2/5
1954	Gainsboro Girl	Lavender Hill	Emardee	23,600	1:57 4/5
1955	Rosemary B.	Crisset	Lavender Hill	24,500	1:49 2/5
1956	Clear Dawn	Miss Arlette	High Voltage	28,950	1:49 2/5
1957	Amoret	Jet Girl	Gay Life	25,450	1:54 3/5
1958	Pardala	Amoret	Gay Life	28,400	1:50
1959	Rosewood	Happy Princess	A Glitter	25,350	1:50 1/5
1960	Royal Native	Happy Princess	Woodlawn	30,160	1:49
1961	Be Cautious	Teacation	Indian Maid	30,095	1:50 4/5
1962	Seven Thirty	Decline and Fall	Smashing Gail	33,215	1:49
1963	Pocosaba	Old Hat	Miss Marcella	31,005	1:49 2/5
1964	Princess Arle	Patrol Woman	Tona	39,455	1:50 3/5
1965	Old Hat	Steeple Jill	Windsor Lady	39,390	1:49 4/5
1966	What A Treat	Alondra II	Tosmah	40,960	1:50 2/5
1967	Mac's Sparkler	Straight Deal	Malhoa	42,250	1:48 3/5
1968	Treacherous	Prides Profile	Green Glade	40,235	1:49
1969	Amerigo Lady	Gay Matelda	Nature II	3,220	1:49 3/5
1970	Taken Aback	Patee Canyon	What A Dream	41,275	1:49 1/5
1971	Swoon's Flower	Golden Or	Taken Aback	41,080	1:49
1972	Alma North	Grafitti	Queen Louie	41,990	1:49
1973	Grafitti	Summer Guest	Bl'ing Ang'ca	41,340	1:49 4/5
1974	Dogtooth Violet	North Broadway	Dove Creek Lady	42,770	1:47
1975	Garland of Roses	Gems and Roses	Eleven Pl's'r's	42,510	1:49
1976	Yes Dear Maggy	Summertime Promise	Katonka	43,680	1:48 2/5
1977	Copano	Imogene II	Frond	42,900	1:49 4/5
1978	Len's Determined	Northernette	C'm L'de L'r'e	44,980	1:49 1/5
1979	Late Bloomer	Time for Pleasure	Excitable	38,545	1:50 2/5
1980	Spr'ng In D'psea	Tempus Fugit II	Jolie Dutch	62,280	1:51
1981	The Very One	Honey Fox	Wayward Lassie	55,800	1:48 1/5
1982	Honey Fox	Endicotta	Shark Song	73,080	1:47
1983	Mistretta	Trevita	Bouncing Back	63,120	1:46 4/5
1984	Sabin	SilverIn Flight	Aspen Rose	96,990	1:47
1985	Isayso	Powder Break	Mre DArgnne	86,205	1:47 1/5
1986	Shocker T.	Lake Country	Dawn's Curtsey	77,250	1:47 3/5
1987	Lotka	Fama	Bonnie Ile	105,000	1:46 4/5
1988	Anka Germania	Fieldy	Black Bracelet	75,000	1:49 4/5
1989	Love You By Heart	Ravinella	Judy's Red Shoes	105,000	1:50 2/5

Note: For 4-year-olds and upward in 1963. Run on main course prior to 1974 and in 1979. Distance 7/8 mile in 1941. Not run in 1943 or 1945.

Florida Derby

1 1/8 miles, 3-year-olds, Gulfstream Park, Hallandale

Year	First	Second	Third	Value	Time
1952	Sky Ship	Handsome Teddy	Sandtop	17,550	1:50 4/5
1953	Money Broker	Blaze	Jamie K.		
1953			Slim	88,000	1:53 4/5
1954	Correlation	Goyamo	Big Crest	100,000	1:55 1/5
1955	Nashua	Blue Lem	First Cabin	100,000	1:53 1/5
1956	Needles	Count Chic	Pintor Lea	95,200	1:48 3/5
1957	Gen. Duke	Bold Ruler	Iron Liege	73,400	1:46 4/5
1958	Tim Tam	Lincoln Road	Grey Monarch	77,900	1:49 1/5
1959	Easy Spur	Sword Dancer	Master Palynch	75,300	1:47 1/5
1960	Bally Ache	Venetian Way	Victoria Park	79,500	1:47 3/5
1961	Carry Back	Crozier	Beau Prince	75,100	1:48 4/5
1962	Ridan	Cicada	Admiral's Voyage	85,800	1:50 2/5
1963	Candy Spots	Sky Wonder	Cool Prince	74,700	1:50 1/5
1964	Northern Dancer	The Scoundrel	Dandy K.	76,500	1:50 1/5
1965	Native Charger	Hail to All	Gallant Lad	79,800	1:51 1/5
1966	Williamston Kid	Bold and Brave	Sky Guy	83,400	1:50 1/5
1967	In Reality	Biller	Reason to Hail	99,400	1:50 1/5
1968	Forward Pass	Iron Ruler	Perfect Tan	94,100	1:49
1969	Top Knight	Arts and Letters	Al Hattab	81,800	1:48 2/5
1970	My Dad George	Corn off the Cob	Cassie Red	103,600	1:50 1/5
1971	Eastern Fleet	Executioner	Jim French	82,680	1:47 2/5
1972	Upper Cas	Spanish Riddle	Gentle Smoke	107,760	1:50
1973	Royal and Regal	Forego	Restless Jet	78,120	1:47 2/5
1974	Judger	Cannonade	Buck's Bid	130,200	1:49
1975	Prince Thou Art	Sylvan Place	Foolish Pleasure	94,440	1:50 2/5
1976	Honest Pleasure	Great Contractor	Proud Birdie	91,440	1:47 2/5
1977	Coined Silver	Nearly On Time	Fort Prevel	68,700	1:48 4/5
1977	Ruthie's Native	For the Moment	Sir Sir	69,900	1:50 1/5
1978	Alydar	Believe It	Dr. Valeri	100,000	1:47
1979	Spectacular Bid	Lot O'Gold	Fantasy 'N Reality	115,000	1:48 4/5
1980	Plugged Nickle	Naked Sky	Lord Gallant	110,000	1:50 1/5
1981	Lord Avie	Akureyri	Linnleur	147,388	1:50 2/5
1982	Timely Writer	Star Gallant	Our Escapade	150,000	1:49 1/5
1983	Croeso	Copelan	Law Talk	150,000	1:49 1/5
1984	Swale	Dr. Carter	Darn That Alarm	180,000	1:47 3/5
1985	Proud Truth	Irish Sur	Do It Again Dan	180,000	1:50
1986	Snow Chief	Badger Land	Mogambo	300,000	1:51 4/5
1987	Cryptoclearance	No More Flowers	Talinum	300,000	1:49 3/5
1988	Brian's Time	Forty Niner	Notebook	300,000	1:49 4/5
1989	Mercedes Won	Western Playboy	Big Stanley	300,000	1:49 3/5
1990	Unbridled	Slavic	Run Turn	300,000	1:52

Note: In 1953 Jamie K. and Slim in a dead heat for third place. Abe's First finished first in 1966 but was disqualified and placed fourth. Run in two divisions in 1977.

Florida Breeders' Futurity

3/4 mile, 2-year olds foaled in Florida, Tampa Bay Downs, Oldsmar.

Year	First	Second	Third	Value	Time
1958	Indian Maid	Mr. Noble	Mad Duchess		
1959	Benell	Bel Centauri	Game Thymus		
1960	My Old Flame	Rare Sport	Arbol Grandee	8,057	:55 4/5
1961	First Banker	General Mark	Princegret	9,548	1:00 2/5
1962	Jewelry	Miss Grey Lee	Count Courier	9,126	1:01
1963	Fair Phina	Cab Stan	Fast Pace	8,853	1:01 2/5
1964	Golden Joey	Record Dash	Winamac	12,259	1:00 1/5
1965	Born Royal	Runagate	Sundestine	20,556	1:00 4/5
1966	Wagon Dance	Laffin Mango	Solid Sender	8,400	1:01 3/5
1967	Fleet Swoon	Let's Hope	Mayor Jerry D.	8,190	1:00 3/5
1968	Gravy Bull	Goencanto	Luminary's Image	7,900	1:00 2/5
1969	Call For Nat	Hum On Jake	Gusty Method	8,265	1:00
1970	Dothan	Sociable Angel	Western Idol	7,425	:59 4/5
1971	Clandustin	Ponderosa Dee	Idol Hand	8,702	1:00 4/5
1972	Kathlon (f)	Miss Hilarious	More Gloves	6,591	:59 3/5
	Osage River (c&g)	Proud and Bold	Tell It Like It Is	7,041	:59
1973	Barb's Charcoal	Spring Feast	Mean Ways	6,535	1:01
	Lizabeth Action (f)	Assunta G.	Gypsy Glory	6,535	1:00 2/5
	Golden G'n'a (c&g)	Wait and Measure	O'Royken	7,060	:59 2/5
1974	Mor Coup (f)	Coldwind	Classy Note	6,525	1:00 2/5
	Big Decision (c&g)	Jandevar	Head Bandito	6,525	1:01
	Tr'k Fiddler (c&g)	Native Praise	One For You	6,525	1:00 1/5
1975	So Magic (f)	Well Recommended	Amposition	7,497	1:00 4/5
	Invader's Baby (f)	Sharpasthewind	Joans Cat	7,372	1:01 1/5
	S'br'ze Jolly (c&g)	Jet Blade	Star of the Sea	7,247	1:01
	Worthy Opponent (c&g)	Safety Harbor Kid	Peggy's Prince	7,247	1:01 1/5
1976	Nasty Nancy (f)	Rough Eagle	Tis An Angel	7,043	1:02
	Steves Fr'nd (c&g)	Streaking Bare	Near Par	6,843	:59 4/5
	Winners Hit (c&g)	Start Something	Chuck Line	6,718	1:00 2/5
1977	Case Ace Queen (f)	Surprise Trip	Careless Pet	5,766	:59
	Sweet L'tle Lady (f)	Stubborn Day	Super Fighter	5,566	:58 2/5
	Sayzar (c&g)	Fire On Three	Lucky 'N Right	5,441	:58 2/5
	Distant Dancer (c&g)	Great Copy	Seminole Warrior	5,766	:59 4/5
1978	Ann's Pleasure (f)	Noon Shadow	Subtropic	7,452	:59 1/5
	Bimbo Belle (f)	Run N'Tumble	Georgia More	7,453	1:00 2/5
	Spy Charger (c&g)	Count Hayai	Art's Bullit	8,053	:59 4/5
1979	Mr. Perfect (c&g)	Pan The Gold	Ward's Intent	7,230	1:02
	Private Girl (f)	HurricaneGlady's	Sw't Shakee Fanny	7,605	1:01 4/5
	Noble Pair (c&g)	Rappett	Woogie		
			He's Blue	7,355	1:00 2/5
	Proudest Bee (f)	Happy Hollie	Sober Jib	7,479	1:00 3/5
1980	Travlin' Edie (f)	My Tressa	Zone O'Silence	6,922	:59 4/5
	Moa (f)	Classie Lanie	Joy of Joy	7,122	1:01
	Silver Dollar Boy (c&g)	Firm Boss	Pruner's Edge	7,522	1:00 2/5
1981	Glory Strings (f)	Miss Tibb	Lady Amber	24,030	1:13 1/5
	Jetabid (c&g)	Broad Minded	Laughing Kas	21,270	1:14 2/5
1982	Best Game (f)	Judge Supreme	Ishudahadthat	17,910	1:13 3/5
	Saucy Lindy (f)	Wrong Answer	Silvered Silk	17,910	1:13 2/5
	Brother (c&g)	Fancy Friend	Striking Prince	21,570	1:12 3/5
1983	Proud Clarioness (f)	Strawberry Road	Black Medallion	21,270	1:11 2/5
	Nite Beat (c&g)	Mo Exception	Real Sharp Dancer	19,080	1:13 4/5

Note: Before 1960, purse under $5,000. Distance 4 1/2 furlongs in 1960; 5/8 mile from 1961 to 1980, inclusive. Divided into sex divisions in 1972 and thereafter. The 1973, 1975, 1977, 1978, 1979, 1980, and 1982 filly sections were run in two divisions. The 1974, 1975, 1976, 1977, and 1979 colt and gelding sections were run in two divisions. O'Quinn's Lassie won the 1975 first filly division but subsequently was disqualified from the purse money. Woogie and He's Blue in a dead heat for third place in second colts and gelding division in 1979. The last two years, 1982 and 1983, the race was run as the Florida Breeders' Sales Futurity. Filly indicated by (f); colt and gelding indicated by (c and g).

FLORIDA STALLION STAKES RACES

Desert Vixen Division

3/4 mile, 2-year-old fillies

Year	First	Second	Third	Value	Time
1982	Crystal Rail	Sugar Gold	Sunburned Baby	36,900	1:07 1/5
1983	Early Lunch	Distant Jig	Casting Queen	27,000	1:12 3/5
1983	Majestic Flag	Luck Touch	Roughlon	27,300	1:13 1/5
1984	French Gold	Nubia	Mellow Glow	51,000	1:15 1/5
1985	Summer Flight	Fleur De Soleil	Happy Cherokee	30,000	1:13 3/5
1985	Regal Princess	Cascade	Thirty Zip	30,000	1:12 3/5
1986	My Nichole	Beau Love Flowers	Foolish Appeal	30,000	1:13 1/5
1986	Blues Court	Jill Of All Trades	Strate Clover	30,000	1:11 4/5
1987	Go Gaiter	Princess Valid	Cantation	30,000	1:14
1987	Crafty Wife	Friendly Appeal	Elbereth	30,000	1:13 2/5
1988	Born Famous	Curia	Great Body	40,000	1:11 4/5
1988	Seaquay	Sez Fourty	Princess Mora	30,000	1:11 4/5
1989	Stacie's Toy	Miss Running Vany	Domestic Goddess	30,000	1:13
1989	Oh My Jessica Pie	Cutlass Envoy	Daring Koluctoo	30,000	1:11 4/5
1990	Nany's Appeal	Tri Gran Maw	Doradoradora	60,000	1:12 2/5

Note: Distance 5 1/2 furlongs in 1982. Run in two divisions in 1983, 1985, 1986, 1987, 1988, and 1989. Sioux Narrows finished third in the 1989 first division but was disqualified and placed fifth.

Dr. Fager Division

3/4 mile, 2-year-olds.

Year	First	Second	Third	Value	Time
1982	El Kaiser	Night Mover	Hello Handsome	37,200	1:05 3/5
1983	No Room	Bou Rullah	My G. P.	27,000	1:13 1/5
1983	Reach for More	Bowmans Express	A London Fog	26,550	1:12 2/5
1984	Emergency Call	Alpha Ridge	Cameo King	25,500	1:13 3/5
1984	Smile	Water Gate	Foundation Plan	25,500	1:13 3/5
1985	True Silver	Sunny Prospector	Ryan's Secret	30,000	1:13 2/5
1985	Sovereign Tom	My First Cut	Princely Lad	30,000	1:13 2/5
1986	Quinkan Country	Wooden Prince	Manhattan's Woody	30,000	1:13
1986	Lord Pergrine	Rushawk	Libretto	30,000	1:12 4/5
1987	Miami Slick	Medieval Victory	Five o'Forbes	30,000	1:11 3/5
1987	Break Par	Stevie's Doctor	Proud and Valid	30,000	1:13 1/5
1988	Reappeal	Sing My Tune	Joey's Hope	51,000	1:12 4/5
1989	American Dreamer	Shot Gun Scott	Time For the Sea	60,000	1:12 4/5
1990	Mot Telbin	Lillycut	Dame in Hand	30,000	1:12 1/5
	What a Cooker	Unreal Currency	Perfect Vodka	30,000	1:12

Note: Distance 5 1/2 furlongs in 1982. Run in two divisions in 1983, 1984, 1985, 1986, 1987, and 1990. Hickory Hill Flyer finished third in 1984 but was disqualified and placed tenth.

Susan's Girl Division

7/8 mile, 2-year-old fillies

Year	First	Second	Third	Value	Time
1982	Crystal Rail	Amber's Desire	Dove Nest	54,600	1:12 4/5
1983	Roughlon	Tis Magic	Most Precious Love	36,000	1:25
1983	Scorched Panties	Early Lunch	Sugar's Image	36,000	1:25 3/5
1984	Stellana	Sheer Ice	Too Nice	39,000	1:26
1984	Micki Bracken	Valid Linda	Check the Time	39,000	1:26 4/5
1985	Cascade	Brief Fame	Happy Cherokee	48,000	1:26
1985	Opera Diva	Thirty Zip	Janjac	48,000	1:25 4/5
1986	Added Elegance	Blues Court	Jill of All Trades	45,000	1:25
1986	Brave Raj	Carols Inheritance	Appealing One	45,000	1:25
1987	Friendly Appeal	Mirna M.	Zingana	45,000	1:26 3/5
1987	Crafty Wife	Bara Linda	Proper Evidence	45,000	1:26 3/5
1988	Sez Fourty	Seaquay	Iron and Silver	84,000	1:25 4/5
1989	Stacie's Toy	Miss Running Vany	Oh My Jessica Pie	90,000	1:24 3/5
1990	Z. Flash Gun	Doradoradora	Nany's Appeal	90,000	1:26 4/5

Note: Distance 3/4 mile in 1982. Run in two divisions in 1983, 1984, 1985, 1986, and 1987. Action Star finished second in the 1987 first division but was disqualified and placed fourth.

Affirmed Division

7/8 mile, 2-year-olds

Year	First	Second	Third	Value	Time
1982	El Kaiser	Gussie's Appeal	Saucy Cloud	21,385	1:12
1983	A London Fog	Appealing Girl	Classy Cut	21,158	1:26 1/5
1984	Smile	Tulindas	Sheila Shine	21,970	1:24 3/5
1985	Tough Talk	Harford Hill	Safe At the Plate	28,535	1:26
1985	Princely Lad	Dessa	Daytime Princess	28,080	1:26 1/5
1986	Baldski's Star	Hopedale O.	Billie Osage	45,000	1:25 1/5
1986	Northstar Prospect	Libretto	Contractor's Tune	45,000	1:24 4/5
1987	Medieval Victory	Break Par	Bold Habitat	45,000	1:25 3/5
1987	In the Slammer	Cutter Sam	Proud and Valid	45,000	1:24 3/5
1988	Valid Space	Truely Colorful	America's Friend	84,000	1:25 1/5
1989	Shot Gun Scott	Swedaus	American Dreamer	90,000	1:25 1/5
1990	What a Cooker	Mot Telbin	Game in Hand	90,000	1:25 3/5

Note: Distance 3/4 mile in 1982. Run in two divisions in 1985, 1986, and 1987.

My Dear Girl Division

1 1/16 miles, 2-year-old fillies

Year	First	Second	Third	Value	Time
1982	My Sweet Baby	Priceless Edition	Silvered Silk	84,000	1:50 1/5
1982	Flawless Diamond	Amber's Desire	Inthethickofit	85,000	1:48 4/5
1983	Early Lunch	Dungaree Dancer	Danderella	180,000	1:48 3/5
1984	Micki Bracken	French Gold	Fritzie Bey	210,000	1:49 4/5
1985	Regal Princess	Cascade	She's Content	114,000	1:48 3/5
1985	Final Reunion	Thirty Zip	Fragrant Princess	114,000	1:49
1986	Brave Raj	Added Elegance	Blues Court	240,000	1:48 1/5
1987	Laurel's Wiggle	Proper Evidence	Stream Colors	135,000	1:49 4/5
1987	Balquiria	Mirna M	Princess Fire	135,000	1:50
1988	Sez Fourty	Seaquay	Georgies Doctor	255,000	1:50 1/5
1989	Miss Running Vany	Stacie's Toy	Voodoo Lily	258,000	1:48 2/5
1990	Doradoradora	Starthorne	Morning Babette	276,000	1:48 3/5

Note: Run in two divisions in 1982, 1985, and 1987.

In Reality Division

1 1/16 miles, 2-year-olds

Year	First	Second	Third	Value	Time
1982	Luv a Libra	Blink	El Kaiser	161,000	1:47 4/5
1983	My G.P.	Reach for More	Scorched Panties	90,000	1:47 3/5
1983	Rexson's Hope	Upper Star	Meal Ticket	90,000	1:48 1/5
1984	Smile	Emergency Call	Covert Operation	260,000	1:45 3/5
1985	Scat Dancer	Sunny Prospector	Snowy Mountain	240,000	1:48 4/5
1986	Never Waiver	Hopedale O.	Quinkan Country	120,000	1:50
1986	Uncle Cam	Regal Togs	Northstar Prospect	120,000	1:49 1/5
1987	Medieval Victory	Sensible Bird	Distinctintentions	300,000	1:48 3/5
1988	Silver Sunsets	Into Bucks	America's Friend	267,000	1:48 1/5
1989	Shot Gun Scott	Unbridled	Swedaus	270,000	1:47 3/5
1990	Pro Flight	Sir Otto	Moment of True	288,000	1:48 1/5

Note: Run in two divisions in 1983 and 1986. In 1984, Smile earned a bonus for winning all three divisions of the Florida Stallion Stakes, which is included in the value to winner of the In Reality Division, last race of the series.

Convenience Division

1 1/16 miles, turf, 3-year-old fillies

Year	First	Second	Third	Value	Time
1984	Lady Mellody	Gentle Screen	Scorched Panties	34,800	1:49 1/5
1985	April Dawn Marie	Merry Cathy	One Dollar Carly	34,200	1:48 2/5
1986	Judy's Red Shoes	She's Content	Talski	33,900	1:47
1987	Munchkin Michele	Wolf Trail	Blues Court	35,400	1:41 1/5

Note: Run on main track prior to 1987.

Roman Brother Division

1 1/16 miles, 3-year-olds

Year	First	Second	Third	Value	Time
1984	Bowmans Express	Amerilad	Rexson's Hope	36,600	1:47 1/5
1985	Racing Star	Crovero	Profit Plus	34,200	1:46 1/5
1986	Annapolis John	Dr. Dan Eyes	Princely Lad	33,900	1:46 2/5
1987	Baldski's Star	Billie Osage	Kindly Court	34,500	1:46 2/5

Note: No Room finished second in 1984 but was disqualified and placed fourth.

Notes on Sources

The following reference works are only a few used in researching this book. Much of the research was done in carefully kept personal scrapbooks. Many Florida-based newspapers, including some no longer in existence, were valuable primary sources but are not always recognized because the scrapbooks contained only clippings, not whole pages. Encyclopedias and general history books were also used as sources. Information contained in the appendixes was supplied by the American Race Manual, Hialeah Park, Gulfstream Park, Tampa Bay Downs, and Calder Race Course.

American Race Horses. Annual publication. Sagamore Press, 1940s.

American Racing Manual. Annual publication. Hightstown, N.J.: Daily Racing Form.

American Turf Register and Sport Magazine. Monthly publication.

Biracree, Tom, and Wendy Insinger. *The Complete Book of Thoroughbred Horse Racing*. Garden City, N.Y.: Doubleday & Co., 1982.

Blood-Horse, The. Journal. Lexington, Ky.: Blood-Horse, Inc., a subsidiary of Thoroughbred Owners and Breeders Association, Inc.

British Race Course. Journal.

Cameron, Frank J. *The Hungry Tiger*. New York: McGraw-Hill, 1964.

Daily Racing Form. Daily publication. Hightstown, N.J.

Domini, Anno. *Ocala, Florida, in Pictures and Prose*. Published privately, 1925.

Dosh, R. Letters, November 1931–February 1933.

Florida. House of Representatives. *Journal of the House of Representatives*. 23d session.

Florida. Senate. *Journal of the Senate*. 23d session.

Florida. State Racing Commission. *Annual Report of the State Racing Commission of Florida*. June 30, 1932.

Florida. Supreme Court. *Syllabus of the Court*. March 9, 1927.

Florida Horse, The. Monthly journal, Ocala, Fla., 1957–.

Florida Thoroughbred, The. Journal.

Florida Thoroughbred Breeders' Association. Minutes. September 11, 1945–.

Florida Times Union (Jacksonville).

Gregg, Charles. "In Support of Winter Racing." *Turf and Sports Digest*. Monthly publication. December 1944.

Horsemen's Journal, The. Journal. Ocala: The Horsemen's Benevolent and Protective Association.

Lexington [Kentucky] *Herald*.

Life Magazine.

Livingston, Bernard. *Their Turf.* New York: Arbor House, 1973.

Maryland Horse, The. Monthly journal. Timonium, Maryland.

Miami Herald.

Miami News.

Montgomery, E. S. *The Thoroughbred.* 3d edition. New York: Arco Publishing Co., 1978.

Morning Telegraph.

New York Times.

Ocala Star Banner.

Ott, Eloise Robinson, and Louise Hickman Chazal. *Ocali Country.* Ocala, Fla., 1966.

Sanford Herald.

Spur Magazine. Monthly journal. Midaleburg, Va.: Spur Publications, Inc.

Tallahassee Observer.

Tebeau, Charlton W. *A History of Florida.* Coral Gables: University of Miami Press, 1981.

Thoroughbred Record, The. Weekly journal. Lexington, Kentucky.

Tilley, Chuck, and Gene Plowden. *This Is Horse Racing.* Miami: Seeman Publishing, 1974.

Turf and Sport Digest. Journal. 1942–43. Baltimore: Montee Publishing Co., Inc.

Update 8, no. 4 (November 1981). Brochure. Historical Association of Southern Florida.

Index